John Matthews's new book on the fiction of William Faulkner is a lively and accessible discussion that offers fresh readings and new insights for everyone. While providing rich historical, cultural, and aesthetic contexts for reading Faulkner's fiction, *William Faulkner: Seeing Through the South* is a pleasure to read; it is the best available discussion of the reach of Faulkner's fiction we have now and will have for many years to come.
Patrick O'Donnell, Michigan State University

William Faulkner: Seeing Through the South is an introduction written by a major Faulkner scholar which both "introduces" and transforms its subject (a difficult trick) . . . The study unfailingly requires that in seeing Faulkner clear, we see him in new and necessary ways.
Richard Godden, University of California Irvine

Matthews lays out brilliantly the ideological systems that solicit Faulkner's fiction. No troubled apologist for the Old South, Matthews's Faulkner engages the challenges of modernity, taking on the disfigurements of colonialism and capitalism. Thanks to Matthews, we have a Faulkner for our time: one who sees through the South – demystifying its collective fantasies – even as he labors to see his region through.
Philip Weinstein, Swarthmore College

Blackwell Introductions to Literature

This series sets out to provide concise and stimulating introductions to literary subjects. It offers books on major authors (from John Milton to James Joyce), as well as key periods and movements (from Old English literature to the contemporary). Coverage is also afforded to such specific topics as "Arthurian Romance." All are written by outstanding scholars as texts to inspire newcomers and others: non-specialists wishing to revisit a topic, or general readers. The prospective overall aim is to ground and prepare students and readers of whatever kind in their pursuit of wider reading.

Published

William Faulkner

Seeing Through the South

John T. Matthews

WILEY-BLACKWELL

A John Wiley & Sons, Ltd., Publication

Registered Office
John Wiley & Sons Ltd, The Atrium, Southern Gate, Chichester, West Sussex,
PO19 8SQ, United Kingdom

Editorial Offices
350 Main Street, Malden, MA 02148-5020, USA
9600 Garsington Road, Oxford, OX4 2DQ, UK
The Atrium, Southern Gate, Chichester, West Sussex, PO19 8SQ, UK

For details of our global editorial offices, for customer services, and for information
about how to apply for permission to reuse the copyright material in this book,
please see our website at www.wiley.com/wiley-blackwell.

Library of Congress Cataloging-in-Publication Data

Matthews, John T.
William Faulkner : seeing through the South / John T. Matthews.
p. cm.—(Blackwell introductions to literature ; 20)
Includes bibliographical references and index.
ISBN 978-1-4051-2481-2 (hardcover : alk. paper)
1. Faulkner, William, 1897–1962—Criticism and interpretation.
2. Southern States—In literature.   I. Title.
PS3511.A86Z89163 2009
813′.52—dc22
2008020118

A catalogue record for this book is available from the British Library.

Set in 10 on 13 pt Meridian by SNP Best-set Typesetter Ltd., Hong Kong

1   2009

Contents

Illustrations

Preface

Faulkner once remarked – in a fit of annoyance at having to provide autobiographical information to accompany an edition of his work – that he wished he might annihilate any knowledge of himself as a human being on the other side of the typewriter. That way there'd be nothing for the reader but the books. To write as if anonymous: that's the dream of an author who put all of himself that mattered into the words on the page. It's true that what we learn about any artist's life and times may enrich our sense of the created works themselves. In the case of Faulkner, readers are fortunate to have a number of excellent biographies, each examining different facets of his outwardly simple but emotionally turbulent life.[1] Most of these also give brief accounts of Faulkner's literary works and artistic career as they interplay with the course of his personal life. As well, Faulkner's stylistic inventiveness and his ability to imagine a whole fictional world full of extraordinary characters and stories have stimulated close study of his technique and themes. Faulkner's art has inspired analysis as wide-ranging, intensive, and original as that of any author in English. Interpretive criticism continues to find fresh meaning in Faulkner's writing and surprising new contexts for understanding its cultural and social environment. I have dealt with the abundance of specialized scholarship on Faulkner by trying to assimilate it as discreetly as possible into my discussions, conceding that it would be impossible to do justice to the many books and articles that constitute the professional body of work on Faulkner. I urge readers to explore the massive archive of criticism to discover how many other "Faulkners" emerge in distinct accounts of this hugely imaginative writer.

In my effort to survey the whole span of Faulkner's creative life, and to introduce readers to the marvels of his artistry, I try to honor his preference for concentrating on the writing itself. I proceed as if the books themselves actually were the essence of Faulkner's life, as I believe them to be. Biographies give us Faulkner's personal and professional life, critical biographies the evolution of his imagination. General introductions offer overviews of Faulkner's key concerns and achievement, while specialized analyses allow readers to pursue particular topics and interpretations of individual works. *Seeing Through the South* attempts something different: I try to present Faulkner's entire imaginative career as a distinctively coherent project. My study reads all nineteen novels and a number of the best short stories as inter-related episodes in a vast chronicle of a world becoming modern; it shows the indispensable rooting of Faulkner's imagination in the place he chose to live all his life; and it emphasizes how the US South was embedded in the history of global colonialism, in doing so suggesting what a Faulkner for our times might be.

Acknowledgments

It would be impossible to identify all the debts I've incurred in writing this book, since it reflects a lifetime of learning about Faulkner from the published work of other scholars, from lively conversations with specialists, students, and fans everywhere (including several on Boston trolleys), and from exchanges with numerous colleagues over work in progress. I wish especially to thank Richard Godden, Patrick O'Donnell, and Philip Weinstein for reading this manuscript so carefully in its final stages, as well as for friendships of a lifetime forged around our regard for Faulkner's art. I've benefited in countless ways from the collaborative teaching of Southern culture, including Faulkner, I've done at Boston University with my colleague Nina Silber, and from her own invaluable scholarship on Southern history. Leigh Anne Duck, Peter Lurie, Anne Goodwyn Jones, Donald Kartiganer, Noel Polk, and Theresa Towner helped me in a variety of particular ways for which I am grateful: confirming my approach, recommending more to read, correcting errors. Although the introductory format of this book prevents a full scholarly apparatus, I have tried to acknowledge sources for all material deriving directly from the work of others, and have attempted to mention as many principal book-length studies on Faulkner as space allowed. Nonetheless, I wrote this book cheerfully if humbly aware of how many other readers' ideas have become indispensable to me as I think about Faulkner. Those companions will see themselves on every page. I trust them to grant me the privilege of transmitting accumulated knowledge to readers just beginning to appreciate the writer we have cared about for so long.

I also wish to thank the many students at Boston University who have come to share my passion for Faulkner's fiction, and whom it has been my privilege to guide as they explored his created world. I've especially loved watching new dimensions of this remarkable writer come into view every few years in response to the changing interests of undergraduates and the shifting intersections of his imagination with the course of contemporary life. I've been blessed as well with superb graduate students through the years; they also will recognize the contributions they have made to my thinking through their hospitable yet tough-minded reactions to my ideas, and through the distinguished scholarship many have gone on to produce themselves.

My editors at Wiley-Blackwell have been extraordinary, beginning with Andrew McNeillie, who first proposed that I do such a book, and continuing to Emma Bennett, whose encouragement and support were unfailing, and thus decisive, as well as Rosemary Bird, Louise Butler, and Hannah Morrell, who superbly oversaw its final stages (which they must often have doubted they'd ever witness).

INTRODUCTION

Seeing Through the South: Faulkner and the Life Work of Writing

We encounter William Faulkner in the twenty-first century as the greatest novelist America has yet produced. He may also be its most paradoxical. If Faulkner has become the United States' most influential world novelist, he did so while setting his most significant fiction in a single obscure county in the Deep South, and spending his whole life in such a place himself. He was a foremost international modernist, yet his subjects and characters are unimaginable apart from the history and sociology of what was the most backward state in the Union. He experimented endlessly with narrative structure, and developed a difficult unorthodox style, yet he described his goal as simply trying to get at the truth of "the human heart in conflict with itself" ("Address upon Receiving the Nobel Prize for Literature," *Speeches, Essays, Public Letters*, p. 119).

Although such contrary features of Faulkner's imagination might seem to indicate the sort of genius that just transcends usual measures – think of him as the American Shakespeare – the purpose of this book is to show how his world's contradictions were a key to Faulkner's originality. Faulkner continues to speak to our contemporary world because his fiction described the seismic upheavals that formed modern life. Such disruptions caused a good deal of confusion and ambivalence, as one predominant way of life gave way to another. These changes seem commonplace now, and their stories familiar ones. But the sheer volume and degree of transformations can hardly be overestimated.

During Faulkner's life (1897–1962), America grew from a disorganized second-rate federation of regions into a modern centralized economic empire and international political giant. A primarily rural and agricultural nation became a vast network of metropolitan centers; capitalism developed from the simple production of goods for local markets into a system of national and international corporations. America expanded its foreign might by seizing its first territories outside the continent in the Spanish-American War in 1898, then pursuing a course through two world wars that made it a Cold War super-power by mid-century. Longstanding civil rights movements brought the vote to many women in 1920 and to most African Americans by the 1960s. Centuries of lawful racial discrimination came to an end. Sexual behavior was transformed by new social patterns fostered by World War I. Developments in technology reinvented almost every aspect of everyday life. Faulkner's father owned a livery stable in their hometown; twenty years later his son was flying airplanes. A child who grew up hearing tales about Civil War battles fought with saber and pistol, became the man who delivered his Nobel Prize speech four years after the US had dropped the first atomic bombs. Moreover, the events of modernity were hardly restricted to the United States. Throughout Western society similar changes were taking place, while across the globe peoples formerly controlled by European colonial empires began the struggle for independence and integration into the modern world.

It is not surprising that Faulkner's fiction should emerge as one of the most valuable imaginative records we have of the changes that created much of our present world. His novels, one by one, take up all the crucial elements of the event of modernization. In *Soldiers' Pay* (1926), his first novel, he concentrates on the way a traditional "provincial" society like the South's was violently inducted into a modern "cosmopolitan" one like the New America's after World War I. *The Sound and the Fury* (1929) tells the story of the eclipse of the South's landed gentry as a heartfelt tragedy; in his multiple novels about the Snopes family (starting with *The Hamlet* in 1940), Faulkner produces a corresponding comedy about the upward trickle of poor folk and the formation of a modern bourgeoisie. *As I Lay Dying* (1930) describes the awkward but determined journey of a family from its dying farm to the alluring town, while *Sanctuary* (1931) probes what Faulkner takes to be the horrific effects of urban mass entertainment and a culture of vicarious spectacle. In *Absalom, Absalom!* (1936) and *Go Down, Moses* (1942), Faulkner descends into the painful history of the plantation system, one whose origins he rightly locates in the earliest violations of the New World by European settlers, whether in North America or the West Indies. Some non-Southern novels take up other alarming features of the modern age, most monumentally, perhaps, in *A Fable* (1954), Faulkner's ambitious meditation on the origins of the 1950s' atomic age military-industrial complex in the America of World War I.

Beyond the power of Faulkner's individual books, his achievement is especially remarkable for its determination to see a great multitude of local and discrete events as parts of a larger inter-related story. Faulkner organizes a lifelong creative project around the saga of an imaginary county in Mississippi that he calls Yoknapatawpha (its name a trace of the Native Americans who first occupied such places). By making so many of his separate novels installments in the description of an entire principality, Faulkner conveys the sense of the importance of region and history in shaping the lives of individuals. This is true particularly for a past-obsessed region like the American South, where many found it difficult to surrender the frustration and humiliation of losing the Civil War, along with a way of life they thought superior. As one of Faulkner's characters memorably remarks, "The past is never dead; it's not even past" (*Requiem for a Nun*, p. 535). But it is also true more broadly for all those global "Souths" that continue to find their way into modernity, confronting histories of colonial exploitation and dependence, struggling with racially complex societies created by the violence of invasion and slaveholding, and learning how to tell new stories in new ways.

Faulkner's situation as an artist and citizen generated tremendous personal conflict, perhaps the decisive element in his temperament as a writer. At the end of *Absalom, Absalom!*, the young Quentin Compson completes his harrowing account of the South by protesting, "I don't. I don't! I don't hate it! I don't hate it!" As Faulkner himself commented about *The Sound and the Fury*, he found himself having to "indict" the South for its grievous sins while longing to "escape" into fantasies of its glorious past. Such powerfully divided sentiments are a product of the massive dislocations of loyalty, faith, and knowledge produced by the shift from one social regime to the next. The bravery of Faulkner's life as a writer and a person was that he did not dodge difficulty. He deliberately chose to live his entire life in Oxford, Mississippi, because it tortured him as much as it nurtured him. Unlike many other modernists who found artistic fellowship in New York or Paris, Faulkner set a solitary course. He lived sharply alienated from almost every intimate relation he forged, including those with his wife, his family, his lovers, his town, and his region. Personally, it was by living as an outsider within the world that had created him that he could represent the nuances of individual dramatic conflict with such authority and precision. Artistically, it was by subjecting his tradition-steeped Southern culture to the alienation of modernist methods for rendering time, language, consciousness, and history that Faulkner could figure out how to retell the stories of a place he knew too well.

Retelling those stories for national audiences became critical at just the moment Faulkner came of age as an artist in the 1920s. The South for a century had been locked into a succession of mythologies that exalted the antebellum ideal of plantation life, the kindness of Southern slavery, the nobility of the Confederate cause, the "natural" hierarchies of race and gender, and the honoring of regional pride over class conflict. In the aftermath of the Great War, the South attracted national attention for its racism (lynching remained a serious problem), anti-intellectualism (the Scopes "Monkey" trial occurred in 1925), and chronic poverty (Franklin Roosevelt called the South the nation's number one economic problem as late as 1938, toward the end of the Depression). Faulkner welcomed the destruction of such injurious myths and behavior, but he remained suspicious of what would replace them.

My subtitle, then, points to the several ways Faulkner fashioned art of universal appeal from his native material. Clearly, he saw human nature through the lens of his own experience, one defined fundamentally by its Southernness. In addition, his writing sought to penetrate the deceptions and delusions of a morally bankrupt and obsolete tradition, to see through its hypocrisies and pretensions. But in committing himself over decades to participating in, and bearing witness to, the difficult evolution of his South, Faulkner also determined to see the place he loved through its troubles.

Not much of this would matter, of course, had Faulkner not written some of the most breathtaking prose in the English language. As in everything, Faulkner made no concessions to simplicity. His conflicted sentiments toward the South, his determination to create the sensation of a long past alive at every point in a unified world, and the inscrutability of deeply-conditioned human motives and behavior – such aspirations place enormous pressure on the descriptive and evocative capacities of language. Faulkner's sentences arc across centuries, rotate endlessly around mesmerizing moments, turn familiar concepts inside out (one character grieves for a "nothusband"), and uncannily render characters' private thoughts as readable script. His characters ache with the burden of unwanted knowledge, their utterances wracked for admitting too much of what they don't want to acknowledge at all. It is the nearly inhuman devotion to making language exceed itself that creates the glory of Faulkner's difficult style. This is not writing for everyone's taste, but there is by now little question that it represents an achievement of the highest order, a coalescence of profound subject matter and originality of expression that embodies consummate literary artistry.

Imagine you are in your early thirties, and you've spent the first ten years of adulthood trying to establish yourself in your career. You won accolades for your early accomplishments, but fewer as you've gone along. One day you learn that your two biggest projects are being rejected, and that you're probably going to be demoted. On top of that, your fiancée announces it's time to get married now.

That was roughly William Faulkner's predicament as a writer in 1929. After concentrating on poetry during his college years, and getting one book of poems published, Faulkner had begun to sense that his real gift was for fiction. In 1925 he had spent some time in New Orleans, where he began to publish prose sketches in a literary magazine there called *The Double Dealer*. Sherwood Anderson, already a famous author, took an interest in the novice writer's fiction, and reinforced Faulkner's sense that he had a goldmine for future novels in the stories and characters the Mississippian had absorbed growing up. Faulkner lived in a small Southern town in an area where his family had been prominent for generations, from frontier times; his world was full of exotic, larger-than-life figures – many of them proud and ambitious, also hot-headed, violent, domineering, lecherous; others longsuffering, resentful, bitter; a few humble, conscience-stricken, honorable. Faulkner had been hearing tales about them from birth, so he always felt like a natural-born storyteller, with things to say about the human condition that his peculiar part of the world could illustrate. By the mid-1920s he became convinced he had a gift for fiction that would enable him to write at the level of the literary giants he so admired, like Dostoyevsky, Dickens, Flaubert, Thomas Mann, and Conrad. And while no one was making money in the 1920s writing poetry, successful short story writers and novelists had begun to earn thousands of dollars publishing in national magazines and getting on bestseller lists. In 1925 Faulkner moved to New Orleans and started concentrating on fiction – first short sketches and stories, then longer pieces. Over the next three years Faulkner made a splash by authoring a pair of well-reviewed novels. This is easy, thought Bill.

But instead of Faulkner's career taking off, it seemed to hit a dead end. His third novel, *Sartoris*, appeared soon, but only after the publisher insisted on radical revisions and cuts – changes so extreme Faulkner agreed to them on the condition that someone else actually do them. He was finishing another novel, and believed it was his best, but he was also making it as true to his vision of what great art should be as he could. The result was a work even his best friends found baffling, and his publisher turned down. Accepting the possibility that this book was too innovative ever to get printed, Faulkner devised a plan to write a *really* popular novel instead, one aimed to capitalize on the recent craze for gangster fiction, laced with gunplay and racy sex. As he turned thirty-two, though, Faulkner got the bad news that his publisher found the new book so obscene he figured they'd both end up in jail if he printed it.

Now what? As bad as his professional outlook appeared, Faulkner's personal life had just gotten a whole lot more complicated too. Ten years earlier, the girl he had first grown infatuated with in grade school, but whose father had forbidden them to marry following high school, had gone on to wed an international lawyer, with whom she had had two children. In 1929, though, Estelle Oldham Franklin and her husband divorced, leaving her free to marry Faulkner. Soon the struggling writer became the head of a household of four; less than a year later he purchased his first home, a ramshackle pre-Civil War "mansion" that he began to fix up himself. In this tight spot, Faulkner called on one of his main traits: perseverance. He acted as he was to do repeatedly during the course of his life as a writer: he just kept writing.

By the time of his marriage in late June of 1929, Faulkner had already received some encouragement; *The Sound and the Fury* would be published in October by a new company headed by one of his former editors, though it was clear that no one involved expected much in the way of general critical appreciation or sales. Just as it was coming out, he began his next novel, *As I Lay Dying*, which he finished quickly, in January. By the time it was published in the fall of 1930, Faulkner had also been surprised with word that his new publisher was now willing to give his pop novel a go; *Sanctuary* appeared in early 1931.

Although Faulkner's career was enjoying a sudden boost, he soon realized that the more "literary" novels he preferred to write were not going to earn him the royalties to be gotten from sensationalistic books, like the ones he aped in *Sanctuary*. Even this one "shocker" didn't sell as well as he'd expected. Faulkner found that his income fell short of what he needed to support his family. By 1932 Faulkner had committed himself to two other sorts of professional writing: short stories and screen plays. Throughout his career these more commercial venues subsidized and informed his novel-writing, even as they interfered with it. Since authors might be paid as much as $2,500 per short story by top mass circulation magazines like *The Saturday Evening Post* – F. Scott Fitzgerald was one well-paid star – Faulkner got himself an agent, took some of the material he was producing for novels, and began packaging it as short stories. Throughout his career Faulkner carefully recycled his creative goods. Sometimes he would split off a piece of whatever he was working on and publish it as a short story ahead of the novel. Other times, since Faulkner was capable of holding vast narratives about whole families and regions of his imaginary domain in his head, he would publish stories years ahead of their eventual integration into novels. And sometimes Faulkner seemed to work backward, taking strands of published novels and developing further (or possibly dusting off) discarded or preliminary versions. Whatever the immediate method, Faulkner always spoke resentfully of the need to cannibalize his fiction, since it was only in his novels that he felt he was creating authentic art.

Faulkner's habitual frugality in the use of his creative work – paradoxical in a way, given the spectacular fertility of his imagination –

leads me to one of the organizational principles of this book. Faulkner's short stories tend to orbit his novels. But since he was designing them to appear in more popular venues, the stories treat their subject matter more directly, with greater accessibility. At the same time, Faulkner's genius never pandered to mass audiences or mindlessly followed commercial formulas; he compromised ingeniously on issues of artistry, never forfeiting the responsibility of presenting his deeply misunderstood part of the country in complex and subtle ways. Many of Faulkner's stories brilliantly recast his subjects from fresh perspectives opened up by commercial pressures. Often the stories play a kind of double game, reflecting on the very market conditions of modern culture under which they appear – especially the mass production and consumption of cultural goods, and the commoditization of human relations.

One of Faulkner's early short stories dramatizes the tension between artistic and commercial obligations. Written in 1931, as he was reconciling himself to the necessity of marketing his fiction to the magazines, "Artist at Home" brings two sorts of authors into conflict. Having struck paydirt with his first novel and bought a comfortable home in the Virginia countryside, Roger Howes represents the successful commercial novelist. Then Howes's prospects cloud; he suffers writer's block as he works on his second novel, while his wife Anne resents the steady stream of struggling writers and painters from Greenwich Village who show up to ask the secret of making art that pays. One of these visitors seems especially unlikely to prosper, a sensitive young man, apparently dying of tuberculosis (once known as consumption, and considered the disease of poets because of its association with John Keats), who writes poems about rejection in love and who scorns the bourgeois conventionality of the Howes's household. The tortured poet eventually declares his infatuation with Anne, who indulges his passion conspicuously enough to stimulate her husband's suspicion. The doomed John Blair expires, though, after standing vigil outside the house on the rainy night he nobly renounces his love for the other artist's wife. It turns out that Howes has been using the episode of his wife's infidelity and the poet's suffering as material for his new story. Inspiration turns out to be little more than finding the right experiences to feed off – the artist as parasite. Even the down-home narrator of the story, a local who appreciates little about the artist-types who invade his rural Virginia town, understands that Howes has rediscovered a "[b]ull market in typewriting, you might say" (*Collected Stories of William Faulkner*, p. 639).

It would be tempting to interpret "Artist at Home" as a little fable about the crassness of the commercial writer, who plunders the lives of others amorally to get a marketable story, versus the high-minded literary artist, who renounces the world out of respect for beauty and love too fine for it. But Faulkner won't settle for such platitudes. In fact, the story suggests that the divide between commercial and literary art is hardly absolute. Blair and his comrades may have contempt for the art market, but, as Anne points out, the only thing the poet wants to know when he shows Howes a poem is " 'Will this sell? not, Is this good? or Do you like it? Will this sell?' " (p. 633). It's true that Howes comes across as a heartless exploiter of others' personal lives, converting intimate matters into entertainment commodities. But Faulkner also satirizes the self-dramatizing poet, who talks too much and writes too little, who shies away from the sheer hard work necessary to get yourself into print, who maybe never gets "mad enough to really write something" (p. 632). Without the friction of domestic or economic challenges, Faulkner suggests, a writer may have too little to overcome ever to write well.

"Artist at Home" derives, ironically, from an episode in Faulkner's own life. As an aspiring poet, Faulkner was introduced to a cultivated young woman named Elizabeth Prall when he lived briefly in New York City in the early 1920s. When Prall married the newly famous writer Sherwood Anderson and moved to New Orleans, she invited the Mississippian to visit. Faulkner revered Anderson's early work, and eagerly accepted the invitation. Faulkner and Anderson became close for a time, with the established writer even recommending Faulkner's first novel, *Soldiers' Pay*, to his publisher. Naturally, there was also a fair amount of rivalry embedded in their friendship, and later the relationship turned sour. In "Artist at Home" Faulkner may be gibing at Anderson, who has figured out how to turn his personal life into paying copy. (As if in confirmation, Anderson wrote a story himself based on an encounter with Faulkner; it's called "A Meeting South.") But Faulkner mocks himself as well in the figure of Howes; Faulkner was routinely censored by his family and friends for violating their private lives and pasts for source material. At the same time, he must also be ridiculing himself in the figure of the fey poet Blair, who suffers like Shelley, rages like Byron, and ends all too tragically like Keats.

Perhaps this story helps exorcise the unworldly poet Faulkner was – one also fond of dramatic posing, while embracing the contradictions and ethical ambiguities of writing for profit.

I'm beginning our investigation of Faulkner's life as a writer by concentrating on a central difficulty for him: the anxiety produced by the sense that he was betraying intimate knowledge of a secluded part of the country in order to satisfy the almost voyeuristic curiosity of a national audience. For numerous historical reasons, the rest of the US had routinely associated the South with gothic weirdness – from the creepy tales of the Virginian Edgar Allan Poe, through the exuberant satire of Mark Twain, to the grotesque comedy of Erskine Caldwell and Flannery O'Connor. In *Absalom, Absalom!*, an elderly woman breaks forty-three years of silence to tell her bizarre story of raging insult and grief to her young townsman, Quentin Compson, who is preparing to leave Mississippi for his freshman year at Harvard. She points out, with amused bitterness, that he could find the story worthwhile, since one day he might "enter the literary profession as so many Southern gentlemen and gentlewomen too are doing," and someday when his "wife will want a new gown or a new chair for the house . . . you can write this and submit it to the magazines" (*Absalom, Absalom!*, p. 5).

The historical moment at which Faulkner comes to maturity as a writer offers him unprecedented possibilities: as Rosa Coldfield suggests above, speaking in 1909, opportunities to capitalize on the national magazines' appetite for regional fiction, especially about the exotic South, had never been better.[1] An important reason for that interest, however, was the growing sense among urban, professional reading classes that regional life was dying out. Sherwood Anderson's hit book, in fact, was *Winesburg, Ohio*, which in 1919 detailed the strange, fading distinctiveness of small town "grotesques." Left behind by the dynamo of commercial, industrial, and technological progress centered in the modern city, the outlying regions of the country looked increasingly like vanishing enclaves to be savored nostalgically. So the conditions of modernity both created new publishing opportunities for writers about region, as well as situated those writers in the crease of modernization, in which old ways seemed to be coming to a close and new ones emerging.[2]

Faulkner could not have written such sustained lamentations about the receding traditional South without witnessing its demise. Such a position reinforced his ethical and imaginative conflict with the society that had produced him; in writing *The Sound and the Fury* he described having simultaneously to "indict" the contemporary South while "escap[ing]" into the "makebelieve region" of "swords and magnolias and mockingbirds which perhaps never existed anywhere" ("An Introduction to *The Sound and the Fury*," in *The Sound and the Fury*, p. 229). Nor could he avoid indicting that makebelieve region either, since the delusion, the nightmare, of a certain South's way of life comes to an end in modern America, and the dreamers must awaken to their guilt and shame and sorrow. It was Faulkner's privilege – such a heavy one, though – to write about the familiar as a stranger, to betray inside stories to outsiders. He became a writer because modern audiences had formed for his stories, and those stories issued from the break-up of a world that, in its very disappearance, became the subject that made his career.

Precisely these anxieties trouble another of Faulkner's early stories, "There Was a Queen," which sketches a few supporting members of the vast edifice of founding families in his imaginary county of Yoknapatawpha. This make-believe region, as we shall see, corresponds in significant ways to the actual county in north central Mississippi in which Faulkner lived most of his life.[3] Lafayette (pronounced in a most un-French fashion, with an accent on the middle syllable and a long "a" there as well: Luh-FAY-ette) County can trace its history back to Native American occupants, primarily of the Choctaw tribe. It eventually developed as a rich cotton-growing plantation realm in the period before the Civil War. Agricultural success went hand-in-hand with commercial prosperity, and Lafayette's county seat became a small hub of market and financial entrepreneurialism. Faulkner's great-grandfather made money as a cotton planter and town lawyer, though the family fortunes did not reach their zenith until after the Civil War, when the Old Colonel (the rank of his Confederate combat service) speculated in railroad-building, and his son, the so-called Young Colonel, founded the first bank in the town of Oxford. In Faulkner's imaginary domain several prominent families embody the ambitions, triumphs, and flaws of this dominant class.

"There Was a Queen" relates an episode that yokes the fortunes of two of the last survivors of the Sartoris clan, perhaps the most elite of Faulkner's plantocracy. Published in 1933, as one of a barrage of stories

Faulkner launched at the market during the decade, "Queen" contrasts the shock of modern ways with the death-like rigidity of an outmoded tradition. Narcissa Benbow has married one of the twin male descendants of Colonel John Sartoris, the major planter and businessman in the town of Jefferson, county seat of Yoknapatawpha. By the time of the story's events in 1926, all that remains of the main family are Bayard Sartoris's widow Narcissa, their child Benbow (Bory), and the ancient Aunt Jenny, the Civil War-widowed sister of the Colonel. The crisis of the story unfolds around the blackmailing of Narcissa at the hands of a federal agent who has come into possession of scandalous letters involving her. Years earlier, Narcissa had been the recipient of a series of anonymous obscene notes from someone in town infatuated with her. The perpetrator turns out to have been a member of a clan of hill farmers, the Snopeses, who have gradually been working their way into the economic and social life of Jefferson. As a book-keeper in Colonel Sartoris's bank, Byron Snopes had begun fantasizing about Narcissa when she stops by on business; finally he begins spying on her, and addressing his longings to her. Narcissa has told no one about the letters, but, somehow intrigued as much as disgusted by the lust she has inspired, she keeps them in a packet in her bedroom. After Byron steals the letters back before he flees town with embezzled bank funds, they are recovered by one of the authorities who pursue him. Years later the agent contacts Narcissa with a proposition about returning them: he wants to exchange them for sex with her.

The crassness of the deal (to which, surprisingly, Narcissa agrees) suggests the heat with which Faulkner was mulling over the consequences of bartering stolen intimate secrets for profit. The dynamic of the story captures a number of conflicting motives and reactions that encode authorial anxieties. From the moment the letters disappear from her possession, Narcissa has been "wild" with the idea that the letters might be made public: "I thought of people, men, reading them, seeing not only my name on them, but the marks of my eyes where I had read them again and again. I was wild" (*Collected Stories*, p. 739). The letters may represent certain dirty secrets of Southern community – that the virginal innocence of the Southern belle (Narcissa refers to herself as a "lady," and dresses in white) masks sexual frustration and even class boredom; that ladies end up splitting themselves between public serenity and private hysteria; and even that there's something therapeutic and enlivening in betraying such secrets to the wider world. Is Narcissa wild with shame, or arousal? In this case, the FBI agent is an outsider – with an exclamation point: Narcissa understands him to be "that Jew" (p. 740), while Aunt Jenny thinks of him as "this Yankee." What matters is that the mystique of Southern community – the ideal of close personal and familial attachments thought to be the glories of fading regional life – appears here as a slipping fiction, under which messier realities like unfulfilled sexual desire and groundless ethnic pride squirm.

To the extent Narcissa's predicament involves what happens to private letters when they become public, it also reflects Faulkner's own activity as one who trades on stories of pollution, or, perhaps, as one whose trading itself is a kind of pollution. All novelists hoard the intimate stories of others, exactly so that their secrets may be betrayed – as letters bundled for strangers to read. By revealing the South's dirty secrets, an author like Faulkner may make himself wild with mortification and regret. At the same time, he may also arouse himself with their sensational icon-smashing force. Like the young Faulkner, and a generation of other Jazz Age escapees from hidebound Southern propriety, Narcissa takes some pleasure in her moment of scandal. She overplays how indifferent she is to the trading of her body to protect her family's name, supremely capturing a modern woman's scorn for the ideal of female chastity fetishized by the traditional South. Faulkner used to parade around Oxford as a spectacularly underemployed, overly boozed dandy – dubbed "Count No 'Count" because he was clearly of no account, and outfitted in full air force officer's regalia from a war he never fought, in a uniform he'd had to buy. He may have venerated the ancients of his family, but he also thought there was something laughably hypocritical and pretentious about the decorousness of Southern "community." As in Narcissa's imagining strange men like the FBI agent reading obscene depictions of her, there must have been something exhilarating in Faulkner's traffic with New York literary agents for the purpose of publishing scandalous tales. Faulkner's anxieties and thrills find their way into Byron's voyeurism and smutty writing; into Narcissa's furtive, compulsive, even autoerotic re-reading; and into an anonymous reader's gratification via commodified letters.

Only the crack-up of a world provides such opportunities for demystification, however. It is precisely because the Sartorises and their class no longer rule that the story can show the flaws in a formerly dominant world view. Narcissa's behavior conveys the conflict between old and new orders: she prostitutes herself in order to save her respectable name, acting, without apparent personal investment, on behalf of her august aunt and the sole surviving Sartoris, her fatherless son. Narcissa's going through the motions like this suggests that the whole set of values and customs formalizing the power of elite families like the Sartorises has now become little more than empty rituals outdated by the shifts of modernity.

At the conclusion of Faulkner's related novel, *Sartoris*, published in 1929, the narrator sardonically describes the foolishness that has constituted Sartoris behavior through the generations: male recklessness, violence, exaggerated honor. "[B]ut perhaps," the narrator concludes, "Sartoris is the game itself – a game outmoded and played with pawns shaped too late and to an old dead pattern, of which the Player Himself is a little wearied" (*Flags in the Dust*, p. 875). We shall see that the "glamorous fatality" associated with the Sartorises is a trait Faulkner diagnoses as a deadly self-destructiveness within the plantation South's design.

In the snapshot of aristocratic decline Faulkner composes in "Queen," the figure of the moribund Old South is Aunt Jenny. With her direct ties to the plantation South's origins in the Atlantic colonies of the Carolinas, Aunt Jenny encapsulates the whole span of Southern slaveholding family plantation history. Dignity and pride have carried her and her kind through tides of fortune, but now she confronts the end of an era. Her rigid form is "framed by the sparse and defunctive Carolina glass" that she has brought from home, like a pioneer who has carried the design of plantation luxury to the frontier. Reduced to immobility by age, she is "tended" to "as though she were a baby" (*Collected Stories*, p. 728). Such regression signifies her obsolescence, but it also exaggerates the arrangements that have always supported dependent lives like hers. Jenny's domestic servant Elnora, an African American, nurses her mistress, whose physical attributes point to an embedded history of relations between whites and blacks in the South: Aunt Jenny is "a thin, upright woman with a delicate nose and hair the color of a whitewashed wall. About her shoulders lay a shawl of white wool, no whiter than her hair against her black dress" (p. 730).

Not only does Jenny's being draped in stark white and black evoke the optics of Southern race, it also suggests the fundamental link between race and labor, mistress and slave. Elnora serves; Jenny is waited upon. Yet something about Jenny implies a "whitewash"-ing, the refusal to recognize the false face of race – race itself a fiction of masters who deny the humanity of blacks while depending upon them for life itself.

Around the edges of the failing edifice of Sartoris domination spills the evidence that condemns the South for laying its cornerstone upon the injustice of slavery. Even in the South of 1926, the denial enabling a dominant Southern way of life continues to falsify human relations. Early in the story we encounter a classic instance of Faulkner's syntactical ambiguity:

> As Elnora crossed the back yard toward the kitchen door she remembered how ten years ago at this hour old Bayard, who was her half-brother (though possibly but not probably neither of them knew it, including Bayard's father), would be tramping up and down the back porch, shouting stableward for the Negro men and for his saddle mare. (p. 727)

We may use this sentence as an example of the way Faulkner's notorious stylistic difficulty is a function of his effort to portray the often confused, even contradictory states of mind of his characters. In this case we have a sentence describing Elnora's memory of a Sartoris patriarch, old Bayard, son of Colonel John, exercising the prerogatives of country master. An owner's force of rule over animals and slaves comes through in the detail of stomping on the porch, which may also imply the kind of irrational violence necessary to establish authority. But the sentence loses its way momentarily when the term "half-brother" comes up, because Elnora is not just the descendant of African slaves; if old Bayard is her half-brother, then her father was Colonel Sartoris, who, in a manner familiar to slaves, must have fathered her by one of his slave women. Elnora's mother is never named. The sentence's parenthetical qualification captures the tangle of knowledge and denial necessary to slaveholding. If "possibly but not probably neither of them knew it," then the narrator is uneasily, indirectly asserting that Elnora and Bayard likely *do know* that they are brother and sister. The dangling phrase, "including

Bayard's father," however, proves hopelessly noncommittal. If the half-siblings know, presumably through Elnora's mother, there is no reason to doubt that the Colonel knew as well. But the ambiguity is telling; it does not matter whether any white Sartoris knows or not about their non-white relations. Even to refer to the Old Colonel as *Bayard's* father is to cancel out the importance of his being Elnora's father too. *Their* father? Impossible. To possess any negro ancestry was to be negro in the slaveholding South (this definition became even more emphatic after Emancipation, and culminated in legal codes defining blackness as the possession of a single "drop" of "black blood." It didn't matter that the concept of black blood has never had a shred of scientific evidence.).[4] To possess any negro ancestry in the slave-holding South was also to be no one in the eyes of the master's law. Thus the "possibly but not probably" underscores, subtly, deftly, the power of social denial in the plantation South. Historically, what whites knew about their inter-relation with black slaves and the reality of mixed families simply was put aside by the force of ideological insistence, which acted to rationalize economic exploitation by a ruling elite. Faulkner sharpens the irony of his insight here by immediately reporting that Elnora's husband is in the penitentiary for "stealing" and that her son Joby had "gone to Memphis to wear fine clothes on Beale Street" (p. 727). Criminalizing a negro's petty thievery obscures the moral obscenity of a master race stealing millions of black bodies and their labor; smiling at a negro's fondness for splashy clothes diverts attention from a national garment industry founded on the raw material flowing from Southern cotton fields, on the raw backs of slaves.

Elnora functions as a transitional figure. Victimized in fundamental respects by the family and system that denies her recognition, she nonetheless defends its core values. She is the one who complains about the last Sartoris, the child Bory, growing up without a sense of ancestral pride, like common "trash." She is the one who refuses to speak Narcissa's name because she looks down on townspeople, and who disapproves of modern violations of decorum. But she is also the one who is going to have to find a new role for herself when the Sartoris name ends. Notice how Faulkner offers a brilliant image for Elnora's function in the Sartoris edifice: "The two women [Aunt Jenny and Elnora] were motionless in the window: the one leaning a little forward in the wheel chair, the Negress a little behind the chair, motionless too and erect as a caryatid" (p. 731). The syntax of the sentence ought to balance Virginia Du Pres as "the one," with Elnora as (the reader might predict) "the other." But Faulkner substitutes "Negress" for "other" in the expected pair "the one/the other." The syntax suggests how Southern habits of identification assume the oneness of a white person, independent and prior, as well as the otherness of the negro, different and secondary. The strange word "caryatid" deepens the effect. "Caryatid" is an architectural term refer- ring to the figure of a woman incorporated into a supporting column, so that it appears as if the upper part of a structure rests upon pillars of women's bodies. The device is used in classical Greek architecture, the term said to derive from the women of the town of Caryae. Faulkner could hardly have found a better word to convey the function of slaves and some women in plantation dynasties. People like Elnora must work silently, as if inanimate components of the monuments built by Deep South masters in tribute to themselves. The unfamiliarity and awkwardness of the word "caryatid" arrest the reader; here is an uncommon term, in which a long history of bondage is secreted away, and whose very obscurity mimics the difficulty, especially for those who have profited from it, of reading slavery's scandal: black women turned into fixtures of labor, humans reduced to stone.

A word to the reader: you can relax. I'm not going to analyze every line of Faulkner with this kind of scrutiny. But at the outset we do need to establish how dense and rich Faulkner's language is, and how his circuitous, polysyllabic style is not just personal eccentricity, or a symptom of alcoholism, or artistic ineptitude, or even some resentful torture of the reader, but an audacious bid to write like no one ever wrote before, and to do so because more than anything Faulkner wanted the reader to feel the world to be as intensely moving as he did himself. That he strained language to its breaking point conveys less a reluctance to communicate anything than a desperate determination to communicate everything. As he put it once, his ambi- tion was to put his whole world in one gigantic sentence, between a single capital and period. "Artist at Home" and "There Was a Queen" illustrate in miniature some of the tensions Faulkner encountered as he began to write about the part of the world he knew intimately, for a public that was curious, often to the point of prurience, about a region that had always seemed backward, strange, even grotesque to outsiders. Faulkner's artistic method tried to encompass the massive, abrupt transformations the South underwent as it became more and more like the rest of the modern nation, even as his art brought the country face to face with Southern ties it had so long sought to deny.

CHAPTER 1

An Artist Never Quite at Home: Faulkner's Apprehension of Modern Life

The prevailing view of Faulkner emphasizes his preoccupation with the past. Faulkner comes across foremost as the descendant of a distinguished family with origins in the Old South's plantation society, creator of the master emblem of modern Southern nostalgia in the person of his character Quentin Compson, and a cantankerous skeptic about many newfangled notions – including, at various times, the onset of a culture of credit, consumption, and labor-saving convenience; the spread of new technologies for communication and commerce; the urgent pace of social change in the South, culminating in women's and black Americans' civil rights; and the relaxation of proper manners and the right to privacy that his class associated with the virtues of a civilized Southern way of life. Recently, some literary critics have even begun to complain that Faulkner's obsession with the Southern past – with its monumental achievements as well as its ruinous evils – stunted modern Southern writing for generations. Faulkner's indisputable greatness as a writer meant, according to this view, that in order to establish their own credentials as Southern writers in a Faulkner-haunted landscape, his successors had to take on Faulkner's subjects – history, race, regional identity, and the despair of one group of individuals (primarily white males of the owning class), who suffer guilt and shame over their past and who fail to create a future. Perhaps this is what Flannery O'Connor meant when she joked about Faulkner's influence on subsequent writers: as one herself, she said, she didn't want her mule and wagon on the tracks when the Dixie Limited roared through.

What I want to argue instead, by way of correcting this portrait of an imagination obsessed by the past, is that Faulkner also responded strongly to the opportunities for novelty presented by the modern age. It is true that perhaps the most famous line in all of Faulkner is a remark made by one of his characters, usually attributed to "Faulkner" himself, that "the past is never dead. It's not even past" (Gavin Stevens, *Requiem for a Nun*, p. 535). But if Quentin Compson feels as a twenty-year-old that his entire life is already over, crushed by the weight of his ancestors' deeds, his head a "commonwealth" of voices that have already said all there is to say, his mind intent on a suicide that feels redundant – for all that, his is not the only fate Faulkner can imagine. Despite the grotesques of passion, greed, indulgence, selfishness, crudeness, and ignorance that populate Faulkner's chronicle of a world becoming modern, he never turns his back on the wondrous capacity of humankind to invent new possibilities for itself. Even a monster of modernity like the rapacious, soulless businessman Flem Snopes impresses his creator with his ingenuity and determination. And Faulkner remarked famously in one of his few comments about his artistic philosophy that "life is motion," and that the aim of the artist was to arrest that motion so that readers years later could make it move again.[1] The changes in the world he knew powerfully affected the young writer Faulkner, and motivated his early efforts to capture change on the tip of his pen. There was something thrilling about what was happening to the world at his moment in time. Faulkner's art responds to the sensation of exhilaration as much as to a sense of horror at these transformations. He asks how individuals process the massive upheavals associated with modernity, and how their varying reactions tell us about their distinct characters, backgrounds, and futures.

In the remainder of this chapter I want to discuss a number of Faulkner's earlier works by considering two main issues we identified in "Artist at Home" and "There Was a Queen." We'll look at some short stories and novels that represent the shock of new forms of social and cultural behavior to the world into which Faulkner was born. The South of the 1920s, after World War I, experienced strong shifts toward modernity: the arrival of automobiles and the building of new roads; the electrification of towns and farms; plentiful consumer goods and the growth of national merchandising through catalogues; the attempt to secure greater personal liberties by black Americans who had fought in Europe and realized that Jim Crow segregation was not universal; the extension of the ballot to women in 1920; a liberalization of sexual mores; the popularity of movies and a culture of celebrity; the power of national magazines and advertising; the modernization of education and public health; the development of local industries, the increase of wage labor, the decline in small farm ownership; and the inevitable rearrangements of wealth, social prestige, and power in communities of the Deep South. These works will help us to see that Faulkner *apprehended* modern life in several senses: he tried to comprehend it by imagining its effects on all sorts of different people; he tried to track down and "indict" what caused suffering in his society, as new evils evolved from past ones; but he was also made apprehensive by modernity even as he granted its ability to excite and liberate. We'll also keep in mind the question of modern cultural forms. What did it mean for Faulkner to think of himself as a modern artist? In what ways did modernist experimentation with literary form and style itself embody the idea of modern change? In what ways might it have resisted them? How did new developments like mass magazines and the movies change the economics of Faulkner's professional life, and how did they affect his subject matter, technique, and sense of audience?

Faulkner seriously committed himself to the vocation of writing during his early twenties. As a neophyte, Faulkner at first sought recognition from individual readers and authors whom he knew; they were critical in affirming his sense of himself as *a writer*. Even when he was in grade school, Billy Faulkner had once answered a teacher's question about what he wanted to be when he grew up by saying that he intended to be an author, like his "great-grandpappy." The Old Colonel, John Clark Falkner (as he spelled his name), had written romance novels about the old South. As Faulkner reached his high school years, he realized that some girls were impressed by artistic types, and he took to composing books of hand-lettered poems, the pages of which he meticulously sewed together and illustrated with pen-and-ink drawings. Faulkner crafted volumes like this for his eventual wife Estelle, as well as for a few other young women he became enamored with.[2] Faulkner also developed a close friendship with a young man from another prominent Oxford family, Phil Stone, who shared his enthusiasm for literature; together they discussed the latest modern verse, experimental fiction, and avant garde literary journals.

When Faulkner began writing himself, Phil Stone was the first audience whose approval he craved. (Maybe a readership of one was good preparation for the size of the audiences for his novels when they first appeared.) Periodically after leaving high school, Faulkner took courses as a non-degree student at the University of Mississippi, in his home town. He studied Shakespeare and French literature, and tried his hand at imitating symbolist poetry. As some of his poems began appearing in the campus magazine, he also latched on to a university theater troupe and started writing scripts for them. One that survives is called *The Marionettes*, after the group's name.[3]

During these years Oxford's townsfolk were puzzled by Faulkner's seeming idleness. A man already in his early twenties, he made money sporadically by painting houses, which left him plenty of time to play golf. He got a job as post-master of the US mail station on the university campus, but spent most of his time playing cards and reading his patrons' magazines. When an inspector finally showed up to fire him, after numerous customer complaints, Faulkner memorably remarked that though he expected to have to work the rest of his life, at least he wouldn't any longer have to be at the beck and call of any son of a bitch with two cents for a postage stamp. Meanwhile, Faulkner was stealing away for long days of reading (sometimes filling Phil Stone's automobile with books and heading to the countryside), and toiling away long nights on his poems and prose fiction. Faulkner's perseverance and Stone's confidence finally paid off in Faulkner's first major publication, a volume of poems entitled *The Marble Faun*. Stone put up money to subsidize its publication by a small Boston firm, and Faulkner saw his book in print in December 1924.

Another reinforcement of Faulkner's calling came when he stayed in New Orleans for six months beginning in January of 1925. In addition to palling around with the Sherwood Andersons, he strengthened his ties with a group of ambitious young intellectuals and artists who had begun publishing a Southern arts magazine. *The Double Dealer* printed work by a number of talented newcomers, including some who like Faulkner were to become major figures, such as Jean Toomer and Hart Crane. Faulkner had gotten to know some of the *Double Dealer* crowd during earlier visits to New Orleans. The editors provided opportunities that encouraged Faulkner's permanent turn from poetry to fiction. He began contributing prose pieces regularly, and also was assigned a few reviews of contemporary authors, including one of

Eugene O'Neill. Although Faulkner was to publish another volume of poetry, *A Green Bough*, in 1933, few of those poems were new; most dated from a decade earlier when he had been concentrating on poetry. In 1925 Faulkner's fresh material mainly involved prose sketches – including experiments in creating colorful first-person narratives.[4] These reflected Joyce's innovative stream-of-consciousness style and the interplay of voices in T. S. Eliot's *The Waste Land*. *The Double Dealer*'s climate of avant-garde experimentation must have been ideal for the primary project Faulkner was working on in New Orleans, a full-length novel he was calling "Mayday" (re-titled for publication as *Soldiers' Pay*).

Everything about Faulkner's first novel signals that he was making his bid to join a new generation of modern artists. Both in subject and style, the book captures emerging sensibilities that became hallmarks of modern literature in Europe and the US. One common element of classic modernist works was the conviction that fundamental changes were taking place in Western society in the first decades of the twentieth century. Besides some of the features of modernization I've already referred to as affecting the US South in the 1920s, earlier and even more basic upheavals followed from late nineteenth-century challenges to principal received truths. Darwin had permanently compromised views of human distinctiveness and the providence of nature; Freud had greatly complicated common sense models of human consciousness and motivation; Nietzsche questioned accepted ideals of morality and truth and urged personal authenticity as the proper measure of a life. New technologies of communication and economic production; the unprecedented geopolitics of colonial expansion and eventual global conflict; and the extension for the first time of full citizens' rights to women and immigrants – all powerfully reshaped Western society. Virginia Woolf remarked that human nature itself seemed to have changed by 1910. Literature of the years just before and after World War I engaged such transformations centrally. Think of William Butler Yeats's involvement in Irish nationalism as British imperial authority was challenged worldwide. Or Joyce's fascination with novelties like urban mass transit, advertising culture, and new sexual permissiveness in *Ulysses* (1922). Or Kafka's prophetic fables of spreading bureaucracy that would threaten the very idea of a private self. Then the war itself became a flashpoint for the way the promise of modernity turned so deadly perverse.

Many of the great works immediately following World War I created portraits of individual and cultural devastation. Readers could find the mood of despair perfectly captured in the poetry of T. S. Eliot. *The Waste Land* (1922) delineated a culture in fragmentary ruins, its myths shattered by modern ignorance, materialism, abandoned faith. Eliot organized his edgy, only partially coherent poem around the murky mythological figure of an ancient fertility god, whose sexually muti-lated body symbolized the need for rejuvenation. The figure of a damaged survivor gets reworked in a number of subsequent novels, including *Soldiers' Pay*. In Virginia Woolf's *Mrs. Dalloway* (1925) we encounter the character Septimus Smith, who suffers from shell shock, and whose condition suggests the war's blows to the invincibility of the British Empire, the superiority of Western moral and cultural values, the purposes of civilized progress. Even a figure like Nick Carraway in *The Great Gatsby* (1925) drifts through a world that has lost its way after the war; on the outskirts of New York City Nick drives through a desolate stretch of working-class Long Island that he dubs "the waste land."

The protagonist of Faulkner's first novel also is a casualty of the war, a young pilot from a small Southern town who returns severely wounded – blind, silent, motionless. Donald Mahon's terrible scar symbolizes the traumatic effects of mass violence, disillusionment, and denial that marked a generation. Like Jake Barnes in Hemingway's more famous *The Sun Also Rises*, which appeared the same year, Mahon lives on as a ghost of himself. Jake Barnes, who suffers a disabling sexual injury, has given "more than his life" (*The Sun Also Rises*, p. 39) according to the Italian officer who awards him a medal; Jake's wound blocks him from intimacy, from satisfaction, from creating a future – he's condemned to a posthumous existence. As for Mahon, a former sweetheart laments that the "Donald she had known was dead; this one was but a sorry substitute" (*Soldiers' Pay*, p. 216). Mahon succumbs altogether to his wounds, while those around him try to adjust to a transformed world. The woman who escorts him back to Georgia from the military hospital herself has lost a lover in the war, and another young cadet who tries to woo her observes that "times have changed since the war . . . the war makes you older than they used to" (p. 221).

"Mayday" is the emergency cry of pilots about to crash. A whole era of confidence and idealism went down in the aftermath of the war. Faulkner's narrator speaks with typical post-war cynicism when he describes the neighbors who come to sympathize with the wreck that is Mahon: "solid business men interested in the Ku Klux Klan more than in war, and interested in war only as a matter of dollars and cents, while their wives chatted about clothes to each other across Mahon's scarred, oblivious brow" (p. 117). If the war in retrospect was revealed to have been urged on largely by the munitions makers and financiers who stood to profit from the death trade – a far cry from the patriotic idealism President Woodrow Wilson had appealed to, other traditional sources of meaning and solace hardly withstood post-war disillusionment either. Mahon's father, a rector, finds little refuge in his church. And the ideal of tight-knit Southern community vaporizes before the severity of Mahon's disfiguration; the generic town seems mainly to have devolved into a bad dream of superficial self-gratification. The occasional act of kindness or generosity stands out, but there's no secure ground for common ethics any more.

For Faulkner, as a young man recently returned from a failed attempt to get into combat, drunk with contempt for the small-town Southern pieties that smothered his genius for audacity, and eager to scandalize those who thought they knew him, this moment of post-war disenchantment must have been sublime. *Soldiers' Pay* proved to be the sort of book in which he could vent his scorn for the old-fashioned mores under which he chafed, scandalously indulge more liberal social and artistic views, sharpen his criticism of modern bourgeois conventionality, mock the frivolousness of an even younger generation that hadn't been scarred by the war, and begin to betray the bizarre, sensational tales his "closed society" tried to keep quiet. In all of these Faulkner found himself perfectly aligned with the latest national fashions in literature. What Faulkner had to say was what a new generation wanted to hear; the way he wanted to say it was what a literate audience thought art should be. Up to a certain point, his early success as a writer derived from the good fortune of this mutual reinforcement. In *Soldiers' Pay* we may appreciate how Faulkner wrote out of deep personal motives, even as he kept an eye on what might win publishers' attention and the rewards of acceptance.

Faulkner finished his manuscript in May of 1925, submitted it to Sherwood Anderson's publisher, Boni & Liveright, and saw his first novel appear the following February. Part of its legend involves Anderson's having agreed to recommend the manuscript on the condition that he not have to read it. Anderson was busy finishing a book of his own, called *Dark Laughter*. The ambitious new publisher Horace Liveright had recently persuaded Anderson to leave his original firm by offering the author of *Winesburg, Ohio* the present-day equivalent of a million dollar advance. As part of his agreement, Anderson promised to be on the lookout for other up-and-coming talent; his conviction about Faulkner's genius evidently did not depend on the detail of actual words on the page. Liveright himself was doubtful about *Soldiers' Pay* after receiving mixed readers' reports, but he went forward on the basis of Anderson's confidence. Anderson never told Liveright that he had not read the manuscript.

Horace Liveright represented the most flamboyant of the so-called new New York publishers. Eager to capitalize on the resurgence of leisure pursuits by a class of prosperous culture consumers in post-war America, several upstart publishing firms aggressively set about developing new sectors of the literary marketplace. In contrast, older houses, even ones that relocated to New York City, tended to retain the aesthetic and business culture of their genteel roots in nineteenth-century New England. Scribner's was one of the few long-time publishers that did manage to keep up with the changing field. Founded in the early 1800s, they were publishers of Henry James, Edith Wharton, and many of the foremost British writers before World War I. The firm also spotted new talent like Fitzgerald and Hemingway after the war, and boasted the greatest editor of the period, Maxwell Perkins. Faulkner was mindful of Scribner's prestige. He had penciled the word "Scribners" at the bottom of the first manuscript sheet of "Mayday" (Karl, 1989, p. 227), and he later urged his wife Estelle to make the publisher her first choice for a manuscript of her own.

If firms like Scribner's could confer legitimacy on a writer by virtue of its time-proven taste and commitment to elite writing, newer publishers happily sought out more volatile sectors of the literary scene, where bolder writers were challenging all sorts of orthodoxies. New companies like Knopf and Harcourt, Brace joined Boni & Liveright in recruiting established writers like Sherwood Anderson, Theodore Dreiser, and Upton Sinclair, who were perceived as prime shapers of a more modern sensibility. Such firms also cultivated fresh writing by a variety of younger artists. The new publishers welcomed work that was experimental in form, and also encouraged the untapped subject matter found in writing by immigrants and African Americans. Though such publishing strategies aimed at expanding the market for

FIGURE 1 Faulkner posing in the Royal Air Force uniform he purchased before returning to Oxford, Mississippi, after flight training in Toronto (July 1918). Cofield Collection, Southern Media Archive, University of Mississippi Special Collections (B1F38).

literature, these publishers also tended to be socially progressive by conviction.

Faulkner's placing of his book with Liveright signifies a connection with a site of cultural production where value accrued to iconoclasm, novelty, and daring. Liveright published the early Ezra Pound, to whom he was committed despite weak sales, Eugene O'Neill, D. H. Lawrence, H. D., Hart Crane, and many others. Whatever Liveright's misgivings about the strength of Faulkner's manuscript, and however much he failed to respond to Faulkner personally (calling him the sort of person he couldn't warm to), there's no question that *Soldiers' Pay* found a congenial place on Boni & Liveright's list. The publisher had defined its mission as wanting to shock bourgeois complacency, offend middle-class notions of propriety, disseminate serious ideas about the liberalization of social mores and economic affairs, and embrace "the modern" however broadly understood.

As a Boni & Liveright book, *Soldiers' Pay* would have been associated with the sexual avant-garde of American publishing. Writing against censorship in 1923, Liveright insisted that "[f]rankness in literature relating to sexual matters never corrupted or depraved anyone, adult or child" (Liveright, "The Absurdity of Censorship," quoted in Gilmer, 1970, p. 75). An early publisher of Freud, Liveright would have liked the boldness with which *Soldiers' Pay* represented sexual behavior. *Soldiers' Pay* and Faulkner's next novel, *Mosquitoes* (also published by Liveright), contain Faulkner's most explicit writing (and thinking) about sexual relations. In the 1920s, many young women took to displaying their bodies more openly and announcing their desires more directly. Recall that the femme fatale of *The Sun Also Rises* is once vividly described as showing off curves as sleek as a racing yacht's. Cicely Saunders in *Soldiers' Pay* parades in filmy gowns that leave little to the imagination. Virtually all of the younger characters offer and accept sexual intimacies openly. Cicely gets out of her engagement to Donald when she realizes how badly he's mutilated; unable to convince the families to release her from her commitment, she gives her virginity to another suitor, in a bid to destroy her worthiness (at least as determined by the standards she wants to defy). A strange character named Januarius Jones spends most of the novel trying to bed any young woman within reach. Faulkner signals that the World War has fundamentally altered the sexual landscape. Girls are "bad" and say what they want. The Southern belle has been consigned to Donald

Mahon's amnesiac oblivion, and the novel daringly entertains sexual attraction between women, between men, and even between races.[5]

These aspects of the novel would have reverberated with other books on Liveright's list, including Frances Newman's pitiless savaging of the Southern belle in *The Hard-Boiled Virgin* (also 1926) and Anita Loos's wildly popular send-up of an empty-headed flapper who outsmarts one sexual predator after the next, *Gentlemen Prefer Blondes* (1925). One wonders if the publication of *Soldiers' Pay* on so progressive a list emboldened Faulkner to explore more frankly the sexual aspects of artistic life in *Mosquitoes*, a book whose original form made such explicit references to lesbianism and sexual matters generally that even Boni & Liveright asked for some taming down.

A second feature of *Soldiers' Pay* that conformed to the sensibility of the new American literature involved its condescending attitude toward small town life. In the wake of the success of Sherwood Anderson's *Winesburg* (1919), the younger writer assured their mutual publisher in 1927 that he was preparing "a collection of short stories of my townspeople" (*Selected Letters*, p. 34). This work became *These Thirteen*, a volume that constituted Faulkner's own attempt at diagnosing the psychopathology of everyday life in the provinces. In *Soldiers' Pay*, the narrator mocks the Southern town to which Mahon returns, its courthouse square peopled by

> the city fathers, progenitors of solid laws and solid citizens who believed in Tom Watson and feared only God and drouth, in black string ties or the faded brushed gray and bronze meaningless medals of the Confederate States of America, no longer having to make any pretense toward labor, [and who] slept or whittled away the long drowsy days . . . (*Soldiers' Pay*, pp. 87–88)

Faulkner affects the kind of cosmopolitan superiority one can also hear in his letters to the worldly Liveright: "I am damned tired of our [F.]99[°] winters of this sunny south. I envy you England. England is 'ome to me, in a way" (*Selected Letters*, p. 34). (It's hard to know what that means. Faulkner visited England with a friend during a six-month Euro-trip, but found London so expensive they left after a few days.) Faulkner remarks in the novel that to "feel provincial" is to find "that a certain conventional state of behavior has become inexplicably obsolete over night" (*Soldiers' Pay*, p. 198). The super-sophisticated

bohemianism running through the novel signals Faulkner's own determination to escape that feeling of being a Southern provincial.

Faulkner's spirit of criticism toward his own South would have been
braced institutionally by Boni & Liveright's record as publishers as well
of politically radical literature. Liveright printed John Reed's widely
read account of the Russian Revolution, *Ten Days that Shook the World*
(1918). He cultivated Greenwich Village radical intellectuals, and over
the course of the 1920s published Max Eastman, Marsden Hartley, and
Mary Heaton Vorse, along with Upton Sinclair. Boni & Liveright's
credits include the most influential proletarian novel of the period,
Mike Gold's *Jews Without Money* (1930). Though Faulkner's personal
politics were mainly centrist (which made them more liberal than most
Southerners'), his steady attention to the legacy of racial oppression,
his sensitivity to class humiliation, and his disgust with the private
ownership of the wilderness (not to mention of humans) would not
have made him out of place among more extreme critics of American
capitalism.

Liveright's profile as a publisher might have contributed to Faulkner's
sense of the literary field in one further respect. In a study of the
Harlem Renaissance, George Hutchinson has focused on the extent of
the new publishers' commitment to writing by African Americans.
No one led more prominently in this project than Horace Liveright. In
1923 Liveright published the earliest and arguably greatest of the New
Negro renaissance works, Jean Toomer's *Cane*. Liveright also solicited
poems from Countee Cullen, and was responsible for the publication
in 1924 of Jessie Fauset's *There Is Confusion*. Liveright's commitment to
representing African American life also indicated directions for white
writers like Sherwood Anderson, whose *Dark Laughter* romanticizes
the easy pleasure-taking and earthy speech of black folk. Liveright
considered it a "great" book and advertised it heavily. *Soldiers' Pay* too
includes some elementary black dialect writing by Faulkner, much of
it in the minstrel vein, and ends with a reference to the "crooning
submerged passion of the dark race" (*Soldiers' Pay*, p. 256) that floats
from a nearby church service. But the more compelling aspect of
Faulkner's representation of race in *Soldiers' Pay* involves a kind of
confession about the incomprehensibility of black experience. Blacks
appear as inscrutable, objects of an historical refusal by whites to comprehend the humanity of a group they have dehumanized: negroes
march by like "a pagan catafalque . . . Rigid, as though carved in Egypt

ten thousand years ago" (p. 119). (Recall Elnora as a caryatid.) At one point, Donald Mahon's aged black nurse attempts to call him out of his stupor: "Donald, baby, look at me" (p. 135). But Mahon's belated response is only to ask "Who was that talking, Joe?" (p. 136). Faulkner scrupulously avoids taking the liberties with black speech and subjectivity that typify *Dark Laughter*. Yet the strong appetite for fiction about African Americans exhibited by his publisher could only have encouraged Faulkner's move toward confronting the South's racial slavery and segregation in the subsequent chronicle of Yoknapatawpha.

Faulkner had headed to New Orleans in January of 1925 intending to book passage to Europe; he planned to travel for six months with William Spratling, a painter he had met through *The Double Dealer* group. Delaying their departure until July, Faulkner and Spratling finally sailed for Italy, though they quickly moved on to Paris. They left only for brief excursions and spent nearly six months there. Faulkner continued to work hard on his writing, concentrating on a narrative set partly in Paris's Luxembourg Gardens. It involved the infatuation of a young man with his sister, and Faulkner was practically intoxicated with its beauty when he described, in a letter to his mother, the sensation of finishing it. (Yes, the tone of intoxication may have had a simpler explanation. It was Paris after all.) The sketch, "Elmer," later was revised, with a small part incorporated into the last scene of the novel *Sanctuary* (1931), and the pattern of a sensitive young man's obsession with his younger sister repeated in *The Sound and the Fury* (1929). Faulkner thought its conclusion was the best prose he had yet written – prose that was "all poetry" – and he was plainly inspired by being in a city associated with the highest achievements of culture. Not only did Faulkner love reading French literature – novelists like Balzac and Flaubert, and modern poets like Verlaine, Rimbaud, and Baudelaire, all of whom he had translated and imitated in his college courses. He also spent hours at galleries and museums, particularly the Louvre, where in the 1920s he might have seen recent post-Impressionists like Cézanne hanging side-by-side with classic paintings from earlier periods.

Faulkner's second novel reflects the continuing effort of a young writer to establish himself as a modernist author. Boni & Liveright published *Mosquitoes* in 1927. Faulkner had worked on the manuscript in New Orleans, where he roomed with Spratling after they returned from Paris. The novel is made up almost entirely of conversations about art and sex, expressing attitudes of bohemian avant-gardism toward both. What Faulkner is up to in this novel is less a sober consideration of various philosophies of art, than a flamboyant dramatization of the scandalous new ways art was being understood as the symptom of emotional and psychological disorders. In a way, *Mosquitoes* subjects art to the sting of demystification, suggesting that sexual frustration and "perverse" desires are the wellsprings of artistic creation. *Mosquitoes* concentrates on the way individual pathology may motivate creativity.

Mosquitoes depicts something like an arts-themed booze cruise. A wealthy patroness of New Orleans cultural life assembles a motley crew of artists – a couple of poets, a novelist, a sculptor; a few aging hangers on – a salesman, a publisher, a donor, a critic; and some attractive young people, for a week's sailing on her yacht around Lake Pontchartrain, just north of the city. What results must resemble features of day-to-day life among the *Double Dealer* circle. Conversations go on apparently for days; earnest discussants have far more opinions than listeners; the older you are the more you drink, the more you drink the more you talk; and various young couples manage to sneak off and hook up sexually to avoid blacking out under the fume of words. The novel mainly suggests the following: life is all about sex, and those who can, do; those who can't, think about it all the time, and some write about it instead. Or wish they could write about it. There's a jokey, spoofy side to *Mosquitoes* that actually tells us a lot about modern attitudes toward art, and Faulkner's willingness to have fun with them.

The dizzy dowager who hosts this expedition, Mrs. Maurier, happily obliges the sponging artists, who care only for the luxury she provides. Mrs. Maurier espouses a traditionally high-minded ideal of art. To the sculptor Gordon, a rude arrogant sort, she blithely extols the ability of the artist to ignore all the "unhappiness" in the world and to "go through life, keeping yourself from becoming involved in it, to gather inspiration for your Work" (*Mosquitoes*, p. 377). Everyone else on board, however, seems to possess more modern worldly views of art. What their naturalistic explanations share is the conviction that the pleasure of making art compensates for other kinds of frustrated desire. Such an attitude reflects Freud's then revolutionary speculation that art is the sublimation of unfulfilled sexual wishes. In *Mosquitoes*, the novelist Dawson Fairchild (generally held to be modeled on Sherwood

Anderson), puts the relation of art to sex concisely: "[I]t's a substitute" (p. 443), he replies, when his friend Julius Wiseman points out that for older people "[n]ot only are most of our sins vicarious, but most of our pleasures are too" (*idem*).

Even a non-artist like the character William Talliaferro, who suffers a disabling terror of intimacy with women, "labors under the illusion that Art is just a valid camouflage for rutting" (p. 312). In his envy of male artists' commerce with naked female models and women admirers, he understands art as a route to, rather than a transformation of, sexual desire. Especially through the art-talk of New Orleans, Faulkner absorbed Freud – who greatly excited the generation of moderns, and notions from his psychology show up in Faulkner's writing throughout his career. In *Mosquitoes*, for good measure, Faulkner tosses in other Freudian hypotheses about artistic production. One is that the pleasure of making art derives from the anal stage of sexual development and is associated with the gratification of making waste. So, the character Mark Frost is ridiculed as "a poet who produced an occasional cerebral and obscure poem in four or seven lines reminding one somehow of the function of evacuation excruciatingly and incompletely performed" (p. 298). Or consider how twins, a brother and sister, exhibit unusual sexual familiarities, which are both expressed and sublimated by artistic activities: as the boy Josh whittles a pipe stem, his sister leans on him, "extending her hand toward the object on his lap. It was a cylinder of wood larger than a silver dollar and about three inches long" (p. 291). Josh finally gets rid of her, annoyed by her open lack of sexual restraint. That art might be motivated by the effort to re-channel bodily drives accords with Freud's premise that the price of civilization itself is the renunciation of natural, unbounded longings, beginning with those conventionalized as incestuous.

Our novelist laughs at himself, too. The nubile Jenny recalls running into an odd little sunburned man on the beach who blurts out that "if the straps of my dress was to break I'd devastate the country" (p. 371). This horny "liar by profession" turns out to be a fellow named "Faulkner." There's a general atmosphere of determined irreverence toward art in *Mosquitoes*; it's as if Faulkner needs to take part in one general goal of modernism, which involved separating art from its earlier exalted purposes as revealing transcendent truth, representing the essence of reality, or expressing the noblest thoughts of humankind. Instead, art for the moderns exposed the relativity of truth, struggled with the elusiveness of reality, and was bound by the ego-centrism of all representation.

Reading *Mosquitoes* as a comic revue inspired by the ways artists sublimate carnal urges may be true to the Freudian spirit of the novel. From this standpoint, art functions as one of a series of sliding substitutes for unavailable objects of desire. But the novel sometimes conveys an intensity of individual dissatisfaction that issues from some more profound black hole of discontentment. In such moments Faulkner's developing sense of desire as unappeasable comes into view. You might say that ordinary desire involves identifying attainable gratifications in place of unattainable ones. But imagine an earlier, fundamental, traumatic event in which every child suffers separation from total love, attention, care, the gratification of every need. With the child's emerging self-sufficiency comes as well this loss of perfect at-one-ness with the mother's body and the material sphere that envelops it. The evidence that, paradoxically, identity is founded on this lack – a rupture that enables selfhood – would appear in adulthood as a sort of causeless, nameless sense of loss. No everyday gratification could possibly address the abyss around which every self forms. This model of how mature individuals harbor the ghost of unappeasable want derives from the psychoanalyst Jacques Lacan, who extended Freud's theories of psychological development. This phenomenon as it appears in *Mosquitoes* adds an important new dimension to Faulkner's view of human nature. It suggests how the feelings we experience as so uniquely our own, are always functions of the processes that socialize us, and how those processes produce selves scarred by the wound of accepting a socially sanctioned identity.

We need these more complex ideas about desire to explain some of the characters' incurable sadness and rage in *Mosquitoes*. For example, the silly Mrs. Maurier, as it turns out, has been the victim of disappointed love early in life. Romanced by a dashing but penniless young man, she is nonetheless forced by her family to wed an older plantation magnate. Mrs. Maurier bears her sorrow behind a mask-like demeanor. Although we infer that Mrs. Maurier was in love with her young "Lochinvar," in fact we learn nothing about her state of mind. Something else, perhaps, having to do with the helplessness of women, under the authority of men, to control their own bodies seems even more deeply to be the issue. Mrs. Maurier's lack of affect suggests powers of suppression required by the most fundamental pain of social life. When Fairchild speculates that her sexless marriage has been responsible for her current flirtatiousness, he describes her body as "no longer remember[ing] that it missed anything . . . the ghost of a need to rectify something the lack of which her body has long since forgotten about" (p. 522). It's that kind of ghostliness, with its memory of the absence of sexual intimacy as the trace of a need addressing a "lack," that hints at the desperate underside to some of Mrs. Maurier's frivolous behavior. Her theory that artists are blessed because they can ignore the world proves more poignant once we appreciate the depth out of which a person's desires may never catch up to her want.

Likewise, even an apparently trivial fool like the lingerie wholesaler Talliaferro, who moons over young women and whines for advice about how to seduce them, manifests scars of a more basic trauma. The opening pages of the novel associate Talliaferro with a strange object: milk bottles – a dirty one that he totes around, which he exchanges for a full one, to be delivered to his friend Gordon, the sculptor. Faulkner makes the image as frankly Freudian as Josh's phallic pipe; here the bottle represents a vestige of pre-sexual maternal well-being. It shows up precisely as Talliaferro suffers extreme sexual agitation over Mrs. Maurier's niece, whom he has just met. As he "covertly" watches the eighteen-year-old's arousingly "sexless" limbs, Talliaferro sits anxiously "nursing his bottle" (p. 270). Talliaferro's arrested development marks a refusal to abandon the female body as pre-sexual nursing mother. In this sense, Talliaferro will never grow up, because sexual fulfillment requires more than just nerving yourself up; it requires accepting the only partial gratification of desire represented by "normative" genital heterosexuality.

Perhaps the clearest version of Faulkner's intuitions about the bedrock of dissatisfaction is Gordon. Often taken as Faulkner's projection of his own artistic sensibility, and perhaps also modeled on his painter friend Spratling, Gordon obsesses over a female figure he's making, a "virginal breastless torso of a girl, headless armless legless, in marble temporarily caught and hushed yet passionate still for escape" (p. 263). This piece of work freaks out everyone who sees it, yet the obviously tortured Gordon insists it constitutes his "feminine ideal: a virgin with no legs to leave me, no arms to hold me, no head to talk to me" (p. 275). The rage, revenge, and perverse idealization that combine in this object point to motives for Gordon's art that cannot be explained by mere sublimation of erotic desire. As Fairchild points out, a woman "may be only the symbol of a desire" (p. 460). At some nearly inarticulate level, Gordon embodies a fuel for art that flows from unknowable unappeasable sorrow: "Only an idiot has no grief, and only a fool would forget it. What else is there in this world sharp enough to stick to your guts?" (p. 524). The narrator concludes that Gordon's sculpture captures "the equivocal derisive darkness of the world. Nothing to trouble your youth or lack of it: rather something to trouble the very fibrous integrity of your being" (p. 263). To grasp art as thrusting back to those conditions under which the very integrity of being forms as the result of a painful separation – this is a moment when the mature Faulkner may be glimpsed, an artist who abandons himself to the anguish of writing about the human heart in conflict with itself, whose greatest works fail to find consolation even in the ecstasy of their own making.

Breaking taboos was a popular sport among the generation that came of age in the post-war years. To feel yourself completely modern you wanted to scandalize your elders, wanted to embrace "the magic of change," as Faulkner puts it in *Soldiers' Pay* – even if that "new world" (*Soldiers' Pay*, p. 15) was the result of lost confidence in everything you'd thought was true. Young people enjoyed new social freedoms in modern America as they defied proprieties of sexual, racial, and class behavior. Young artists experimented with new imaginative forms in their own spirit of rebelliousness. As we have seen in most of Faulkner's youthful fiction, unconventional sexuality, frankly presented, becomes both the embodiment and the emblem of a modern sensibility. There are good reasons for this. By the end of the nineteenth century, critics of the growing dominance of Western industrial capitalism had begun to grasp the connection between economic advantage and other forms of social oppression. Marx had observed that the profit made by successful factory owners arose from the gap between what they paid their laborers and the prices they charged for their products. Marx considered actual slavery only the most extreme version of the way capitalists steal from laborers the "surplus" value that constitutes profit. The power of owners over workers reflected a more fundamental injustice in the division of goods and labor according to Marx's collaborator, Friedrich Engels. In his study of the origins of the family, Engels proposed that the modern father-dominated household replicated, at the level of domestic organization, the foundation of Western society upon male control of resources and the exploitation of women's labor. Charlotte Perkins Gilman, an American suffragist writing in the 1880s, went so far as to call marriage itself a form of prostitution. In this context, rebellion by modern women against restraints on their sexual inclinations carried an economic as well as erotic charge. To defy the law of the Fathers regarding proper romantic behavior was not only to insist on the right to do what you liked with your own body sexually. It was also to have seen through a general ideology of paternalist (or masculinist) organization responsible for maintaining social inequities. Faulkner imagines a variety of areas in which young people acted out their challenge to paternal dictate through sexual rebelliousness.[6]

The modern young woman as sexual renegade preoccupies Faulkner's imagination. We have already encountered instances such as Narcissa Benbow Sartoris, Cicely Saunders, and the libidinous teenagers of *Mosquitoes*, Patricia and Jenny, but a particularly desperate version of the type appears as the protagonist of the short story "Elly." We might think of Elly's predicament as a variation on Mrs. Maurier's marital calamity: Elly has accepted a marriage proposal from the town bank's staid assistant cashier, a "grave, sober young man of impeccable character and habits," who courts her with "a kind of placid formality" (*Collected Stories*, p. 213). Looking at a future made up of "the monotonous round of her days," she contemplates life as a zombie: "At least I can live out the rest of my dead life as quietly as if I were already dead" (*idem*). So awful yet common a fate seals the heartbreaking self-denial required of many women; this story imagines how one victim-in-waiting stages a last ditch act of refusal.

Dreading her ordained lot as a Stepford Wife, Elly does everything she can to scandalize her family's expectations. Elly's defiance of Southern small town propriety begins with her appetite for making out, all but indiscriminately – "youths and young men of the town at first, but later with almost anyone, any transient" (p. 208). Realizing the futility of such petty acting out, though, Elly advances to the gates of the South's ultimate taboo: she takes up with a suave visitor from New Orleans, Paul de Montigny, whose allure to Elly is enhanced by the rumor of his "having nigger blood" (p. 209). Elly relishes what effect that piece of information would have on her straitlaced grandmother: "A nigger. A nigger. I wonder what she would say if she knew about that" (p. 210). Elly's grandmother occupies the place of conventional social authority in the story. When Elly comes home bruised by her petting sessions, it is her grandmother whose disapproving eye she must meet in the morning. When Elly allows Paul nearly to have his way with her in the shrubbery outside her house, it is her grandmother Elly imagines outraging – "I wish she were here to see!" – then a moment later Elly realizes that the old woman is in fact spying on them, her face materializing above them, Elly's indecisive surrender of virginity interrupted. It is the grandmother, tellingly, who enforces paternalistic authority. The old woman is described as "sitting bolt upright, sitting bolt and implacably chaste in that secret place, peopled with ghosts" (*idem*). "Bolt," repeated, conveys the imprisoning rigidity and fixedness of woman's place under Southern patriarchy; her status as "implacably chaste" hints both at the impossibility of the standard of purity exacted of women, as well, perhaps, as the frustration it causes its adherents; ghosts show up here as kindred spirits to the traces of unfulfilled desires haunting Mrs. Maurier.

In the sexual bliss Elly approaches with Paul, she gets a foretaste of what so extreme a flouting of conventional morality might mean: "for that instant Elly was lost, her blood aloud with desperation and exultation and vindication too" (p. 211). For a white girl to lose her virginity to a black man, one who moreover makes it clear he has no interest in marrying her (presumably by passing for white), is to violate every canon of behavior Elly's people espouse. Doing so creates a sense of "exultation," the thrill of being "lost" to accepted mores and the "vindication" of one's own will. Elly's grandmother suffers from deafness, a condition that requires Elly to shout and pantomime her subversive intentions. The old woman represents Elly's future as the past, in which women become proxies for the very powers that bolt them to their chairs. The grandmother reproves Elly's violation of racial protocol – "bring[ing] a Negro into my son's house as a guest" (p. 217), as she has earlier cast a condemning eye on her grand-daughter's sexual escapades. For reasons associated with the history of relations between the sexes and races under slavery and later segregation, racial identity and sexual behavior could never be disentangled in the South.

Faulkner himself contributes one of the greatest meditations on the double helix of race and sex in his novel *Light in August* (1932; composed after "Elly," but actually published two years before the short story appeared). What matters to Faulkner's brief study here is the way that miscegenation (sexual relations between members of different races), still outlawed in Faulkner's 1930s South, becomes a badge of modern rebellion. Elly's girlfriend informs her of Paul's rumored mixed "blood" by observing that her infatuated friend must have "queer taste" ("Elly," p. 209). In 1934 "queer" hadn't yet become synonymous with "homosexual," though it was beginning to be used that way; rather, the force of Elly's taking up with Paul involves doing something that will "queer" normal knowledge, make the familiar strange, make the fixed transient. Trying to talk Paul into marrying her after all, Elly exclaims, "If it's that story about nigger blood, I don't believe it. I don't care" (p. 222). Not to believe that Paul is black is one thing; not to care is something else altogether, something once impossible for a young white woman in the South to say about her lover – despite the hypocrisy of a regional past in which white slave masters populated their plantations with children of mixed race by their slave concubines. Talk about the "uncountable and unnamable" ghosts that people grandmother's "place" (p. 210)! In violating norms of sexual chastity and racial "purity," Elly aims a blow at Southern white paternalism's nerve.

For all her brazen defiance, though, Elly cannot think her way out of the dead end her life heads toward. She gets some measure of revenge by recruiting her hapless fiancé to drive her to a rendezvous with her lover, but when it comes to figuring out what she really wants, Elly is stuck trying to inveigle Paul into marriage, albeit of a sort rarely seen. Elly is reduced to old tricks to try to get her way: offering herself in "voluptuous promise" (p. 221), threatening pregnancy. One could argue as well that Elly's fetishizing of Paul's "nigger blood" ends up reinforcing racialist thinking, even as she uses it to scandalize racists. Elly's capacity to envision a genuinely different future comes up short: "She seemed to feel her eyeballs turning completely and blankly back into her skull with the effort to see" (p. 219). As a consequence, Elly's last act turns hopelessly destructive. Driving home with Paul and her grandmother, Elly finds herself trapped between an uncompromising past and an unimaginable future. Suddenly, she lunges across the old woman's body and throws herself at the steering wheel, the car hurtling into a ravine, where Elly finds herself the only apparent survivor of a wreck. Sitting among the shards of glass, and bemoaning her invisibility to the passing traffic above,

Elly has at least vented the schizoid rage that drives modern woman's will to kill the past.

Faulkner's sympathy for the figure of the female renegade no doubt owed something to the willful young woman he fell in love with growing up in Oxford. Estelle Oldham made a name for herself as an attractive, flirtatious, headstrong young woman. That she wanted to marry Billy Faulkner, though, proved too much for her parents, especially Judge Oldham, who appreciated Faulkner's pedigree but doubted this pup would ever hunt. He forbade their marriage when they were high school sweethearts, and disapproved of the idea again when as adults they finally wed, the year Estelle divorced her solid lawyer husband Cornell Franklin. What's intriguing about the possibility of her reflection in Elly is that the story was actually first composed by Estelle, not Bill. Estelle had been a writer of women's romances for English language newspapers in the Orient, where Cornell's business interests had taken their family for extended stays. At Bill's urging, Estelle drafted a short story based on the idea of "Elly" soon after they were married. When the piece was rejected by *Scribner's Magazine*, Estelle gave up on the whole prospect of further submissions and possible revision; Faulkner offered to take over, and he remade the story. Nothing survives of the earlier version, so it is impossible to say how much of Estelle's original composition Faulkner used. But the several passages of free indirect discourse in which Elly's thoughts are imagined ring with authenticity – authenticity that might have been earned by someone who knocked heads with her family because she found a sullen rude artist-type far cooler than the three-piece-business-suit her father had in mind.

Faulkner's most fully rendered versions of the rebellious young woman prove to be two of his most memorable characters, Caddy Compson and Temple Drake. Each makes herself a modern girl to escape the smothering constraints of Southern Victorian mores. Caddy's flight contrasts with the rigor mortis of her family; Temple's bad trip exposes the dark side of modernity. Caddy (dis)appears in Faulkner's masterpiece, *The Sound and the Fury* (1929), which surveys the ruins of one of Yoknapatawpha's leading ancestral families. The Compsons descend from the planter elite, of a kind with founding clans like the Sartorises, whom Faulkner began writing about in earnest after *Mosquitoes*. Such families resembled Faulkner's own in many ways, and a major part of his novelistic project was dedicated to portraying their rise, fall, and eventual oblivion. At the moment Faulkner began writing, he realized that these dominant lines were reaching their end; that was in part what made the transformations of modern life so personally urgent to his imagination. One set of interlocking novels and stories in Faulkner's Yoknapatawpha fiction chronicles the demise of the slaveholding plantation classes. They include works from his early years like *Sartoris* (1929) and *The Sound and the Fury*, which begin to search out the flaws in the South's design and the nation's encompassing destiny: the atrocities of human enslavement, the genocide of indigenous people, and the national disavowal that wrought the doom of Civil War and the century of racial warfare that followed. Novels as late as *Go Down, Moses* (1942) continue Faulkner's probing into the South's past. As we shall see in Chapter 2, the prevailing stance of this fiction is a shamed repudiation of the sins of the fathers, accompanied by a keen resistance to the shifts of modernity. By contrast, fast young women like Caddy Compson rush out of that obsolete world, leaving the old guard at a standstill.

Temple Drake, our other modern girl, also the daughter of a prestigious family, similarly tunes out the wagging tongues of the old fogies, and hops a train to where the action is. But she suffers a horrific initiation into a new world that turns out to be mostly a bad dream of the old one. If the morose Quentin Compson loses sight of his sister Caddy because he's looking backward when she's way out ahead, the local elite searching for Temple Drake can't find her because they don't think to look down. Temple falls into an underworld that apes what's cool – racy pop culture, frivolous youth culture, mesmerizing movies, city seductions. When in 1929 Faulkner first tried to write a book that would appeal to mass audiences, he had little direct experience with popular taste. Yet somehow, even before he began designing stories for mass circulation magazines in 1930, and before his first scriptwriting job in Hollywood in 1932, Faulkner had fathomed modern mass culture. In Temple Drake Faulkner not only creates a character who exemplifies how young people were being conditioned by the new pop culture, but also shows how the worst versions of that culture reduced the female body to the status of screened image, onto which men could project economic, emotional, and sexual fantasies. In *Sanctuary*, Faulkner suggests that some of the new forms of social and cultural expression promising liberation actually end up reinforcing powers of patriarchal, commercial exploitation. Temple finds there is no sanctuary from the commodifying, dehumanizing, misogynistic violence of a money- and sex-driven society. In this bleak view, women fall in love with their own debasement, men with their power to abuse.

Temple takes advantage of the 1920s new sexual freedom to experience power once reserved for men. Young women flaunted their bodies in the era's more revealing fashions, began to speak more openly about sex, and asserted a newfound sense of command over their erotic lives. Temple is repeatedly described with an eye toward her "long legs blonde with running" (*Sanctuary*, p. 28); the flash of flesh vaporizes any leftover Victorian decorum about proper ladies hiding their ankles, while her running accents a headlong rush toward the modern. There's a touch of masculine self-possession in Temple's look: "cool, predatory and discreet" (p. 29). The co-ed recalls the star power one of her dorm sisters attains when she swears she's actually had intercourse. Even as Temple is falling into sexual danger she won't be able to handle, at an abandoned house where she and her boyfriend accidentally discover a coven of Memphis bootleggers, she still thinks her campus-style boldness will do the trick. She challenges the nastiest of the gangsters "with a grimace of taut, toothed coquetry" (p. 48), as if she can tame him with mock sexual power.

Faulkner has Temple represent the modern emancipated young woman, in the vein of Cicely and Elly. But the novelistic scale of *Sanctuary* allows him to explore whole regions of cultural change that behavior like Temple's derives from and reinforces. Throughout *Sanctuary* girls like Temple are associated with new forms of consumption and entertainment. Temple's face displays "two spots of rouge like paper discs pasted on her cheek bones, her mouth painted into a savage and perfect bow, also like something both symbolical and cryptic but carefully from purple paper and pasted there" (p. 284). This was the age of Clara Bow, the "It Girl," whose flirty appeal captured both the seductiveness of the day's bold young women as well as the new media in which they appeared. If Temple's face is a cheap magazine cover, it is also a starlet's screen image. Knowing that one of the thugs is outside spying on her as she prepares for bed in the house where she and her date have taken refuge, Temple nonetheless begins to disrobe. Though she can't see her audience in the dark, Temple seems to follow "the passage of someone beyond the wall" (p. 69) while looking "directly" but unseeingly at her voyeur. Such a scenario brilliantly dramatizes the relations structuring cinema. The actress looks out from the screen as if at a viewer, her body offering visual gratification; the audience member projects his desire onto the screened image, consuming vicariously what is and is not meant for him. Temple derives a strange power from this self-display, in a way that might evoke the spell cast by a new phenomenon – the female screen star – in Hollywood's emerging film industry.[7]

Temple's grasp of formerly masculine power corresponds to the endangerment of all sorts of traditional authority in *Sanctuary*. Just before she endures a monstrous sexual assault by the gangster Popeye, Temple fantasizes a strange self-defense: "Then I thought about being a man, and as soon as I thought it, it happened" (p. 220). Delirious with fear, Temple pictures herself dressed as a bride lying on a coffin; when the bad man begins to fondle her, she convinces herself that her vagina has turned into a penis – "it made a kind of plopping sound, like blowing a little rubber tube wrong-side outward" (*idem*). Turning a vulnerable cavity into a menacing protrusion, Temple's fantasy captures the desperate will of women to invert the terror of male domination. But it also suggests the transformative possibilities of Temple's (and Faulkner's) historical moment. In an important respect, Temple's fantasies of empowerment point to a wide array of attempts by subordinated people to switch places. In *Sanctuary* the most obnoxious example may be Clarence Snopes, a country boy turned small-time politician who thinks he's entitled to easy familiarity with the lawyer Horace Benbow, a First-Family-of-Oxford sort repulsed by everything smacking of the lower classes. But other hierarchies are in the process of dissolving under the flow of modern change as well. The narrator sneers at the country folk who make their way to town as first-time wage earners, consumers, even pop culture producers:

> The sunny air was filled with competitive radios and phonographs in the doors of drug- and music-stores. Before these doors a throng stood all day, listening. The pieces which moved them were ballads simple in melody and theme, of bereavement and retribution and repentance metallically sung, blurred, emphasised by static or needle – disembodied voices blaring from imitation wood cabinets or pebble-grain horn-mouths above the rapt faces, the gnarled slow hands long shaped to the imperious earth, lugubrious, harsh, and sad. (p. 112)

There's a kind of begrudging sympathy here, but the prevailing tone underscores how artificial and ugly the product is, how stupefied the consumer. Even at this early stage in Faulkner's commerce with mass culture, he bemoans its capitulation to formula, surface effect, simplicity. He extends the critique by describing a jazz recording as sounding "[o]bscene, facile," the two saxophones "quarreling with one another like two dexterous monkeys in a cage" (p. 202). Nor is it an accident that the embodiment of pure evil in the novel plays his part as if he's acting in a faddish film noir: "Tommy watched [Popeye's] face flare out between his hands, his cheeks sucking; he followed with his eyes the small comet of the match into the woods" (p. 68).

The comparison of a jazz duet to monkeys quarreling plainly has a racist tinge. That blacks were leaving their accustomed places also contributes to the convulsions wracking *Sanctuary*. In a comic sub-plot, two of Clarence Snopes's nephews show up in Memphis, looking for a cheap hotel, but unknowingly taking a room in a brothel. Clarence mentors the boys by pointing out that when they do decide to indulge, there's a better bargain at a nearby establishment employing negro prostitutes. Clarence casually declares that cash itself is "color-blind," and so presumably are the sexual favors it can buy in Memphis. At any rate: country folk in the city; blacks and whites enjoying sexual commerce; women acting like men; two-bit thugs building commercial empires – things in the modern South have been set flowing. In fact, that sense of fluidity infiltrates the imagery of the novel by becoming the hallmark of Temple's condition. Her hair "spills," her voice wails, her bladder leaks, but most of all her body bleeds and bleeds. She's in a perpetual state of hemorrhage, somehow both the agent and victim of violated intactness.

Like any popular sex symbol, from Greta Garbo to Marilyn Monroe to Madonna, Temple Drake tries to make the trap itself the key to freedom. But it's a risky path to liberation that lies through more extreme sexual captivity. To enjoy the only kind of power Temple can imagine, she requires male menace. There would be no "cool, predatory" air without an audience of gaping boys, "like a row of hated and muffled busts cut from black tin and nailed to the window-sills" (p. 29). The film theorist Laura Mulvey describes how the power relations of gender replay themselves in the typical cinematic dynamic of desired female screen object and desiring male viewer.[8] Probably the most horrific feature of Temple's obsessively described face is her eyes, said to look like holes (pp. 69, 92). These are hollows made by the penetrating male gaze. Temple suffers an unspeakable physical assault, one that, as we shall see in a later work, permanently traumatizes her. But what all of her mistreatment by men has in common is its root in voyeurism. No character in fiction is as compulsively *watched* as Temple Drake. "He was watching me!" (p. 90) might be exclaimed on any page. Leering guys from campus and town, lusting thugs at the Frenchman's Place, the rheumy-eyed Pap looking at her blankly, the whinnying Popeye ogling her, and Red in the brothel, Horace wide-eyed as Temple narrates her violation, her father and brothers fixing her in their protective oversight at the trial – all this watching throws Temple onto the screen of male voyeuristic fantasy. Even Popeye's assault – performed with a corn cob, because he is impotent – must essentially be an act of visual gratification to him, something he does to watch, since there is no sensation to be had otherwise. Temple's status is so purely a product of being looked at, that even she relates to her own body visually: "For an instant she stood and watched herself run out of her body, out of one slipper. She watched her legs twinkle against the sand" (p. 91). It's as if she cannot escape the pornographic movie her life has become.

Popeye is Faulkner's grotesque portrait of the moviegoer. Fredric Jameson has remarked that the essence of movies is pornography, since their pleasure depends upon penetrating the visible and staging vicarious gratification. That Temple's eyes cannot return the male gaze, that they're just holes, captures the violence done to female subjectivity in much mass culture. Temple is a wound, a morselized body of delectable parts, a blur of teeth and legs and hips and loins, never a full human being. She and Popeye each represent half of the mechanism of mass culture that Faulkner caricatures in *Sanctuary*: the object of desire, the voyeuristic consumer. The cultural critic Guy Debord coined the term "society of spectacle" to describe the way modern life under late capitalism began to prefer spectatorship to actual participation in social activities. Images are consumed for themselves, rather than what they stand for; vicarious gratification must satisfy those many who lack the means to actually acquire a vast new array of luxuries; and media like the movies condense present experience as well as history into a series of simplified frames.

In *Sanctuary* Faulkner not only gives us a fable that illustrates the forces at work in modern mass culture – the fetishization of the young female body and its prurient exploitation by a paternalistic culture industry. He also shows us how such fantasies are *used* by certain audiences to embody and work through their own relation to shifting conditions. Faulkner does this by rooting the origins of Temple's story as much in the fantasy-life of one of its spectators as in objective reality. What happens to Temple is a kind of fictional projection of what Horace Benbow fears may happen to his own step-daughter, another sexual adventurer. Faulkner devises Temple's story as a revved-up version of several genres of popular fiction: the gangster story, the sex shocker, the cult-of-cruelty tale – with flashes of film noir. Such formulations of dread and debasement reflected the nightmarish sense among some contemporary readers that their familiar, comfortable way of life was becoming endangered. In the case of *Sanctuary*, Faulkner portrays the middle-class lawyer and family man Benbow as hysterical over the wickedness and vulgarity of the new age. Horace uses Temple's story as a surrogate to project his own desires, anxieties, and rage at modernity.

Horace goes into shock when he realizes how much things have changed from the apparently innocent world he knew growing up in a small Southern town. Ostensibly, Horace gets hung up on his teenage step-daughter's sexual boldness. Like Temple, she's far more public about her sex life than Horace is used to (think how he obsesses over Temple's name being penciled on bathroom walls around Oxford). Little Belle once talks to her parents by phone while her boyfriend audibly paws her in the background, and when Horace looks closely at her photograph, he sees the "travesty of the painted mouth" that typifies "a face older in sin than he would ever be" (p. 167). Horace reacts with "horror and despair," partly because he's beginning to respond erotically to the image himself, "the delicate and urgent mammalian whisper of that curious small flesh" (p. 166). Here Benbow as step-father doubles Popeye's violation of female innocence – "Give it to me ... Daddy" (p. 236), Temple once blurts out to Popeye in the depths of her depraved captivity. The trappings of paternal incest in the battle for Temple – from Popeye's brutal invasion, to Horace's projective empathy, to Judge Drake's eventual reassertion of fatherly command – indicate the symbolic connections between the various forms of modern paternalism. In a novel of about the same time, *Tender*

Is the Night (1934), F. Scott Fitzgerald similarly uses paternal incest – in this case, the literal act – to symbolize the persistence of men's power over women. Fitzgerald explores how influential new cultural institutions like the movies, the medical establishment of psychoanalysis, and a culture of consumption all provide fresh opportunities for men to capitalize on feminized objects of desire.

Although Horace gets all swoony over the bare arms, swinging hips, and suggestive talk of modern college girls, his real anxieties run to more fundamental threats to the privileges he and his kind have enjoyed for generations. Faulkner characterizes Horace's longing to recapture a lost innocence, to arrest time before "purity" was "corrupted," with a contrasting mode of incest, this between brother and sister. As we shall see, Horace's veneration of his sister replicates Faulkner's most famous exploration of the refusal to accept modernity: Quentin Compson in *The Sound and the Fury*. In both cases, young men project the fantasy of eternal innocence and self-preservation onto their virginal sisters. Horace recalls how in childhood "he and Narcissa paddled and splashed with tucked-up garments and muddy bottoms" in the unimproved street outside the family house: "He could remember when, innocent of concrete, the street was bordered on either side by paths of red brick tediously and unevenly laid and worn in rich, random maroon mosaic into the black earth" (p. 122). Horace's nostalgia (a word that literally means homesickness) expresses grief at a broader social loss, not just yearning for individual childhood. The sexual assertiveness of young women represents the upheaval of an entire social regime. Horace's family, part of a professional class that formed around the plantation elite in the Deep South, faces its historical demise. Horace feels himself to be rushing toward an unfathomable future. Driven onto the darkened grounds of his ancestral home at one point, he has the sensation of speeding into an "unpruned tunnel as though into the most profound blackness of the sea" (p. 125). Later this feeling gets crystallized in an uncanny identification with Temple's initiation into an unmanageable, horrific new world. Recalling the account of her assault, Horace suddenly *becomes* Temple:

> But he had not time to find [the light] and he gave over and plunged forward and struck the lavatory and leaned upon his braced arms while the shucks set up a terrific uproar beneath her thighs . . . She was bound naked on her back on a flat car moving at speed through a black tunnel, the blackness streaming . . . (p. 223)

Temple's hallucination of acquired manhood corresponds to Horace's assumption of female victimization. The sensation of hurtling into a black future is Horace's response to the array of terrifying things that together have bound him on the train to modernity.

Horace's "ruined house" stands for a whole way of Southern living that involved cultivating the land a certain way, conceiving of black people a certain way, controlling white women, making money, defining what it meant to be a man, all in certain ways. Yet if Temple and Popeye play out the abuses of a new era, Horace's own passage through a modern underworld prompts an even more jolting conclusion: that modern methods of exploitation descend from standing lines of power. Horace's initiation into modernity leads him to see traditional ways in a new light. Faced with the filth of contemporary sexual depravity, rapacious greed, and brutal violence, Horace realizes that the South's most cherished values and beliefs cloaked equivalent practices of dominating women, the land, the poor, and the weak. The "innocence" he so values simply amounts to the obliviousness of affluent white male privilege. *Sanctuary* reveals the tendency of modern social and cultural change to strengthen the very sources of authority it challenges.

Horace at first believes himself to be above the wantonness of modern culture. When he stumbles across the Frenchman's Place one afternoon, Popeye accosts him and forces him to wait until dark before leading him to the house. The bootlegger suspects the trespasser of carrying a gun: "What's that in your pocket?" Horace is actually packing poetry; it's a book in his pocket, he explains, the "kind that people read. Some people do" (p. 5). Horace doubts low-lifes like Popeye read books, and that confidence in his superiority carries over into Horace's moral beliefs as well. He prides himself on his idealism: he represents without payment the man falsely accused of assaulting Temple, looks after Lee Goodwin's penniless wife and infant, defies mere respectability, tries to protect Temple from the humiliation of testifying, acts the good father to his step-daughter and the good husband to his manipulative wife, and most of all champions the sanctity of "the law, justice, civilization" (p. 132). What makes *Sanctuary* so unnerving a book, however, is that it offers no assurance that the worst practices of modern Southern society are new, only that they are newly visible.

In other words, *Sanctuary* is not a fable about how modernity violates the virtuous South. That has been one standard way of interpreting the rape of Temple as historical allegory. Think of Popeye described as ultra-modern: a "modernist lampstand" (p. 7), his silhouette like "stamped tin," his eyes like rubber – a city fellow scared to death of country creatures, yet all too willing to victimize them. But Horace's transit through Temple's story shakes any confidence in the traditional South as a sanctuary from modernity. Instead, Horace begins to realize that even during the South's heyday of leisure, innocence, and refinement, the grossest sorts of violation were taking place out of sight. For example, Horace envisions his sister Narcissa as "living a life of serene vegetation like perpetual corn or wheat in a sheltered garden instead of a field" (p. 107), a description that connects agricultural possession of the land to command of the female body. One of Popeye's crew wonders whether Temple's boyfriend has "laid any crop" by her yet (p. 41), a figure of speech for impregnating her, but one that also reinforces the link between male domination of agricultural and human reproduction. That Temple is raped by a corncob, in a barn, on a former plantation, deepens Faulkner's probing into what the relation is exactly between the beneficiaries of the South's plantation regime, who live in "sheltered gardens," and those out in the "field." When, at the moment of greatest danger, Temple tries to imagine the impregnability of her family's security, she pictures her father the judge "sitting on the porch at home, his feet on the rail, watching a negro mow the lawn" (p. 51). Safety and leisure are the products of others' labor, the South's virtues never far from its vices. What I'm arguing is that *Sanctuary* does not tell the story of the invasion of alien modern ways, so much as lifts the scales of self-deception that exalted the South as an exception to the story of national exploitation.

There was Southern idolatry in the air in the 1930s. A group of Southern intellectuals had decided that the ridicule of the South's backwardness and shameful history had gone on long enough – it culminated in H. L. Mencken's mockery of Southern ignorance during the so-called Scopes Monkey trial in 1925 – so they organized a defense of Southern values as antidotes to the excesses of both northern industrial capitalism, on the one hand, and communist state collectivism, on the other. The Agrarians, as they called themselves, included some prominent writers: Allen Tate, John Crowe Ransom, and Robert Penn Warren. They published the movement's manifesto, *I'll Take My Stand*, in 1930. A novel like *Sanctuary* as much opposes the Agrarians' deification of the traditional South, as it condones their complaints about the evils of modernity. Faulkner's relentless "indict-ing" of the land he loved produces the deepest kind of insight into the willful blindness that accompanied the development of regional and national greatness. We might take Temple's ravaged face, "sullen and discontented and sad" (p. 317) upon return to her father's custody, as a badge of such denial. The closing scene, set in the Luxembourg Gardens of Paris, exudes the restoration of privilege, paternal control, indifference. Families like the Drakes seem to have righted themselves yet again. But perhaps not everything is back to normal; around the forlorn couple "the dead tranquil queens in stained marble mused" (*idem*), indications of unwanted knowledge perhaps, particularly musings on women's stained deaths and all they might represent.

Horace sustains his final shock when, against all odds, and all truth, his client Lee is found guilty. Goodwin is summarily lynched by an aroused mob, although they immediately undercut the ideal of defending female chastity by implicating themselves in the logic of violation:

> "Who was she?"
> "College girl. Good looker. Didn't you see her?"
> "I saw her. She was some baby. Jeez. I wouldn't have used no cob."
>
> (p. 294)

Horace staggers home, having given up on the cause of justice. None-theless, the novel leaves us with a residue of unsettling insight. For one thing, though Goodwin is white, his murder evokes the practice of lynching blacks, an atrocity that was generating more and more outrage and political activism during the 1920s and 1930s. This racial blot against the South's image as "sheltered garden" is related to the fundamental misogyny beneath it too: not only were white women objectified as female victims by the insistence of Southern white men after emancipation that they had to be protected from the "black beast rapist" (Williamson, *Rage for Order*, p. 82); such women had earlier been commandeered by the planter elite before the Civil War to produce male heirs to property and fortune. The high value placed on virginity and chastity fundamentally guarded the economic privileges of fathers and husbands. The obsessive watching of women may be related to their fetishized value in the social reproduction of the master class. Planter wives were to safeguard the purity of blood and lineage;

maintain domestic order; cover up the master's own transgressions of blood and rank with his slave concubines; transform brute wealth into elegance by acquiring the right things; embody all virtue and refinement. Such women were regarded as icons of beauty and innocence, but they were also watched carefully to ensure compliance. It's as if Popeye still repeats such habits of fetish and surveillance without understanding where they come from. A name like "Little Belle" may underscore the capacity of new forms of social exploitation to take over from past ones, as *Sanctuary* further suggests that the shock of the modern discredits the "innocence" that enabled past injustice.

The course of legal justice promises to rejuvenate the power of men. The judge in Goodwin's trial encourages Temple to "speak out": "Let these good men, these fathers and husbands, hear what you have to say and right your wrong for you" (p. 285). Temple does so speak out, but only to tell a lie that protects her family. She leaves the courtroom in the company of her father and brothers, who close ranks around her in reassertion of their rights over a "father's only daughter" (*idem*). Faulkner sees through the particularities of Southern planter culture to grasp a larger phenomenon here: patriarchal and paternalistic societies of all sorts are predicated on the control by men of women's bodies and sexual reproduction. This "traffic in women" establishes the foundation of wealth, power, and the division of labor in the differentiation of gender. In a way, Western societies require the illusion that such social differences are natural and inevitable; that's the purpose of ideology – to provide ideas, images, narratives that make human customs seem like eternal laws.

In Faulkner's modern South a whole set of traditional values and ways of living collide with new realities. But even as new institutions like the culture industry reconfigure masculine power, its subjects aren't entirely overwhelmed. The fetishized object of female beauty and innocence, represented by Temple's hole-like eyes, momentarily comes to life. At the trial, Temple does something that never gets explained. As she testifies, she appears to be "gazing at something in the back of the room" (p. 284). She moves her head when her sightline is obstructed, but we never learn what she's looking at. It could be her father, of course, whose presence may remind her to lie about Goodwin, to keep the case simple and not involve the fugitive Popeye. But as Judge Drake walks down the aisle to retrieve his daughter from the witness box, she continues to look at the back of the room.

Interestingly, her behavior has been prefigured by an effect Horace notices when he is looking at Little Belle's photograph: the face looks like it is "contemplating something beyond his shoulder" (p. 167). That Temple (and Little Belle) can *look back* suggests a powerful reversal. After a life in which she has been the object of others' gaze, here Temple gets to originate one. Moreover, the face that actually occupies the position she and Belle are looking toward is *ours*, the readers', just over the narrator's shoulder. To what extent does Faulkner's highly self-conscious use of pop culture method and material include a reminder that the gratified consumer of this very novel stands implicated in Temple's exploitation?

Edith Wharton once called Temple Drake Faulkner's "cinema girl." After a few years of actually writing for the Hollywood film industry, Faulkner had a lot more to say about the world of movies. Faulkner's short story "Golden Land" focuses on the mid-life worries of a Beverly Hills real estate mogul, a heavy-drinking deal-maker plagued by a shrewish wife, an addled mother, fiendish foreign house servants, and a pair of already debauched young adult children. The story is practically a cartoon of Hollywood vices. It describes all the repellent behavior that amuses satirists like Nathanial West in *Day of the Locust* and F. Scott Fitzgerald in *The Last Tycoon*, though Faulkner prefers a sort of furious disgust to their tone of savage mockery. Ira Ewing's bad day begins with newspaper headlines summarizing the latest developments in a trial involving his daughter, an aspiring screen star: "APRIL LALEAR BARES ORGY SECRETS" (*Collected Stories*, p. 705). This cinema girl is a professional, though, not a mere fan like Temple. April changes her name when she enters the business, and determines that she will be one of those girls who, as her father puts it, "will do anything to get into the pictures" (p. 714). That includes cavorting naked in a hotel room with another woman and a casting director, the result either of "just having a good time" or, as the director contends, "trying to blackmail him into giving them parts in a picture" (p. 713). "Extra parts," Ewing sneers, unwittingly accenting the industrial process that requires an endless belt of starlets to keep up with the production of commercial culture. In any event, LA sleaze has begun to ooze.

April Lalear's new name reminds us how cinema girls are just things to leer at (you do have to wonder about the story's prophetic powers when you think of a name like Heather Locklear). The prostitution of his daughter to the movie industry corresponds to another kind of

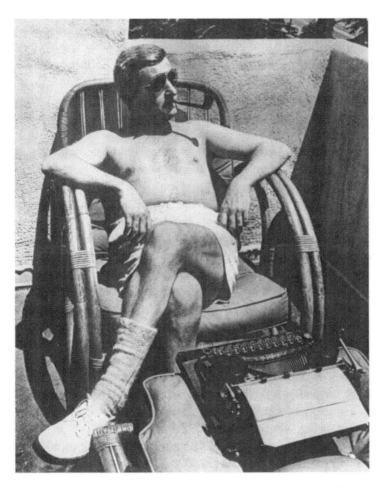

FIGURE 2 Faulkner in Hollywood (December 1942) by Alfred Eriss/ Stringer/2870705/Getty Images.

corruption that enrages Ewing, the effeminacy of his son. The aptly named Voyd taunts his father with a "veiled insolence that was almost feminine" (p. 709). His characterization owes something to the 1920s stereotype of the "fairy" – Voyd parades all but naked in a pair of straw-colored shorts, "his body brown with sun and scented faintly by the depilatory which he used" (p. 707). But if Voyd prefigures Holly-wood caricatures of gayness, it is not simply his homosexuality or even gender ambiguity that troubles the story. It's more the vacancy of Voyd's life, a symptom of the decadent hedonism of the whole LA scene. Ira's wife blames her husband's drunken oblivion for the way both children have turned out, but every member of the family acts hopelessly lost. Mrs. Ewing herself rattles around in a trophy villa with nothing but her husband's infidelities to think about; Ira's mother lives in Hollywood like the simple Nebraska plains woman she is, miserably befuddled by the California lifestyle. Even the Asian maids and gardeners seem mainly to be busy reading scandal tabloids.

There's something fundamentally perverse, Faulkner suggests, about this unreal city, a place of golden dreams where not a single thing feels authentic. Of course, that LA is artificial and full of greedy soulless people is a pretty banal insight. There's a good deal of rage about his own bondage to the Babylon of Hollywood that Faulkner vents in writing a story so outrageous yet predictable in its complaints. But you can sense that the artist is worried more broadly about what he sees coming in commercial mass culture. The Coen brothers capture the threat perfectly in their brilliant movie *Barton Fink*, which is based on Faulkner's experiences in Hollywood. The idea that a production company could actually *own* the contents of a writer's head, and that the industrial manufacture of movies by the studio system – as opposed to the artistic ambitions of the earlier cinema – appealed to lower and lower tastes troubles the playwright-turned-scriptwriter Fink. As it did Faulkner. Whenever he felt forced to take Hollywood's outlandish money (sometimes $1,000 a week), Faulkner complained in his letters about having to "whore" himself. Beyond jeopardy to art, "Golden Land" also points to profound shifts associated with the movies' celebrity and youth culture: "young people . . . precursors of a new race not yet seen on the earth: of men and women without age, beautiful as gods and goddesses, and with the minds of infants" (p. 721).

The last monstrous act of the story sparks the connection between the two commercial enterprises that create golden land's prosperity: the movies and real estate. Since all publicity is good publicity, Ewing pays for a legitimate newspaper to print a special edition, to be sent to his client mailing list. The front page will have a photograph of himself, identified as both the father of April Lalear and the president of the Ewing Realty Company. Ewing figures the notoriety will be good for business. In effect, Ewing prostitutes his own daughter to a money-making scheme. The act echoes the suggestions of incest in *Sanctuary*, and deepens Faulkner's suspicion that new forms of financial and cultural power perpetuated longstanding patterns of domination. As it turns out, Ewing's father had been something of a small town Nebraska success story, and his mother points out that making money is just too easy for Ewing men. Faulkner proposes a continuum between the pioneering force that conquered the country's land, and the entrepreneurial drive now creating film and realty empires. This savage little story wonders whether there are any limits to the capitalization of human relations and the debasement of imagination.

For all the loathing in *Sanctuary* and "Golden Land" of industrial pop culture, and the whole transformation of contemporary life for which it stands, we should keep in mind that the modern age disgusts those who are losing advantages rather than those who've been closed out in the past. Even when the disapproval of modernity seems to come in Faulkner's own voice, we need to read the stories carefully for a wider array of responses to the possibilities of the new age. It is true, for example, that Faulkner wrote introductions to *The Sound and the Fury* and *Sanctuary* in which he bemoaned some of the changes overtaking the South. He complains that the contemporary New South is no South at all, but "a land of Immigrants who are rebuilding the towns and cities into replicas of towns and cities in Kansas and Iowa and Illinois, with skyscrapers and striped canvas awnings instead of wooden balconies" (*The Sound and the Fury*, p. 229). Economic nomadism, urban life, homogeneous replication: these are regional symptoms of the modern ills portrayed in "Golden Land." Similarly, Faulkner confesses his own implication in commercial culture, saying he conceived *Sanctuary* for a mass audience – "a cheap idea" that would perhaps lure 10,000 of "them" into buying it. Faulkner sounds like Horace Benbow, or, as we shall see, Quentin Compson: skeptics regarding the new order, but helpless defenders of a way of life that has not only been historically eclipsed, but seriously discredited in the process.

Yet, for all his mooning over modern life's tawdry excesses, a good measure of Faulkner's empathy runs toward characters who, by playing fast and loose, attempt to get out from under the weight of the past's monumental decrepitude. The rebellious young woman constitutes the type; the Estelle he'd fallen in love with had been one herself. I think the Faulkner who scandalized his townsmen with his drinking and joblessness; who was so determined to fly that he invented a British identity and headed to flight school in Canada during World War I; and who fled to New Orleans, New Haven, and New York to find the new art – that Faulkner kept looking for the freeing possibilities of the modern age.

If we recall, then, the more exuberant attitude toward change that some of Faulkner's characters display, we can appreciate what Faulkner is doing in much of the fiction lying outside the Yoknapatawpha sagas of historical decline. The notion of modernity as a high-spirited adventure inspires one of Faulkner's early short stories from the 1930s. In "Turnabout," written just before he went to Hollywood for the first time, Faulkner has some fun with the disruptiveness of World War I. Americans flocked to the Great War in Europe because travel and danger seemed so exciting to a generation raised in prim Victorian households, many in sleepy provincial towns. The war let you *move*. You could see Europe; sexual mores relaxed under the realities of fleeting romances and ever-present death; African Americans got out of the Southern countryside or Northern cities and were amazed at the freedoms they could enjoy abroad. Emblematically, the world mobilized. We know about Hemingway and other soon-to-be-celebrity writers like John Dos Passos who tried to get to the action even before the US had joined the hostilities. Gertrude Stein learned to drive an automobile so she could visit troops on the front lines in France. And a short twenty-year-old tried to mask his Mississippi drawl behind a fake English accent, added a "u" to the spelling of his last name to make it look more British, and got himself into pilot training for the Royal Air Force in Toronto.

"Turnabout" pivots on a little rivalry that develops between a young British boat crew and a pair of American aviators. The Americans find their English counterparts lacking in professionalism; the boatmen seem to do nothing but zip playfully around the harbor by day, then sleep on the streets like hobos when their vessels are stored under docks at night. To impress their new chums with real danger and bravery, the pilot Bogard invites the sailor Claude to accompany him on a bombing mission. Claude shows nerve beyond his years on the flight, impressing the pilots, and then completely unnerves his US mates when he compliments them on having landed with an un-released shell dangling from one wing. That Claude is so calm about the mishap – he could see what was happening, they couldn't, but he coolly says nothing – weak-knees Bogard, who then accepts an invitation to see what the boat crews do. The story's "turnabout" involves the American's realization that the boatmen's tasks require bloodcurdling courage; the tiny vessel hurtles toward a German tanker, veering off at the last minute, under gunfire, and releasing a torpedo. Often the torpedoes jam, requiring them to be winched back into the firing mechanism, the suicidal launch process to begin again.

Faulkner's story grasps the war as a spike in modernity's contradictory development. On the one hand, the war effort prompted greater consolidation of state and industrial powers, leading to wider regimentation of individuals. On the other, the might of modern social and economic institutions hardly turned out to be total; there were opportunities to play turnabout with it. One threat posed by the demands of modern "world" warfare in 1914 involved the emergence of a military-industrial complex serving manufacturing and financial interests. World War I enriched munitions makers, bankers, and numerous other suppliers of war material; they pushed for American intervention in the European conflict, which came in 1917. We may recall comments in *Soldiers' Pay* suggesting that the war was motivated more by economics than politics. In his novel *A Fable*, written in the early 1950s, at the outset of the Cold War, Faulkner returns to the circumstances under which the US became the century's dominant commercial, political, and military power as a result of World War I. In "Turnabout" he senses the gathering force of state authority and industrial technology, but shows how it provokes resistance too.

"Turnabout" culminates with an act of fury at military order. Having learned that Claude and his crew are missing in action, Bogard rages at war's senselessness as he wings toward his present target. Closing down on a German headquarters, the pilot risks self-destruction as he gets close enough for a direct hit on the chateau, regretting only that he couldn't have wiped out the warmongers on both sides: "all the generals, the admirals, the presidents and the kings – theirs, ours – all of them" (*Collected Stories*, p. 509). Ironically, Bogard receives a medal for his bravery on the mission, though he'd have been court-martialed for his recklessness had it failed. Faulkner suggests how noncompliance gets muffled within the rigid enforcements of state authority, the protest of duty perversely turning into its very performance. Likewise, though failures of modern combat technology draw attention to the limits of advanced industrialism, as in the torpedo device that repeatedly jams, the sailors ingeniously figure out how to make it work rather than junking it and reverting to more primitive means. Another tantalizing thread of unorthodoxy in the story involves the kind of sexual crossovers we've seen elsewhere. In this case, erotic attraction springs up among the rank and file. Claude in particular appears as "girlish" (p. 476), "with a pink-and-white face and blue eyes, and a mouth like a girl's" (p. 475). There's a note of soldierly homoeroticism here, men with men, as war must have it. But Claude's girlishness also indicates the hybrid elements of one's sexuality that are more openly released around the war's upheaval and the immediate aftermath of modern adventure. Faulkner sees the war as a moment of crisis for absolutes of all kinds, including those of gender – freeing people to greater experimentation, variety of experience, questioning of restraints. Yet he also understands the war as an event that strengthens the hand of the modern capitalist state to regulate desire and enforce assignments of gender and class.

The growing power of modern agencies of social conformity – the military, the culture industry, national state-regulated production and consumption, international finance – continues to concern Faulkner in a series of novels and stories he writes during the 1930s. "Turnabout" advanced Faulkner's intimacy with these developments by initiating his direct relations with Hollywood. A literary agent had come across Faulkner's story in *The Saturday Evening Post* in 1932, and recommended its author as an upcoming talent to his brother, Howard Hawks, the ambitious head of MGM Studios. Hawks was always on the lookout for promising new writers, and he offered Faulkner his first scriptwriting contract. Desperate for money, his father having recently died, his family responsibilities acute, and his novel-writing far from profitable, Faulkner headed west.

Unsurprisingly, Hawks asked him to begin his duties by adapting "Turnabout" itself for the screen. Faulkner had already encoded the filmic potential of his story in its language; for instance, sometimes its imagery borrows from movie effects: as the boat crew circles close under the looming steamer Bogard feels that "[h]igh above them the freighter seemed to be spinning on her heel like a trick picture in the movies" (p. 504). Stylizing war as already a kind of movie also shows Faulkner making a connection between two major modern enterprises. Moviemaking does resemble warfare in a certain way – with its logistical co-ordination of theaters, units, teams, supplies, campaigns. Both depend on intricate chains of command to direct complex operations and deal with vast numbers of people. Moreover, as early critics of industrial culture pointed out, popular mass movies were devised as working-class diversion, gently disciplining an army of laborers to forget their troubles. At the same time, Faulkner's coding of his war story as already a movie points to the dangerous capacity film possessed for representing combat as thrilling and glorious. It's not just that war movies of this early era downplayed violence and death, but also that the very novelty of moving screen-images so captivates and excites, that whatever is represented borrows the magic of the medium itself. D. W. Griffith invented the movie "spectacular" by appreciating the enthralling effect of being able to experience swirling armies and charging cavalry in your theater seat. The pleasure of watching a war movie has something to do with the visceral pleasure of watching lots of powerful things move fast. War movies became a Hollywood staple partly because the maximal visual and aural effects of the medium could be shown off in techniques developed to capture aerial maneuvers, fields of sweeping infantry, underwater action, and exploding planes, ships, bridges, brains. That war movies end up making war itself seem less real suggests there are also ideological consequences to be reckoned with.

Faulkner's experience transforming "Turnabout" into an MGM movie – it was released under the title *Today We Live* in 1933 – triggered a career-long conviction that Hollywood mutilated literary art. Faulkner worked on the adaptation through a few versions; he was reassigned toward the end of the process, but not until he'd had to deal with MGM's surprising insistence that a female part be added in order to fulfill an obligation to Joan Crawford, who was under contract for a set number of pictures per year. Faulkner's droll response to the news – "I don't seem to remember a girl in the story" – didn't prevent him from thinking up a way to use the new character to exploit the opportunities of the new medium. For one thing, Crawford's character, Ann, introduces an awkward third between Claude and Ronnie, the boat captain, whose sister she becomes; the result is to defuse the homoerotic charge of the story's wartime fraternization and to relocate it in Ann's aggressive sexuality. Ann behaves like many of Faulkner's young women, making a bid to control her own erotic life and challenging patriarchal authority. In the film script Faulkner worked on, Ann hooks up with Claude while making it clear she doesn't love him. Ultimately, though, the movie tames the subversiveness it has entertained. Bogard ends up marrying Ann, and instead of firing off his anti-war sentiments directly to the reader, he murmurs them encircled in Ann's protective embrace. The movie domesticates, literally, the political insubordination of the short story, as it also pulls Ann's wayward sexual independence back under marital authority.

Faulkner's involvement in the Hollywood film industry influenced his fiction in several long-lasting ways, as we shall see. We've already noticed how Faulkner used the movies to symbolize key shifts associated with modernity. Over the course of the next two decades, Faulkner not only continues to write intermittently for the studios, he also creates his greatest novels. His fiction conducts an ongoing dialogue with the forces of modernization, and Hollywood gave him direct access to the latest leading features of modern culture. In a number of stories, as well as in two subsequent novels, *Pylon* (1935) and *The Wild Palms* (1939), Faulkner draws on a sense of the seismic shifts in social and sexual mores, cultural forms, mass behavior, and economic relations that his life in the Hollywood film colony cued him to.

One of Faulkner's strangest novels, *Pylon*, tries to capture the dizzying sensations of a modern age in the making. The novel focuses on the unconventional lives of a new breed of entertainer, barnstorming aviators who traveled the country staging races. Their line of work – a civilian version of the breath-taking aerial combat waged by celebrity "aces" during the war – seems like nothing their audiences have ever seen. A newspaper reporter, a timid observer of life who tends to romanticize the barnstormers' freedom, exclaims that they "aint human": "No ties; no place where you were born and have to go back to it now and then even if it's just only to hate the damn place good and comfortable for a day or two" (*Pylon*, p. 805). Faulkner himself emphasized the novelty of the pilots' existence: "To me they were a fantastic and bizarre phenomenon on the face of a contemporary scene" (Gwynn and Blotner, p. 36). The nomads defy norms thrillingly. Their daring flying stunts theatricalize their disregard for social, especially sexual, customs. Faulkner emphatically associates them with modernity, as if they are a fleeting avant-garde of future society.

The idea that the barnstormers never stop anywhere for long, that, in effect, they actually live in the air, might make them especially intriguing to a writer who felt inescapable ties to the place where he had been born. In fact, Faulkner turned to the flyers' tale when he got stuck writing his most ambitious and challenging novel about the South, *Absalom, Absalom!*, and decided he had "to get away from it for a while" (*idem*). *Absalom*, as we shall see, relentlessly traces the origins of the contemporary South back to its earliest roots in European colonialism. Faulkner had to discipline his powers of moral concentration heroically to excavate the South's awful story; what emerged was a complex set of partial and conflicting narratives, each conditioned by the way its teller understood the demonic origins of the plantation South. *Absalom* suggests how every inch of Southern soil is saturated with centuries of bloody history, every individual tied oppressively to all that precedes him or her. Faulkner thought "to get away" from this condition by turning to the "contemporary scene" he explores in *Pylon*. If *Absalom* proves to be about the sins of the father, lines of descent, a society's decline, and the burden of the Southern past, *Pylon* takes up the irrelevance of sin (not to mention fathers), lines of ascent, a society's transformation, and a weightless future.

The aerialists are futuristic. The reporter marvels that their cold precision makes them as much machines as the planes they fly: cut one and it won't be blood but cylinder oil that leaks out (*Pylon*, p. 804). One of the hallmarks of modernity involves the body's extension by technology. As photography came to preserve the human image, and phonographs the human voice, modern technology begins to dream of supplementing the biological organism. *Pylon* signals this evolution in the constant intrusions of the air announcer's amplified voice, which transcends the limits of the human organ, but does so as eerily "disembodied." Technology, Faulkner foresees, will extend human presence, but only as it deconstructs it too. In the moment of fantasizing the liberating effects of technology in *Pylon*, there's something mesmerizing even about such disembodiment, whatever the menace, as if this, too, is a way to break the ties of a single body, to a single place. The utopian note comes through in the early description of the airport as "a mammoth terminal for some species of machine of a yet unvisioned tomorrow, to which air earth and water will be as one" (p. 786).

A few years earlier, Faulkner had written about a desperately stuck rural family, the Bundrens, who manage to get moving from their failing farm only when the mother dies and they must honor her request to be buried in town. As we shall see, *As I Lay Dying* (1930) is very curious about the expansion of human consciousness represented by technology. One of the Bundren brothers fancies a new-fangled graphophone, which he figures would comfort him fine at the end of a long work day. Other characters similarly have picked out mechanical devices that might ease their lots: a toy train for the deprived tot, an abortifacient for the tricked teenage daughter, new false teeth for the worn-down father, and so on. When the dead mother Addie actually begins speaking as one section's narrator, we have the equivalent of Cash's talking box – the novel as mechanical reproduction of voice, as phono-graph. I draw in this feature of *As I Lay Dying* here because it does suggest Faulkner's fascination – even if it's sometimes skeptical – with the way modern technology might create new structures of human feeling, new relations to one's own body and place, and new possibilities for human imagination. Faulkner became an amateur pilot, and eventually bought his own flying machine. The sensation of lifting off from the Old Colonel's postage stamp of native soil must have been exhilarating.

Faulkner codes the pilots' sexual behavior as futuristically machine-like too: "It aint adultery; you can't anymore imagine two of them making love than you can two of them aeroplanes back in the corner of the hangar, coupled" (*Pylon*, p. 933).[9] The plot of *Pylon* involves the encounter of a reporter for a New Orleans newspaper with one team of performers who participate in an air show celebrating the opening of the "modernistic" new Feinman International Airport. The reporter falls for the whole exotic ménage: the pilot Roger Shumann, his wife Laverne and their child, the parachutist Jack Holmes, and their mechanic Jiggs. Laverne's open sexuality knocks the repressed reporter off his pins, and he moons around after them, lending them money and fantasizing himself amid their mysterious intimacies. Laverne represents the furthermost evolution of the sexually defiant young woman in Faulkner's fiction. In fact, she's way over the top. Shumann recalls how Laverne learns to perform aerial stunts when she first takes up with him. Her gimmick is to climb out of the cockpit once the bi-plane is airborne, walk along the wing, then parachute onto the field. The two deliberately capitalize on Laverne's femaleness by having her perform in a skirt. But just before she is to make her first jump, Laverne startles Shumann by climbing into the cockpit first, and having "wild and frenzied" sex with him as they maneuver around the joystick. Though that might have been sufficient to making the point about Laverne's revolutionary attitude toward sexuality, Faulkner goes on to have her catapult from the plane, naked under her skirt, and float to earth like a heavenly vision to the spectators below. Her generosity doesn't prevent her from being apprehended for public lewdness. What's typical about this bizarre incident is the brazenness of Laverne's defiance: she's scared at first of jumping, but that changes into "a wild and now mindless repudiation of bereavement" (p. 908). The mid-air ecstasy, in other words, is a spectacular metaphor for the impulse to be caught up above the ties to earth, a place, the past, and to repudiate them in an act of defiant, willful self-gratification.

It's a little hard coming down to earth after all that, but the barn-stormers remain true to their refusal to be bound by convention wherever they wander. The reporter can't figure out the family relations in the group at first, and his confusion turns out to be well-founded. He learns that Laverne has settled her child's paternity with a cast of the dice, literally; at the infant's birth, both Shumann and the parachutist Holmes are summoned, and when the pilot rolls high he gets the honor of marrying her and "becoming" the boy's father. Laverne herself turns the uncertainty of her son's fatherhood into a joke by teasing him, "Who's your old man?" Laverne flouts the law of the fathers by exposing how male control over women's bodies is a matter of chance, vulnerable to female sabotage. The open mechanics of sexuality here dispel the ideological mystification that usually veils it in Southern culture. Sex as practiced in *Pylon* has no greater point than physical pleasure, unlike the elaborate labyrinth of social significance enclosing it in the plantation world of *Absalom, Absalom!*

There's a carnivalesque atmosphere loosed in *Pylon*. The novel takes place during Mardi Gras, as had the actual events Faulkner modeled his novel upon. Faulkner put aside *Absalom* to travel to New Orleans early in 1934, partly because he'd gotten to know some of the pilots who were to perform at the dedication ceremonies; he'd also met a newspaperman named Herman Deutsch, upon whom he modeled the anonymous reporter of the novel. Faulkner lost himself in the festivities, as he wanted, but I think his preoccupation with *Absalom* ended up affecting *Pylon* in unanticipated ways. Despite the bald challenge to conventional morality and economics in the novel, the barnstormers hardly lead free lives. The reporter romanticizes the pilots' disregard for money, preferring to believe they risk their lives for thrill and fame. But the aerialists themselves – for all their non-conformism – are desperately grounded in the economic circumstances of the 1930s. That is, though the reporter embodies Faulkner's wish to imagine individuals exempt from ties to place, their predicament suggests that the future is planted firmly in the past.

The fundamental condition afflicting the barnstormers is their poverty. They work under extreme danger – Schumann is the second pilot to die in a crash during the races – and are paid little. The novel shows the pilots staging a strike to get prize money restored when the sponsors try to deduct unexpected expenses from the competitors' pot. The barnstormers are constantly looking for financial help, and insinuations are drawn about Laverne's willingness to trade on her body for necessities. The aviators become emblems of Depression-era workers – forced into nomadism, reduced to bare-bones existence, too often disorganized and disadvantaged to challenge their employers, and treated as depraved by those better off. Jiggs is spellbound by all the consumer goods to be had in New Orleans; he sidles up to a display window "like a boy's approaching for the first time the aerial wheels and stars and serpents of a nighttime carnival" (*Pylon*, p. 779). There are serious matters of economic deprivation underlying the spectacular entertainments of "aerial wheels" and "carnival" over the course of the novel. Faulkner's sense of the barnstormers as pure "ephemera," "no place for them in the culture, in the economy" (Gwynn and Blotner, p. 36), doesn't fully jibe with the novel's presentation of them as products of a long-standing history of economic exploitation. *Pylon* seethes with class resentment. The investors who build the airport, headed by the "sewage board Jew" (*Pylon*, p. 924) Feinman, provoke working-class hatred. Jiggs literally offers his back as a desk to a wealthy patron in order to get a credit agreement signed that will enable Schumann to buy a used plane and earn the group's living again.

Behind the novel's setting in "New Valois" stands the New Orleans of Huey Long's heyday. The actual city's new Shushan Airport was named for one of the "Kingfish's" chief lieutenants, his director of public works. Long, governor of Louisiana and later US Senator, vaulted to power on a "share the wealth" platform. He memorably declared "Every man a King" as he electrified 1930s crowds with his radical populism. Long's ability to mesmerize audiences frightened his opponents. In *Pylon* the announcer's disembodied, authoritarian voice hints at the scary potential of new technologies like amplification and radio to bring mass audiences under the sway of a single speaker. Long's actual legacy is complex. Doubtless a demagogue, he also understood that working-class suffering during the Depression had been caused by greed on Wall Street and fecklessness in the White

House. The rise of German nationalist socialism expressed similar kinds of resentment in Europe, and if Faulkner was reading the newspapers in New Orleans during his visit, he would have found reports about the rise of Hitler and German Nazism bordering columns about the local air show. Though matters of finance and labor in the plantation South of *Absalom, Absalom!* are left behind when Faulkner interrupts himself to start a new novel, *Pylon* ends up confronting other class conflicts troubling the Depression-era nation. Faulkner sees fascism as a modern threat arising from ongoing exploitation of the working poor. The barnstormers' lawlessness reflects unrest on several fronts during the decades following World War I – unrest stirred by promises of political, economic, and social enfranchisement for white women, blue-collar workers, and African Americans.

Faulkner's goal in *Pylon* is hardly political commentary, though. If he's interested in exploring the contradictions of modernity, as I've argued, he does so in a typically creative way. Neither the plight of the working class nor the abuses of modern captains of finance and culture tempt Faulkner to polemics. Instead, he uses the filter of the enthusiastic but befuddled reporter to focus on the difficulty of comprehending modernity-in-the-making. We might think of this character as a funky alternative to Horace Benbow or Quentin Compson, who snobbishly turn their backs on change. Perhaps he's something like a more determined version of Ernest Talliaferro in *Mosquitoes*. For the author who believed that "life is motion," refusal to imagine the future amounted to a death sentence. At the same time, willing but ill-equipped moderns like Talliaferro and the reporter embarrass themselves comically by failing to appreciate just how unsuited they may be to modern life. As another kind of writer who reckons awkwardly but hopefully with modern ways, the reporter serves as Faulkner's proxy.

The way Faulkner tries to identify with a futuristic world is as an artist, writing in an unmistakably "modernistic" style. *Pylon* signals its allegiance to an exuberant modernism. In some modernist works, the abandonment of straightforward narrative and the shattering of individual consciousness and voice denote despair, as in *The Waste Land*, or *To the Lighthouse* and *Mrs Dalloway*, or even *The Sound and the Fury*. Instead, *Pylon*'s modernist mood more resembles Joyce's, or Hart Crane's, or Dos Passos's – engineered to catch modern life's startling transfigurations, and committed to their synthetic and creative possibilities. (One chapter of *Pylon* is entitled "The Love Song of J. Alfred Prufrock," which here seems to be a joke on the reporter's desperate efforts to join his new mermaid Laverne, and maybe a snicker at Eliot's cosmic futility.) *Pylon* pops with Joycean puns and manufactured new words: "the garblement which was the city . . . ."; the "clatterfalque [for catafalque, a coffin stand] Nilebarge"; "the hydrantgouts gutterplaited with the trodden tinseldung of stars" (*Pylon*, p. 918). Faulkner wants to amplify the innovativeness of an emergent era of the machine, mass production, mass culture, and consumption by linking it to a conspicuously innovative way of writing.

Notice how the following lines evoke classical painting in a neologism ("Rembrandtgloom") that suggests how new sensations require an innovative lingo. A store is illuminated by a single kerosene lamp

out of whose brown Rembrandtgloom the hushed bellies of ranked cans gleamed behind a counter massed with an unbelievable quantity of indistinguishable objects which the proprietor must vend by feel alone to distinguish not only object from object but object from chiaroscuro (p. 901).

Emergent human sensibilities are on display here – like the ability to distinguish by feel between identical mass-produced objects; the anthropomorphic cans take on human aura ("bellies"); and to tell the difference between object and chiaroscuro underscores the distance between Rembrandt's world and this one, even as it suggests a continuum between art and modern mass production. *Pylon*'s style emphasizes modernity's capacity to surprise, delight, liberate, and lift. Faulkner is certainly not naïve about such transformations, and he exposes their disappointments plainly, as we have seen. There's plenty of suffering for *Pylon*'s band of avant-garde mavericks, and it's a misery that comes directly from the new deadliness of the machine age. But there's also that ecstasy of soaring beyond earthbound limits.

As the Great Depression deepened during the 1930s, depictions of its suffering became more urgent, and remedies for its ills more extreme. Those with leftist leanings were convinced the present crisis in capitalism signaled its imminent demise; inspired by the Bolshevist revolution in Russia, which had established a communist government in 1917, they believed the US working class would likewise challenge the inequities of capitalism. A world-wide proletarian uprising would be underway. The marginal existence of the barnstormers in *Pylon* may be taken as an emblem of the misery forced on working classes all over the country, from farmers to factory workers: nomadism, families devastated by illness and death, abject poverty. After three years in which the Republican President Hoover hoped for a natural economic "correction," the Democrat Franklin Delano Roosevelt was elected to address the crisis more aggressively. FDR soon organized federal agencies to distribute aid to the poor, set up government employment programs, and developed measures for restoring the nation's financial health. Leftists welcomed the relief, but also understood FDR's interventions as intended to save capitalism from itself. Those on the right criticized the unprecedented growth of the federal government, and worried about its damage to their ideal of "rugged individualism."

Though the effects of the Depression were widespread, it took a while for Americans generally to appreciate how many regions and groups of people were going under. Numerous artists, some of them eventually supported by government programs, spread out to portray the suffering of the poor in photographs, films, painting, audio recordings, and literature. Working-class individuals were themselves encouraged to document their experiences. This effort became a kind of aesthetic movement of its own: proletarian (or working-class) art. Autobiographical novels written by blue-collar workers began to appear, but "the proletarian novel" also encompassed works about class conflict and economic conditions more generally. Proletarian fiction typically sympathized with socialist solutions to the problem of poverty; often they encouraged and dramatized the formation of class consciousness (the awareness that the disadvantages of the working class are the result of the way the system of capitalism creates profits for owners by paying the lowest wages possible to workers), and frequently described the growth to political activism of their protagonists. Examples include Mike Gold's *Jews Without Money* (1930) and Jack Conroy's *The Disinherited* (1933). A related project involved exposing the decadence of the bourgeoisie (or middle class) – their complacency, materialism, spiritual hollowness, and indifference to the poor. Novels like *The Great Gatsby* and *Tender Is the Night* would be good examples, although Fitzgerald, unlike many other writers of the time, such as Hemingway and Dos Passos, never affiliated with leftist political organizations.

At the end of the decade, Faulkner wrote a novel that shows the influence of proletarian fiction as it reflects on the catastrophic effects of the Great Depression.[10] He conceived an unusual form for *The Wild Palms* [*If I Forget Thee, Jerusalem*][11] (1939): a double narrative that counterpoints stories of working-class suffering and middle-class decadence. The result is a distinctively modernist take on the way several key features of modern life in the 1930s now may be seen to intersect: class conflict, an economy of waged labor and mass consumption, sexual freedom, and the influence of popular culture.

The Wild Palms sets Faulkner's familiar theme of sexual rebellion in fresh circumstances. Here the domestic lives of married couples interest Faulkner more than the wild adolescents of his earlier fiction and the alien sex-forms of *Pylon*. The prison in *The Wild Palms* isn't the cult of female purity and male procreation stemming from plantation patriarchy; instead, it is the numbing emptiness of modern middle-class existence that cries out for a revolt of the passions. Faulkner introduces the problem starkly at the outset of the novel: a middle-aged physician makes a cameo appearance that allows Faulkner to establish the sterility of a settled life. The doctor lives in his home town, has married "the wife his father had picked out for him and within four years owned the house which his father had built and assumed the practice which his father had created" (*If I Forget Thee, Jerusalem*, p. 496). Two decades of marriage produce no children. Proprietor of summer beach cottages as well, this burgher physician has been summoned by a young couple renting one of the units. Charlotte has fallen ill, the result of a furtive abortion botched by her lover, Harry, also a doctor. The episode takes place at the end of their affair; the novel loops back to recount its course. Faulkner frames the couple's romance by contrasting it to the loveless marriage of the older married pair, a fate Charlotte and Harry have desperately sought to avoid.

Harry Wilbourne's youth has disappeared into the years of self-denial his medical training has cost him. Frugality and self-discipline have gotten him through school and into an internship, but he realizes in his late twenties that gone are "the years for wild oats and for daring, for the passionate tragic ephemeral loves of adolescence" (p. 517). In fact, he contemplates a life even more seriously deprived than his older double's at the cottage; he is resigned to "that peace with which a middleaged eunuch might look back upon the dead time before his alteration" (*idem*). Harry's hopelessness derives in part from his conviction that without money (he's a lowly paid staff member at an urban hospital), he'll have no shot at love. But his gloom at being excluded from even modest bourgeois happiness gets rocked by a woman he meets at an artists' party. Charlotte Rittenmeyer has reached a comparable dead end; an amateur sculptor, she has settled in to predictable wifery to a wealthy husband, an apartment in an "irreproachable neighborhood," two children, a maid.

Faulkner brings his lovers together through their passion for art – Harry amazed by the leisure and self-indulgence represented by every painting, Charlotte aroused by the pleasure of creating something real, "something you can touch" (p. 521). Although Faulkner qualifies their romance by noting its immaturity – the pseudo-sophistication of the artists' colony that brings the lovers together, the juvenile sauciness of Charlotte's saying she really would have preferred to marry her brother – the author nonetheless treats the extravagant escapade with respect. Charlotte sacrifices her children to run off with Harry, and the pair throw over everything they've worked for to take flight with each other. Faulkner empowers their love with both a strong charge of anti-bourgeois non-conformity (they never marry, and Harry performs illegal abortions on both Charlotte and another young woman traveling with her lover), and the passionate intensity of artistic creativity. It's love-making and art-making that drive the two to the wilderness, and permit them ecstatic touches of the Real:

> you are one single abnegant affirmation, one single fluxive Yes out of the terror in which you surrender volition, hope, all – the darkness, the falling, the thunder of solitude, the shock, the death, the moment when, stopped physically by the ponderable clay, you yet feel all your life rush out of you into the pervading immemorial blind receptive matrix, the hot fluid blind foundation – grave-womb or womb-grave, it's all one. (p. 589)

Harry's talking about sex, but the words also encompass Charlotte's rapture at making something real in her art of clay.

If Charlotte and Harry stage a jail-break from bourgeois proprieties, their story is shadowed by a second narrative of literal imprisonment and escape. The "under"-story to the main romance recounts the adventures of two convicts from Mississippi's Parchman Penitentiary, members of a prison work crew released temporarily to aid in rescue efforts during the Great Flood of the Mississippi River in 1927. Set ten years earlier than the love story (which is roughly contemporaneous with Faulkner's present), the convicts' tale touches on another quest for freedom during the intervening decade: working-class liberation from economic bondage. Parchman operated as a profit-making state-owned plantation. Prisoners farmed cotton fields under armed guard, their lot also symbolizing the permutations of coerced labor throughout the history of Southern agriculture – from African slaves to post-Emancipation debt-peons, tenants, and actual leased convict labor.

While he's out, one of the convicts gets a tantalizing taste of American freedom. At one point he takes up with a Cajun alligator hunter; they become partners, and the convict savors *"how good it is to work"* (p. 673). Real work involves labor you're not alienated from – represented here by grappling with a primitive beast and taking its life yourself. It also means getting paid and keeping the money. In contrast, labor at Parchman – whether the plantation is an image of state collectivism or state capitalism – is nothing but "toil" (*idem*) because neither the profit, nor the land, nor the labor belongs to the worker. Once adrift, the escapee travels back to a primeval scene in which men and women do for themselves. Separated from his work detail in the chaos, the Tall Convict encounters a pregnant woman stranded in a tree. They fend for survival, subsist by the efforts of their own hands, and perform the most natural of labor together, bringing the woman's child into the world. Experiences of this sort have a utopian tinge, even if utopia never materializes.[12]

Actually bringing about the kinds of emancipation figured in the lovers' rebellion or the convicts' release proves very difficult to accomplish. The convict recoils from the immensity of the upheaval engulfing him – a future freedom embodied by the deluge-born infant: "it was not the woman at all but rather a separate demanding threatening inert yet living mass of which both he and she were equally victims" (p. 599). If the emerging child constitutes an "inert yet living mass," it may signify several kinds of mass formations of the period: women amassing for political enfranchisement; workers for greater rights; communists to overthrow capitalism; and so forth. Yet there is something finally "inert" about both plots of rebellion in *The Wild Palms*. In the labor narrative, the Tall Convict never quite develops the will to challenge the authority that deprives him of his freedom. Faulkner sympathizes with the unfair conditions that have made the criminals victims themselves. The short convict, whose crime no one in the novel ever learns, has been sentenced to one hundred and ninety-nine years, a term so "savage" that the narrator concludes it "certainly abrogated justice and possibly even law" (p. 511). Moreover, the convict himself has been forced to decide between Parchman and a conventional penitentiary, making his incarceration a mockery of "free choice and will." The Tall Convict, a lean man with a "sun-burned face and Indian-black hair" (p. 509), runs afoul of the law because he takes the dime Westerns he's been reading literally. He tries to hold up a train but gets arrested almost immediately.

You can see Faulkner establishing the symbolic import of the convicts: a weakly educated slave of popular culture, a descendant of decimated peoples; a helpless target of an elite class's "blind" "outrage and vengeance" (p. 511). The Tall Convict rails at the simple inaccuracy of pulp fiction, as if he's been issued a bad instruction manual, but Faulkner wants to suggest more fundamentally how pop industrial culture puts false dreams of agency and success before the minds of the working class. And it's not just "the impossible pulp-printed fables" that have infected the Tall Convict's imagination, it's the movies, too: "who to say what Helen, what living Garbo, he had not dreamed of rescuing from what craggy pinnacle" (p. 596). Stuffed with such fantasies, the Tall Convict can't be expected to think through the conditions that trap him. Or so Faulkner suggests at the end of a sour decade writing filmscripts, commercial short stories, and even the odd detective tale to make money. The Tall Convict is repeatedly described as lacking self-awareness, and he remains so persistently duty-bound through the flood that his behavior continues to be more perverse literal-mindedness than authentic honorableness. It's no wonder he passively accepts the truly perverse imposition of an additional ten-year sentence (on bogus charges) so that he won't walk free, as a technicality turns out to make possible. Having been launched into freedom, the convict decides he wants no part of it: he's happy to "return to that monastic existence of shotguns and shackles where he would be secure" (p. 599), and where "the plow handles felt right to his palms again" (p. 723).

Temporarily freed prisoners still bound to do the state's bidding may suggest the fate of the proletariat during the 1930s. Though the

Depression engulfs the US in a disorienting flood of destruction, suffering, and loss, working-class self-determination turns out to be just an interlude; as with the convicts, there's eventually a retreat to a familiar state of confinement. Laboring America only briefly surfaces in the public's notice: surveying the sheet of water covering the oldest plantations bordering the Mississippi, one convict thinks of "the generations of laborious sweat, somewhere beneath him" (p. 592). The most popular metaphor in documentary accounts of the Great Depression was the flood. Writing at the end of the decade, Faulkner watches the water recede and the prison doors swing shut again, to leave a US still firmly in the hands of modern industrial, commercial, and financial complexes.

By no means was Faulkner writing from the standpoint of a committed proletarian novelist, but he does take up both principal strands of the sub-genre – working-class exploitation and bourgeois decadence – to describe what was happening in the 1930s. The lovers' voyage of liberation also fails to locate a sanctuary where passion may be purified of modern decadence. Disgusted by the separate ways they've been corrupted by money – Harry indebted to his sister for bankrolling his education, Charlotte entrapped by her husband "Rat"'s riches – the rebels make a cult of self-subsistence. They turn their backs on money culture just as they defy sexual mores. When Harry and Charlotte first run off, they set up a love nest that soon degenerates into a mere replication of the "bourgeois standard" of marriage. Harry concludes that it is "what we call the prime virtues – thrift, industry, independence – that breeds all the vices – fanaticism, smugness, meddling, fear, and worst of all, respectability" (p. 585). Fleeing their new little jobs – Charlotte as department store window decorator, Harry as writer of pulp fiction for girls – the lovers head for the woods, where they can for a time abandon themselves to "Nature the unmathematical, the overfecund, the prime disorderly and illogical and patternless spendthrift" (p. 572). Like proto-hippies on the way to Walden II, the lovers luxuriate on a lake in northern Wisconsin, swimming naked, drawing pictures, making love.

Idyllic as this interlude is, though, Faulkner dooms it to the interference of economic necessity. Just as the danger of bourgeois routine periodically menaces them (Charlotte makes a little figure she calls the Bad Smell to keep them on the alert), so the need for money compromises the purity of their renunciation. Indeed, Faulkner suggests that the lark of middle-class bohemianism is itself a kind of luxury made possible by affluence. When Charlotte cheerfully declares on the way to the woods that "We've lost our jobs!," she doesn't show much awareness of what unemployment meant to real working folks. In this novel, a private sexual utopia for two seems more a lucky indulgence than a blow struck against oppression. The selfishness of bourgeois habits of mind clouds even imagined alternatives. That Charlotte ends up having been infected by contaminated surgical instruments symbolizes the difficulty of getting cured with dirty tools.

Faulkner guides the lovers' comparatively self-centered repudiation of modern decadence toward a recognition of working-class desperation. The counter-pointed plots come close to intersecting when Harry and Charlotte find themselves serving as the medical staff for a mountain mining colony in the West. They soon realize that the laborers, European immigrants who can't speak English and "don't understand dishonesty" (p. 622), are being exploited by the absentee owners, who have stopped sending payroll. Past mistreatment has stirred mild protest, but this version of the proletariat settles for a few handouts from the commissary rather than a real revolution in their labor relations. "They're like kids. They will believe anything," the manager observes sympathetically (p. 623). It's up to Harry and Charlotte to enlighten them about the futility of their situation. Charlotte literally sketches out their predicament on a pad – a kind of ersatz proletarian art – to incite them to raid the commissary a last time and flee the camp before the fatal snows set in. Harry and Charlotte hardly become fomenters of revolution here, but we do feel Faulkner strengthening an identity between the beset working class and the bothered bourgeoisie. The lovers' predicament becomes graver, more desperate, while the comic effects shift over to the plot of the convicts' senseless but welcomed return to incarceration.

Harry Wilbourne ends up in the same Parchman that houses the convicts, so the final scene of imprisonment does at last let the plots intersect. Harry comes off as a self-pitying sort, and for all his sorrow over losing Charlotte, he spurns her ex-husband's offer to help him commit suicide, resolving to stick out his life sentence – famously: *"Between grief and nothing I will take grief"* (p. 715). (Faulkner once amended this for another occasion: "Between whiskey and nothing I will take whiskey." Which may be a better deal.) Harry's ruminations conclude a career in which he has had his own run at a more authentic lifestyle, and gotten a taste of the conditions blocking both proletarian and bourgeois revolt. He's had a surprisingly crucial role to play symbolically in the collapse of both romances of freedom. To pitch in to the lovers' finances, the ex-doctor once takes up romance writing. Harry has nothing but contempt for the "moron's pap" he comes up with, tawdry "sexual gumdrop[s]" that subject their readers to "the anesthesia of his monotonous inventing" (p. 578). It's this job that convinces Harry he has himself fallen into the mass of mere wage workers, "thinking of nothing, . . . thinking only of the money" as he sits in front of his typewriter (pp. 580–581). When he announces to Charlotte that they must leave Chicago to flee respectability, Harry makes it clear that it is their status as alienated commercial artists that he finds intolerable: his pulp, but also Charlotte's shop window figurines, turned out like conveyor-belt objects for Saturday's payday. At the end of the 1930s, that is, Faulkner notices that cultural workers themselves had become members of a subset of the proletariat. Like Barton Fink, in the Coen brothers' film about Faulkner in Hollywood, they've sold the contents of their heads, the "moronic fable[s]" (p. 578) stupefying both their creators and consumers.

The double romance of *The Wild Palms* suggests that there are no commodity-free zones in modern American society. Even the primeval Cajun alligator hunter runs afoul of state officials who want to regulate his catch and take a percentage of his profit. In effect, these particular visions of both unalienated labor and unfettered sexuality themselves prove to be cheesy romances, products of the cultural fantasy factories that pander to working-class resentment and middle-class ennui. *The Wild Palms* comes out of Faulkner's own discomfort at his complicity with the engines of industrial culture. The novel bristles with references to the movies, perhaps beginning with the title's evocation of the golden land's emblematic palm tree. The mayhem in the mining camp strikes Harry as "a scene like something out of an Eisenstein Dante" (p. 621). The mention of the Russian filmmaker is suggestive since Eisenstein fashioned a method of cinematic montage in which scenes from separate narratives were inter-cut to suggest thematic connections. But unlike Eisenstein's confidence that montage would contribute to his audience's class consciousness and inspire a progressive politics, Faulkner's reference seems to indicate that montage has become just a special effect, a kind of extra theatricality.

Hollywood Bill's self-incrimination no doubt involved a personal dimension as well. In December of 1935 he had returned to Twentieth-Century-Fox at Howard Hawks's invitation. During this stay he met a young woman employed as a script clerk by the studio. Meta Carpenter was also from Mississippi, and she and Faulkner soon began a passionate affair. Their romance continued on and off for nearly two decades, through Bill's absences, Meta's frustration at his refusal to divorce Estelle, and even Meta's eventual marriage. The novel's annoyance with bourgeois respectability must reflect Faulkner's own disenchantment with his marriage, and his regret at the duties to Estelle and, most of all, to their daughter Jill that he felt bound to honor. Faulkner and Meta permitted themselves a flagrantly defiant relationship (Faulkner once went so far as to invite Meta and a decoy date to dinner at his house while Estelle was visiting, a stunt his wife saw through immediately). Their affair evidently created unprecedented ardor and intimacy for both of them, but Faulkner's novel, at least, implies that merely insulting respectability is a pretty small gesture of rebellion. Meta Carpenter's account of their affair, *A Loving Gentleman*, published after Faulkner's death, exalts their doomed relationship with heartbreaking dignity and sadness.[13] Yet it uncomfortably reads like an innocent teenage romance itself. In a certain respect, Meta *was* Faulkner's Hollywood – young, seductive, modern, emancipated, and even Southern. He loved her, but he couldn't bring himself to give up his past love (or love of the past?) for her.

In this first chapter we have explored Faulkner's efforts to envision the massive transformation of his world – and the Western world at large – by the event of modernity. We've seen a side of Faulkner that welcomed the freeing new social life-forms offered by modernization to a place like post-plantation Mississippi, once called "the closed society" by James Silver, a prominent historian of Faulkner's era. At the same time, the seductiveness of sexual, racial, and economic revolutions also alarmed the writer, because he saw in them the outline of renewed powers of exploitation, aggrandizement, and disregard for individual worth. As we might expect of a creative sensibility so deeply committed to telling the whole story of everything he writes about, Faulkner's reflections on the most encompassing crisis of his age – the set of changes that constitute twentieth-century modernity – probe numerous aspects of these new conditions, scrutinizing them passionately, skeptically, ambivalently. When Faulkner spoke of the artist's calling as writing about the human heart in conflict with itself, he meant to emphasize the enduring human values of courage, honor, shame, love. But of course those virtues generate conflict only when they encounter the messy, ambiguous circumstances of lived life. As Faulkner imagined those circumstances, he more and more realized he was chronicling nothing less than the passing of one world and the emergence of another.

CHAPTER 2

That Evening Son Go Down: The Plantation South at Twilight

I deliberately began this introduction to Faulkner's writing by focusing on his receptive attitude toward modernity. I did so because too often Faulkner is simply identified with the opposite view, in which the past seems more heroic, intense, and passionate than anything modern life has to offer. To many readers, including a number of influential professional critics, Faulkner's fiction has seemed limited by the burden of the Southern past, however eloquent his characters' lamentations over lost glory, or however edifying their guilt and shame about the means through which regional and national grandeur were attained.[1] In the 1930s, Jean-Paul Sartre set the tone for this view of Faulkner; he saw the character Quentin Compson as representing Faulkner's attitude toward time: Sartre likened Quentin to a passenger in an automobile rushing toward the future, but, Sartre jokes, with the rider facing backwards. Faulkner's belief that the past conditioned every feature of human existence, from the most apparently instinctual of our feelings to the texture of the very soil we tread and the objects we handle, was indeed a principle of his descriptive imagination. But that the past haunted the present hardly meant it had to destroy the future. Chapter 1 attempted to shift our approach to Faulkner out of the channel of his alleged imprisonment to the past by showing how widely he explored and even embraced modernity, as well as its accompanying new modernist ways of making art. Now, however, we do come to the topic that elicited some of Faulkner's most deeply empathetic writing: the decline of the plantation families that had created the world he and his clan lived in for generations, and the place he made home throughout his life.

One of Faulkner's most brilliant short stories, "That Evening Sun" (1931), is a miniature version of the massive canvas Faulkner devotes to the subject of loss in *The Sound and the Fury*. The rebellious moderns we have been concentrating on in the preceding chapter provoke a reactionary response in a class of Southerners who feel their familiar world slipping away from them. Rather than welcome aspirations toward progress, these individuals turn their backs on the future and stiffen themselves against change. We have already seen an example of this attitude in Horace Benbow, whose recoil from the worldliness of boldly modern girls like Temple Drake and his step-daughter Little Belle sends him into a nostalgic funk. The middle-aged Horace represents the second stage of the type; he's a grown-up version of the late adolescent Quentin Compson, who embodies Faulkner's fullest and most sympathetic portrait of a man undone by modernity. If a less morbid Harry Wilbourne decides at the last that between grief and nothing he will take grief, Quentin, seeing no future for himself and his kind, chooses the nothingness of death over the prospect of ceaseless bereavement. Quentin's sense of doom shadows *The Sound and the Fury*, Faulkner's masterpiece about the agony of change and the tragedy of loss. About the time Faulkner was composing the novel – as a succession of "failed" short stories, he said – he was also sketching out other tales in Quentin's voice. Besides "That Evening Sun," Quentin narrates "A Justice," in both looking back from his mid-twenties to recount episodes from childhood that prefigure the end of the familiar world.

Faulkner artfully uses the device of an older narrator looking through the filter of his younger self in these stories. One of the central tensions in Faulkner's account of the South's plantation society involves how little its beneficiaries acknowledged the injustice to others that their way of life depended upon. In the layered format of the Quentin stories Faulkner provides a formal equivalent for the state of simultaneous knowledge and "innocence." The child Quentin doesn't fully understand the events and stories circulating above his head, while the older Quentin has learned more about the South's ills than he wants. In the stories, the two points of view create a double perspective – naïve and knowing at once. It's as if the Southern master class has been willfully childlike in its ignorance. Moreover, the innocent narrative works as more than just a foil for the older Quentin's insight; it also allows Faulkner to get at experiences more mature observers have been conditioned to disregard. By looking at his world through the eyes of a child, Faulkner notices things that happen to black people and poor people and certain kinds of women – none of which mattered much to the class of well-off white men who ruled the plantation regime.

"That Evening Sun" signals immediately that it is a modern story about a black person's suffering, and will include the sound of black people's voices. The title phrase comes from a blues song composed by the legendary W. C. Handy, and made popular in the 1920s by the singer Bessie Smith. Both artists were African Americans born in the South. The opening lines of the "St. Louis Blues" lament a lover's abandonment: "I hate to see that evening sun go down / 'Cause my baby he's gone left this town." Faulkner twists the blues of loss into ones of dread, though, since the irony of his story involves a young woman's terror that her vengeful lover *has* come back. Nancy, an African American who works as a paid domestic in the white Compson household, believes that her man, named Jesus, has returned from St. Louis to threaten her life. He's enraged because Nancy may be pregnant with another man's child. She has apparently earned extra money by prostituting herself to white townsmen, and Jesus suspects one of them, a Baptist deacon no less, to be the father. Jesus rails at his own impotence: "White man can come in my house, but I cant stop him. When white man want to come in my house, I aint got no house" (*Collected Stories*, p. 292). Nancy's blues issue from the even more woeful plight of a poor black woman in a viciously racist society. A white customer punches out her front teeth when she publicly confronts him over his failure to pay her. She and Jesus both have been reduced to terrified, dangerously cornered prey. Jailed after the public altercation, she tries to commit suicide, having spent a long night "singing and yelling" out her cell window. It's that kind of barred expression that Faulkner seems determined to listen to in this story.

The child narrator Quentin recounts the scenes of Nancy's anguish in a way that both lets its reality come through while also reproducing the capacity of white people to deny black suffering. Nancy is so afraid of what Jesus will do to her that she decides to use the Compson children as shields; when Mrs. Compson refuses to allow her to spend the night in the main house, Nancy insists that the children accompany her to her cabin. Walking through the woods, she pretends to be talking to Mr. Compson too, in hopes of deceiving the lurking Jesus. Nancy's terror is raw and real; her shaking hands jar the coffee from her cup as she tries to entertain the oblivious children, and she gags when she finally gets it to her lips. Because Quentin the child can't grasp the full implications of Jesus's indignation – its sexual outrage and genuine murderousness – he mainly registers the inexplicability of Nancy's behavior. Her state of preoccupation strikes him as "[l]ike she was living somewhere else, waiting somewhere else" (p. 302). He can't decipher her utterances: she whispers "oh or no, I dont know which. Like nobody had made it, like it came from nowhere and went nowhere . . ." (p. 296). Faulkner uses Quentin's incomprehension to indicate the social barriers obscuring what abused people like Nancy have to endure. Quentin's childlike circumlocutions indicate his unfamiliarity with black life, as the story dramatizes the childish self-centeredness of the Compsons. Made anxious by Nancy's bizarre behavior, the seven-year-old Jason knows enough to reassure himself in a tried-and-true Southern way: "I aint a nigger . . . Am I . . .?" (p. 298). The innocence of childhood unattractively matures into the obliviousness of the master class: personally sympathetic, Mr. Compson nonetheless refuses to take Nancy's plight seriously – "Nonsense" he keeps saying to her. Meanwhile, Mrs. Compson huffs that "I cant have Negroes sleeping in the bedrooms" (p. 299), a Southern propriety that apparently does not cover centuries of slave women summoned to masters' beds, or white deacons' ministrations to black servant girls.

Better-off whites like the Compsons misrecognize the injustice of a segregated society and the historical damage of racial slavery. Nancy's attempted suicide is chalked up to her suspected use of cocaine, for example, and the story misleadingly shifts the cause of her suffering from the longstanding conditions of white abuse in the South to the phenomenon of black-on-black domestic violence. Moreover, since Jesus never actually appears in the story, the effect is of a hypothetical, even imaginary, danger. That Nancy may be making up her menace discredits black fear. Nancy's employers downplay her predicament for their own reasons: they don't want to be inconvenienced by the breakdown of her service to them. White people prefer not to take black suffering seriously in this 1920s Mississippi town, because to do so would be to acknowledge the wrongfulness of past behavior toward them, and to accept the emergence of a new order.

Indeed, it is just that upheaval that turns out to be the underlying concern of Quentin's recollection. For the blues he's really affected by aren't finally Nancy's, but his own. The opening paragraphs of "That Evening Sun" convey Quentin's distaste for the surreal transformations of modernization – the first streetlights looking like they are "bearing clusters of bloated and ghostly and bloodless grapes," "the irritable electric horns" of automobiles, the fading of "old custom" (p. 289). When, in the story's last lines, Nancy has at last fled for her life, Quentin the child wonders, "Who will do our washing now, Father?" (p. 309). The South's interest in preserving custom is mainly an interest in preserving the conditions for white leisure and black labor. Once, Quentin looks so intently at the terrified Nancy, that it seems she has actually disappeared into her own image: "it was like Nancy was not there at all; that I had looked so hard at her eyes on the stairs that they had got printed on my eyeballs, like the sun does when you have closed your eyes and there is no sun" (p. 296). The South's violent Jim Crow regime was scaring black people out of the region in unprecedented numbers in the first decades of the twentieth century. Who *would* do the washing – and the tilling, planting, tending, picking, hauling, stacking, feeding, fixing, cooking, serving, cleaning – turns out to be a question many white people were asking. Quentin sees his world at twilight, when the sun dropping below the horizon creates a virtual image, an object visible but already gone. What Quentin is truly grieving for is not Nancy and the setting sun of black terrorization, but himself, a dying son of the plantation South.

Faulkner first thought his story about the decline of the Compson family ought to be entitled "Twilight." He wrote that word on the top line of a sheet of paper, and composed ten pages about children being sent outside to play during their grandmother's funeral. The mood of the entire novel that grew out of that initial sketch proves funereal – from Damuddy's death, through Mr. Compson's, Quentin's, a confusing array of assorted animals' (including one called Nancy), and Jesus's (well, that *other* Jesus, as Jason might put it in "That Evening Sun") – this one the divine Jesus whose death inspires not just indignation at unjust suffering but the promise of resurrection to the faithful oppressed. Faulkner intensifies his experiment with innocent narration by making the childlike Benjy Compson the first teller of the tale. Without explanation or guidance, Faulkner traps his reader in a severely curtailed perspective for the entire long first chapter of what became the novel *The Sound and the Fury* (1929). Benjy registers events and sensations primitively; though he is thirty-three years old, his mind has not progressed beyond childhood, and so he lacks the ability to generalize about his circumstances or to manage the raw fluctuation of daily existence through rational abstraction and prediction. In "That Evening Sun" there is no mention of a Compson brother named Benjy (or Maury, his given name), and his appearance first in *The Sound and the Fury* not only suggests that the other related Compson short stories may have been written before the novel, but also that Faulkner may have invented the youngest Compson as much as a formal device for narrating the story as an added family member. Benjy reports *what* happens to him without any apparent comprehension of why it does, or what it may mean. It is as if Faulkner wants to convey the immediacy of life – the most direct sensations of what constitutes reality – prior to the intrusions of ideas, beliefs, even language itself. And what constitutes Benjy's reality, as Faulkner imagines this cradle of human consciousness, is the experience of loss, lack, pain. Consciousness of self is born in the twilight of an awful rupture – in a separation from the ambient nurture of the mother-world.

Benjy experiences life as a perpetual loss of maternal love. The woman called "Mother" is cold and remote; Mrs. Compson pities her defective child, but cares more about family pride and proper behavior than the needs of her offspring. She delegates the most intimate duties of mothering to the black household servant Dilsey, who plays the longstanding Southern role of "Mammy," and to the Compsons' only daughter, Candace (called Caddy), who tries to fill in for her withdrawn mother. Caddy reassures Benjy that he'll be all right: "You're not a poor baby," she insists. "You've got your Caddy" (*The Sound and the Fury*, p. 6). But Benjy is definitely not all right. His life is all misery: he howls from the beginning, when he hears a golfer call a word he mistakes for the name of his beloved sister, to the end, when, in a pathetic tangle of half-memories, Benjy conflates the death of his grandmother, the disappearance of his sister, the unavailability of his mother, and the dismembering of his own body. In this novel, the sound of fury at the pain of loss begins as Benjy's ear-splitting wail, and continues through the succeeding monologues of his brothers, who find their own ways to rage at exile from all-encompassing motherly love.

Since Benjy's world hardly seems bigger than the sphere of a single organism, we might be tempted to read his predicament narrowly as the result of an individual mental deficiency, or at most as the outgrowth of a particular family's pathology. But Benjy has never fit clinical definitions of mental retardation or autism (though he may have been modeled on an impaired townsman Faulkner knew, the brother of his beloved first grade teacher). Rather, the literal traits of the Compson family, as I suggested in our reading of "That Evening Sun," serve more as emblems of a whole class's values and behavior. What Faulkner does seem intent on doing in his study of Benjy is to probe as deeply as he ever did the origins of conscious selfhood. Benjy is less a person than the possibility of personhood. Over the course of the first three sections of *The Sound and the Fury*, Faulkner gives us a kind of time-lapse, freeze-frame development of a composite self. Section by section, the novel draws back from the peep-hole of the single mind to the expanse of the historical production of selves. *The Sound and the Fury* captures, with heart-rending eloquence and beauty, the special idiosyncrasies of every individual self, yet it also grasps how even the most intimate of feelings and thoughts are undeniably woven from the fabric of social life. As such, it anticipates Faulkner's lifelong concentration on the tension between one's private self and one's community, between the individual and history, a person and his or her people.

Benjy occupies the space between, on one side, the infant's unity with the mother as a total supporting environment, and, on the other, an eventual detachment from her that produces the freestanding self. You may remember that in discussing *Mosquitoes* I outlined a psychoanalytic model for this process that Freud first hypothesized and Lacan developed in more detail. The crux of human subjectivity for Lacan involves the toddler's realization that he or she is a separate organism, a recognition precipitated by social reflections (literal mirrorings in physical surfaces or figurative ones in others' speech and treatment). Paradoxically, the moment of self-constitution – "That's *me*!" – cannot be experienced apart from an accompanying realization of self-alienation – "*That's* me!" To come into possession of your self is also to lose the bliss of pre-conscious wholeness, to be parted from the all-enveloping gratification of every want. From then on, according to Lacan, conscious desire is the condition of perpetual *dis*-satisfaction, every individual doomed to seek pleasure in provisional objects of desire, condemned always to fall short of the state of total satisfaction from which he or she has been parted.[2]

Faulkner's text reflects this general pattern of how selves originate. The discourse of the novel's first section represents something like a field of sensations and articulations out of which a person might one day emerge, a hypothetical person who would be known as Maury Bascomb Compson, youngest son of the Jason Compson family of Jefferson, Mississippi. But Maury gets stuck as he tries to negotiate his way toward maturity, a snag symbolized by his getting caught on a nail when he tries to get through the "broken place" of the fence on the first page of the novel. Rather than advance, this eternal infant is arrested; he dwells as much in the past with his sister Caddy as in the present with his custodian Luster. As one character jokes, the youngest Compson isn't thirty-three years old, as his birthday celebration in 1928 might suggest; it's more like he's been three years old for thirty years. Snared at the juncture when individuals typically begin to organize socialized selves in the face of removal from mother love, when they begin to internalize the state of discontentment that underlies mature sexual and other forms of desire, Benjy fails to move beyond that first raw separation from the condition of blissful total dependence. Benjy is preliminary to selfhood. Predictably, he does not quite know what to do with mirrors, since he never reaches that key stage of self-organization; he fails both to connect and differentiate reflected images. At one point he does confront his own image in a mirror, but instead of seeing the outline of a whole body, which might normally trigger the sense of an autonomous ego, Benjy notices only that something's missing – manifested in the scar of the surgical castration he has undergone. That's a telling loss, moreover, because it suggests that Benjy will never assume full-fledged masculine identity in his society. Benjy remains at the stage of traumatic wound. His very name has been changed; the honorific "Maury," after his mother's brother, has been withdrawn, and the destiny of recognized family membership will be withheld from him.

The idea that we fall from a state of blissful innocence into self-conscious experience of the world is a very old story. It is not surprising that Faulkner evokes the Biblical account of Adam and Eve's exile from Eden to suggest how fundamentally humankind associates a sense of selfhood with the sensation of loss. As Benjy watches his sister climb a tree to spy on their grandmother's funeral, they re-enact the Biblical couple's transgression of God's command not to touch the Tree of the Knowledge of Good and Evil. In Faulkner's version, the serpent shows up in jokes about snakes under the house, and in Dilsey's offhand reproach to Caddy as a "Satan" who'd better come down from the tree her "paw" told her to stay out of. Faulkner threads this central Western myth through the novel, reminding us that later psychological models themselves derive from Freud's and Lacan's appreciation of mythology as the expression of collective unconscious truths. Freud acknowledged as much by drawing key psychoanalytic concepts from the story of Oedipus, for example, and Lacan's Catholicism doubtless reinforced his scientific observation that the essence of our humanness is a kind of original fall, alienating us from perfect love and sentencing us to irredeemable unhappiness. The only structural principle that governs Benjy's seemingly random discourse rests on his preoccupation with death – funerals, marriages as the little deaths of disappearances, a welter of objects that go away, perhaps never to come back – as if the first inkling of consciousness is already overshadowed by the fact of human mortality. The dread of human flesh stripped away in death underlies Benjy's morbid preoccupation with acts of undressing (the dead horse Nancy's carcass flayed by buzzards, but also Caddy's "fallen" body disrobed after she muddies herself with carnal sexual experience). Benjy can smell death, as one character notices, and there's nothing he summons to mind that does not impress upon him that the fundamental condition of life is loss.

Benjy never finds his way to the consolations of symbolic thinking. If most individuals sustain the passage into social identity as a kind of injury or loss, they recover as fully as they do because they manipulate language and other sign systems to represent and so partially master the trauma of constituting the self. But Benjy is pre-symbolic; he remains without speech, and the best he can manage is to try to refill the void of lost maternal bliss. In a primitive, if sporadically effective way, Benjy consoles himself with physical substitutes for the open wound of his existence. Caddy makes a bid to function as mother – feeding and protecting him, enfolding him in her body as they lie in bed, even trying to educate her "natural" brother (as the mentally retarded were then called). And when Caddy vanishes, eventually obeying the dictates of her own maturation, Benjy finds miserable substitutes for the substitute: his sister's discarded slipper, the shards of broken bottles he arranges as a crude private burial plot – ferociously guarded tokens of her presence. Benjy is practicing a psychological habit known as fetish, in which a physical object associated with a departed person is cherished as the lost thing itself. Freud associates such behavior with a state of arrested development, and here we can see Faulkner using Benjy's ritualism to embody a primitive denial of change and loss.

Even more precisely, fetishism typically seeks to remedy the frightening knowledge of sexual difference. If the male child happens to notice that his mother differs anatomically from him, according to Freud he tends to interpret that difference as an absence. To be female is to "lack" a penis – a lack the male unconsciously associates with the threat of castration. This is a central precept in modern psychological theory, even though many Freudian claims have since been modified or discredited. The threat of castration figures in the male child's evolution toward adult identity because it represents the enforcement of social prohibition. Symbolically, the father stands for the social law that incest between mother and son is forbidden, and that the price of such a transgression would be sexual disablement. However much credence we put in the specifics of Freud's poetic account here, the point is that every individual must accept the authority of society to determine which desires are permitted and which prohibited. It is all the more telling that Benjy should suffer an actual castration, since it confirms his failure to enter the realm of symbolic thinking. He chases a neighbor girl one day when he confuses her with his long-gone sister Caddy, for whose return he waits year after year at the gatepost. The iconography of incest organizes Benjy's fascination with Caddy's sexuality. He smells her sexual adventuring in her perfume and the aroma of the trees where she makes her trysts, and, like his brothers, Benjy gets transfixed by Caddy's muddy drawers, looking and looking at the place that makes her a woman. But Benjy fails to progress into a whole system of social forms and symbolic consolations prepared to process this emergent new self. Neither incest nor its prohibition means anything to him. But neither does anything else, except the imponderable instant at which consciousness befalls us as already the condition of loss.

Understanding Benjy as lost in transition, then, exiled from maternal dependency but never to enter the social order, may enable us to appreciate how thoroughly Faulkner wants to imagine what it means to conceive a self. Why do we carry with us the sensations of child-hood pain and pleasure? How do mothers condition the fashioning of one's mature self, and why do they remain such lifelong influences for so many? (Fathers, too, for sure – but that's another story, to be taken up in *Absalom, Absalom!*) How do the components of identity – the affiliations of racial, gender, class, family, national, and religious personhood – get set? Why do so many individuals suffer in adulthood from a nagging sense of discontentment, of unfulfillable desire, even depression? These were all issues that plagued Faulkner in his personal life, too, as they do so many of us, and it is not surprising that his richest exploration of human consciousness engages them so frontally. Faulkner spoke of Benjy as a kind of "dumbshow" for *The Sound and the Fury*, recalling the silent performances that mimed the action of the full-scale play in Elizabethan drama. (Hamlet stages a dumbshow about a murderous king to try to frighten his usurping uncle into a confession.) Benjy's section lays out many of the key themes that the rest of the novel will take up, so in that sense it does function as a pantomime of the rest of the novel. In another sense, Benjy's lack of speech confines him to only partial or preliminary selfhood, and makes him less a fully human character than a mute gesture to-ward one.

The preliminary state of Benjy's self-consciousness accounts for the many confusing features of his section. We might think of what we read on the page as Faulkner's effort to create an analogue in words for Benjy's condition. Though the section is written in the first-person, the "I" is obviously only a very rudimentary marker, something like a "not-you." Benjy does not tell stories, analyze behavior, or conduct self-reflection. Like his developmental condition, his discourse is nothing but transitions: one fleeting memory turns into another; embryonic narratives go nowhere; conversations break up and inter-fere with one another; even characters seem to morph into each other. Every reader gets puzzled at first by the references to Quentin as male and female, to more than one Jason, more than one Maury, and so forth. Faulkner tries to give us the visceral experience of life before conscious selfhood has been mobilized by the social definitions that we inherit: time as linear advance; identity as fixed by racial and gender grids; family as generational continuity; and so on. A related impulse leads to Benjy's surprising descriptions of sensory stimuli as if the organs of sense were all one rather than separate: "my hands could see the slipper" (p. 46). This is known as synesthesia, and it was once thought to be a vestige of primitive thought processes.

Admittedly, the formal experiments upon which Faulkner stakes his novel were radical and risky. He understood that he was attempting a kind of modernist art so extreme that, as he boasted to his editor and longtime friend Ben Wasson upon finishing the manuscript, it "might not be published for a hundred years." In one sense, Faulkner was right about the interval, partly because *The Sound and the Fury* today, as we approach that century mark since its publication, seems so thoroughly cinematic in its artistic procedures. Consider its perspectivalism (each narrative tied to a single focal consciousness); its quick cuts, fades, and flashbacks; its uncanny voice-over narrations (how can Benjy narrate if he can't use words, and how can Quentin if he's apparently already dead?). Today's readers may nearly have caught up with Faulkner, after experiencing a vast aesthetic revolution he helped orchestrate. Few of Faulkner's narrative tricks surprise viewers familiar with the films of David Lynch or Quentin Tarantino.

Twilight is the oldest Compson brother's time, too: Quentin muses, "I could see the twilight again, that quality of light as if time really had stopped for a while" (p. 107). As "That Evening Sun" confirms, it is Quentin, and his family, and the plantation society they represent, whose day is drawing to a close. Quentin's fascination with the illusion of stopped time is just that – an elaborate "as if" that eventually will lead him to the imagined solution of suicide. Mr. Compson understands his son's desperate determination to flee the torture of loss, Quentin bidding to halt time's erosion at the moment of self-extinction: "you are contemplating an apotheosis in which a temporary state of mind will become symmetrical above the flesh" (p. 112). Yes, Quentin agrees, "was the saddest word of all there is nothing else in the world its not despair until time its not even time until it was" (p. 113). If Quentin mourns a passing world, he, too, does so in the person of his lost sister. But Faulkner begins to widen the novel's aperture as we move into Quentin's section. What has been explored as the trial of emergent selfhood in the first section now gets placed in broader social contexts. Quentin, arrested in late adolescence, struggles self-consciously with opposing scripts for the sort of adult he might become. Like a latter day Hamlet, he weighs and wavers, overborne by the dictates of the fathers, but tempted to improvise something new and freeing.

Still, there's so much to be overcome. Quentin feels like he's been born dead. He can't open his eyes in the morning without checking the march of time's shadow across his bedroom wall, nor can he enter the day's dawn without remembering that the sun has already set on him and his kind. His grandfather's watch ticks in Quentin's Harvard dorm room, where this most promising of the last three bearers of the Compson name has "come East" from Mississippi to begin his freshman year in 1909. But the watch serves less as the proud memento of a family's past exploits than what his father calls it when he passes it along to his departing son: "the mausoleum of all hope and desire," a token that "reveals to man his own folly and despair" since "victory is an illusion of philosophers and fools" (p. 48). The sentiments may be understandable coming from Mr. Compson, himself a disillusioned heir of the Confederacy's Lost Cause, but it's not much of a send-off for a college freshman. The death-haunted Quentin ends up drowning himself in the Charles River, which borders the Harvard campus; virtually every detail of his section forecasts his doom. By the time he speaks his monologue, he's presumably already dead, a situation that makes him in effect a posthumous narrator. The idea of Quentin as a voice from the grave underscores the perhaps deliberate discrepancy between the Quentin-narrated short stories and *The Sound and the Fury*; from the novel we learn that Quentin dies in June 1910 (a fact confirmed by a chronology Faulkner appended to *Absalom, Absalom!*). But "That Evening Sun" and "A Justice" indicate a narrator in his early twenties. Perhaps what looks like a literal contradiction in his age more symbolizes Quentin's status as a ghostly afterword to his own life.

In *Absalom, Absalom!*, he is described as actually

two separate Quentins now – the Quentin Compson preparing for Harvard in the South, the deep South dead since 1865 and peopled with garrulous outraged baffled ghosts . . . and the Quentin Compson who was still too young to deserve yet to be a ghost, but nevertheless having to be one for all that, since he was born and bred in the deep South. (*Absalom, Absalom!*, p. 4)

Upon hearing the ticking of his grandfather's watch Quentin immediately thinks of "the long diminishing parade of time" (p. 49), an image that then prompts the recollection of a remark his father has made about Jesus walking through light rays down a corridor and about the last moment of St. Francis's life, in which he calls out to "Little Sister Death." If Benjy's discourse works by rapid transitions, Quentin's displays more complex patterns of association. Benjy's connections operate mechanically: a physical location or a spoken word triggers every event related to it. His mind functions like a rapid search engine. Quentin's mind operates both more conceptually and expressively. In the example above, the strands of the ticking watch, Christ, and St. Francis continue to knot around Quentin's preoccupation. A few lines later he thinks: "Father said that. That Christ was not crucified: he was worn away by a minute clicking of little wheels. That had no sister" (*idem*). A puzzling cluster: the crushing inescapability of Father's voice – a sound that pre-empts every original thought Quentin might have; a belief that it was the clock killed Jesus, killed a precious son; death as a figurative sister that shadows every mortal. Quentin's associations acquire layers of meaning. Later, as he meanders through Cambridge on his final day, he encounters a dark-complexioned little girl whom he takes to calling "sister." He can't shake her; she shadows him as the projection of the very body he wants to cast off in suicide – "Niggers say a drowned man's shadow was watching for him in the water all the time" (p. 57). But she also shadows him as the reincarnation of his little sister Caddy, who comes to represent the passing of an entire world. Quentin identifies the clock as his mortal enemy, and throughout his last day takes secret pleasure in trying to discredit its authority: he notices that all the clocks in a jewelers' window display a different time; he ignores the campus bells before he realizes that his body is already counting; and in a final act of fury at the sound of his grandfather's watch, he tries to destroy it once and for all, succeeding only in shattering the crystal, wounding himself in the process, and finding that the wheels continue to wind down anyway.

The shifts of modernity that Quentin observes in the opening passage of "That Evening Sun" swell in the novel into seismic shocks to his very sense of self. Quentin's consciousness has been jarred from its familiar footings:

> I could feel water beyond the twilight, smell [the honeysuckle] . . . I would lie in bed thinking when will it stop when will it stop. Sometimes I could put myself to sleep saying that over and over until after the honeysuckle got all mixed up in it the whole thing came to symbolize

night and unrest I seemed to be lying neither asleep nor awake looking down a long corridor of gray halflight where all stable things had become shadowy paradoxical all I had done shadows all I had felt suffered taking visible form antic and perverse mocking without relevance inherent themselves with the denial of the significance they should have affirmed thinking I was I was not who was not was not who. (pp. 107–108)

Quentin's twilight less symbolizes a stillborn identity like Benjy's than one already suffering rigor mortis, failing to reinvent itself at the close of his family's historical day. The corridor he looks back into evokes the line of his descent – the parade of grandfathers and fathers ticking down to him. But in all sorts of ways the modern world refuses to support folks like the Compsons, and Quentin is faced with changing or vanishing. You can feel Quentin's acceleration toward disaster in the way Faulkner writes passages like these; the flow of thoughts and images, without any punctuation to slow things down, suggests a person losing control. Quentin is like the driver of a runaway car, barely hanging on, racing past unfamiliar objects. Retired to his bed, trying to fight off anguish by hoping sleep will make "it stop" (like Benjy at the end of his section), lost in a maze of self-assertion and self-extinction ("I was I was not"), Quentin doesn't inspire optimism.

What has turned Quentin's world "shadowy paradoxical"? One source of disruption involves the kind of rebellious assertiveness by young women we've already seen associated with modernity in some of Faulkner's other fiction. Like her precursors Elly, Cecily, Temple, Little Belle, and others, Caddy chafes against the paternalism and out-right misogyny of Southern genteel culture. Although we have access to Caddy's feelings and desires only through the filter of male accounts, her menace to traditional society comes through loud and clear. Quentin recalls the shock of discovering that Caddy has a sexual life of her own. In one of the most initially confusing passages of the novel, Faulkner presents fragmentary exchanges from several of their con-versations in a way that suggests how powerfully Quentin projects his insecurities onto his sister. When Caddy takes Quentin aside to confess that she is pregnant by one of her lovers, Quentin immediately reacts to deny Caddy her desire. He demands, "did you love them Caddy did you love them," but Caddy replies disconcertingly that it was all about pleasure, not love: "When they touched me I died" (p. 94). Died, exactly, since Caddy's sexual "promiscuity" does make her dead to the "ideal" of female "purity" (Quentin recalls Mrs. Compson dressing in black when Caddy is first caught kissing a boy). His last resort is to hope she's been forced: "did he make you then he made you do it let him he was stronger than you and he tomorrow Ill kill him I swear" (p. 95). But this jumble of insistence on male domination, female shame, and a code of masculine honor defended by violence gallops in from an antique past. Quentin is playing Sir Galahad, except that it's 1909, and it's hardly surprising that when he imagines confronting Caddy's lover, Dalton Ames, he begins to talk, idiotically, like a movie cowboy ("I heard myself saying Ill give you until sundown to leave town" [p. 101]). Then he just faints "like a girl" (p. 103). Quentin can't stand the paradox that it is Caddy who is sexually experienced, like a boy ("you've never done that have you / what done what / that what I have what I did" [p. 95], and he who is the virgin, like a good Southern girl ("In the South you are ashamed of being a virgin. Boys. Men. They lie about it" [p. 50]).

If modernity reverses traditional gender roles, it also unsettles familiar terrains of race and class. As the small-town Mississippian makes his way around Boston and Cambridge on the inter-urban rail system, he rehearses how his attitudes toward black people must change: "When I first came East I kept thinking You've got to remember to think of them as colored people not niggers" (p. 55). Quentin is hypersensitive to the strangeness of Northern racial customs. Coming from a world of Jim Crow segregation, he has to adjust to having black people take familiarities with him in public. He's used to proximity with African Americans, but on his terms, not theirs. The black character named Deacon jolts him with his take-charge attitude toward white Harvard students; his roommate Shreve initiates him into the way the rest of the world holds every white Southerner responsible for slavery ("Just look at what your grandpa did to that poor old nigger," he jokes about Deacon wearing a Yankee uniform in a parade); and Quentin is finally driven to fantasize a return to the South when he will see blacks in their "proper" places ("there was a nigger on a mule . . . like a sign put there saying You are home again" – "Hey, Uncle," a relieved Quentin greets him [*idem*]). Quentin responds to the way new conditions challenge his racism, but only to a point; he eventually concludes: "That was when I realized that a nigger is not a person so much as a form of behavior; a sort of obverse reflection of the white people he lives among" (*idem*). Quentin means this as a putdown – that servile blacks like Deacon conform themselves to white expectations to get what they want. Mainly though, Quentin just wants to wash his hands of race troubles: "I learned that the best way to take all people, black or white, is to take them for what they think they are, then leave them alone" (*idem*). Considered a little further, Quentin's point about a "nigger" as an "obverse reflection" of whites might have suggested to him how a racist term like "nigger" falsifies the human being behind it, relegating African Americans to objects rather than persons. But if Faulkner is on the way to grasping the long history and hurtful consequences of racial stereotype, Quentin never thinks to question the color line.

In moving to a northeastern city for his education, Quentin also encounters shades of future class and ethnic transformations. The courtly Quentin buys an extra breakfast bun for a bedraggled little girl he comes across in a bakery shop, then sends her on her way; but he soon discovers the sticky Italian immigrant is here to stay. The waif's poverty unsettles Quentin, the metallic smell of a damp coin wrapped in the girl's "worm"-like fingers nauseating him. The "jumbled," "heterogeneous" neighborhood where he thinks she might live amid the "new Italian families" disgusts him in its vulgarity (one house is festooned with "a garment of vivid pink"). The little creature shadowing him increasingly gets on Quentin's nerves. Her constant chewing and apparent ignorance of English trigger a startling mental blurt: "Land of the kike home of the wop" (p. 79).

Quentin's sense that the nation is being overrun by "foreigners" exemplifies a widespread nativist movement of the period dedicated to defending Caucasian "purity" against an influx of darker middle European and Asian immigrants. But the young Southern gentleman's sentiments derive from more than an ideal of ethnic solidarity. Quentin understands that he represents a once-genteel family's last bid to reclaim fortune and prestige in a rapidly changing economic landscape. The Compsons derived their ancestral wealth from the cotton plantation system. The first Mississippi Compson arrived in 1811 and soon took possession of the square mile of land that became the center of Jefferson; his son became governor, and his grandson, Quentin's grandfather, a slaveholding planter, lawyer, and decorated Confederate general. Quentin arrives in Cambridge a hundred years removed from his frontier ancestor, feeling the pressure of expiring fortune. The

Compsons have had to sell off their last parcel of land to finance Quentin's tuition: "Benjy's pasture," now a golf course. Caddy reminds her brother of his responsibility to Benjy and the rest of the family: "your school money the money they sold the pasture for so you could go to Harvard don't you see you've got to finish now if you don't finish he'll have nothing" (*idem*).

But times have changed, and Quentin finds no frontier to seize, no domain to found. This ossified son of the South cannot figure out how to compete amid foreign wage laborers, crafty "colored" people, and modern finance types. He blows off Caddy's fiancé when he offers him a job in his bank – "To hell with your money" (p. 70), – and laughs hysterically when he realizes he's been sentenced to pay the Italian girl's brother cash in compensation for the hour's wages he loses trying to track down his "stolen" sister. Of course, Quentin's disdain for commerce couldn't be more ironic given his past. Like all cotton plantation owners, the Compsons would have been fully engaged in market practices – from getting commercial advice about what strains of cotton to plant and retaining agents to procure the best prices for their crops, to trading in slaves (both acquiring and selling, as Faulkner makes clear in other novels), to speculating in related transportation and banking services (Faulkner's planter grandfather founded the first bank in Oxford and built the first railroad in the state). What Quentin can't stand is not just the loss of wealth but the loss of superiority that goes with it. The condition of being dependent on a fortune accumulated through the exertions of others, masquerades as the hauteur of independent wealth. That Southern grand manner seems laughable outside of the remote past (or the movies); Quentin knows enough to see the "cavalier" (p. 109) Gerald Bland and his mother as caricatures from a former time. But he has no clue about what will take its place.

It's at this point I want to make a connection with the psychoanalytic account of Benjy's troubles I introduced. With Quentin, Faulkner takes the question of the grounds for identity to the next stage, asking how exile from the bliss of total dependency might be understood as afflicting adults historically and socially. That is, in what way might the trauma each of us experiences as we move into our mature identities be duplicated for a whole group of people who have enjoyed the historical equivalent of womb-like total support? How is Benjy's condition also an emblem for a class of individuals who experienced the bliss of innocent reliance on others to meet their every want? Who arranged an environment that sustained them in the illusion of utter entitlement and effortless gratification? Quentin behaves as if he, too, has been parted from mother love, and longings for the remote Mrs. Compson burst on him as well: "if I'd just had a mother so I could say Mother Mother" (*idem*). And like Benjy, he ends up doing little more than grieving over what he has lost. You get the feeling that he, too, is trying to staunch the hemorrhage by holding on to Caddy; however, it's not just as a surrogate for her mother that she matters to Quentin, but as the embodiment of an entire way of life.

Quentin is as obsessed with Caddy as Benjy is, but her symbolic value to the Compson household grows clearer in his section as we see him associate specific elements of a fleeting world with her vanishing body. If Benjy primitively accepts any object ever associated with the absent Caddy as a token substitute, Quentin morselizes her memory into fetishized attributes. The scene that Faulkner said generated the novel – Caddy climbing into the tree to look at Damuddy's funeral while her brothers watch below – crystallizes her meaning to Quentin. He sees her drawers, muddied from sitting in the water of the branch (or stream), and realizes that they indicate sexual difference. Yet a difference with a difference, since gender roles are reversing, and the brave little tomboy Caddy is the one climbing the tree and taking lovers, while the timid Quentin weeps that he is still a virgin. Caddy always wants to be in charge, and there are many hints in Quentin's monologue that he considers her the manlier of the two. In one strange exchange, Quentin and Caddy seem to be on the point of conducting a murder/suicide, the result of their doomed attraction to one another. But Quentin remembers asking Caddy to "push it harder," to "touch your hand to it," while he ends up crying and finally dropping the knife. The phallic overtones assign masculine agency to Caddy, while, later, Quentin imagines having no sex organs: "Versh told me about a man who mutilated himself . . . But that's not it. It's not not having them. It's never to have had them then I could say O That That's Chinese I don't know Chinese. And Father said it's because you are a virgin: don't you see?" (p. 73).

Quentin also exhibits abnormal sensitivity to matters of blood. He fusses over his cut finger and the blood stain on his vest; he hears the blood pumping in his ears as he confronts Caddy's lover, then gets his nose bloodied when he takes his rage out on the suave Gerald Bland of Harvard (Shreve jokes, "I think you lost caste with [Gerald's mother] by not holding your blood better" [p. 105]). Quentin cares about blood for its symbolic value as, exactly, what defines "caste." Blood signifies the prominence of his family, race, class. Caddy's muddied drawers may also evoke, then, without actually being, the blood of menstruation – the sign of the female's role in the reproduction of a family's bloodlines. Quentin returns repeatedly to Caddy's purity, virginity, innocence, not because he's hung up on his sister's sexual behavior per se, but because their loss constitutes the loss of his own power, privilege, property. Caddy is so precious and so white and so purely the Compsons'; she represents every attainment a family like theirs can boast. Even Quentin's fantasy of incest suggests the narcissism of a clan in love with itself. But Caddy is not just an arbitrary symbol; in the past, she would as a woman have had social functions to fulfill that involved protecting the value of her family: the domination of genteel women's sexuality guaranteed the purity of male descent; unblemished lineage safeguarded the transmission of property and fortune; women's uncompensated labor augmented the value of plantations, and so forth. Quentin may gravitate to Caddy reflexively, but his fetishizing of her muddied drawers profoundly expresses a master class's infantile denial of loss – the "unmastering" of sexual difference, the "dirtying" of sexual reproduction, the transfer of phallic authority, the pollution of blood. Losing all that echoes the self's first awful fall from Edenic bliss into unwanted independence.

To want to stop it, though, is to want to stop life itself, since, as Faulkner famously remarked, "life is motion." Quentin is left behind, a tiny shrinking "i" that finally abandons itself to the flood of time. Though it is not time in general that does Quentin in, as he thinks; it's actually history. Quentin once recalls how he daydreamed through a history class in grade school and had to be awakened to a question about the Spanish "discoverer" of the Mississippi River. The arc of colonial history begins with the Conquistadors and may one day end with what's left of the Compsons. Surely the contemporary twenty-first-century South, for all the vestiges of its plantation past, has energetically fulfilled Quentin's prophesy: it teems with immigrants from around the world, especially from global South origins like Latin America and Vietnam, themselves earlier objects of colonial domination. Quentin seems to take the demise of his Compsons – a great clan of lords and governors proud in their Scottish ancestry – as worthy of the exalted language of Shakespearean tragedy. When he complains about his life turning "shadowy paradoxical," he's actually rewording one of Macbeth's soliloquies. Quentin speaks of "all I had done shadows all I had felt suffered taking visible form antic and perverse mocking without relevance inherent themselves with the denial of the significance they should have affirmed" (p. 108). Macbeth, usurper of the Scottish throne, hearing that his wife is dead, and accepting his own imminent defeat, offers this:

> Tomorrow, and tomorrow, and tomorrow,
> Creeps in this petty pace from day to day,
> To the last syllable of recorded time;
> And all our yesterdays have lighted fools
> The way to dusty death. Out, out, brief candle!
> Life's but a walking shadow, a poor player,
> That struts and frets his hour upon the stage,
> And then is heard no more: it is a tale
> Told by an idiot, full of sound and fury,
> Signifying nothing.
> *Macbeth* V, v: 19–28

Faced with the reversals of privilege threatened by modern times, Quentin gives up. As we shall see, another of the Compson brothers struggles doggedly, if futilely, to retool. But the final word on all their efforts comes late in the novel, when Dilsey, the Compsons' ancient African American servant, summarizes the rise and fall of a family, and perhaps a whole historical era: "I seed de beginnin, en now I sees de endin" (*The Sound and the Fury*, p. 185).

There is one Compson, though, who'd be more than happy to ditch the family baggage. Toss grandpa's watch in the river, not yourself (You can't *swim*!); ship the slobbering half-wit to an asylum (He's the Great American Gelding! What's the point?); get the rest of the household on the program (Show up for dinner on time! Quit playing hooky from school! And leave the town squirts alone! Look what happened to your mother!). Oh, and forget that Harvard dope sitting backwards in the car: buy your own Ford and learn to drive it! It's the future! "I'm a different breed of cat from father," Jason IV boasts jazzily. This Compson gambles everything on looking forward. The only problem is that he's as anchored to the past as either of his brothers, he just doesn't realize it. Jason's mad rush into the future is fueled by a resentment of slights and injuries so profound as to disable him; his section is a gusher of rage, paranoia, jealousy, envy, persecution, bigotry, contempt, and self-pity. His life just goes in circles. Jason embodies the conflict of spanning a period of historical transformation; he embraces modern ways, but with obsolete reflexes and values. The result is a kind of replication of his brothers' torture at twilight – except that their tragedy, repeated unconsciously by Jason, turns into comedic farce. The Compsons' drop from gentry (landowning wealth) into the petit-bourgeoisie (the class of merchants, clerks, etc.) provokes another massive exercise in denial, this one proving just how insane apparent sanity can be.

Jason functions in daily life, as his brothers do not. He holds a job, fulfills family responsibilities, pursues ambitions, and even creates a love-life of sorts. But as he spouts his vile opinions to the reader, Jason reveals how crazy a once-revered past actually was. Jason tries to update all the presumptions about masculinity, paternalism, whiteness, and ownership that defined the Southern gentry he descends from. But as that old order gives way, the violence that was always necessary to maintain it gets flushed to the surface, and the contradictions its ideologies papered over now break through and discredit it.

Jason responds to a decline in masculine authority, for example, by beating up on every woman in his life. He's obsessed with the injuries to himself and his family that he attributes to Caddy's betrayal, but he identifies her prime offense as the inability to deliver a job he has been promised by her husband. When Herbert Head discovers that his bride is already several months pregnant, he throws her out and rescinds the offer of a position in his bank for Jason (the job Quentin turns down so contemptuously). Jason is enraged both by needing to depend upon his sister and for her failure. Once it's clear Caddy will be of no use to him, he insists: "Do you think I need any man's help to stand on my feet? ... Let alone a woman that cant name the father of her own child" (p. 164). Jason obsessively prides himself on acting like a man – "At least I'm man enough to keep that flour barrel full" (p. 130), he hurls back at Dilsey, who has challenged his heartless treatment of his niece Quentin (Caddy's illegitimate daughter, who has been sent home to live with her mother's family after the divorce). This fading male potentate physically and fiscally tries to exercise total authority over women: he steals money Caddy sends to her daughter; he polices and bullies his niece; he deceives his mother over their finances; and he explains his view of gender relations succinctly with regard to the woman he keeps in Memphis: "That's the only way to manage them. Always keep them guessing. If you cant think of any other way to surprise them, give them a bust in the jaw" (p. 122). There's plenty of false bravado in Jason's mouthing off, but the violence of which he does prove capable reveals how "natural" superiority in fact requires the forcible subjugation of everyone else. "Once a bitch always a bitch, what I say" (p. 113) sounds like Jason's version of a law of nature, but the "what I say" reminds us that power depends upon the discourse and practice of violent assertion. Underneath all the idolatry of female chastity and beauty, it turns out the Southern gentry was mainly intent upon making sure there were no bastards, no slip-ups in the wealth alliances called marriage.

Jason expresses similar resentment toward other rising groups who threaten his privilege. More openly than Quentin, Jason voices repugnance toward graspy newcomers and "uppity" blacks. He spews contempt for freed African Americans, whom he finds lazy and dissolute. He rages at what he takes to be his obligations as master of a household, and rails at the disappearance of worthwhile field labor: "I have to work ten hours a day to support a kitchen full of niggers in the style they're accustomed to and send them to the show where every other nigger in the county" (p. 150) is headed. Toward the end of his section he describes how he torments Dilsey's grandson, Luster, by destroying before his very eyes tickets to that show; Jason has gotten free passes, which he offers to sell to the penniless Luster. Slowly dropping the tickets into the stove, Jason performs a cruel ceremony of humiliation upon Luster to make a petty point about economic power. Jason dreads falling into the wage-earning class, and the language of "slavery" permeates his constant complaints about having become an hourly worker. As he tries to maintain his advantage over those below, Jason also rages at those who've vaulted above. Southern economy after the Civil War came to depend on Northern capital and credit. New York City represents just the latest intrusion on Southern affairs by Yankees. Jason figures to get in on modern stock market speculation, putting small sums of money into cotton futures. But he's also suspicious that hayseeds like him, stuck thousands of miles from the center of things and dependent on slow information, are probably being screwed by insiders. For him, those insiders are stock-in-trade stereotypes of Jewish businessmen: "a bunch of dam eastern jews I'm not talking about men of the jewish religion" (p. 120). "But I'll be damned if it hasn't come to a pretty pass," he goes on, "when any dam foreigner that cant make a living in the country where God put him, can come to this one and take money right out of an American's pockets" (p. 121).

Jason's preoccupation with money would seem to be a more mature solution to the family's problems than his brothers' fixation on their sister's body. Jason was never part of the inner circle of Caddy, Quentin, and their father anyhow, and was favored instead by Mrs. Compson, who thinks of Jason as one of *her* people, a true Bascomb. Jason acts as though reversing the Compsons' economic decline might fix what's wrong with them all. I've been interpreting Benjy's and Quentin's fascination with Caddy as evidence of their effort to deny historical conditions of loss through the over-valuation of their sister's change-lessness. If this is a kind of fetishizing of Caddy, we might expect Jason's acknowledgment of economic hardship at least to spare him from self-deception. But in fact Jason labors under heavier delusions than either of his brothers, and the reason involves his deeper invest-ment in another kind of collective fantasy. As the South modernized, certain formerly privileged individuals and groups suffered traumatic loss. It's important to state up front that the so-called traumas experi-enced by such advantaged people were slight and secondary when contrasted with the massive damage done to native and slave popula-tions over the course of colonial plantation society in the New World. On the other hand, the crisis of modernity for privileged groups did cause soul-searching, and eventually the acknowledgment of wrong in many of those newly cast down. What we see in *The Sound and the Fury* is precisely such a jolt toward ethical awareness in Faulkner's reckoning with the world his ancestors had made. By the fourth section of the novel, the injustice done *to* the victims of Southern plantation society comes to the fore, and Faulkner will advance through the next major stage of his career to an exploration of the devastating consequences of historical oppression for all those involved – materi-ally to its victims, spiritually to its perpetrators.

Jason gets nowhere near such recognitions, though, despite his focus on economics. In fact, what Jason illustrates instead is the com-promising of another kind of self-deception, upon which the region's identity was based: the fantasy that the profits to be earned in the market for plantation output had nothing to do with the social violence necessary to produce it, and that the wealth so gained by the plantation elite could be transformed without taint into refinement, status, and culture. The root of such an ideology lies in the nature of market exchange. According to Marx, goods that are exchanged must first be subjected to a system of common valuation. I regard the value of something I have made for myself by how much use I get from it. But how do I know how much of your corn to ask for my bale of cotton unless we quantify the labor that goes into producing each? Once exchangeable goods are made equivalent, however, the material circumstances of production drop out of the equation. As soon as we determine cost, we turn even bartered goods into abstractions. The next step in the development of a market economy involves the assignment of a monetary price to each commodity that constitutes its exchange value. From there, cost may fluctuate as a factor of scarcity or other functions of the marketplace. This process moves us from value determined by use to that determined by exchange. In order for market capitalism to work, the sleight-of-hand that reduces use value and actual labor to the abstraction of price must be ignored. Instead, we treat marketed goods – or commodities – as if they themselves *possessed* intrinsic value that is really determined arbitrarily, and which suppresses or hides the social realities of production (who did what labor to make the products). Marx dubs this status of goods "commodity fetishism," because the object is taken as a stand-in for all the relations and labor that produce it, and allows buyers and sellers to "forget" that the profits of market exchange derive from a questionable appropriation of the difference between what the laborer is paid and the price charged. I've taken some time to explain this concept because it figures importantly in a number of Faulkner's novels in the 1930s, and it will help us see a relation between the fetishistic practices of racial and sexual psychology, and those of capitalist economics.

It's telling that commodity fetishism should be unmasked in *The Sound and the Fury*, because Faulkner's subsequent great novels of the South's decline concentrate on the most extreme and unfathomable form of commodification: the rendering of human beings as goods under chattel slavery. Historians have long studied the direct links between the growth of slavery and the rise of capitalism among

European colonial powers; Eric Williams has argued that the "surplus" profits accruing from the use of unpaid labor on colonial plantations around the world were critical to the rise of Euro-American prosperity, and that the accumulated capital eventually led to the industrial revolution, the decisive event in the development of Western global domination. The horrific incoherence of human commodification still makes Jason's world quake; its enormity survives in the abuse of freed black people, of foreign laborers, of women economically bound to their sexuality. While once his kind *owned* black people, now Jason has to hire them to do his bidding. He fumes at having to bargain with a young African American to get him to drive him home, for example, and repeatedly ridicules what he takes to be blacks' wasteful ways with money. Jason refers to his infant niece *as* his job when Caddy sends her home and he realizes his sister's marriage is over and his chance to get the bank position lost. Later he "sells" Caddy a minute's time with her daughter, and foully accuses his sister of prostituting herself as the only way she could have "gotten" both her bastard child and the $100 he charges her. Eventually he turns the family mansion into a boarding house, the last step in the relentless conversion of everything Compson to cash. Every human relationship is commodified for Jason, as if the age of finance capital has already overtaken the town of Jefferson and Jason is its man of the future.

Jason captures the irrationality of capitalist logic when he explains his philosophy of money: "After all, like I say money has no value; it's just the way you spend it. It don't belong to anybody, so why try to hoard it. It just belongs to the man that can get it and keep it" (p. 122). Jason spends his life acting at financial cross-purposes. He invests in the stock market, but liquidates his share in his employer's hardware store, preferring the immediate gratification of a new car. He throws money around Memphis, but tight-fists everyone in Jefferson, beginning with his family. He dedicates himself to restoring the family fortune, but expects to cash out when his mother goes. As with the other components of the fantasy that once structured his world, Jason can't get his economic life to reconcile either. He's being traumatized by the backwash of a system that his family once worked entirely to their advantage, and, after a few years of just hanging on, his efforts will fizzle out (as Faulkner relates in the later Appendix to the novel).

In describing the Agrarian movement earlier, I pointed out that some Southerners of this period prided themselves on the South's indifference to money, touting the region as a "traditional" society devoted to refinement, cultivation, and leisure, while attributing money fever to crass Yankees. But Jason's behavior suggests that the profit motive comes with the bloodline, that the South was always deeply invested in capitalist enterprise, and that it took mighty acts of denial to believe otherwise. Faulkner's sweeping novel of plantation ambition, *Absalom, Absalom!*, never forgets that for all the rhetoric about racial pride, family dynasty, and gracious living, it was always mainly a matter of "getting rich."

What's distinctive about Jason's response is that, unlike his distraught brothers – one fetal, the other fatal – Jason constructs a full-fledged narrative to account for his life. He takes actual pleasure, for example, in repeating to the sheriff the story of how his niece has stolen his (embezzled) nest egg. Jason's description of his misfortunate life is wildly entertaining; it makes you cringe, for sure, but it's also among the funniest things Faulkner ever wrote. Jason takes the reader into his confidence, begging someone to side with him, sympathize with his indignation, share his scorn. Jason's narration is a perfect illustration of how people keep themselves marginally sane by displacing traumatic events rather than confronting them and working through them. If you take Jason at his word, his misery has been caused by the persecution of treacherous women, Jews, blacks, abusive employers, no-good co-workers, and so on. Jason's story functions as a suit of armor against his daily woes.

But once or twice his glib self-narration slips, and we glimpse undigested fragments of more fundamental suffering. For example, Jason reports "thinking about when we were little and one thing and another and I got to feeling funny again, kind of mad or something" (p. 127). That unprocessed feeling seems to be associated with memories of his father's funeral, with a child's fear of death, and with the presence of Uncle Maury, Caroline's ne'er-do-well brother. The cluster of associations may indicate a mental scar that has formed around a deeper anxiety. Jason's parents are sensitive about their class status – Jason III secure in the Compson name, though now bereft of fortune, Caroline less sure of her Bascombs, but proud of their superior manners. And Maury represents the awkwardness of financial insecurity – he's constantly asking to borrow money, nakedly on the make with assorted schemes. Perhaps the trauma of an irreversible historical overthrow of former elites like the Bascomb-Compsons has infiltrated Jason's earliest formation of relations to his parents, extended family, and community. Such insecurity becomes the irritant around which Jason's self-sustaining narrative accretes – a coherent fantasy of petty persecution that blinds him as completely to his historical circumstances as do the incoherent self-accounts of his brothers.

After being confined to the myopic narratives of the three Compson brothers – as if the reader were stuck looking between Benjy's railing rods for hundreds of pages – we are given a more inclusive panorama in the last section of *The Sound and the Fury*. As "April Eighth, 1928" opens, we watch from a distance as Dilsey emerges from her cabin on an Easter Sunday morning, enveloped by the dawn's "moving wall of gray light out of the northeast" (p. 165). Standard third-person narration gives us the sensation of aerial freedom after what we've been through. The impersonal, more objective narrator provides contexts and explanations for behavior that until now we've been able to access only through distorted single minds. Maybe the most startling effect involves the sudden depiction of characters' appearances. Having dwelt so exclusively in inner worlds, how strange to picture Dilsey's paunchy, caved-in body, or Benjy's bear-like shuffle and "dead looking" "hairless" skin. It's as if Faulkner wants us to appreciate retrospectively the relativity of the earlier accounts, to appreciate the extent to which the individual imagination actually *produces* its reality. The special interests of the Compson brothers, so kindred in their values and states of emergency, now may be seen as just one life-form in a complex, variegated social world. What the Compson family takes to be a universal tragedy proves to be only a single chapter in the procession of human history. Dilsey's conviction that Rev. Shegog's Easter resurrection sermon has given her a vision of a beginning and an ending suggests how out of the conclusion of one story new ones may emerge.

There's a shift of voice within Rev. Shegog's sermon that corresponds to a structural shift in the novel as a whole. At first the guest speaker from St. Louis addresses Dilsey's "countrified" congregation in his city-educated voice: "he sounded like a white man" (p. 183). His audience admires the "virtuosity" of his performance, but his words remain "cold"; they listen to him as a curiosity, as "they would have to a monkey talking" (*idem*). Shegog adjusts, though, and connects with his listeners by easing in to their vernacular: "They did not mark just when his intonation, his pronunciation, became negroid, they just sat swaying a little in their seats as the voice took them into itself" (p. 184). That voice goes on to spell out the power of the Easter story – the whole arc of God's divine protection of His chosen people, from bondage to the eventual salvation accomplished by the "Blood of de Lamb." The novel's architecture prefigures a shift in Southern story-telling, from the voicing of white masterly complaint like that of the early sections, to the urgent sounds of black recollection and protest arising in the last. Tales of the Compsons (or the Faulkners, for that matter) will give way to stories of others in the South – of African Americans, and eventually Native Americans and immigrant Southerners.

Shegog's sermon relies on a traditional trope of black Protestant faith: the parallel between the Biblical plight of the Old Testament Israelites and the bondage of African Americans. Even after US emancipation, the long trek to the freedom of equality continued to require such inspiration. Martin Luther King's famous "I Have a Dream" speech draws deeply from this rhetoric, and Shegog knows its power too: "I sees de light en I sees de word, po sinner! Dey passed away in Egypt, de swingin chariots; de generations passed away. Wus a rich man: whar he now, O breddren? Wus a po man: whar he now, O sistun?" (*idem*). Shegog preaches eternal recompense for earthly injustice, but he also inspires faith in more immediate freedom. Dilsey conveys this when, as she stumbles home, tears creasing her cheeks, she instructs her daughter to "tend to you business en let de whitefolks tend to deir'n" (p. 185). Dilsey sees in the 1920s that the bondage of black to white, the dependence of white on black, is slowly coming apart. When Faulkner writes an epilogue to the novel in 1945, he imagines how Dilsey has moved to Memphis to live with her daughter Frony. Removed from the world of Jefferson, Dilsey chooses to have nothing to do with a painful past. Once, someone comes across a newspaper photograph of what appears to be Caddy in a Nazi general's staff car; when Dilsey is consulted, however, she simply refuses to respond, as if years – centuries – of white misrecognition like Quentin's ("a nigger . . . the obverse reflection of the white people he lives among" [p. 55]) deserve reciprocal non-recognition.

A reader might notice how Shegog's sermon glosses the fall of the masters – those like the once rich Compsons who lose their station,

their houses pierced by "de wailin of women en de evenin lamentations" (p. 184) over dead sons and brothers. But Shegog insists that
his sermon addresses the needs of the oppressed, not the oppressor.
He points to the children in the congregation: "Look at dem little
chillen settin dar. Jesus was like dat once" (p. 184). When he goes on
to describe the nightmare of Roman soldiers seeking to kill Mary's
precious son, it's clear the sermon means to fortify and console victims
of present racial terror under the hellishness of Jim Crow segregation:
these children, sitting *there*. In accord with Shegog's exhortation to see
the resurrection and the light, Dilsey's determination to *make* something of her circumstances leads to her aura of triumph. Far from being
simply a victim of white cruelty – amply embodied in the last section
by Caroline's unfeeling abusiveness and Jason's physical violence –
Dilsey seeks to advance against her enemy. The emblem for her creativity comes in Faulkner's first description of her wearing "a stiff black
straw hat perched upon her turban, and a maroon velvet cape with a
border of mangy and anonymous fur above a dress of purple silk"
(p. 165). The stiffness signals her fortitude, the purple the royalty of
her personal dignity. She accepts the hand-me-down clothes of her
white "betters," learning how to arrange them into a style of her own.
Dilsey practices a kind of syncretism, selecting, reworking, and syn-
thesizing expressive elements descending from a dominant culture.

Faulkner evokes a mood of new beginnings even if the novel doesn't
get much beyond acts of escape. Caddy remains at large, never to
return to her unforgiving family; her daughter Quentin absconds with
her Uncle Jason's ill-gotten patrimony, in a sharp blow to masculine
control; and African Americans of Frony's generation enjoy greater
freedom to move away, as the Great Migration of blacks out of the
South in the 1920s proved daily. Meanwhile, the futility of being the
last sane Compson catches up with Jason, whose closing gesture
underscores his desperation. Hearing Benjy erupt one day outside his
place of business, Jason realizes that Luster has decided to drive the
Compson wagon around the town square in the wrong direction.
Jason bolts out of the store and takes a stick to the insubordinate black
boy, forcibly reversing his course and at least momentarily restoring
order. Faulkner makes the scene emblematic, for Benjy's eyes are
described as becoming "empty and blue and serene again as cornice
and façade flowed smoothly once more from left to right, post and
tree, window and doorway and signboard each in its ordered place"

(p. 199). Benjy's serenity returns to match another figure's – the monument of the Confederate soldier, who "gazed with empty eyes beneath his marble hand in wind and weather" (*idem*). Together they represent the tranquility of a dead order.

The power of Faulkner's work of imagination in *The Sound and the Fury* involves subjecting his doomed characters to a radically innovative and modern treatment. That is, while the Compsons prove stuck in the past, Faulkner's artistry can't wait to get to the future (remember his boast about being a hundred years ahead of his readers). It's precisely in the friction between a backward social order and a progressive aesthetics that Faulkner gets imaginative traction on the world that has produced him. The modernism of the *The Sound and the Fury* has to do with Faulkner's effort to represent reality in a new way. He's not writing abstractly or expressionistically; his goal is *mimetic*, to reproduce reality using experimental techniques. Faulkner derives the novel's methods from major innovative technologies of representation: photography, sound-recording, cinema. Walter Benjamin has a famous essay on the work of art in the age of mechanical reproduction in which he discusses the capacity of film, for instance, to "see" things never seen before: to slow down and dismantle time, break down body movements and facial expressions, construct composite points of view, and so forth. Such modern techniques of representation perform a critical service: they make the familiar object-world strange, inviting us to examine and resist the commodification of everyday life under modern capitalism, a pervasive trend Benjamin identified as the defining feature of the modern world.[3]

I have space here only to suggest how Benjy's discourse hints at experience before it has been "reified" (turned into the objects and categories we experience as already *things* preceding our arrival on the scene). For example, Benjy's ears are full of voices; they sound different, and he can identify them all, but they never *mean*, say, a person's race to him. He doesn't organize his world by social categories like race – or gender: otherwise we wouldn't have so much trouble figuring out when he's talking about the male Quentin and when the female. And think about how the quick-cuts between fragmentary sensations suggest a different way of experiencing time: not as the steady linear progression of increasing knowledge, value, mastery (what we might call "capitalist" time), but as an expanse organized around sensation, indulgence, intimacy. Likewise, Benjy's sensory apprehension of the world resembles a primitive unified experience, as we discussed earlier. His hands can "see" things. Here I'd like to note that such primitivism was an important feature of modernist writing generally. Many modernist artists sought to imagine pre-capitalist mentalities (even traveling to find them, as in Gaugin's sojourn in Tahiti). What they wanted was a kind of relation to the world before nature and other humans had been turned primarily into functions of the marketplace as laborers, producers, and consumers of goods. Such features of Faulkner's original style of writing in *The Sound and the Fury* at least suggest how modernist art resisted social degradations imposed by modern economy. As he told the tale of a dying order's decline, Faulkner's artistry invited his readers to abandon familiar ways of making sense of the world and to attend closely to what new methods of representation could show them.[4]

It was Faulkner's commitment to a thoroughly modernist aesthetic that electrified his career. We can appreciate what *The Sound and the Fury* achieves by comparing it to Faulkner's other novel of planter decline written about the same time, entitled *Sartoris* (also 1929). Faulkner had returned from his trip to Europe full of energy and optimism about his writing career. He had already published two well-reviewed, if not so wide-selling, novels, and he had a publisher who believed in his talent; he'd seen a book of verse into print; and he'd connected with a literary crowd in New Orleans that led to publications in an important avant-garde art journal. Sherwood Anderson had taken a personal interest in him, and urged him to concentrate on writing about the exotic Mississippi the young artist knew so intimately. After setting his first two novels, respectively, in a nondescript Georgia town and in New Orleans, Faulkner decided to try his hand at telling the story of his own place. Eventually he conceived an entire imaginary county, Yoknapatawpha, to correspond to the one where he lived, Lafayette.

From the outset, Faulkner seemed to imagine his task as telling the stories of the county's distinctive clans. By mid-1925, he had already started a book about the Snopeses, poor hill folk who begin to give up on tenant farming and make their way into village commercial life. Breaking off *Father Abraham* (later to be resumed as a whole trilogy in the 1940s and 1950s), Faulkner turned to a more familiar kind of family: the planter elite that his own ancestors belonged to. Throughout antebellum Mississippi, every family lived its own permutation of plantation society, and throughout the Deep South, the social life and economics of plantation agriculture varied a good deal, from the rice plantations of the eastern seaboard in the Carolinas and Georgia, to the sugar estates of the Caribbean and Louisiana, to the cotton fields of Alabama, Mississippi, and later Texas. I should reiterate that in writing so concretely about Southern places and times, Faulkner does not end up offering broad generalizations about "the" South. He is absorbed with writing about individual human beings in their fundamental contention with social and natural environments. Faulkner was neither an historian nor a moralist; he was an artist determined to record as creatively, memorably, and movingly as possible what it meant to be alive, at the time and place that happened to be his.

Faulkner's first move in creating Yoknapatawpha was to imagine something like family chronicles: the Snopeses as a farcical new chosen people led by their father Abraham to the promised land of financial success; the Sartorises as a founding planter dynasty worn away by the shifts of modernity. As he completed the manuscript of his first Yoknapatawpha novel, Faulkner was very excited by what he had accomplished. He considered it the novel by which his reputation would stand or fall, and he must have been especially satisfied with having gotten so many of Yoknapatawpha's storylines under way: the Snopeses appear in the form of Byron (who plays out the subplot of infatuation with Narcissa Benbow leading to the events recounted in "There Was a Queen"); Horace Benbow, as an inhibited young man preoccupied by notions of sexual and racial purity, represents a traditional society's fears of modern change; years after emancipation, African Americans still serve in principal white families, members of subterranean clans composed of unacknowledged mixed race offspring; and the Sartorises bestride the novel as a first family of Mississippi, a multi-generation dynasty – its males remembered as romantic heroes and reckless fools, its women as longsuffering helpmeets and stoic widows. Faulkner called this big book *Flags in the Dust*, to capture the sweeping fate of a vainglorious Southern past.

Imagine our author's shock when he heard back from his always supportive publisher Horace Liveright that the firm considered the manuscript a sprawling mess – rich with promising stories, to be sure, but at least six different novels struggling to be one. Faulkner reluctantly agreed to allow his longtime friend and editor at Liveright, Ben

Wasson, cut the manuscript to size – like making a cabbage into sauerkraut, the author sniffed contemptuously. The shortened book was eventually published as *Sartoris*, although after Faulkner's death a copy of the original manuscript was discovered among his papers and published in 1973 as *Flags in the Dust*. Having seen what Faulkner was to do with the subject of a distinguished family's decline in *The Sound and the Fury*, we might conclude that the problem with *Flags in the Dust* was not so much that Faulkner tried to tell too many stories in it, but that he was relying on storytelling at all. *Flags in the Dust* is a much more traditional narrative even than either of Faulkner's first two novels; it employs an impersonal authorial voice; it authoritatively recounts events, presents characters, dramatizes conversations, and describes settings; and it makes unchallenged generalizations about the action it presents. Notice, for example, how the narrator confidently summarizes the foolishness of the Sartoris passion for risk and bravado:

> The music went on in the dusk; the dusk was peopled with ghosts of glamorous and old disastrous things. And if they were just glamorous enough, there would be a Sartoris in them, and then they were sure to be disastrous. Pawns. But the Player and the game He plays . . . He must have a name for his pawns, though, but perhaps Sartoris is the name of the game itself – a game outmoded and played with pawns shaped too late and to an old dead pattern, and of which the Player Himself is a little wearied. For there is death in the sound of it, and a glamorous fatality, like silver pennons downrushing at sunset, or a dying fall of horns along the road to Roncevaux. (*Flags in the Dust*, pp. 874–875)

Faulkner makes his modern cynicism plain here, distancing himself even as he lavishes ornate prose on a lost world. Compare this externalized perspective on the glamorous ghost of Sartoris with Quentin's creepy stream-of-consciousness recollection of the same Southern icon:

> It used to be I thought of death as a man something like Grandfather a friend of his a kind of private and particular friend like we used to think of Grandfather's desk not to touch it not even to talk loud in the room where it was I always thought of them as being together somewhere all the time waiting for old Colonel Sartoris to come down and sit with

them waiting on a high place beyond cedar trees Colonel Sartoris was on a still higher place looking out across at something and they were waiting for him to get done looking at it and come down Grandfather wore his uniform and we could hear the murmur of their voices from beyond the cedars they were always talking and Grandfather was always right. (*The Sound and the Fury*, p. 111)

In the passage from *Flags in the Dust* Faulkner writes from a position of superior judgment: "Sartoris" is an "outmoded" "game" that's over. It's an empty ritual now, and was responsible for "disasters" once, but it hardly seems menacing or even of much consequence to the voice that says farewell to it here. In *The Sound and the Fury*, on the other hand, the uncanny horror haunting these planter families deranges point of view and even syntax. Grandfather is dead, yes, and so he is a familiar of death. But what about that sense of not being able to "touch" or "talk loud" about death in the same way you weren't supposed to touch the desk or talk loud in the planter-lawyer's office? Might a descendant like Quentin harbor unprocessed anxiety about his family's past traffic in deadly unspeakable things like slavery? Then there's Colonel Sartoris staring eerily into space at "something" while General Compson stands waiting in his Confederate uniform, the two of them apart but also conversing – murmuring – out of the family's earshot, and Quentin remembering his grandfather as always right. Another suppressed memory of a social psychosis? The planter presided over his world by looking but not seeing; the masters colluded in sheltering their dependents from unwanted knowledge; the elders instituted taboos of silence and untouchability (the way you might manage relations with human commodities like slaves) that established their rightness, not to mention their rights.

In *Flags in the Dust* Faulkner gets seduced into trying to tell tales as a way of penetrating a society expert in spinning its own self-protective fictions. The narrator eases into the familiar role of storyteller, generously allowing characters to perform their own recitations, and imitating tried-and-true effects of an oral tradition in his own narration. There's something comfortably conversational about the narrator's manner, though the voice never becomes embodied (as it will in Faulkner's many subsequent dramatized narrators).[5] The limitation of this method is that the narrator never gains enough distance from what he's describing to question his own implication in the behavior he judges. Although the narrator succeeds in evoking the surprising variety of life in a deep South small town, nothing in the assorted stories of aristocratic pride, suicidal daring, family narcissism, racial privilege, masculine domination, or pervasive violence disturbs the narrator's confidence in his own authority to represent them, or the capacity of story to comprehend them. Faulkner's reaction to writing *Flags in the Dust*, experienced as a crisis of authorial confidence, may have compelled him in *The Sound and the Fury* to reassess the authority of narrative, to identify with states of mind rather than describe them, to *write* about a storytelling culture in such a way as to weigh the social implications of its acts of self-representation. *Flags in the Dust* manages to describe in thick detail a world Faulkner sensed was at the point of disappearing from the historical scene, but its traditional realism lacks the staggering effect of *The Sound and the Fury*, which seizes upon modernist techniques of representation to render that world as it could never have been apprehended by *any* individual member of it.

Flags in the Dust begins in the mouth of a storyteller, with a rollicking anecdote by Old Man Falls about the Confederate "Cunnel" John Sartoris. It's a story Falls repeats ritualistically to Old Bayard, the Colonel's now ancient son. Teller and listener are described as "cemented by a common deafness to a dead period" (p. 543), yet as a result of their telling, John Sartoris "seemed to loom still in the room." Falls's vignette celebrates the Colonel as a trickster who outwits Yankee soldiers come to capture him. The novel elaborates on the Sartoris legend by passing it from mouth to mouth. Aunt Jenny takes up the incident of the Colonel's foolhardy death: he gallops into the midst of a Yankee encampment to filch a tin of anchovies fancied by his General, only to be shot in the back. What's additionally pertinent about the story is that the narrator collaborates with Aunt Jenny in telling it. Some of the story appears in her quoted words, but most of it is paraphrased by the narrator. The result is a seamless rendition. When she ceases her "dream"-y tale of Confederate derring-do, and her voice is described as "proud and still as banners in the dust" (p. 556), there's no separate word from the narrator.

We might say that Faulkner's narrator in *Flags in the Dust* is overly invested in the world he is describing. In view of how prominent matters of race were in the South, and how Faulkner increasingly acknowledges their prominence over the course of *The Sound and the*

Fury, let's turn first to the question of how race relations are depicted in *Flags in the Dust*. The Sartorises exhibit the unthinking racism of their class and era. As a former slave-owning family, they illustrate how white masters got used to faulting black people for the very behavior slavery had caused. Aunt Jenny, for example, whose age links her most closely to the plantation past, constantly ridicules the black servant Isom for his perceived laziness and stupidity: "Isom made his living by being born black" (p. 580). Yet it's the narrator who later refers casually to "the shiftless fashion of negroes" (p. 661). It's a redneck white who insists that there must "be some kin between a nigger and a animal" (p. 646), but the narrator who knowingly explains that blacks emit "an animal odor" (p. 638). And it's the narrator who offsets Caspey's impatience with continued Jim Crow racism by giving the Uncle Remus-like Simon the last word on race in the novel: "Yessuh, de olden times comin' back ergain, sho'. Like in Mars' John's time, when de Cunnel wuz de young marster en de niggers f'um de quawtuhs gethered on de front lawn, wishin' Mistis en de little marster well" (p. 864). Even if we know Simon to be slyer than he sounds – and no doubt he is mocking such sentiments even as he pumps them out – still, Simon represents a distinctly unthreatening response to Southern racism, and his outward submissiveness fits in to the novel's non-confrontational treatment of it.

The young Bayard Sartoris of *Flags in the Dust* functions like Donald Mahon, Quentin Compson, and Horace Benbow to register the modern changes that have overtaken a traditional South. Bayard has returned from the Great War distraught over the death of his twin, John, lost in aerial combat. Bayard's temperament varies slightly from his cohort of faint young moderns, however, since the glamorous Sartoris past has been nothing but a burden to him – inciting desperately reckless behavior and ruining him for the quiet gratifications of marriage and family. Bayard leaves a trail of mayhem and pain until he manages to kill himself piloting an experimental aircraft. Bayard's self-absorption makes him an instructive contrast to Quentin, who, though equally narcissistic, comes face to face in *The Sound and the Fury* with a whole society's self-destructive flaws, which have plunged his beloved South into twilight. Bayard, on the other hand, proves oblivious to such evidence. At one point in *Flags in the Dust* he gets lost in the countryside and demands the assistance of a black family. He offers a generous payment for their hospitality and spends the night, but the utter squalor this tenant family lives in – the narrator notices the children "licking solemnly" at a "stick of peppermint candy to which trash adhered" (p. 842) – never gets through to Bayard. Offered a chair, he drifts off, "lost in a timeless region where he lingered unawake" (p. 843) until the wife rouses him for dinner. That kind of sleepy inattention symbolizes the open disregard by better-off whites for the degradation and inequity lived every day by blacks in a Jim Crow South.

The narrator seconds this dreamy incomprehension of racial reality when he describes the "negroes" and Bayard sharing a meal "amicably, a little diffidently – two opposed concepts antipathetic by race, blood, nature and environment, touching for a moment and fused within an illusion – humankind forgetting its lust and cowardice and greed for a day" (p. 843). The narrator seems to be insisting that although "negroes" and whites differ antipathetically as the result of "opposed concepts," they can occasionally achieve moments that leave behind the divisions caused by the illusion of their difference. Through such unselfconscious intimacy, presumably, blacks and whites can become one in their "humankind"-ness. Well, nice sentiment, but the scene doesn't dramatize anything like that, the guest rushing off as soon as he's eaten, and the family forgotten immediately as Bayard and his host head out in the commandeered wagon.

Later, the unflappable narrator encounters a spectacle of the neo-slavery imposed upon black workers after emancipation. A street is being paved:

> Along it lines of negroes labored with pick and shovel, swinging their tools in a languid rhythm. Steadily and with a lazy unhaste that seemed to spend itself in snatches of plaintive minor chanting punctuated by short grunting ejaculations which died upon the sunny air and ebbed away from the languid rhythm of picks that struck not; shovels that did not dig. (pp. 851–852)

To the lightly attentive narrator: simply languor and laziness – but not a word that shows any interest in the laborers' actual circumstances. Such workers were likely convicts leased by private contractors from the state prison. This was a common practice, and black men were often arrested on trumped up charges of vagrancy so that they could be assigned to such work crews. Blacks were kept out of mischief, the state made money, the work got done cheap, and everyone was happy. All right, maybe not everyone.

The narrator's tone remains serene as it surveys other features of Yoknapatawpha's terrain. *Flags in the Dust* contains many striking descriptions of the beauty of the Mississippi land. Late in the novel this extravagant picture of a single rose:

> now though persimmons had long swung their miniature suns among the caterpillar-festooned branches, and gum and maple and hickory had flaunted two gold-and-scarlet weeks, and the grass, where grandfathers of grasshoppers squatted sluggishly like sullen octogenarians, had been pencilled twice delicately with frost, and the sunny noons were scented with sassafras, it still bloomed. Overripe now, and a little gallantly blowsy, like a fading burlesque star. (p. 778)

The last sentence acknowledges that both Mississippi nature and Faulkner's prose are a bit over the top, on the edge of burlesque even, but the precision of the description ("caterpillar-festooned," "pencilled" with frost) can't be separated from the lavishness of the narrator's stylistic attentions (the heavy alliteration and arched syntax). Such lyrical interludes – and there are quite a few – establish the authority of nature in the world being described. That authority tries to lend itself to social realities as well. Notice, for example, how the Sartoris mansion is described in such a way as to make its social standing an extension of the natural order: "The fine and huge simplicity of the house rose among thickening trees, the garden lay in sunlight bright with bloom, myriad with scent and with a drowsy humming of bees – a steady golden sound, as of sunlight become audible . . ." (p. 584). The narrator approves of the mansion ("fine") and counts it among the natural glories of the place; the garden, favored with "bright" sunlight, "myriad" with scent, and filled with a "golden sound," embodies the successful efforts of a family to bring increase to the land and prosper.

If such descriptions of nature in effect "naturalize" the status of an elite class, others suggest that hierarchies of race and gender also are facts of nature. One of the most famous passages in *Flags in the Dust* is Faulkner's tribute to the Southern mule. The beast of burden labors patiently, without hope of betterment, consigned to reproductive oblivion, and doomed to the indignity of being sent in the end to a glue factory. The praise is tongue-in-cheek, of course, but it takes on an odd metonymic resonance at one point when the narrator observes that the mule is "[m]isunderstood even by that creature (the nigger who drives him) whose impulses and mental processes most closely resemble his" (p. 780). Such a connection ought to shame the narrator, but he never notices that in describing the lowly mule he has also in effect described the abused, longsuffering, and often resentful negro slave through plantation history. (Or perhaps the passage instructs us in the art of disregard.) This is the sort of fantasy about black folks as naturally subordinate that Quentin sees discredited in the wider world. But in *Flags in the Dust* the narrator still stands by the assumptions of a society that passes itself off as a natural fact.

The same projection of manmade values onto nature characterizes ruling attitudes toward gender as well. We recall how Caddy's innocence is prized in *The Sound and the Fury* as the symbol of a whole nexus of beliefs, behavior, and personal relations that delineate an elite class. In *Flags in the Dust* a young Horace Benbow reveres his own sister in much the same way, for the same reasons. Returning from a war that has up-ended life as his generation knew it, Horace finds a way to express his flight from the modern. As a non-combatant volunteer in France, Horace has learned the art of glassblowing. He displays one of his creations, "a small chaste shape in clear glass . . . fragile as a silver lily" (p. 677). These "tragically beautiful" vases, "[l]ike preserved flowers . . . inviolate; purged and purified as bronze, yet fragile as soap bubbles" (p. 678) are fetish objects to Horace. They correspond to his sister Narcissa, or at least his fantasy of her, and culminate in "one almost perfect vase of clear amber, larger, more richly and chastely serene . . . which he kept always on his night table and called by his sister's name" (p. 686). The physical form of the vase evokes both male fantasies of regression to female cavities and dread of anatomical vacancies. Horace notes that glassblowers work in caves, the walls of which are "wet" and feel "just like blood" (p. 677). The blood cuts both ways – as image of uterine nurture/as sign of sexual wound. Horace's vases carry the painful knowledge of sexual difference, even as they substitute for the corruption of actual bodies. They work like fetishes, avowing and denying loss – soap bubbles, something and nothing. The contradictory uses of women's "natural" sexuality produces the same kind of schizophrenic treatment of them as we saw in *The Sound and the Fury*: women are supremely chaste and inviolate, at the same time they are naturally "dirty" (pp. 711, 713), each a devouring tigress gaping with "cavernous pink gullet" (p. 804). The schematics of gender tend to bifurcate individual characters, making Narcissa both inviolate and corrupt, and locating the same division in Horace's teenage stepdaughter, Little Belle. But male ambivalence also generates doubled characters – pairs of good women/bad women like Horace's respectable wife Belle and her wild sister, with whom he has an affair. I stress that such characterization originates in male fantasy, and like the other projective dynamics we have considered, Faulkner struggles in *Flags in the Dust* to get a handle on it.

Flags in the Dust turns out to be a vast exercise in equivocation. In the narrator's memorializing of Sartoris generations, nothing – however foolish, hurtful, self-destructive, mistaken, or violent – manages to discredit the awe-inspiring project that was the plantation South. Notice how unwilling the narrator is to condemn the dream:

> Old Bayard held the rapier upon his hands for a while, feeling the balance of it. It was just such an implement as a Sartoris would consider the proper equipment for raising tobacco in a virgin wilderness . . . And old Bayard held it upon his two hands, seeing in its stained fine blade and shabby elegant sheath the symbol of his race; that too in the tradition: the thing itself fine and clear enough, only the instrument had become a little tarnished in its very aptitude for shaping circumstances to its arrogant ends. (p. 614)

"Arrogant ends," perhaps, but the thing itself – "his race," "the tradition" – still "fine and clear enough." This insistence upon paying honor to a collapsing past even while acknowledging its flaws characterizes Faulkner's uneasy approach to the remnant plantation society into which he had been born. He will go on, as he once put it, to both "indict" and "escape" from that world. The son of the South who suffers the most from a schizoid relation to a place capable of barbarity in the name of civilization, human commodification for the sake of human cultivation, brutal violence for the end of ethereal fineness – is Quentin Compson. It is no wonder he can get a full view of his beloved country only from far away: *"If I had been there I could not have seen it this plain"* (*Absalom, Absalom!*, p. 155) – first from Cambridge, then from the realm of the dead. *Flags in the Dust* retells familiar tales in such a way that it eventually dead ends storytelling itself. *The Sound and the*

Fury decides that its is a tale that cannot be told at all without sounding like an idiot, and abandons the comfort of traditional narrative for the disorienting effects of modernist aesthetics.

One other short story narrated by an older Quentin Compson also illustrates the strain on narrative exerted by Faulkner's challenge to a Southern storytelling tradition that tends to self-glorification. Not only did his own family members regale each other with tales about their magnificent if slightly daffy forefathers, but numerous Southern writers also attempted to portray plantation culture as the highest attainment of civilized life, whatever its minor imperfections. Before the Civil War, partisans like John Pendleton Kennedy treated Northern audiences to entertaining and sympathetic descriptions of plantation life, initiating a sub-genre of US fiction known as the plantation novel. His *Swallow Barn* (1832) is one of the best known, but there were many, and Faulkner's great-grandfather even wrote a couple himself. After the Confederacy's defeat and Reconstruction, advocates of a lost Southern way of life arose to extol at least the values of plantation culture; at the turn of the twentieth century, racists like Thomas Dixon, Jr. told tales of aristocratic ruination at the hands of beast-like freed blacks and Yankee carpetbaggers, while several new waves of plantation fiction through the 1930s turned nostalgically from the harshness of modern urban industrial and commercial life to fantasies about strong personal ties and intimacy with the natural world once fostered by plantation communities.

Against such a celebratory tradition skeptical writers spoke back, to be sure; not only did former slaves expose the brutal hypocrisy of plantation idealization in autobiographical and fictional narratives (such as those by Frederick Douglas, Harriet Jacobs, and William Wells Brown), but "anti-plantation" fiction materialized (such as the Northern writer Harriet Beecher Stowe's notorious *Uncle Tom's Cabin* in 1852 and the expatriated Southerner Mark Twain's lampooning tales of plantation folly in novels like *Pudd'nhead Wilson* in 1895). We'll see that Faulkner tries to negotiate these extremes as he writes modernist versions of the plantation novel in *Absalom, Absalom!*, *The Unvanquished*, and *Go Down, Moses* into the early 1940s. But as he makes his way back to that pre-Civil War world, he must pass through its ruined heirs.

In "A Justice" (1931), Faulkner imagines Southern plantation origins through the filter of the "posthumous" narrator Quentin Compson.

Though this fact might not be apparent to all readers of the two Quentin short stories, by the time of their publication, *The Sound and the Fury* had already appeared, and Faulkner simply presents us with the unexplained discrepancy. In the case of "That Evening Sun," I argued that Quentin's deadness (or at least ghostly continued life) suggests that he experiences modernity as a member of an expired social class. This makes sense for "A Justice" as well, but in it Faulkner somersaults back to pre-Civil War days, complicating narrative format by having Quentin serve merely as a pretext for yet another teller's only partially intelligible recollections, themselves second-hand.

What we get in "A Justice" is a kind of scrambled version of ante-bellum plantation society. The kernel story focuses on a peculiarity of Native American history in the South that involved Indian ownership of African slaves. The Cherokee, for example, developed large slave-worked cotton plantations in the southeast, partly in an attempt to demonstrate the "red man"'s capacity for assimilation into white dominant culture. The tribes of Mississippi would have been Choctaw and Chickasaw, but all of Faulkner's stories about them make clear that he takes liberties with their history even as he draws on the tradition of Native American slave-owning.[6] The dramatic conflict of the story involves a dispute between a negro slave and a Choctaw tribe member over a woman. The tribe's chief, and master of its "Plantation," has won six new slaves in a gambling trip down river. But Doom, as the chief is known, doesn't really want more slaves, and forces them upon two of his constituents, one of whom is pleasantly surprised to find an attractive young woman in his lot. Problems begin when one of the male slaves claims he is already married to the woman. The slave threatens to defend his rights violently; the challenger, Craw-ford, backs down, but the antagonism continues to simmer. Eventually, after a cock-fight fails to settle things by proxy, the slave appeals to Doom a final time to render justice, on the urgent occasion of the woman's giving birth to a son of suspicious color. The slave figures his "copper"-colored neighbor Craw-ford must be the father of this "yellow" child, and wants redress. Doom equivocates on the paternity question, but resolves the dispute by requiring Craw-ford to erect a fence around the slaves' cabin too high for him to scale. Doom makes the child's blurred origins into a joke, declaring that he will be known henceforth as "Had-Two-Fathers." But Doom's interventions may

FIGURE 3 Faulkner in 1930. Publicity still for *Sanctuary*. Cofield Collection, Southern Media Archive, University of Mississippi Special Collections (B1F1).

mask a deeper joke, since the story insinuates that it is Doom who in fact may be helping himself to the comely slave girl, and hence is the secret author of the anomalous child.

Faulkner's deliberately eccentric version of the plantation regime in "A Justice" creates two major effects: the second is an act of displacement, stimulated by the first, which is the discovery of a truth. The notion of Native American slaveholding is so surprising and atypical that it distracts from the institution as it was normally practiced. Plantation slave-owning appears in the form of a novelty, and the way the tale is told transforms sinister, even deadly actions into an amusing anecdote. In that sense, "A Justice" suggests how the anguish of slavery gets softened and disavowed as it makes its way from the remote past. A figure like Quentin, because of his generational distance and class insulation, can hardly detect the notes of terror and rage in the story of a humiliated slave, or understand what Sam Fathers must feel about being a comical "Had-Two-Fathers" (and really *three*), in a world where power was proudly patrilineal.

But beyond the denial encouraged by a funny story about Indians trying to be slave-owning plantation masters, there's also the recognition deep down that such history jeopardizes the distinctiveness of the Southern elite's racial and economic status. Plantation society might not rest on the natural superiority of a people who generously bring their inferiors into civilization from darkest Africa; instead, it looks like a vicious and fundamentally unjust exercise of power and spectacle: hardly a matter of justice. Edouard Glissant has distinguished two fundamental mentalities in Faulkner's Yoknapatawpha plantation society: one is *atavistic* – the longing to prove that your people descended in a pure line from the founding great figures of your world's creation; the second is *composite* – the realization that all peoples are mixtures of ethnicity, blood, race, class, etc., and that the ideal of purity is a fiction itself.[7] Glissant believes that Faulkner's planters form a composite class that deludes itself into believing it is atavistic. "A Justice" illustrates this nicely, since when Quentin starts hearing actual tales about the old people – told by Sam Fathers, a blended product of that society, who speaks as a member of the Compson plantation – the scenes he discovers are full of composite figures, indeterminate origins, and questionable rights.

Because Native Americans assume the role of landowners and slave masters, we can't help noticing their mimicry of European colonial behavior. Doom decides that the nearest approximation to an authentic plantation mansion he can find is a stranded steamboat, which he orders his slaves and underlings to carry overland. As it inches along, the master rides on its front porch: "Doom sat in his chair, with a boy with a branch to shade him and another boy with a branch to drive away the flying beasts" (*Collected Stories*, p. 354). The spectacle makes fun of typical plantation mastery by showboating the unfeeling usage of laborers and pointless consumption of leisure. By the time he takes over the tribe, Doom is already something of a European/Native American amalgam. He spends seven years "abroad" in New Orleans (at that time a "European city" ["Red Leaves," *Collected Stories*, p. 317], and returns not only attired in the latest French fashion, but educated in political treachery. It turns out that the nickname "Doom" has evolved from the French equivalent for the Native American term for head man: "the Man": "du homme"/"doom." The chief's given name is Ikkemotubbe, but "Doom" works as a fair warning, since the first thing he does upon his arrival is to stage the poisoning of a puppy, then of his only rivals, his uncle and infant nephew. Again, Faulkner seems to be pointing to the ferocious violence of the plantation order, however disguised in this Indian costume drama.

It's as if whoever is responsible for telling this story – and we'll get to that in a moment – needs to screen anxieties about the plantation behind comic high jinks. These are mimic plantation and slave masters, so their violence, rapacity, and decadence never directly implicate their models. If we trace such displacement back through the narrative levels, we see concentric circles of evasion at work. The story is told originally by one of the Indians, a man named Herman Basket who is a friend of Craw-ford. He subsequently tells the story to the "yellow" child in order to fill him in on his origins. "Had-Two-Fathers" grows up to be a legendary figure in the wilderness sagas of Yoknapatawpha, the man named Sam Fathers. Sam works as a carpenter on Grandfather Compson's farm, where he befriends Quentin, but his real life exists in the big woods, where Fathers honors his ancestral spirits by practicing the rites of hunting. Sam cherishes the story of his nativity because it constitutes proof to him that he is something more than the negro he is commonly treated as. Quentin seeks out Sam's stories, curious about this ancient figure who defies familiar categories. White people call him a "negro," but "the negroes call him a blue-gum" (according to folk knowledge, a person born with discolored gums, capable of a poisonous bite). Quentin sees that Sam talks "like a nigger" too, but he doesn't look like one. The closest Quentin can come to defining what Sam is, is to state what he is not: "he wasn't a Negro" (*Collected Stories*, p. 343). Quentin seems drawn to the anomalies of Sam's story, to the gaps that trouble origins. Sam's history represents the mixed or *creolized* realities of plantation society, a fact denied by the ideology of family and racial purity, but slowly revealed to the survivors of that fantasy's collapse. The participants in this particular version of "the Plantation" combine indigenous birth and colonial manners, the positions of ethnic oppressed and racial oppressor, the submissiveness of slaves and the rights of masters.

As we might expect, Quentin cannot take all this in. Not only do the successive tellings of the story muffle its serious import, but Quentin experiences on behalf of the reader a certain incomprehension at this peculiar variant of slaveholding. The adult narrator pleads that he "was just twelve then, and to me the story did not seem to have got anywhere, to have had point or end" (p. 359). Quentin does admit that the import of the story finally comes clear, but "I would have to wait until I had passed on and through and beyond the suspension of twilight. Then I knew that I would know. But then Sam Fathers would be dead" (p. 360). Of course, the knowledge Quentin comes to possess by then ensures that he will be dead too, having passed beyond his own twilight.

CHAPTER 3

Come Up: From Red Necks to Riches

The social and economic changes overhauling the South after the Civil War – which so jeopardized advantaged groups like the Compsons and Sartorises – offered splendid new opportunities to others once down-trodden. From the earliest inklings Faulkner had about Yoknapa-tawpha in the early 1920s, he knew a central transformation to be reckoned with was the rise of some so-called "rednecks" from the dead end of tenant farming into the ranks of a newly-forming middle class. When Faulkner began entertaining his best friend Phil Stone with comic inventions about over-reaching hillbillies who try to Horatio Alger their way into money, these two sons of distinguished Oxford families just found the whole thing good for a laugh. The idea that a clan of dirt poor creatures might evolve into successful rivals of planter elite descendants seemed unimaginable. Barely into his twen-ties, Faulkner was reacting to actual historical shifts with the reflexes of his class. He bestowed the "Snopeses" with a name ugly enough to suggest their sneaky dopey invasion of village and town, and described each new family member as a tall tale critter – a serpent, a cow, a mink. Like most other members of the plantation gentry, the Faulkner family had had to endure such encroachments on their power: Faulkner's grandfather had reluctantly identified a brilliant ambitious young man from the hills, Lee Russell, taken him as a partner in his law office, and helped sponsor his ascent to the governorship – all the while holding his nose at the need to capitalize on new blood, con-stituencies, and schemes supplied by folk he considered hopelessly uncivilized.

Faulkner's first effort to capture the Snopeses on paper resulted in an embryonic novel, entitled *Father Abraham*. By early 1927 Faulkner seems to have set the project aside to concentrate on *Flags in the Dust*, but a few years later he took the kernel of the manuscript – an episode recounting the auction of some flamboyant Texas ponies to the hard-working farmers of Frenchman's Bend – and turned it into a free-standing short story, published in 1931 as "Spotted Horses." Initially, Faulkner seems mostly just repulsed by the naked money-grubbing of the Snopeses. Underneath his derision lies real disgust:

> The Snopeses sprang untarnished from a long line of shiftless tenant farmers – a race that is of the land and yet rootless, like mistletoe: owing nothing to the soil, giving nothing to it and getting nothing in return; using the land as a harlot instead of an imperious yet abundant mistress, passing on to another farm. Cunning and dull and clannish, they move and halt and move and multiply and marry and multiply like rabbits: magnify them and you have political hangerson and professional office-holders and prohibition officers; reduce the perspective and you have mold on cheese, steadfast and gradual and implacable: theirs that dull provincial cunning that causes them to doubt anything that does not jibe with their preconceived and arbitrary standards of verity, and that permits them to be taken in by the most barefaced liar who is at all plausible. (*Father Abraham*, pp. 19–20)

The narrator admits no knowledge of the economic hardship that forced tenants into nomadism, or drove desperate offspring to more stable public service jobs, or would expose landowners as the actual parasites on the labor of their debtors (like that mold on the cheese). The Snopeses' chief offense to the unidentified narrator (who in later stories will get separated out as an independent antagonist named Ratliff) involves their monomaniacal pursuit of profit. The faux patriarch of this up-and-coming clan is Flem Snopes, the "Abraham" of a new chosen people. He's a creature of the market – his nephew is named Wallstreet Panic Snopes – and swindle is his trademark.

The deal that preoccupies *Father Abraham* and "Spotted Horses" dramatizes the essential deception at the heart of trade; Faulkner eventually makes it the centerpiece of the last section of *The Hamlet* (1940). A string of "gaudy" (*The Hamlet*, p. 300), "harlequin"-spotted (p. 303) horses parade into the hamlet on the hand of a trader from

Texas. Although Flem is rumored to be their actual owner, he remains behind the scenes, allowing Buck Hipps to inflame the curious farmers with the spectacle of the gorgeous, spirited creatures. Everyone recognizes that the horses will be useless as work animals, but as consumers they conspire with the auctioneer in a "hallucination" of their desirability (p. 302). In *Father Abraham* and "Spotted Horses" Faulkner suggests how such commercial theatrics loose a "contagion" of mass indulgence upon the hamlet. By *The Hamlet* (1940), Faulkner has seen more deeply into the mechanisms of commodity fetishism and consumption. As tricked up consumer goods, the horses have been abstracted from their use value. Their dreamy, almost erotic appeal derives from the thrill of competitive acquisition itself, the hamlet's first glimpse of them taking in their resemblance to "vari-sized and – colored tatters torn at random from large billboards – circus posters, say" (p. 299). Figments of primitive advertising, promoted by the auctioneer's market savvy as he gives away the first horse in exchange for a bid on the second to get things going, these goods represent the concentration of value in the mystery of consumer desire. The purchasers tap deep cravings for fulfillment beyond the narrow world of alienated labor they occupy, and these particular objects of yearning represent the exercise of the imagination and the pleasure of play. The horses are bought and owned, but, significantly, never used, since most of them escape into the countryside when their new owners attempt to take possession of them. Faulkner identifies crucial elements of an emergent culture of merchandising and consumption as he portrays the new prominence of commercial life in a region long dominated by agricultural production.

We have seen how Faulkner's unusual imaginative sympathy enables him to explore both the promise and disappointments of modernity. As he pursues the saga of the rise of the rednecks, he becomes more and more attuned to the desperation of their poverty and the poignancy of their ambition. Another short story spun off from the Snopes material charts the painful choices confronting those determined to escape a legacy of degradation. Published in 1939, at the end of the nation's most serious economic depression, "Barn Burning" displays Faulkner's sensitivity to the rage and despair of the poor. The story recounts an act of violent revenge by a tenant farmer insulted by his landlord's suit over damages to a carpet deliberately ruined during a visit by the new worker. Ab Snopes, spoiling with resentment at his reduction to tenancy, insists that his son Sarty accompany him when he goes to introduce himself to Major de Spain, with whom he has signed a season's contract. Snopes wants his son to see first hand the gulf between rich and poor, to educate him in class loyalty: "I reckon I'll have a word with the man that aims to begin tomorrow owning me body and soul for the next eight months" (*Collected Stories*, p. 9). Ab's status has been destabilized by the cessation of slavery. Ab lets on that during the Civil War he was a proud soldier of the Confederacy, even naming Sarty after his commander, Colonel Sartoris, the eminent Jefferson planter. The story's last lines correct Ab's fantasy, reporting that Snopes was nothing but a horse thief who traded with both armies, and whose only loyalty was to the "booty" of war. What has transpired since then, to be sure, is Ab's loss of racial solidarity with better off whites, as a result of slave emancipation. With freed blacks often considered more desirable tenants than poor whites, given their vulnerability to violent intimidation under Jim Crow laws, Ab's condition as a laborer now can hardly be distinguished from a slave's. Catching sight of De Spain's mansion, he exclaims to Sarty: "Pretty and white, ain't it? . . . That's sweat. Nigger sweat. Maybe it ain't white enough yet to suit him. Maybe he wants to mix some white sweat with it" (p. 12).

Ab's response to his confinement as a landless wage laborer without hope of advancement, is to lash out destructively at his perceived antagonists. Ab takes to burning down the barns of his landlords. Extreme as the act may seem, Faulkner is actually drawing on historical precedent; arson was a measure some tenants used to protest unfair treatment. Ab turns out to have a well-earned reputation as a barn-burner, and we'll see that when he shows up in Frenchman's Bend, one landlord tries to take advantage of his trail of terrorism. The story acknowledges that Ab performs these acts as a "weapon for the preservation of integrity" (p. 8), but the son's recoil at his father's endangerment of life and property suggests how obsolete such a code of honor and violence has become. To Sarty, Ab looks stuck in primitive routines of class confrontation. Ab tromps about on a foot "stiff" with an old wound, and after reflexively stepping in manure on his way into De Spain's house, he smears his tracks onto the pristine French carpet, in a gesture of resentment that he's nothing but excrement in the eyes of a landlord. Ab has no other means to express his rage – "he said something unprintable and vile, addressed to no one" (p. 5) – so these crude pantomimes manage only to convey his agitation in "outrageous overstatement" (p. 15). His fouling of the rug and the subsequent rock-scrubbing that ruins it leave "water-cloudy scoriations resembling the sporadic course of a lilliputian mowing machine" (p. 14). The image richly distills Ab's felt littleness in the scheme of things, the all but invisible tracings of his labor on the landlord's field of luxury, the absence of anything but the faintest indication of the tenant's transient presence.

Sarty tries manfully to accept his father's creed of blood and class loyalty: "our enemy," he thinks about an earlier landlord, "ourn! Mine and hisn both! He's my father!" (p. 3). But the story pivots on Sarty's decision to betray his father's plan to torch De Spain's barn; he escapes from his sympathetic mother's detention – Ab is already suspicious of Sarty's resolve – and alerts the landlord's family to the just-kindled blaze. Sarty and the reader are left with the impression that Ab has been killed by shots De Spain fires. Conflicted as the child is, Sarty casts his lot with the future, confident that a little walking will "cure" his own "stiff"-ness after a night of hiding. Parting words: "He did not look back" (p. 25). Sarty's revolt against Ab's deadly ways arises from his identification *with* De Spain's affluence. Sarty responds to the "peace" and "dignity" and "safety" bespoken by the mansion, and recognizes that somehow right is on the side of might: "Hit's big as a courthouse" (p. 10). Earlier his father strikes him when Sarty betrays some sympathy for a landlord's entitlement to justice. Given the family's endless deprivation and insecurity, which Ab's class warfare does nothing to alleviate, Sarty concludes there's more sense in enriching yourself than attacking the wealthy. The opportunities offered by modern commercial life open an avenue to prosperity for some members of a generation willing to leave the land. "Barn Burning" begins with Sarty's disorientation at being called forward to testify in a suit involving his father. The itinerant Justice of the Peace has set up court in a store, and Sarty must make his way past cheese he can smell and tins of food "whose labels his stomach read" (p. 3). The scene suggests that the route to justice, or at least relief, for a lucky few may lie through the aisles of Wal-Mart.

As Faulkner pursues his account of poor white ascent against the backdrop of planter decline, the Snopeses come to represent Yoknapatawpha's major brand of modernity. Faulkner reworks both "Spotted

Horses" and "Barn Burning" to incorporate them into *The Hamlet* (1940), the first of three novels devoted to Flem Snopes's rags-to-riches rise. A sleight-of-hand by Faulkner underscores the disruptive new ethos embodied by the Snopeses. When Ab and his family show up in the opening pages of *The Hamlet*, Sarty has disappeared, scarcely even remembered. Instead, a "new" older son named Flem has taken his place. This Snopes shows no signs of the ambivalence or regret that tinge Sarty's rebellion. He's impassive and calculating, coolly parting ways with his family's flammable self-destructiveness: "Aint no benefit in farming. I figure on getting out of it soon as I can" (*The Hamlet*, p. 25). Flem announces this intention to Jody Varner, the son and heir-apparent of the most powerful man in the counties surrounding the tiny village of Frenchman's Bend. The remark serves as both a statement of general ambition and a specific warning that the Varners may be in for some competition.

The Varners have built their fiefdom through shrewd financial speculation, so Flem identifies a precedent for his self-making. Will Varner, introduced by the narrator as "the chief man of the country," "the largest landholder and beat supervisor in one county and Justice of the Peace in the next and election commissioner in both" (p. 5), presides over his dominion as "a farmer, a usurer, a veterinarian" (p. 6). Will recognizes the advantage of horizontal integration, annexing interconnected realms of power – legal, political, financial, even livestock medical. For all his hearty good humor, Will's success owes to sharp dealing. With the profits from his general supply store he exploits the chronic lack of credit available to small farmers; he extends loans and mortgages to landowners, but also profits from supply arrangements with sharecroppers who work the farms Varner seizes when those mortgagees default. Jody emulates his old man's ruthlessness, immediately sizing up, for example, the newcomer Ab's potential vulnerability to rumors about his barn-burning past. Jody hopes to blackmail his tenant into leaving after he does the work of planting but before harvest (and pay day). Flem identifies a counter-vulnerability, though, offering himself as clerk-in-training to the Varners in exchange for keeping their property off his father's hit list. The Varners lose this preliminary round. Flem's victory augurs his relentless ascent over the next forty years to the presidency of Jefferson's Merchants and Farmers' Bank.

On the surface, Will and Jody's rudimentary mercantile capitalism retains enough flexibility not to ruin the community's cohesion. Devotion to profit doesn't prevent Will from savoring the intangible pleasure of outwitting a trading partner, or even being outwitted by one, and he buddies up with another clever small-time entrepreneur, V. K. Ratliff, who enjoys a comfortable life selling sewing machines door-to-door as he circulates through the region in a home-made horse-drawn cart. Will indulges a "Rabelaisian" appetite for food and sex, his friend Ratliff contributes a taste for the well-told comic tale, and both seem to engage in commercial trade as much as an entertaining pastime as a source of income. On the one hand, we might think of the hamlet's primitive capitalism as representing the mixed attributes of a transitional stage between economic regimes. Will Varner derives from an apparently simpler world of barter and occupant ownership of land; he trusts his customers at the store with a self-pay box, and generally exhibits a relaxed attitude toward money. Will prides himself on his middle-class modesty in contrast to the "baronial splendor" dreamt of by the planter elite, another obsolete economy, rooted in feudalism. Will comes from peasant stock, migrants from the northeast who settled on small farms and worked their own land. Though he's bought the now-abandoned Old Frenchman's Place, the county's first and foremost slave-run cotton plantation, Will can't fathom the lordliness it represents: "I like to sit here. I'm trying to find out what it must have felt like to be the fool that would need all this" (p. 7).

On the other hand, Will's insouciance masks a relentless predatory mercantilism. He has already introduced the hamlet to the harsh reality of profiting from your neighbors' ineptness or bad luck. While the Varners extend "long credit" to their community, the farmers nonetheless know "they would pay interest for that which on its face looked like generosity and open-handedness" (pp. 62–63). Faulkner makes it difficult to locate kindness in a market economy, even in its embryonic stage. And when Flem arrives, deciding on his own that he will no longer allow credit to the chronically dependent, Will is outraged – undoubtedly more because such a policy would choke off a revenue stream than out of any good-heartedness. Varner's little empire feeds on his debtors. Who really is the mold on the cheese?

If Faulkner's portrait of the Varners fails to convince there's a humane decency capable of offsetting the blind brutality of market economics, Ratliff himself does come as close to "good" capitalism as Flem eventually does to "bad." I draw that distinction from John Gray's study of globalization, *False Dawn*, in which he distinguishes a form of capitalism that preserves commitment to general social welfare, even if the bottom line suffers, from a kind of absolute free marketry that pretends social protections will simply emanate from competitive self-interest.[1] Salesman Ratliff is always looking to turn a profit, and isn't above seducing poor farmwives with easy credit to do it. But his sewing machines also provide a convenience that, historically, eased the lives of many rural women. He's also willing to suffer a loss when he thinks some good will come of it. Ratliff's most impressive gesture of ethical commerce involves his interventions on behalf of a mentally deficient Snopes named Ike, who has become enamored of a neighbor's cow. This pitiful man-child longs Benjy-like for his true love, but his pathetic perversion gets capitalized upon by a relative, Lump Snopes, who stages for the villagers' amusement Ike's acts of coupling with the cow in a barn stall. Outraged, Ratliff admits that this "aint any of my business" (p. 219), but he closes down the "engagement" anyhow and arranges to extract money from various Snopeses to "buy" the cow from Ike and destroy it. Earlier, Ratliff has donated to Ike's custodian the equivalent of his profits on a trade with Flem so that the distraught "lover" can purchase his beloved from its original owner. Ratliff forces everyone involved to confront the "moral value" of the money that passes hands, and seems especially anxious about the voyeuristic dimension of the cow-diddling: "does he make you pay again each time, or is it a general club ticket good for every performance?" (p. 217). There's something about a mass audience assembled around a pornographic spectacle, enjoying it vicariously, that unnerves even a traveling salesman. It's as if Ratliff foresees the destiny of commercial mass media to provide artificial gratification through voyeuristic fantasy. The episode prefigures the sleazy trickery of the spotted horses' auction, too, though the disapproving Ratliff decides to sit that one out.

Ratliff delivers Faulkner's most eloquent denunciations of economic exploitation, yet his own dependence on merchandising and consumption makes it impossible for him to establish complete moral separation. When Ratliff realizes how heartlessly Flem means to enforce the strict letter of market law, he fantasizes a scene that captures the store clerk's utter rapacity. Ratliff imagines a penniless black girl come up from the fields to trade her body for some lard, but who, as Flem has at her, spies more exotic goods above the clerk's bobbing head: "Mr Snopes, whut you ax fer dem sardines?" (p. 182). Ratliff's anger also inspires a breathtaking set piece at the end of Book Two; there the salesman pictures Flem as a claimant before the Prince of Heaven himself – Snopes a law-spouting Faust who has bartered his soul for worldly riches but now refuses to be condemned to Hell until he redeems his soul, as the contract stipulates. This only semi-coherent episode reflects Ratliff's conviction that the Varners, father and son, have no chance of stopping Flem, and that the odious little creature plans on laying siege to "Paradise" itself – the ultimate possession Ratliff associates with Eula Varner, Will's imagination-beggaring beauty of a daughter. At the same time, Ratliff's rage must derive from his own sense of guilt at spreading the contagion of speculation and consumption. He affiliates himself with older, more personal modes of trade, even celebrating Ab Snopes, in one instance, as the champion of the sort of horse-swapping meant to defend the honor of his county against outsider raiders like Pat Stamper. But Ratliff also admits that Ab has "soured" over years of uncured poverty, and *The Hamlet* presents a whole gallery of poor white farmers who, as chronic victims of market manipulation, have lost their land, their pride, their purpose.

Ratliff's sympathy for such losses stimulates a sort of compensatory fantasy that attaches to the person of Eula Varner. The region's collective trauma involves the displacement of small subsistence farmers from their individual plots of land by speculators like Varner. Such consolidation leads to wider tenancy, and eventually to takeover by large-scale agribusiness.[2] Faulkner's remark in *Father Abraham* about the Snopeses treating the land like a harlot rather than a mistress suggests the corruption spread by mere commercial valuation of the soil. It also hints at an extended trope in *The Hamlet* by which the land is personified as the figure of an overwhelmingly seductive, explosively fertile female. From the first reports by Europeans about the vast beckoning New World wilderness, the habit of associating the continent's open land with a woman's receptive body seems the defining feature of the way males imagined American nature.[3] Think of Terence Malick's movie *New World*, which shows how the founding myth of "Pocahontas" and John Smith embodies the colonial fantasy that an unspoiled land and people would fall in love with their ravishers. Faulkner refines the trope to express a new imaginative solution to later historical changes in the occupation of the land.

For Ratliff, who sees farming despoiled by exclusively mercantile interests, Eula becomes a kind of fetishized substitute for pleasures the land no longer affords. To the hamlet's menfolk, Eula is an object of fantastic desire. She's courted by half a dozen young men, but dreamt of, Ratliff jokes, by every male up to Old Man Hundred-and-One McCallum. Eula possesses feminine charms to excess – at least the excess of an excitable male's prose: "her entire appearance suggested some symbology out of the old Dionysic times – honey in sunlight and bursting grapes, the writhen bleeding of the crushed fecundated vine beneath the hard rapacious trampling goat-hoof" (p. 105). Even as an adolescent Eula is "a kaleidoscopic convolution of mammalian ellipses" (p. 111), her exposed thigh "profoundly naked as the dome of an observatory" (p. 112), her whole body "a moist blast of spring's liquor-ish corruption" (p. 126), a veritable "seed of the spendthrift Olympian ejaculation" (p. 164), and – okay, you knew this had to be coming – "the supreme primal uterus" (p. 126). The point is not that Eula actu-ally *is* some earth goddess promising orgasmic fulfillment and boundless fruitfulness, but that she needs to be fantasized as one by her seriously deprived admirers. Why? Because the dispossessed menfolk project onto Eula a longing for their land lost, as well as a refusal to believe it is lost.

Eula's body morphs into the earth itself: the bursting grapes, the fecundated vine, the seed of Olympian ejaculation. As such, she embodies the land before it became commodity. Ratliff despairs not only because no single individual deserves sole ownership of abun-dance such as Eula's, but also because, worse, she falls into the hands of the least worthy possessor, Flem Snopes himself. Eula has gotten pregnant by her young lover, Hoake McCarron, who flees at her urging, and Will in effect sells his daughter off to the only person with the means to support her and salvage her reputation. Flem sees in the ruined Eula nothing but an opportunity to advance himself in Will's favor, with career benefits. So the deal gets made, to Ratliff's horror. The narrator spells out the connection between the land and Eula, both imperiled by the rule of property and the "dead power of money." An earlier admirer of Eula prophesies the sort of husband who'll claim her:

He would be a dwarf, a gnome, without glands or desire, who would be no more a physical factor in her life than the owner's name on the fly-leaf of a book . . . the crippled Vulcan to that Venus, who would not possess her but merely own her by the single strength which power gave, the dead power of money, wealth, gewgaws, baubles, as he might own, not a picture, statue: a field, say. He saw it: the fine land rich and fecund and foul and eternal and impervious to him who claimed title to it, oblivious, drawing itself ten fold the quantity of living seed its owner's whole life could have secreted and compounded, producing a thousand fold the harvest he could ever hope to gather and save. (pp. 132–133)

There's a deep conviction in this passage that Eula, like the rich fields, will somehow prove inexhaustible to the arrogance of ownership. In projecting their feelings about the shifting conditions of land property onto Eula, the menfolk of the hamlet practice a trick of equivocation. On the one hand, they imagine the body of the land as incorruptible, beyond the capacity of human touch to harm, and capable of recovering its original plenitude. On the other, they recognize that the land fell into commercial proprietorship long before they occupy it. The ruined shell of the Frenchman's Place gestures to the intricate edifice of plantation economy – the acquisition and administration of vast parcels of land, not to mention a reliance on human property. Eula's contradictory qualities allow the contradictions of Southern land use to be held in mental suspension; that is why Eula is both incorruptible and a blast of corruption, why she embodies at once infinite promise and foreclosed desire, why she combines in a single word the "implications of lost triumphs and defeats of unimaginable splendor" (p. 165).

Eula's mythic stature expands around the event of her engagement to Flem. The narrator proposes her Olympian pedigree just as Ratliff learns the news of the betrothal deal. The inexhaustible potential of Eula's beauty speaks to Ratliff precisely when the "froglike creature" claims his new wife with all the passion of "cashing a check, buying a license, taking a train" (p. 164). That is, those who lose out on Eula hallucinate her transcendence, in much the way dispossessed farmers romanticize the land before property and ownership. Eula's love story doubles as a fable of the land. Faulkner goes out of his way to fill in the background of the boy who impregnates her. Hoake McCarron is the son of a widow who has inherited her father's plantation, which Hoake now oversees. When he spies Eula in the village one day, he begins his pursuit, eventually chasing away his punier rivals, who are jokingly dismissed as "foreclosed bankrupts" in the Eula sweepstakes. Her courtship takes place across a "long summer," the season of crop growth, and concludes with her marriage to Flem at "harvest, the money-time" p. 165). The imaginary link between Eula and the land gets stronger when we learn that Will has transferred the title of the Frenchman's Place to Flem as part of Eula's nuptial agreement.

Eula's contradictory symbolic meaning – in that she stands for the land both before its ruination and after its loss – reverberates with other glimpses of women in *The Hamlet*. Ab's cousin Mink Snopes takes a mistress in a logging camp where he once works – or, more accurately, Mink is taken by her, since as the owner's daughter she makes a practice of summoning laborers for her pleasure. Their violent lovemaking feels metaphorical:

> Afterward it seemed to him that that afternoon's bedding had been the signal for that entire furious edifice of ravished acres and shotgun houses and toiling men and mules which had been erected overnight and founded on nothing, to collapse overnight into nothing, back into the refuse – the sawdust heaps, the lopped dead limbs and tree-butts and all the grief of wood – of its own murdering. (p. 264)

Mink's lover adds to the symbolic association of ruined women with the desecrated land, but here the fantasy is that the land itself desires such abuse. If the lovemaking is a "signal," it communicates both the defilement for profit of the wilderness, along with the self-justifying dream that the land may be a mistress rather than a harlot, as Faulkner puts it in *Father Abraham*. Ravished for cash, yes, but wanting it all the while?

Once we appreciate how the figment called "Eula" is produced as a compensatory fantasy by male anxieties about the loss of land ownership in *The Hamlet*, we might notice an even broader symbolic role she plays in the collective imagination. Eula represents a desperate effort to hypothesize something exempt from the very principle of capitalist exchange. A community increasingly dominated by mercantile mentality comes up with a fantastical creature they believe transcends market logic. Faulkner actually uses a concept drawn from Marx's analysis of commodification, "exchange value," to describe this imputed attribute of Eula's: "that quality . . . which absolutely abrogated the exchange value of any single life's promise or capacity for devotion, the puny asking-price of any one man's reserve of so-called love" (p. 131). As a fetish object, Eula both transcends economics (being beyond the exchange value of any one man's love) and gets assigned value within economics (the terms used to exalt her derive from the market: "asking-price," "reserve"). Eula tantalizes with the halluci-nated possibility that she supersedes equivalence, even as the towns-folk also see that she is just another merchandised female in a society run by males. Descriptions of Eula emphasize how it is her excess that makes her so desirable. Her body itself is just too much – "too much of leg, too much of breast, too much of buttock; too much of mam-malian female meat" (p. 111). She's the "spendthrift" seed, we recall. A poor young schoolteacher named Labove falls in love with her when she's his twelve-year-old student. To this inhumanly disciplined young man on the rise – he's already escaped his "dirt-farmer" (p. 128) origins to gain a university degree, and has his sights set on the governor's mansion – Eula's promise of "Dionysic" self-abandonment threatens to blow up his "monklike" exercise of self-denial. From childhood the heavenly Eula is notorious for her immobility: she seems to do nothing, and even has to be carried to school by a manservant. Eula functions as an extravagant fantasy-creature of limitless leisure, self-indulgence, contentment, and eros – all the things repudiated by industrious, ascetic, scheming, neutered little market men epitomized by Flem.[4]

Faulkner reinforces the idea that Eula has been made into a fantasy by repeating the pattern in the story of Ike's love for the cow. Book Two ends with Eula's marriage to Flem, the couple's disappearance from the hamlet (to wait out the birth of Eula's illegitimate child), and Ratliff's caustic vision of Flem gaining "Paradise" in a deal with the panicked Prince of Heaven. Book Three opens with a narrative episode that takes a while to believe: a man romancing a neighbor's cow – described in some of the lushest, most lyrical language Faulkner ever wrote. The notion itself reflects centuries of barnyard humor, of course, and Faulkner once before had tried a comic tale about love for a cow, making the human protagonist, one Ernest V. Trueblood, an aspiring author, and using the gimmick of his infatuation to suggest the delusional quixotism of literary ambition. "Afternoon of a Cow" amounts to a fledgling author's self-parody. But in *The Hamlet*, Faulkner shapes this crude material into another kind of fable, one concerning the dream of exemption from a monetary economy. The novel has already traced several arcs portending the rising "power of money" – in Ab's defeats by a professional trader, then by his own craftier son; in Ratliff's enjoining Flem in market wars; and of course in Eula's reduction to commodity in the matter of her marriage. Eventually, the madness of commodity consumption floods the countryside as a result of Flem's equine auction. But in this bovine interlude, Ike enacts a utopian fantasy of life free of even the concepts of use and exchange value.

Ike earns his keep by doing small chores for the proprietor of a rooming house, Mrs. Littlejohn. But when Ike finishes his work, he flees the village for idyllic trysts outdoors with his beloved. In the purity of his devotion to the cow's well-being – he frees her from Houston's fields, leads her on jaunts through woods and streams, lies luxuriantly with her in meadows – he represents all that the hamlet is forsaking as it heads toward modernity. Ike experiences these pastoral moments as distinct from his labor: "Because even while sweeping he would still see her, blond among the purpling shadows" (p. 186). Ike's mental "deficiency" blesses him with the ability to be at peace with toil: "There is no work, no travail, no muscular, and spiritual reluctance to overcome, constantly war against; yesterday was not, tomorrow is not, today is merely a placed and virginal astonishment at the creeping ridge of dust and trash in front of the broom" (p. 183). Never cursed with the awareness that paid labor may alienate you, Ike is free to indulge his passion for the cow as a labor of love. The misty vision of the animal "planted, blond, dew-pearled," "the flowing immemorial female," makes him feel "serene and one and indivisible in joy" (p. 183). In his own act of extravagance, Faulkner gives us here a second version of fetishistic power to accompany Eula's, this one a pastoral comedy, to counterpoint her village tragedy. Faulkner's "spendthrift" (p. 203) style in the episode enriches his sympathy for Ike's wandering off from the dull, stingy utilitarianism of commercial life.

Ike uses the cow as Ratliff and his fellows use Eula, or, for that matter, as the Compson brothers use Caddy and Horace uses Temple: as screens upon which to project male anxiety. We saw in Chapter 1 how Faulkner feminizes the force of rebellion against a masculinist society. In Chapter 2, we focused on how elite classes find ways to pretend their world is not coming apart. In his exploration of how poorer people's lives changed as modernity approached, Faulkner identifies a similar (perhaps universal?) tendency to internalize imaginary explanations and consolations in dealing with realities they lack the power to change. Some social theorists have defined the concept of ideology in just such terms – as the way a group or community actually *produces* the reality they experience through an imagined relation to "the Real" (understood as the material conditions of a society: its economic system, social structures, political institutions, etc.). What makes Faulkner's confrontation with such mental technologies distinctive – as they were tooled particularly for the South – is his determination to expose them *as* imaginative ruses, to see through them.

If we return to Ike's fantasy for a moment, we might notice in Faulkner's paean to the natural life a small blot. Ike doesn't seem to know what a coin is, let alone sense the intricate network of financial transactions that whirl over his head. But once, when Houston reclaims his cow and confusedly tries to compensate Ike by tucking two quarters in his pocket, Faulkner complicates Ike's innocence. Ike digs out one of the coins, places it on his hand, then a moment later notices his palm is empty, "who to know," the narrator speculates, "what motion, infinitesimal and convulsive, of supreme repudiation there might have been" (p. 197) in the disappearance. Yet a moment later, we find Ike searching for the quarter, though now "watching him you would have said he did not want to find the coin" (p. 197). I think Ike may indeed intuit that the coins have value, an indication that even this last figure of innocence has finally been contaminated by money-thoughts. The narrator, against his own evidence, insists that Ike remains pure, however; Faulkner exposes how even his own narrative is tempted by the hope that something might be free of the hamlet's degrading obsession with commerce. Likewise, Ratliff also finally admits to having projected such a wish onto Eula. After all, he is himself a merchant, having forsaken the land and life of his farmer fathers. Maybe he's been wrong, he thinks, about Eula being "wasted" on Snopes, "on all of them, himself included" (p. 166). Maybe Eula has been nothing after all but a "figment" (*idem*). It is intriguing that Faulkner brings an end to cow fantasies by staging an actual ritual of primitive fetishism. Ratliff hears that you can cure bestiality by killing the animal and feeding it to the afflicted. He not only insists that Ike's relatives fork over cash so that Ike isn't left indigent by the loss of the cow; he also requires them to participate in an act of fetishistic exorcism. Afterwards, Ike is given a tiny cow trinket, but no aura of fantasy adheres to this mere toy. It's as if Faulkner is determined to de-fetishize a South that believes itself innocent of mercantile ways.

Virtually every sub-plot in this generously plotted novel involves a question of economic conflict. Jack Houston submits himself in marriage to a woman desperate to push upward from meager origins; she sets the couple on a course to bourgeois security, yet all the while Houston chafes under the bit of respectability. When Lucy dies prematurely, Houston loses his way altogether, though there's evidence he subconsciously caused her death by making her the gift of a wild horse. Houston meets his end when he runs afoul of the vicious Mink Snopes, with whom he has an altercation over the wintering of a stray heifer. Mink tries to pull a fast one on Houston, but when he's challenged and defeated by his neighbor, Mink decides to cure his insult by ambushing Houston and blasting him out of his saddle. The thick mood of economic resentment comes through Ab's next thought about the corpse: "What he would have liked to do would be to leave a printed placard on the breast itself: *This is what happens to the men who impound Mink Snopes' cattle,* with his named signed to it" (p. 242). We have seen the same rage course through Ab as he takes on his landlords. *The Hamlet* teems with the mix of implacable anger and hangdog despair that can pin down the poor.

In this first Snopes novel, however, all the dramatic energy accrues to future ambitions rather than past slights. Mink is left waiting and waiting for Flem's expected assistance in getting the charges of murder dismissed; but his influential nephew never attempts to intervene, having already calculated there's no benefit in associating himself with a criminal like Mink when Flem aspires to move on to a life of affluent respectability in town. Later in the trilogy Mink gets revenge on Flem, after waiting out a forty-year prison term. But the whole force of the novel suggests how the Snopes phenomenon directs our attention toward the future, swinging Yoknapatawpha from preoccupations with planter decline and poor white resentment. *The Hamlet* concludes with Flem's sweet taste of triumph. The focus of attention shifts back to Flem's ongoing contest with Ratliff, this last round going to the challenger. Flem deceives Ratliff with an effective but surprisingly obvious trick; he pretends to search clandestinely for Civil War-era treasure long rumored to be buried on the grounds of the Old Frenchman's Place. Making sure that Ratliff and his partners notice what he's doing, Flem then arranges to sell the place for an exorbitant sum to the three money-mad speculators. Ratliff is the first to notice, after several digging sessions of meager success, that even the coins they've unearthed are part of Flem's trick: they've got recent mint dates and have been planted by Flem to heighten the realism. Naturally, this defeat unsettles the previously invincible Ratliff, and we begin to appreciate that Flem's talents may take him as far as he wants to go. What that will be remains uncertain at this point, but the tilt of unfettered ambition seems captured in the very last words of the novel, directed by Flem at his mules when he heads off, newly bankrolled, to try his luck in Jefferson: "Come up" (p. 406).

Flem may be riding high when he leaves Frenchman's Bend, but he suffers a comeuppance in the first scheme he attempts when he reaches town. Faulkner relates this installment of Flem's saga in a short story entitled "Centaur in Brass," published in 1932, nearly a decade before *The Hamlet* appeared in 1940, and over twenty years before he resumed the trilogy in *The Town*. Faulkner must have envisioned the full trajectory of Flem's career by the mid-1920s, when he conceived the Snopeses in the embryonic *Father Abraham* manuscript. "Centaur in Brass" begins with a rehearsal of Flem's doings in the hamlet, complete with the details of the spotted horses auction and the trickery over the Old Frenchman's Place that Faulkner had sketched out in *Father Abraham*. The short story permits an instructive glimpse into Faulkner's workshop. Faulkner's depiction of Flem in "Centaur" still seems preliminary; this Flem shows little of the cold genius that inspires dread as *The Hamlet*'s Faust-in-a-machine-made-bowtie. In "Centaur," Flem is banal without being evil.

What may strike readers of *The Hamlet* is how clumsily the Flem of "Centaur" goes after what he wants. In the novel, Flem's menace accrues from his mystery; he's sly and slippery, hidden behind the scenes, his motivations a puzzle. Although Ratliff first speculates that Flem's lust must involve a kind of eroto-mercantilism – recall the scene he imagines of a behind-the-counter sexual transaction between the new clerk and a black female customer – both Ratliff and the reader come to realize that this apparently glandless droid seems to have no human appetites at all, even the love of money. In "Centaur in Brass," Flem's behavior is attributed flatly and simply to "greed," the narrator inferring that Flem must be after a buck for the same reason anyone else would be: for the pleasure it can buy. In Greek mythology a centaur was a fabulous creature, half man, half horse, associated with Dionysian sexual indulgence and drunkenness. However, in the voice of the anonymous town narrator, Faulkner struggles to grasp the enormity of the different kind of creature Flem seems to be, one who displays no passions, who operates like a bland automaton of opportunism. If you could imagine Flem getting off on *something*, being a centaur of any kind of revelry, you'd at least have a comprehensible adversary. "Centaur in Brass" begins to wonder, as the rest of the trilogy will continue to ponder, just how far the pointless pursuit of money can carry a person.

The narrator is perplexed that his new townsman remains so bizarrely business-like in the face of events that would stir up any normal person. Snopes begins brazenly enough; having learned Eula's economic value through the marital transactions he conducts with his father-in-law, Will Varner, Flem proceeds to dangle his voluptuous wife before the appreciative eyes of Jefferson's mayor. Hoxey quickly takes up the offer, beginning an affair with Eula in exchange for appointing Flem superintendent of the town power station. (The story's total obliviousness to Eula's response at being passed around like this erupts in *The Town*, when the poignant anguish of her frustration and despair leads to an awful end.) The narrator puzzles over the friendly terms maintained by the adulterer and the distinctly unaggrieved spouse: such "amiable cuckoldry . . . seemed foreign, decadent, perverted: we could have accepted, if not condoned, the adultery had they only been natural and logical and enemies" (*Collected Stories*, p. 151). What the narrator fails to see, and what Faulkner is beginning to grasp for the purposes of his trilogy of capitalism, is that money trumps honor, money trumps sex, money just trumps.

In fact, the cause of Flem's downfall in "Centaur" is that it never occurs to him that someone might actually prefer a tumble in the hay to making hay. Flem's grand scheme involves an act of naked theft; he notices that the brass fittings on the plant's boiler system might yield him a side profit if they could be stripped and replaced with cheaper material. Acting in his new role as industrial manager, Flem tries to pull off the pilferage by playing his two African American subordinates against each other. He gets Tom-Tom to hide the purloined scrap metal at his cabin, then, when auditors discover the brass is missing, Flem calmly indemnifies the town in cash, without explanation. Figuring he's now free to sell the goods at a higher price, he dispatches the second worker, Turl, to retrieve the brass, motivating the junior worker with a promise of the preferred day shift. Flem's design fails to anticipate the power of sexual distraction, however; Tom-Tom's young wife is a temptation too good for the legendary tom-cat Turl to pass up, and it takes him two weeks not to find the brass he's not looking for. What he eventually does find is one irate husband, though, who has gotten wind of his betrayal and who hides in his bed to surprise the amorous Turl one night. Next you'd expect a swirl of knives and the crack of bones, but in fact the confrontation ends up in another vignette of "amiable cuckoldry," this one leading the two victims of Flem's shenanigans to turn the tables on him. Tom-Tom and Turl haul the pirated brass to the water tower, into which they dump it in mock fulfillment of an earlier ruse Flem invents to hide what he's stealing.

"Centaur in Brass" leaves the impression that incipient Snopesism might be contained, if not exactly stopped cold. The town is treated to the spectacle of a hillbilly over-reacher getting trashed by two clever negroes – the stance of the story set by Harker, the plant engineer, who laughs condescendingly at the doings of such lesser folk, much the way Faulkner and Phil Stone hooted over the Snopes menagerie early on. Even though he's put together a string of wins in the minor leagues, Flem gets whupped in his first start in Jefferson. The town officials decline his anonymous offer to buy the brass-filled tower outright, and Flem is left to contemplate a private monument to a costly miscalculation for as long as he lives in Jefferson. On the other hand, Flem's balked opening gambit, his first sally into the town's money-making mentality, and an act that posits the noxious continuity between outright theft and capitalist speculation, just ends up goading this epitome of American winner-take-all-ism. Flem slowly devours the town anyhow, ending up president of the bank, his feet propped on the mantel of his remodeled Georgian mansion, no one, least of all himself, any closer to figuring out why someone would sell his soul for something that means nothing.

The rise of a few fiercely determined poor white farmers who realized they'd reached a dead end on the land – epitomized by Flem
Snopes, but also represented by Labove in *The Hamlet* – rearranged the
social topography of the Deep South. As we have seen, a new bourgeoisie began to emerge, many of them drawn from the countryside
to small towns, where they elbowed aside sinking remnants of the
plantation gentry. Many who succeeded in these new pursuits left
farming in the later decades of the nineteenth century, as Reconstruction policies redistributed land to freed slaves, and former sources of
capitalization dried up. With the decline in small family-owned subsistence farms, tenancy became the bitter fate of many who refused to
leave the land. Flem arrives at the decision that there's no longer any
"benefit" to farming sometime in the 1890s, when opportunities to get
in on the ground floor of new commercial ventures began to multiply.
A few decades later, Southern agriculture had plunged to its nadir;
farmers still trying to wring a living out of cotton, the price of which
had risen during World War I shortages, now confronted a full-scale
economic depression, years before the collapse hit the rest of the
country in 1929. Like many writers of the 1930s, Faulkner produces
a sympathetic portrait of the South's white tenant farmers, who come
to be the very face of Depression-era poverty for the rest of the
nation.

All but en-coffined in a dead way of life, the Bundren family of
Faulkner's novel *As I Lay Dying* (1930) struggle to understand the fatal
blow they've been struck. If the Snopeses jump on modernity's band-
wagon early, the Bundrens remain stuck decades later on a mule-
bound hearse. Under the pretext of honoring their dead mother's last
wish, the rest of the Bundrens haul her body from their remote farm
toward Jefferson, where her people bury, but also where tantalizing
novelties await them. This is a long-delayed and only fleeting visit to
town, but it suggests all they're missing out on back home. Even the
youngest Bundren, eight-year-old Vardaman, has metropolitan dreams;
his is a toy train he once saw displayed in a store window on an earlier
expedition. When a neighbor helps the child and his family cross a
flooded river on this journey, Tull gets an odd sensation gazing across
the divide at the farm behind him: "When I looked back at my mule
it was like he was one of these here spy-glasses and I could look at
him standing there and see all the broad land and my house sweated
outen it like it was the more the sweat, the broader the land" (*As I Lay*

Dying, p. 139). Tull registers the fatigue and futility of a dying breed; he's sweated too much, too long, for too little. Vardaman, on the other hand, beckons as an emissary of future possibilities, "[l]ike he was saying about a fine place he knowed where Christmas come twice with Thanksgiving and lasts on through the winter and the spring and the summer, and if I just stayed with him I'd be all right too" (*idem*). Might there be a consumer utopia where laborers are freed from the bonds of seasonal fortune and the grind of production?

If there is, it's going to come too late for the adults of *As I Lay Dying*. The novel is a study in belatedness, the majority of its characters dead or mad or doomed without knowing it yet. From the title forward you get the sense that this is a book of talking corpses. The phrase "as I lay dying" comes from a line in the *Odyssey* in which the murdered Greek hero Agamemnon complains about the indignity of not having had his eyes closed for him in death. Here is the Bundrens' father, Anse, reacting to his wife's death: "He looks like right after the maul hits the steer and it no longer alive and don't yet know that it is dead" (p. 61). Anse never expects Addie to quit on him, so his state of mind certainly registers some kind of personal loss, but her disappearance also makes palpable that other profound loss farmers like him can hardly believe: the flickering out of their land and livelihood: "His eyes look like pieces of burnt-out cinder fixed in his face, looking out over the land" (p. 32). For farmers like Anse, Tull, and the others who populate this central Mississippi hill country, a crisis threatens to destroy their world in an apocalypse equivalent to fire and flood, make the land all but unrecognizable ("the road too had been soaked free of earth and floated upward, to leave in its spectral tracing a monument to a still more profound desolation" [p. 143]), and strand them from a future they may not be able to bridge. Surveying the rising tide, one Bundren concludes: "It is as though the space between us were time: an irrevocable quality. It is as though time, no longer running straight before us in a diminishing line, now runs parallel between us like a looping string, the distance being the doubling accretion of the thread and not the interval between" (p. 146).

Unlike the small-time farmers of *The Hamlet*, such as Mink and Ab Snopes, who have been reduced to tenancy, or Jack Houston, who has fallen into irreversible mortgage debt to Varner, the Bundrens, Tulls, and their neighbors have managed to hang on to their land, perhaps because their hill country plots are among the region's least valuable and because they have figured out how to make a little money apart from farming. The bottoming out of US cotton prices in the early 1920s after the Great War proved catastrophic for the many Southern farmers who had put every available acre of land into cotton production when prices had skyrocketed a few years earlier. The sorrow of grieving farmers may be heard as a constant undertone in *As I Lay Dying*. It speaks of nature's whimsy, but acknowledges a governing historical logic:

> Well, I be durn if I like to see my work washed outen the ground, work I sweat over. It's a fact. A fellow wouldn't mind seeing it washed up if he could just turn on the rain himself. (pp. 90–91)

> It's a hard country on man; it's hard. Eight miles of the sweat of his body washed up outen the Lord's earth, where the Lord Himself told him to put it. (p. 110)

> Darl . . . sits at the supper table with his eyes gone further than the food and the lamp, full of the land dug out of his skull and the holes filled with distance beyond the land. (p. 27)

The Bundren family's difficulty negotiating a terrain made unfamiliar by forces of nature provides a metaphor for their historical circumstances. Caught in the current of the swollen stream, they struggle to maintain "slipping contact" with the ground beneath: "What had once been a flat surface was now a succession of troughs and hillocks lifting and falling about us, shoving at us, teasing us with light lazy touches in the vain instants of solidity underfoot" (p. 148). The water mimics the very earth it savages ("hillocks"), taunting and mocking its land-loving victims.

In their desperate efforts to save a doomed way of life, farmers were often driven to self-destructive remedies. We learn that Vernon Tull has sold much of the timber on his non-arable land in order to pay off a mortgage. His friends find this admirable in their exceptionally industrious neighbor, but they also joke ruefully about the general futility of their lot: "Most folks that logs in this here country, they need a durn good farm to support the sawmill. Or maybe a store" (p. 143). It's as if the whole natural order of things has gotten reversed, with farming a mere support for commercial activities. And it's all the more ironic that logging should subsidize farmers, since it actually contributes to the "natural" disasters that befall them, with logging companies stripping bare the countryside and leaving it open to flash floods. Although Anse and his comrades suffer what they consider an act of God, they also sense the connection between taking out the trees and the land's "profound desolation" as it stands covered in flood water. Anse goes further in his analysis of the farmers' plight, grasping that the problem is fundamentally economic:

> Nowhere in this sinful world can a honest, hardworking man profit. It takes them that runs the stores in the towns, doing no sweating, living off of them that sweats. It aint the hardworking man, the farmer. Sometimes I wonder why we keep at it. It's because there is a reward for us above, where they cant take their autos and such. Every man will be equal there and it will be taken from them that have and give to them that have not by the Lord. (p. 110)

Anse vents working-class resentment here, though he's a little myopic in identifying the adversary. It's not simply Jefferson bankers and merchants who exploit farmers like him, it's a national economic system that historically positioned Southern agriculture as a colonized source of raw material for the Northern metropolises of global industrial and commercial empire.

As I Lay Dying is Faulkner's most probing exploration of the effects of modernization on the rural poor. The engulfing currents of change he identifies prove hallmarks of modernity. Arjun Appadurai in *Modernity at Large*, a study of global modernization, argues that world populations in underdeveloped countries experienced modernity most forcefully as a new capacity to relocate globally, spurred by new connections to mainstream hegemonic culture via electronic media.[5] This intersection of migration and mass communication may be seen as principal components of the forces disarranging (and deranging) the Bundren family. The death of the farm wife precipitates a move to town – even a visit like theirs anticipates the flow of urbanization in the modern South. Town represents new opportunities for consumption: the toy train Vardaman wants, but also the false teeth Anse covets, the abortion medication Dewey Dell has been sent for, the graphophone Cash longs for, even the imported bananas that substitute for less attainable goods. Some of these products are first known to the Bundrens by virtue of the mail order catalogues that find their way down recently constructed paved roads. The Bundrens have been contacted by the modern world, not the least traumatic consequence of which has been Darl's drafting into the army to join the troops fighting in France.

These subsistence farmers find themselves stumbling into a new era of cash and commodity. Cora's comic misadventures on the cake and egg market introduce the desperate farmer's naïve schemes for making money: we also have the aptly-named Cash falling off a roof during one of his turns as a wage laborer; Jewel working night and day to buy a luxury vehicle (one of the infamous Snopes spotted horses); Anse taking a gamble that Addie will last long enough for his boys to make one more wagon run because they so need the $3 it will bring; the family holding back on summoning Dr. Peabody because Anse doesn't want to spend the $10 until he absolutely must; the fumbling efforts of Dewey Dell to negotiate an impersonal retail transaction of the most personal and embarrassing kind – and one that eventuates in her commodifying her sexuality as the only currency left her; even Anse counting on the retention of old ways of hospitality and lending to counteract the modern town habits of constant purchase and sale. Cash stages his own resistance to commodification by lavishing his labor freely and limitlessly on the crafting of his mother's coffin. It's precisely because no one will see or care about the quality of the workmanship that Cash is so determined to do it right, to work like a jeweler on the golden boards. To make a beautiful object intended never to pass into economic circulation constitutes the idealism of Cash's artistry, and it makes a stand against the capitalization of all labor. Anse's unfeeling robbery of his own children suggests the deepening monetization of personal relations, even if it also hints that the nuclear family has always been a social form primarily keyed to particular economic requirements, in this case the reproduction of a large force of "free" in-house domestic and agricultural labor. Still, whatever the economic origins of the farm family, its massive disruption and sensed disintegration are suffered by its members as a traumatic shock, a shattering of maternal nurture, sense of self, and intimacy.

The Bundrens and their neighbors have been islanded in a "primitive" rural sub-culture; now they're being pressured to change, and the novel understands how they must strike more "advanced" moderns as only half-evolved grotesques. Once the family gets to more civilized environs, they're made to look like aliens: a witness in one town reports, "They came from some place out in Yoknapatawpha county, trying to get to Jefferson with [that corpse]. It must have been like a piece of rotten cheese coming into an ant-hill, in that ramshackle wagon that Albert said folks were scared would fall all to pieces before they could get it out of town, with that home-made box and another fellow with a broken leg lying on a quilt on top of it" (p. 204). A broken leg they want to cast in *concrete*, let's not forget. The strangeness of town ways and the sense of metropolitan superiority are not lost on these self-conscious rustics. As the cavalcade enters Jefferson, Jewel (mistakenly) thinks he's been insulted by a townsman; Jewel fumes, "Thinks because he's a goddamn town fellow . . . Son of a bitch" (p. 230).

What makes *As I Lay Dying* so richly unsettling a novel is that Faulkner expertly fathoms the contradictory desires and emotions provoked by modernization. On the one hand, precious things will be lost. Dewey Dell's touching private moment with her mother's dead body captures the genuine, if largely inarticulate, grief that the whole family, whole community, suffers in this epitome of a disappearing way of life. The farmers' lamentation over the land is answered by the women friends who sing hymns at Addie's funeral: "In the thick air it's like their voices come out of the air, flowing together and on in the sad, comforting tunes. When they cease it's like they hadn't gone away" (p. 92). Addie's long dying reminds Dr. Peabody of a regional fate: "That's the one trouble with this country: everything, weather, all, hangs on too long. Like our rivers, our land: opaque, slow, violent; shaping and creating the life of man in its impalpable and brooding image" (p. 45). His remark isn't about the turning of an era here, but Peabody is mindful of how conditions are changing, elsewhere mentioning the "worry about this country being deforested someday" (p. 42).

As it has under different circumstances for Quentin Compson, the transformations of modernity produce severe trauma for the rural poor as well. Darl, for example, as the one Bundren who has had the most experience with the modern age, ultimately suffers a mental breakdown. Darl has fought in the war, and his psychological torment may perhaps have some connection to the sort of trauma modern psychiatry began to diagnose as shell-shock in veterans of combat. Like

Virginia Woolf's Septimus Smith in *Mrs Dalloway*, Darl is afflicted by some sort of self-alienation. He gets inside other folks' heads but hardly seems to have a home mentality of his own. He claims he doesn't have a mother. Like Quentin, he possesses an ego riddled with existential doubt:

> Beyond the unlamped wall I can hear the rain shaping the wagon that is ours, the load that is no longer theirs that felled and sawed it nor yet theirs that bought it and which is not ours either, like on our wagon though it does, since only the wind and the rain shape it only to Jewel and me, that are not asleep. And since sleep is is-not and rain and wind are *was*, it is not. Yet the wagon *is*, because when the wagon is *was*, Addie Bundren will not be. And Jewel *is*, so Addie Bundren must be. And then I must be, or I could not empty myself for sleep in a strange room. And so if I am not emptied yet, I am *is*. (p. 80)

Darl already manifests here schizophrenic tendencies that will surface more pronouncedly later, when his family arranges his incarceration and he begins to speak of himself in the third person. (Only US super-star athletes may do this without being considered psychotic.) Darl loses his purchase on the life he has known, his mother's death somehow letting the linchpin of identity slip out. The family's centrifu-gal whirl out toward cash mania and consumer-drives seems to under-lie Darl's addling. Notice how it is the peculiar suspended non-existence of the load of lumber – in transit among owners and conveyers on the market – that precipitates Darl's confusion. It's as if notions of the Cartesian self as the property of consciousness, based on the simple idea of things being used and owned by those who make them, have been unmoored by the fetishistic mysteries of commodity exchange.

It's not surprising, then, that the simplest Bundren, the child Varda-man, instinctively finds consolation in an act of primitive fetishism. Catching his first fish the same day his mother dies prompts Vardaman to associate the two events magically. The bleeding fish becomes a totem of his mother, her vanished body commemorated in the flesh of the fish "cooked and et," like some homemade Eucharistic rite, her coffin an object that does briefly turn into a fish that has to be retrieved, Osiris-like, from the waters of the flood. Anse complains that all his troubles began when roads invaded the countryside, making bodies lurch into unnatural motion. Cora Tull edges into new marketing ventures with her cake business, but has so completely been befuddled by commodity logic that she fails to assign any monetary value to her own labor, accepting the mysterious abstraction of price as the only index of expense. Much like the Compsons, then, the characters of *As I Lay Dying* sustain reverses that cry for consolation and recompense. Both novels figure social setbacks in the loss of a matrix figure, and both suggest fetishistic reflexes of denial. In *As I Lay Dying*, though, Faulkner can see more clearly how the loss of a way of life cherished by one group actually provides desperately sought opportunities for others. Faulkner captures the grotesque ambivalence provoked by modernity: a sense at once of mourning and adventure; of orphanhood and independence; of self-commodification and consumer empowerment.

Not everyone in *As I Lay Dying* thinks the past is worth immortalizing. Some who have enabled Southern fantasies of organic, well-ordered families and communities – many of them women – prove to be seething with rage and resentment at the sacrifices demanded of them. *As I Lay Dying* has appealed powerfully to at least two well-defined global audiences: those who read in it a sharply felt, sympathetic effort to render laboring class poverty under broadly colonial circumstances; and those who hear in it a male artist's eloquent determination to give voice to the "hard lives" of women.[6] Faulkner figures out the connection between the abuse of women and the abuse of agricultural laborers under global capitalism. The shock of *As I Lay Dying* lies in the sound of a dead woman talking. Addie's section opens a space for her utterance as *The Sound and the Fury* does not for Caddy. Addie's complaint speaks for all those whose lives have been ruined by the lordship of others: "I could just remember how my father used to say that the reason for living was to get ready to stay dead a long time" (p. 169). For Faulkner's women, especially, but also for "weak" sons like Quentin, *father says* is the kiss of death. In *Absalom, Absalom!* Rosa Coldfield is another father-haunted ghost. Addie's fury at all the men in her life originates in their repeated efforts to use her for their own purposes. Anse professes love, but turns out to practice it as a hard reproductive regimen. When Addie tries to call a halt to her relentless self-division child by child ("I was three now," she thinks when she learns she's pregnant with her second), Anse crudely corrects her: "you an me aint nigh done chapping yet, with just two"

(p. 173). What Addie wants is to recover a sense of her own self; in her affair with Rev. Whitfield she exults in the prospect that "I would be I" while her husband has been "negatived" as "not-Anse," made "dead" by her betrayal (pp. 174, 173).

Addie understands that a discourse of masculine power long precedes her arrival, and is responsible for insisting that she yield to its authority. When she tries to recall the "shape of my body where I used to be a virgin," all that occurs to her is that it "is in the shape of a   and I couldn't think *Anse*, couldn't remember *Anse*" (p. 173). That Addie's most intimate space should in effect be colonized by male command evokes again the connection between female bodies and the land. Addie underscores the syndrome by naming her child "Dewey Dell," and it's worth remembering that the word "colony" and its derivatives all come from a Latin word for "farmer," "colon." Faulkner senses the deep identity between masculine conquests of foreign spaces and domestic places, the prerogatives that seize lands as well as women's bodies as territorial possessions. If Addie at least turns her dying into a form of belated revenge, she's perpetrating a kind of silent anti-colonial terrorism, striking at the will of Oedipal power. Deleuze and Guattari observe that the anti-colonialist should be anti-Oedipalism's best friend.[7] As many subsequent subaltern and so-called Third World readers were to sense in its pages, *As I Lay Dying* illuminates the alignment of Western colonialisms: domestic, of the female body; regional, of the rural South; global, of the world-producing classes. In the disruptions caused by modern transformations, protests against colonial domination erupt, and confusing but instructive contradictions become visible, such as the double position of men like Bundren who are exploited by town merchants while treating their wives like mules.

Dewey Dell attempts the next stage of female defiance of Oedipal law by seeking to terminate her pregnancy. Although she is blocked by men like Moseley, who advises her to entrust her problem to "your pa or your brothers if you have any or the first man you come to in the road" (p. 202), Dewey Dell goes as far as she dares, even trading her body for pills she knows won't really emancipate her. Still, her determination outlines a course of action for women unwilling to reproduce their subordination without at least protest. Likewise, Jewel rebels against Anse's authority, indemnifying himself for his illegitimate status under a law of paternal exclusion by buying a horse to substitute for the licit affection he is denied. Even Cash chafes at Anse's meddling, but this quiet son's need for "balance" helps him adjust to the re-engineering of life under modernity and the renovation of Oedipal order: "meet Mrs Bundren." Seduced by what he hears as the entirely life-like reproduction of music by the phonograph, Cash accepts the costs of updating. He accommodates himself to Darl's committal, and gets rewarded when Anse's new wife brings as part of her dowry exactly the sort of graphophone Cash has coveted before his father robs him to buy new teeth.

Faulkner imagines the numerous individual styles by which people engage the conflicting components of an event as complex as modernization. Faulkner's earlier experimentation with perspectival narrative and first-person discourse in *The Sound and the Fury* gives him a flexible instrument for rendering diverse, often ambivalent states of mind. In one respect, Faulkner achieves an unprecedented range of identification with quite different personalities and temperaments. He partners his language with the sensibilities of an inarticulate hill farmer, a depressed wife, a cheerful Protestant saint, an illiterate eight-year-old, an overwhelmed pregnant teenager, a furious bastard son, a clairvoyant schizophrenic, and so on. Each narrative creates the impression of a distinct human voice belonging to a real person, who otherwise might mean nothing to cultivated readers beyond an abstract illustration of rural poverty. On the other hand, each section also sounds like Faulkner's own voice, a highly stylized, emphatically literary rendering of sensibilities too culturally impoverished to command such aesthetic resources. So Dewey Dell compares the big-bellied Dr. Peabody to her own heaviness: "He is his guts and I am my guts. And I am Lafe's guts. That's it" (p. 60). But also, she thinks, "The cow breathes upon my hips and back, her breath warm, sweet, stertorous, moaning. The sky lies flat down the slope, upon the secret clumps" (p. 63). In one sense, Faulkner indemnifies these subaltern subjects by giving them access to the richest language he possesses. On the other, he veers toward speaking *for* them, putting him in the position cautioned against by Gayatri Spivak, who points out the inauthenticity, however well-motivated, of representing those whom colonialism has "silenced" and whose vernacular identities and languages it has refused to recognize.[8] Here we may admire Faulkner for staging such complexities so uncompromisingly.

In much the same way, we might see the perspectival narrative structure as both replicating and trying to overcome the centrifugal tendencies of family and even individual self. The Bundrens are rapidly degenerating into a clump of isolated wage-earning consumers, each pursuing his or her own interests, co-operating only as far as their selfish objectives may be advanced. On the other hand, Faulkner takes these modern monadic selves and manages to incorporate them around their central lack, putting them into communication with each other and folding them into a single narrative they execute as a united entity. The novel imagines a much more sustained merging of individuals than, for example, the fleeting moments Virginia Woolf salvages from the flux in *To the Lighthouse*. It is this kind of endurance despite itself that distinguishes the Bundrens as a kind of heroic family, or at least one capable of pulling off a comedic (in Dante's sense of redemptive, as well as comic) denouement. As the Bundrens gamely recover their balance at the end of *As I Lay Dying*, we come to realize that the characters who survive have always been all about gratifying desire rather than mourning loss, about the future, however belatedly arrived at, than the past. Even Addie understands this, making the burial of her corpse the matter of a protracted journey down the road ahead. Once we get to town, the novel shows its hand; we never get to the presumptive climax of an actual burial scene, but instead witness a frenzy of acquisition, the most notable success Anse's unexplained procurement of a [new] Mrs. Bundren to replace the one he wore out. Like many other members of the modern work force in the second and third decades of the twentieth century, Southern farmers were being converted from producers into wage laborers, their salaries expected to fuel an emergent consumer culture. The personal disorientation and social disintegration sustained by newly mobile, mass media-shaped, nationally conscious populations were balanced by a new sense of enfranchisement ("I reckon we can stop to buy something same as airy other man," Anse declares [p. 204],), as well as new sources of consolation ("But now I can get them teeth. That will be a comfort. It will" [p. 111]). The novel shrewdly observes how modernity fills the very holes it has itself dug.

Dying prospects throughout the South in the decades following Reconstruction put many country folks on the road to town, where swelling mercantile and service economies offered them new opportunities. By the 1880s, as we have seen, ambitious farm boys like Flem Snopes had begun filing in from the countryside. A generation later, by the 1920s, social tectonics in small towns had shifted; besides sealing the doom of many of the plantation South's dynastic families, like the Compsons, the influx of newcomers had upset the social positions and sleepy routines of established professional and working-class families. Merchants and craftsmen found themselves competing with strangers from unfamiliar places – whether remote Mississippi hill farms or the even less imaginable origins of Northern laborers and foreign immigrants. In increasing numbers, African Americans began leaving the "closed" South altogether; they streamed out of the Deep South during the second and third decades of the twentieth century as war labor shortages in the industrial North drew them to better jobs and let them escape the violent racism of Southern segregation. Some blacks who stayed took advantage of the demand for reliable tenant farmers and steady wage laborers (think of Tom-Tom and Turl in "Centaur in Brass"), managing a fragile grasp on the bottom rung of the working class. Shamefully, even such meager successes too often provoked the resentment of threatened poor whites, who hated "good negroes" as competitors to be kept down in their places, and resorted to racial intimidation – most viciously the lynchings that cost hundreds of African Americans their lives.

Southern legislation establishing public segregation was touted by whites as a *modern* innovation for managing the threat of racial intermixing associated with the wider circulation of people throughout the South, and the gathering migration to towns. Beginning in the 1890s, the passage of so-called Jim Crow laws enabled states to separate the use of public facilities on the basis of race. The test case that eventually affirmed the lawfulness of segregation involved, significantly, an issue of public transportation; when Homer Plessy, a light-skinned black man from Louisiana, took a seat in a train car restricted to whites only, he identified himself as a negro and was promptly arrested. His challenge, arranged and backed by civil rights activists, ended up inducing the Supreme Court to uphold separate-but-equal racial accommodation. (Needless to say, there was little commitment to the "equal" part of the equation anywhere such rules of apartheid were applied.) Restraint on African American freedom to travel may serve as a larger emblem of the white South's determination to hold blacks in place –

socially, as well as economically, since they provided an indispensable source of cheap labor, and would do so into the 1940s. Many Southern communities passed so-called vagrancy laws that allowed the arrest of individuals deemed to lack permanent homes or jobs. Such bogus laws sent many blacks to prison, from which they could be leased out as convict labor gangs to private contractors. The thrust of Southern apartheid was to prevent blacks from moving – either up or away.

Faulkner pictures the violent clashes that result from the increasing mobility of populations in the modern South. In the extreme symbolic landscape of Yoknapatawpha, social motion may be turbulent: individuals and whole families decline, some vanishing; others seem to materialize out of thin air, a few rocketing to success; blacks improve their positions, suffer extermination, or disappear into the North; white women leap off their pedestals or slip their harnesses and head for the open road. Such volatility often called up reflexes of vicious self-defense that worried Faulkner as he chronicled the South's troubled metamorphoses. In one of his most powerful short stories, "Dry September" (1931), Faulkner probes the fantasies that mediate the modern flux of racial status, sexual mores, and class relations. The story centers on the lynching of a negro named Will Mayes, who is executed vigilante-style when a white woman insinuates that he has committed some indecency toward her – whether a gesture, a word, an actual sexual assault, or nothing at all is never determined.[9] Faulkner presents the story as a study of racial and sexual delusions in intricate counterpoint, while exposing both as expressions of anxiety about social standing.

Minnie Cooper's explosive accusation of sexual attention from a black man originates in her own sense of declining erotic, and underlying economic, value. Unmarried and approaching the age of forty when she makes her charge, Minnie has suffered a slow descent into disreputability. She comes from "comfortable people – not the best in Jefferson, but good people enough" (*Collected Stories*, pp. 174–175), and she parlays this decent start into early ascendancy, drawing on a "hard vivacity" "for a time to ride upon the crest of the town's social life" (p. 174). Eventually, though, minute gaps in status begin to matter; Minnie finds herself the object of "snobbery," and soon fades from the "shadowy porticoes and summer lawns" of her betters. Thrown off the path to marriage and family among the upper-middle-class set she'd projected herself into, Minnie makes a late bid to avoid spinsterhood by taking up with a bank cashier. But he won't marry her, so she gets "relegated into adultery by public opinion" (p. 175), and when the clerk takes a promotion in Memphis, Minnie further descends into furtive alcoholism, relieved only by a complementary addiction to the movies.

Minnie triggers a tried-and-true imaginative mechanism when she cries rape. The modern South predicated racial segregation on the fear that emancipated black men posed a sexual threat to white women, and that new regulations had to replace the protections of slave codes. In part, such fantasies of black sexual predation reflected white anxieties about black revenge for planters' abuse of slave women. As well, the need to protect women from imagined sexual danger may also have expressed men's fears about no longer being able to provide for their families under the economic hardships of the post-Civil War era – which struggling white men sensed as failures of potency and entitlement. Moreover, as some white women asserted greater control over their own sexual and economic lives during this period of social reordering, men sought to re-imagine that they were still needed to protect the women they wanted to depend upon them. Lastly, the defense of female chastity hypothesized a commodity whose value had much declined, if not disappeared altogether. Think of Caddy, whose virginity no longer commands patrimonial value among her defunct class.

In suggesting that she has been defiled by a negro, Minnie perversely gets some of her sexual cachet restored. She has fallen into erotic irrelevance – "men did not even follow her with their eyes any more" (p. 175) – but when Minnie presents herself as a violated object, those same men "followed with their eyes the motion of her hips and legs when she passed" (p. 181). In effect, Minnie's ruined racial chastity erases her earlier adultery, and she flushes with recovered sexual "fever" herself, dressing for display in the "sheerest underthings and stockings and a new voile dress" (p. 181). Minnie's accusation taps in to racialized sex fantasies, while she is further eroticized by casting herself as a helpless white woman in need of vigorous male defense. Faulkner's brilliant treatment captures how the whole disgusting scenario leading to the execution of an innocent man springs out of projections of "furious unreality" (p. 175), many of them deliberately enflamed by the mass culture industry.

The movies supply vicarious gratification for Minnie and her set of similarly frustrated middle-aged women. To recuperate after her shock,

Minnie's friends take her to the theater, where they lose themselves in "beautiful and passionate and sad" "silver dreams" (p. 181), while actual young lovers slip into seats around them. The women grasp the continuity between screen image and imaginary reality, coaxing Minnie to tell "everything" "he said and did" to her, thrilling with prurient curiosity: " 'Do you suppose anything really happened?' their eyes darkly aglitter, secret, and passionate. 'Shhhhhhhhhh! Poor girl! Poor Minnie!' " (p. 182). The connection of racial and sexual fantasy to the movies is more than just an analogy; films about the South were hugely popular in the 1920s, with the infamous *The Birth of a Nation* (1915) establishing the appeal of racial/sexual sensationalism. (Derived from the notoriously racist novel *The Clansman*, written by Thomas Dixon, Jr. in 1905, and the live touring theatricals based on it, D. W. Griffith's film delivered electrifying images of black sexual menace, white female victimization, and rejuvenated white male solidarity.) In the lethal mixing of social anxieties and cinematic projections of racial and sexual redress, Faulkner identifies a fresh reinforcement for the hallucinatory nature of Southern phobias, imaginary transgressions, and spectacles of restored order.

To hear everything that happened, but to doubt anything did: that's the space in which self-protecting fantasy turns unforgivably murderous. The only white person of conscience in the story, a barber named Hawkshaw, tries to talk sense into the lynch gang by pointing out that Minnie has circulated similar unfounded insinuations in the past. But stuffed with their own figments of racial revenge and male assertion, Will's executioners obey complementary fantasies. The townsman who heads up the lynching expedition is a combat veteran of World War I who returns to Jefferson aroused by the need to keep insurgent blacks in their places. His answer to the lack of evidence implicating Will perfectly captures the delusional quality of a racist mentality: "Are you going to let the black sons [of bitches] get away with it until one really does it?" (p. 172). Faulkner takes care to include the key historical ingredients contributing to the disastrous outcome: the lead vigilantes, for example, all betray insecure social positions. A second loudmouth is described as looking "like a desert rat in the moving pictures" (p. 170). Faulkner underscores the ragtag quality of the lynchers; the desert rat identifies himself as "only a drummer and a stranger," but one who's ready to fill the gap "if there aint any white men in this town" (*idem*).

Marginal whites typically tried to solidify their standing by identifying with the only trait they shared with their betters: race. We may notice that Will Mayes's execution emphasizes the need to immobilize "good nigger[s]" (p. 169). At the ice plant where he works as a night watchman, Will is handcuffed "as though he were a post," and eventually hurled down an abandoned brick kiln "without bottom" (p. 179). The lynchers want to make sure negroes like Mayes get pushed as far down as they can go. Of course, imputed racial insubordination reinforces other kinds of domination in the modern South. When the brutal "soldier" McLendon gets home to his "neat new house," freshly defended by his act of racial intimidation, he's enraged to find his wife waiting up for him, strictly against orders, reading a magazine. He grabs her hard enough to hurt, then "half struck, half flung her across the chair," in a spasm of violence addressed to that other population who refuse to stay in their places and obey a man's commands.

Faulkner suffuses his story with unbearable heat: Jefferson is an airless tinderbox of self-delusion and frustration. The inescapable staleness represents the airtight fantasies organizing the Deep South's closed society. Faulkner resolutely confronts the deceptions upon which the racial and sexual arguments of segregation rested. In his reading of Jim Crow, as for most historians now, frenzies over the sexual intermixture of the races served to screen, as ideology will, the economic realities upon which Southern society had long been based: the coercion of labor from Africans, first under slavery, then under a host of extractive legal measures. Obsessions like virginity, blood, color, miscegenation, and so on, mystified more basic realities. When the lynchers cram themselves into an automobile with Mayes, they recoil from "his sweaty reek" (p. 178). White Southerners habitually complained that negroes smelled bad; they tended to suppress the fact that the "reek" might have something to do with the manual work that makes one "sweaty." The deeper reasons for racial abuse do come clear in an uncanny moment toward the end of Faulkner's story. As Minnie breaks down into hysterical laughter, her worried friends try to cool her feverish skin: they press "cracked ice" to her temples, and "ministered to her with hushed ejaculations, renewing the ice and fanning her" (p. 182). The ice they use must come from the plant where Will Mayes was employed. It turns out that Minnie is touched intimately by a negro after all, but only via a commodity that has "forgotten" its origin in the labor of a dead black body. Such a relation goes unnoticed by its beneficiaries, but Faulkner conveys a whole history of suppressed relations between the races in the ironic ambiguity of the phrase "hushed ejaculations." The fetish of white female untouchability turns inside out the truth that unwanted liberties of all sorts were taken with black bodies in order to found and sustain a way of life.

When McClendon erupts with his irrational challenge not to let black men get away with rape until one actually happens, Faulkner underscores the way prejudice and stereotype can *produce* reality. If you believe that all negroes are "black beast rapists"[10] – the fantasy inspiring Jim Crow legislation – then you don't need to wait until one *does* something to act as if he already *has*. Stereotype insists that the behavior of others is wholly predictable because determined by nature. Stereotype is a way to impose order amid confusing times and shifting relations, to insist on absolute difference and hierarchy when reality suggests nothing of the sort. (Isn't it interesting that dominant groups view those they subordinate through stereotypes, but never think of themselves in such terms?) Stereotype disciplines feelings, as well, attempting to police subversive relations between individuals.

In the novel he wrote just after "Dry September," *Light in August* (1932), Faulkner treats the powerful forces of change rearranging the traditional South. The arc of Faulkner's concern with modernization carries into the turbulence caused by new phases of emancipation for black men and poor whites, especially women, in the South of the 1920s. Loosed from longstanding constraints, such individuals roamed more widely, congregated more freely, and endangered, too seriously to ignore, the social and cognitive structures organizing Southern life. In reaction, those who were threatened often resorted to the meanest of stereotypes to try to keep others in their places. *Light in August* is Faulkner's most socially panoramic and least resolved work of fiction. It describes the desperate heartbreak of those seeking only to lead lives unburdened by the massive communal delusions of the past. And it hints at routes of escape some may stumble upon as they flee an imploding society.

Light in August depicts a crisis of unhoming. Its principal characters leave homes, lose them, never have them, steal them, create makeshift ones – and, in a spectacular instance, burn one down. The novel's whole world whirls in perpetual motion, its unmoored occupants struggling to catch up to new lives they can imagine but can't quite take possession of. Faulkner lays out a sprawling double narrative to encompass two vast areas of social life undergoing change in the modern South: relations between sexes and relations between races.[11] As we have seen in "Dry September," their exploration is complicated by their entanglement – both historically and in the present, since the South will not move into the future without numerous backward glances. As he does in the short story, Faulkner oscillates between two major narratives – one primarily about a black man, the other about a poor white woman – to give a sense of their thematic and social interplay, as well as to suggest a virtual structure they might share. In *Light in August* Faulkner extends his consideration of how class frames race and gender, by thinking about what it means for new kinds of middle-class values to be gaining ground in a South long-dominated by ways of thought that had benefited plantation elites.

Faulkner recalled that when he began *Light in August*, he knew "no more about it than a young woman, pregnant, walking along a strange country road" (*The Sound and the Fury*, p. 226). Lena Grove on the loose: but to get there she's had to escape from a familiar kind of cage. As for so many of the women we've encountered in Faulkner's South, Lena feels trapped by the life the men in her world expect her to lead. Addie Bundren – nailed shut in a coffin, her life nothing but a slow dying – is the most graphic image of what the narrator in *Light in August* calls the "labor- and childridden wife" (p. 5). He's referring to Lena's sister-in-law, the wife of an older brother who takes Lena in when their parents die and leave her an orphan at twelve. Lena sees her fate in this over-borne woman; before long Lena appears to have reproduced it for herself. She gets pregnant by a happy-go-lucky local named Lucas Burch, who promptly disappears, but Lena soon declares her independence, climbs out her lean-to window under cover of night, and blithely heads off to rejoin Lucas, confident he must have had a good reason not to send for her sooner. The narrator points out that no one, least of all her brother, much cares that Lena is pregnant or even that she's left. Contrast the panic over Caddy's lost virginity and her daughter's later going fugitive. Families like Lena's have less reason to value chastity, since their interests are less served by the sexual and racial barriers that guard privileged status.

Lena hardly represents a modern emancipated woman, but her unconventional behavior does make people think of such novelties. One farmer, startled into helping this openly pregnant, obviously unwed "strange young gal walking the road" (p. 13), generalizes that when you

> just let one of them get married or get into trouble without being married . . . right then and there is where she secedes from the woman race and species and spends the balance of her life trying to get joined up with the man race. That's why they dip snuff and smoke and want to vote. (p. 15)

Armstid offers Lena shelter for the night; his wife offers her something more. Mrs. Armstid is one of those labor- and childridden wives, now furiously resentful at the hard life she's had to lead. She gets mad at Lena for not being married yet, and for scandalizing community standards by parading around so brazenly. But this desperate housewife also sympathizes deep down with a young woman who wants to find a husband-to-be even as she gets the chance to explore the open road. Mrs. Armstid takes her cache of saved-up egg money, shattering the china rooster bank she keeps it in, and insists that Lena accept it – in a gesture of unspoken female solidarity.

Lena is the first to outline a pattern common to female vagrancy throughout *Light in August*; acts of resistance begin by reproducing well-worn customs, but sometimes end up drastically altering or altogether discrediting them. In the case of Lena, though she starts out by affirming her confidence that God will see to the proper reunion of mother, father, and child when the time comes, the more Lena travels, the more open she grows to unanticipated possibilities. We'll consider how far she gets by the end of the story, but for the moment we can see Faulkner pointing to the contrary nature of her project. Overwhelmed with fatigue, she accepts a ride on Armstid's wagon, which she spies across the landscape long before it arrives. So slow it moves, she thinks, that it appears to "hang suspended in the middle distance forever and forever, so infinitesimal is its progress" (p. 8). There's something in that image of gradual progress that corresponds to Faulkner's preferred rate of social change – patient, steady, somehow in tune with natural rhythms, "peaceful." As Lena depends on one man after the next, her independence slowly awakens. It will take a while for Lena to appreciate how far she's come.

Plenty of other women try to negotiate lives ruled by masculine authority in Faulkner's portrait of 1920s small town life. The saddest tale may be that of a woman whose name we never even learn, the wife of Rev. Gail Hightower, Jefferson's Presbyterian minister. Never much interested in church teachings, Hightower has instead made a religion out of his forefathers' Confederacy. The cleric's worship of the South's so-called Lost Cause corresponds to historical realities; in the 1880s, after Reconstruction, some whites determined to rehabilitate the image of the secessionists. Protestant ministers and their war widow parishioners were especially caught up in such efforts, and Hightower illustrates the type: he daydreams obsessively about his grandfather's daring feats during the war, and spins sermons "full of galloping cavalry and defeat and glory" (p. 63). Even his sympathetic female supporters begin to realize he's fallen into "sacrilege," but they continue to enable Hightower's patriotic idolatry. Mrs. Hightower remains an enigmatic figure – a woman without a purpose, her misery invisible to her husband's preoccupations. We see only that she edges into and out of her husband's congregation, having already been groomed by her seminarian father for duty as a pastor's wife. Before long she's sneaking off to Memphis. Then one weekend word comes that she's fallen from a hotel window, her drunken male companion arrested at the scene. Following her burial in Jefferson, Faulkner notes, after other mourners have left, a lot of "the younger ones . . . remained . . . looking at the grave" (p. 69). This rebel's death must touch a generational nerve in those subject to the tyranny of the past.

Hightower's wife represents a whole company of women in *Light in August* punished for their waywardness. A young woman employed as a dietician in the orphanage where the novel's co-protagonist Joe Christmas once is housed indulges a flustered sexual liaison with a fellow employee, only to be wracked by pathological guilt and terror at exposure. Christmas grows up an orphan because his mother has been allowed to die in childbirth by her own father, who cannot forgive either her pregnancy or, worse to him, the rumor that the baby's father is a negro. Joe's grandmother endures the delusional racist tirades of her husband, and is forced by him to part from the grandchild she would love whatever his race. Joe's foster parents exhibit another marriage based on extreme male authoritarianism; Mrs. McEachern sympathizes – doubtless even identifies – with the poor child's torture under her husband's harsh discipline. She confines herself to furtive acts of charity to Joe, who will have nothing to do with them, despising her weakness and fearing contamination by it. Even a prostitute Joe takes up with must be reminded by her pimp that she is a sexual commodity, and won't get away with having a love life of her own. In this pattern, men oversee women's lives – overlooking them when obeyed, overpowering them when defied.

Joanna Burden also endures ostracism as the price of challenging Jefferson's mores. Sole survivor of a family of anti-slavery New Englanders who arrive after the Civil War to help with the enfranchisement of negro freedmen, Joanna remains an outsider in her home town:

> She has lived in the house since she was born, yet she is still a stranger, a foreigner whose people moved in from the North during Reconstruction. A Yankee, a lover of negroes, about whom in the town there is still talk of queer relations with negroes in the town and out of it, despite the fact that it is now sixty years since her grandfather and her brother were killed on the square by an ex-slaveowner over a question of negro votes in a state election. But it still lingers about her and about the place: something dark and outlandish and threatful, even though she is but a woman and but the descendant of them whom the ancestors of the town had reason (or thought that they had) to hate and dread. (pp. 46–47)

Joanna suffers primarily for her race activities, but she's also sneered at for being an undomesticated woman in Jefferson. The use of the word "queer" in the passage above illustrates a sub-theme associating "deviant" sexual behavior with the refusal to conform to racial custom. Dismissed as a sexless old maid, she's also suspected of unspecified "queer relations" with negroes. Mixing in with black peoples' lives to arrange opportunities for education and training for them – little of which actually gets described by the narrator – Joanna grows into a public agent of progress revered by Jefferson's negroes. For that, the town's whites will never forgive her, and when one day she is found savagely murdered, her body nearly decapitated, the spectators, following the dictates of stereotype, "believed aloud that it was an anonymous negro crime committed not by a negro but by Negro and who knew, believed, and hoped that she had been ravished too: at least once before her throat was cut and at least once afterward" (p. 288). Faulkner lets the prurience and projective rage of stereotype declare themselves here. The town folks' collective fantasy punishes Joanna sexually for her willingness to mix racially, but also for her refusal to confine herself to wifely domestic activities. We may begin to see how motives of racial and sexual containment interlock in the single stereotype of white female chastity menaced by negro lust.

As an ostensibly white teenager, Joe Christmas joins several other town boys for a traditional, if repellent, rite of initiation into manhood. The group arranges to have intercourse serially with a young black girl. When Joe's turn comes, something goes wrong; he suddenly attacks the negro girl, exploding at what's "prone, abject" in her eyes. The narrator speculates that Joe revolts at being "enclosed by the womanshenegro" (p. 156), a fusion of words that conflates two violated groups: both "woman" and "negro" are "she" to the power exerted by white males. Joe may be reacting to the suspicion that his own subjugation at the hands of McEachern in effect has reduced him both to a woman ("Woman's muck" he screams at Mrs. McEachern when she smuggles him food) and to a negro (McEachern treats him like a newly acquired slave, renaming him, introducing as "home" a place Joe's never seen before, and trying to civilize and save his soul as only a headstrong Calvinist can). To be powerless is to be that which is repudiated, polluted, abject, prone – and to assault its embodiment is to deny any similarity. Deny it, though, precisely because you *do* sense the similarity. Joe's fury is triggered because when he looks into the girl's eyes, "he seemed to look down into a black well and at the bottom saw two glints like reflections of dead stars" (*idem*). Those "glints" unsettle Joe both because they suggest a human spark in a creature he and his kind are treating like an object, and because "like reflections" they return Joe's own dead gaze – indicators of what you have to kill in yourself to believe that you are human and others are not.

Later in his life Joe struggles to affirm an unambiguous racial identity; he feels entirely comfortable nowhere, and though he's drawn to the negro section of town, he panics as a suffocating blackness begins to envelop him:

> About him the cabins were shaped blackly out of blackness by the faint, sultry glow of kerosene lamps. On all sides, even within him, the bodiless fecundmellow voices of negro women murmured. It was as though he and all other manshaped life about him had been returned to the lightless hot wet primogenitive Female. (p. 115)

Even as he lives the life of a white man, Joe recognizes that he wants to return to something black and female "within him," something he has had to expel in order to be (or become or remain) white and male. That is, simplistic racial or gender identity requires disavowing the complex mixtures – biological, social, historical – of which we're all made. The very language used to express Joe's state of mind betrays the excesses of stereotype. All that beckoning black fecundity and mellowness and Female-ness suggests an ambivalence at the core of racial fantasy. Joe is not a black man passing for white (there's no conclusive evidence that he has any negro ancestry), or even a Southerner whose whiteness is impugned (no one would listen to crazy Hines's claims about black blood, and Joe is adopted and raised by the McEacherns as a white child). Joe is a white man who develops doubts. And part of why he questions what he is involves his sense that to be either one thing or the other, you end up damaging yourself badly in the very process of creating yourself. The extravagant worth of blackness, then, paradoxically interlocks with its extreme devaluation under racism. The white subject dismisses what is black "within," even as he comes to miss what he repudiates; likewise, to become "manshaped" he exiles what is feminine within, only to wander unhomed from the "primogenitive Female."

Faulkner attends closely in *Light in August* to the ways societies reproduce themselves physically, psychologically, and socially. The process of finding yourself within the material and imaginative locales into which you are born unfolds unevenly, over a period of time. It depends upon acceptance of communal conventions through volitional acts of identification with the possibilities on offer. But the fact that becoming a person is part of a social dynamic also means that the process can go off track, or get stuck, or otherwise result in faulty reproduction. In *Light in August* the mechanisms of social reproduction are subjected to immense strains by new historical conditions, and by anomalous individuals who present problems to the scheme of things. If many of the women in the novel chafe under standard expectations (led by a naïve young woman who improvises cleverly even as others try to box her in to stereotype – what a very odd sardine-fancying earth mother!), it is also true that Joe Christmas balks before the mortal stakes of racial identity under Jim Crow. The irony of the 1920s South was that never had racial differentiation been more flimsy and voluntary, yet never had the consequences been so absolute and deadly. To "be" a negro meant that you possessed as little as the fabled single drop of black blood (itself only a figure of speech, of course, since racial "blood" is as much a physiological fiction as "race" itself), and that you were known in the community as black (could there be a more naked tautology than that?). The "problem" with Joe is that, like many of the characters in *Light in August,* he refuses to be any one thing or stay in any one place.

Once his grandfather uproots Christmas and leaves him in an orphanage, Joe remains in transit for the rest of his life. The rhythm of nomadism is set as Joe is seized in the middle of the night from this new home, flees with his grandfather again, is brought back, watches another orphan get spirited off, then eventually is released to McEachern. When Joe finally flees the farm after murdering his adoptive father, he sets out on "a street which ran for thirty years" (p. 339). In all that time, Joe realizes at the end of his life, he has gotten nowhere, the street nothing but a circle, and he "still inside the circle" (*idem*). Joe roams the continent on that street – from Oklahoma to Mexico to Chicago and Detroit, becoming "in turn laborer, miner, prospector, gambling tout" (p. 224), even briefly an army enlistee, until he deserts. Joe goes AWOL from life because there's no place he can be himself; when he finally shows up in Jefferson, he looks "rootless," "as though no town nor city was his, no street, no walls, no square of earth his home" (p. 31). If the closest he comes to being settled is the domestic arrangement Joanna Burden offers him, the irony is that his stay only reinforces Joe's conviction that homes are the factories where stereotypes are reproduced. Born into a house pulsating with denunciations of women's "bitchery and abomination" and "yelling against niggers" (p. 378), landing in an orphanage where an authority screams "nigger bastard" at him (p. 125), enduring virtual enslavement at the McEachern chapter of Future Farmers of America, he deserves better than to get sucked into the Burden House of Southern Gothic Horrors.

An object of communal hatred herself, however, Joanna turns the reproduction of social truth inside out, exposing stereotype as collective fantasy, an artifice of prohibitions meant to preserve the status quo. Joanna insists on rendering Southern phobias actual: she casts Christmas as the "black beast rapist" and herself as the ravished virgin secretly lusting after a negro lover. Joanna has "invented the whole thing deliberately, for the purpose of playing it out like a play" (p. 259). It's as if Joanna wants to defy the hold of Southern taboos by making the imaginary real. Mimicking long gone plantation mistresses, Miss Burden begins to leave dinner for Joe after he moves into one of the former slave cabins on the grounds of her house. She insists that he play-act the whole erotic-racial scenario by climbing in a window, eating the food that's "set out for the nigger," and entering her bedroom "like a thief, a robber" to "despoil her virginity each time anew" (p. 234). As he follows this script, though, it begins to come apart. Joanna resists Joe, he realizes, not as a maiden defending her chastity, but as a man wrestling "with another man for an object of no actual value to either, and for which they struggled on principle alone" (p. 235). Or, Joe revises, "it was like I was the woman and she was the man" (*idem*). Here stereotype begins to implode, Joanna's whiteness trumping Joe's blackness, her racial maleness his femaleness, the values defended by chivalric racism emptied of their worth. The roles are destabilized in this overly self-conscious effort to perform them. In a subsequent "stage" of this bodice-ripping plantation romance, Joanna acts out her own defilement under the logic of fetishized female purity, abandoning herself to obscene language and "the wild throes of nymphomania" (p. 259). Joanna and Joe break every taboo, indulge every forbidden desire, as they seek to reconnect with all that Southern prohibitions make people give up. What they do is an open secret, moreover, meant to scandalize the town, folks noticing immediately when Joe moves to the cabin, and "wondering where he slept at night" (p. 79).

The tragedy of the lovers' desperate affair is that even the most private intimacies between two people are subject to the thunderous abstractions organizing social life: there's no sex free of communal strictures regarding race; no pleasure outside regulations protecting family, blood, class; no individual variation exempt from absolute categorization. In *Light in August*, women and people of color menace social definitions with their perceived fluidity. Joe is stunned when he finds out about female menstruation, for example, picturing it ever after as an urn leaking a dark liquid. When he accidentally witnesses a sex act between the dietician and her lover, Joe has furtively been squeezing pink toothpaste from its container. The novel is filled with sex- and race-triggered violations of bodily integrity: vomiting, slashing, shooting, finally a castration. Insinuations of homoeroticism abound in the novel, marking queerness as a category-buster, and betraying the ambivalence at the core of all stereotype. The sheriff jokes about the "wife" Joe Christmas has taken when he sets up house with Joe Brown (Lucas Burch's road pseudonym), and recall that Joe and Joanna embrace like two struggling males. When Hightower finally renounces his daffy Lost Causism, he atones for its racism by employing a negro woman as a domestic, and later a negro man as his cook; the town believes Hightower has had "unnatural" relations with both of them. (Byron Bunch tries to talk Hightower into providing an alibi for Joe based on those suspicions: "You could say he was here with you that night. Every night . . .," Byron pleads [p. 390].) Any flouting of rigid black/white or male/female dualities calls down general ridicule or condemnation. Rock is turning to sand in Jefferson, but old truths die hard.

The vise of stereotype also gets propped open temporarily by Joe's racial ambiguity. He's a categorical anomaly, a "white nigger" (p. 344), a subject of Jim Crow law that "never acted like either a nigger or a white man" (p. 350). And that, the narrator concludes, "was what made the folks so mad" (*idem*). The fact that Joe has learned identity to be arbitrary, an effect of performance, constitutes the gravest menace to Southern order. When Joe finally gives up his fugitive life, he succumbs to the South's insistence that he be deemed one thing or the other. Joe turns himself in as an accused negro rapist murderer, and with that he is "recognised" (p. 337). Immediately he notices "the gauge definite and ineradicable of the black tide creeping up his legs, moving from his feet upward as death moves" (p. 339). Definition moves to cover Joe, but, arrested, Joe himself can't move. The terror inspired by Joe's knack for mobility – the mistress of the orphanage frets, "We must place him. We must place him at once" – has to be addressed repeatedly, the last time by the white-supremacy crazed Percy Grimm, who plays out the black vs. white contest as if it were a game of chess, with Percy the white knight permitted the closing gambit of checkmating his opponent to death.

Light in August constantly suggests the community's paranoia about individuals who go off script, who elude powers of surveillance.[12] The novel's most memorable, if also most enigmatic, assertion – "Memory believes before knowing remembers" – points to the overpowering effects of social conditioning. Just after its appearance as the topic sentence of Chapter 6, which begins the extended flashback relating Joe's early life, comes a description of Joe's sensations in the orphanage. This "home" becomes a symbol of the disciplinary tasks performed by all families to the extent that they reproduce law-abiding citizens. Faulkner's Dickensian vision of a "grassless cinder-strewnpacked compound surrounded by smoking factory purlieus," resembling a "penitentiary or a zoo," the uniformed orphans "in and out of remembering but in knowing constant as the bleak walls" (p. 119), suggests the reach of the state into the organization of personhood. In the emphatic case of an orphan like Joe, "factory purlieus" augur preparation for the working class. But the general principle involves the bombardment of children by social instruction, such that imparted belief eventually works as a reflex, before it can even materialize as conscious memory or knowledge. Faulkner represents the instruments for such indoctrination in metaphors of the word and the gaze.

Joe's indeterminate racial status makes the process of accepting a prepared identity more difficult for him than for those who do not question. The ways a community thinks and talks await each person born into it. As individuals become aware of the possibilities they have been trained to believe they must choose among, a process of recognition takes place: each subject answers a call to claim certain elements of identity, to personalize a script from the social archive. Joe senses this discursive atmosphere: "he was hearing a myriad of sounds . . . voices, murmurs, whispers: of trees, darkness, earth; people: his own voice; other voices evocative of names and times and places – which he had been conscious of all his life without knowing it, which *were* his life" (p. 105, emphasis added). Joe becomes Bobbie's lover through language: "[i]t was as if with speech he was learning about women's bodies" (p. 196). Joe's face is regularly described as having a "dead parchment color" (p. 34), as if inviting the stroke that will define his legal race. To feel recognized is to acknowledge the legitimacy of the collective gaze. The more independent-minded characters of the novel often sense the eye of the community trying to fix them in place. Lena has to traverse a "battery of maneyes" (p. 27) that see through her bluff and denude her as a sexual object. In the orphanage for white children, Joe begins to be called "Nigger" by the others when they sense that he is the object of special "watching" (by his grandfather, masquerading as a custodian). Even the narrator of *Light in August* functions as the voice and eye of the community, reflecting the values and biases of Jefferson's white middle-class majority.

More characters than just Joe Christmas and Joanna Burden demonstrate the inadequacy of the South's outmoded ways of thinking.

Byron Bunch, a simple, hard-working young man employed at the town sawmill, gets all mixed up in Lena's attempted reunion with Burch/Brown, with Joanna Burden's murder, and with his mentor Hightower's fearful re-emergence into the community. At one point, having decided the ethical course is to arrange for Lena to meet with Brown, despite having fallen in love with her himself, Byron climbs high above Jefferson as he heads out of town. He looks down on the charred outline of the Bundren plantation house, then looks upward to imagine an inviting horizon where things might lose the very language that ties them to present necessities: "Where trees would look like and be called by something else except trees, and men would look like and be called by something else except folks" (p. 424). Joe's grandmother also wishes for "one day like it hadn't happened. Like folks never knew him as a man that had killed . . ." (p. 388). Both struggle to articulate the need for new discursive realities to accommodate, even foster, new social realities.

The novel does in fact propose at least one new word to counter a noxious discourse of sexual and racial segregation preoccupied with purity and pollution, white blood and black, rape, and lynching. Instead, as Hightower drifts into an exhausted reverie after Lena's childbirth and Joe's execution, he envisions a wheel or "halo" of all the faces he's encountered. Surprisingly, those faces, representing some of the South's most violently maintained social differences, "all look a little alike, composite of all the faces which he has ever seen" (p. 491). Startlingly, Hightower sees that the two faces least able to free themselves from each other are Christmas's and Grimm's, black victim and white executioner. The fused image suggests to Hightower that Joe's fate has finally passed beyond the recent "confused" "throes" of "a more inextricable compositeness" (*idem*). Compositeness points to a Southern future beyond blunt racial dualities, beyond racialist notions of biological hybridity, beyond racist watchwords like "miscegenation" and "amalgamation."

On the novel's other front, Lena Grove withstands yet another desertion by her husband-to-be, and decides to push further down the untraveled road of unwed motherhood. Courted now by Byron, she's in no rush to climb into the confines of labor- and child-ridden wifedom. She hops on a vehicle heading in slow motion toward the future, happy to relish the freedom of movement again. "My, my. A body does get around," remarks Lena, neatly summing up the novel's restlessness (p. 507). The furniture salesman who amuses his wife by telling her about Lena's adventures represents a kind of healthy middle-class hospitality to women's efforts to improve their lots. Less encouraging remained the outlook of African Americans, who continued to encounter the murderous violence of racism. For those who witness Joe's death, his slaughtered body, the narrator assures us, will "rise soaring into their memories forever and ever" (p. 465). But its meaning remains indecipherable: "musing, quiet, steadfast, not fading and not particularly threatful, but of itself alone serene, of itself alone triumphant" (*idem*). Perhaps the communal memory of lynching goes into hiding, unattended but never forgotten, to be recalled when a society is finally prepared to acknowledge its guilty past and make atonement.[13]

CHAPTER 4

The Planting of Men: The South and New World Colonialism

As Faulkner described the startling transformations that modernity brought to his part of the world, he formulated one of his core beliefs: that life itself is motion. We have seen how modern rebellion against oppressive manners and mores engaged Faulkner. Captivated, and no doubt a little intimidated, by the boldness of contemporary young women, Faulkner returned again and again in his early fiction to their nervy acts of defiance, and to the often violent punishments they suffered for clashing with the paternalism of the South's entrenched white families. Without overstating the region's – or even the nation's – willingness to accept the claims of all under-enfranchised groups, we can say that beginning in the 1920s the South did begin to undergo changes that would lead to greater social, economic, and political freedom for white women, African Americans, and many of the poor. It would take decades for some of these people to attain just minimal rights: not until the mid-1950s, for example, did Southern segregation laws finally get struck down.

Faulkner's fascination with how his traditional society dealt with upheaval stimulated his imagination. In observing the trials of selfhood experienced by those gaining power as well as those losing it, Faulkner learned how fluctuating social circumstances conditioned even the most fundamental features of individual personality; how those in states of crisis vividly displayed the essential drama of human nature: what he called "the human heart in conflict with itself"; and how any given world looked radically different according to what was happening to you in it. That last insight may help us connect the first three chapters of this book: as Faulkner describes the volatility of contemporary life in Yoknapatawpha and the greater South, he notices the frantic discontentment of many young women; the imaginative bankruptcy of a once dominant, now moribund planter elite; the blithe materialism of an ascending class of "rednecks"; the courageous gestures of resistance or acts of escape performed by African Americans – all of these people occupying the same space, but making very different senses of place out of it.

One dimension of Faulkner's project in telling the stories of his "own postage stamp of native soil" remains to be considered: the broader history that had shaped the people and communities of his contemporary South. When most people think of William Faulkner today, they picture a bourbon-sipping, slow-drawling, "Missippi" writer whose overwrought novels are tangled up in a Southern gothic past. I have tried to approach Faulkner from other perspectives to show the inadequacy of this view. Nonetheless, it is true that the two most famous sentences Faulkner ever wrote are: "The past is never dead. It's not even past." Southern writers in general are often seen as distinctively preoccupied with the past as a result of the lingering effects of the Civil War – which ultimately proved traumatic for almost everyone in the region. For Faulkner, though, the catastrophe of civil war more truly *culminates* the history of a flawed historical design, as opposed to initiating a region's cause for grievance. The ghosts of slavery and racism that continue to haunt the modern South descend not just from its defeat over the "peculiar institution" in 1865, but from the antecedent project of European colonialism that began encompassing the so-called New World in 1492.[1]

In *Absalom, Absalom!* (1936), a young American finds himself in the country of Haiti, already by the 1820s a place soaked in centuries of racial bloodshed, the whole island a theater of past rebellions and massacres, with the stage now set for another imminent insurrection. Yet Thomas Sutpen in his ignorance of New World history remains oblivious to the very ground beneath his feet, "not knowing that what he rode upon was a volcano" (*Absalom, Absalom!*, p. 202). The narrator movingly imagines what the novice plantation overseer does not fathom: that the fields of sugar cane rise from "soil manured with black blood from two hundred years of oppression and exploitation" (*idem*), soil compacted of "the planting of men too: the yet intact bones and brains in which the old unsleeping blood that had vanished into the earth they trod still cried out for vengeance" (*idem*). And not only "the torn limbs and outraged hearts" of African slaves to be recounted, but also the corpses of French plantation masters executed during Haiti's slave revolution two decades earlier, the island still "breathed over by the winds in which the doomed ships had fled in vain, out of which the last tatter of sail had sunk into the blue sea, along which the last vain despairing cry of woman or child had blown away" (*idem*).

The ruinous social and moral consequences of much New World colonial history are evoked by these images: its very cradle, on an island named Hispaniola by Christopher Columbus, where the native Arawak people became the first victims of New World enslavement; the acts of revolt by the island's next enslaved population, the Africans first imported in the early seventeenth century when the Indians had died out, and their establishment of the New World's first black republic in 1804 (promising to end those "two hundred years" of exploitation); the tremors of slave rebellion felt in the US plantation South; and, during the time Faulkner was writing the novel, the just-ended US military occupation of both states on the island, Haiti and Santo Domingo, the troops deployed to provide security for American investors (much of it still in sugar agriculture). After witnessing the misery caused by the plantation system – for everyone it touched – one of its participants concludes that in the Civil War "the South would realise that it was now paying the price for having erected its economic edifice not on the rock of stern morality but on the shifting sands of opportunism and moral brigandage" (p. 209).

Faulkner's plantation fiction unflinchingly confronts what it means for the South to have been misbegotten in slavery. Its enormity ripples in every direction. In *Absalom, Absalom!* Faulkner imagines how the initial insult of reducing human beings to instruments of labor and commodities of exchange dooms a society to concussions of brutality, domination, and revenge. In *Go Down, Moses* (1942) Faulkner portrays slavery as a function of the general delusion of property-owning, a tragic wrong stemming from the worst kind of hubris – as if you could hold title to a piece of the earth's surface any more than to the body of another human being. In a small set of short stories about the Yoknapatawpha Indians, as well as in sidebars throughout his plantation novels, Faulkner also touches on the long ignored acts of deception and force that "cleared" plantation land of its earlier occupants. In *The Unvanquished* (1938) Faulkner explores the systems of belief that supported and disguised the atrocity of slavery: the fabled code of honor and shame that orchestrated conduct among white plantation masters and between white classes, and that simultaneously muffled the outrages upon which US slave culture rested.

In Chapter 2 I suggested that Faulkner's struggle to tell the story of Yoknapatawpha's plantation families involved his being too close to them, too familiar with their own sense of importance and their habits for rationalizing privilege. In *Absalom, Absalom!* Quentin Compson concludes that the only way he has finally been able to understand the South has been to get away from it: *"If I had been there I could not have seen it this plain"* (*Absalom, Absalom!*, p. 155). If the narrator of *Flags in the Dust* fails to achieve critical detachment from the dream of the plantation South, and if *The Sound and the Fury* subsequently abandons traditional narrative altogether because survivors of a corrupt ideal have become estranged from familiar stories of self and community, then we might see *Absalom, Absalom!* as inventing a kind of narrative discourse that *incorporates* the conflict between being too close and too far at the same time. Faulkner's magnificent achievement in *Absalom* arises from his recognition that the only way to tell the story of the South is to tell it as the story of many stories. "The" South encompasses a host of narratives, some told, others not, about those who made, and later unmade, the flawed society upon which a conflicted nation had been founded. The narrators are by turns self-defensive and ashamed, oblivious and curious, vulnerable and hostile. They shape their stories around their own requirements as well as the needs they sense in their auditors. What is once called "the marriage of speaking and hearing" intimates the dynamic of exchange and collaboration at the heart of storytelling, and also at the heart of how communities are constituted.

Faulkner's greatest novel suggests how social reality is always a matter of telling the story that will best serve you and yours, that history is always a matter of relating the past according to present interests, that life itself is a Sisyphean struggle to impose your own design on reality:

> You get born and you try this and you dont know why only you keep
> on trying it and you are born at the same time with a lot of other people,
> all mixed up with them, like trying to, having to, move your arms and

legs with strings only the same strings are hitched to all the other arms and legs and the others all trying and they don't know why either except that the strings are all in one another's way like five or six people all trying to make a rug on the same loom only each one wants to weave his own pattern in to the rug, and it cant matter, you know that, or the Ones that set up the loom would have arranged things a little better, and yet it must matter because you keep on trying or having to keep on trying and then all of a sudden it's all over . . . (pp. 100–101)

We might see *Absalom* as reconstructing narrative by absorbing its modernist failure. From his consummate modernist work, *The Sound and the Fury*, which he once called his "most splendid failure," Faulkner brings back some of the Compsons to try their hands once more at the game Quentin has grown so weary of as a freshman at Harvard: *"Tell About the South"* (p. 142). The stories that emerge prove flawed by outlandish bias, unmanageable emotions, willful misinterpretation, and crucial absences of fact. Nonetheless, each story at least tells the story of itself, and in so doing suggests how we are all composed by narratives we tell ourselves and others, within collective fantasies accepted as truth. The jostling of contrary stories also invites us to reckon with every individual's bid for self-creation, within whatever community that person recognizes as his or her own. Of course, Faulkner's novel never stoops to platitudes such as these; instead, it creates breathtakingly eloquent images like the following for the way action cannot be separated from response, past from present, event from representation, individual consciousness from communal mentality:

Maybe happen is never once but like ripples maybe on water after the pebble sinks, the ripples moving on, spreading, the pool attached by a narrow umbilical water-cord to the next pool which the first pool feeds, has fed, did feed, let this second pool contain a different temperature of water, a different molecularity of having seen, felt, remembered, reflect in a different tone the infinite unchanging sky, it doesn't matter; that pebble's watery echo whose fall it did not even see moves across its surface too at the original ripple-space, to the old ineradicable rhythm . . . (*Absalom, Absalom!*, p. 210)

Let's start with the ripples. The first voice to dominate the novel belongs to Rosa Coldfield, who has broken a silence of forty-three years in order to enlist the attention of her young townsman Quentin

Compson. We do not learn from Rosa what caused her to seclude herself in 1866, but in September of 1909 she finds herself needing Quentin's help to solve a mystery. Rosa suspects that her long-fugitive brother-in-law, Henry Sutpen, has returned to the family mansion to die. Henry, Thomas Sutpen's son, has been missing since 1866, when he abruptly murdered his sister Judith's fiancé at the gates of Sutpen's Hundred and became a fugitive. She believes she will have to force her way into the house, past the ancient servant Clytemnestra, who will be guarding her long-dead master's son. Quentin protests to his father that the mysterious Miss Coldfield is practically a stranger to him, but after Rosa unleashes a torrent of pent-up rage, frustration, and self-justification in the course of explaining what she wants, Quentin can appreciate Mr. Compson's hypothesis that Miss Coldfield considers Quentin obliged by ancestral association:

> She may believe that if it hadn't been for your grandfather's friendship, Sutpen could never have got a foothold here, and that if he had not got that foothold, he could not have married Ellen. So maybe she considers you partly responsible through heredity for what happened to her and her family through him. (p. 8)

Mr. Compson speaks here in the novel's trademark rhythm of historical interconnectedness, the present tracing its origin to events of long-ago, the ripples pointing back to that first dropped stone. Quentin also learns every Southerner's lesson – and it ought to be one every American takes in – that you can be responsible for circumstances you benefit from (like slavery, say), even if you had nothing to do with setting them up.

Rosa narrates most of *Absalom*'s first chapter, though her quoted speech is interrupted by Quentin's periodic recollection of his father's commentary as well as by an anonymous narrator. The next three chapters return to Quentin's house, where he waits for darkness (Rosa wants to sneak into the Sutpen mansion under cover of night) by talking over with his father what he's heard. The fifth chapter completes the phase of the narrative that takes place on that single September day; in it the narrator seems to reproduce the rest of Rosa's story as Quentin has absorbed it. It's as if we're overhearing Quentin's mental recapitulation of what Rosa has said to him. Rosa refuses to name the trauma that sends her into a half century of shocked silence.

Yet in every word she utters the essence of that event burns through. What has happened to her is both the origin and the consequence of some unspeakable insult. Faulkner begins the effort to relate how a certain kind of abusive mentality was responsible for the South's misconceiving, perpetuated itself through rippling acts of brutalization, and so thoroughly infected its victims that they ended up replicating its horrors even as they sought to redress them.

Rosa circles around the outrageous thing Thomas Sutpen does to her soon after the aging Confederate colonel returns from the Civil War and begins rebuilding his ruined family and mansion. Toward the end of her furious diatribe, Rosa insists that the town gossips are wrong in their belief that she never forgave Sutpen for whatever it was he did:

> But I forgave him. They will tell you different, but I did. Why shouldn't I? I had nothing to forgive; I had not lost him because I never owned him: a certain segment of rotten mud walked into my life, spoke that to me which I had never heard before and never shall again, and then walked out; that was all. (p. 138)

The "nub of the insult" (p. 139) has something to do with Sutpen's addressing to her "bald outrageous words exactly as if he were consulting with Jones or with some other man about a bitch dog or a cow or mare" (p. 136). We have to wait until Quentin's roommate at Harvard, the Canadian Shreve McCannon, rehearses this episode to learn that Sutpen, feeling at age sixty that he might have only "one more shot" left in "the old cannon" (p. 224), and desperately in want of a son to whom he can bequeath his restored plantation, proposes to Rosa that "they breed like a couple of dogs together" (p. 147), he to marry her if they succeed in producing a male. Understandably, Rosa considers this proposal a bit lacking in tact. Sutpen's behavior is no surprise: he announces his courtship by putting his hand on Rosa's head and confessing that he's already been a bad husband to her deceased sister. And then he makes his bid to breed first, with all the tender regard, Rosa observes, of somebody saying "Come" to a dog (p. 135).

In the particular "molecularity of having seen, felt, remembered" that is Rosa, the unspoken insult to women at the base of the planter ideal shockingly gets spoken: Rosa recoils in horror, and when she finally does speak, she can hardly make her way against the thicket of emotions and loyalties that have been bred into her. She understands herself to have been a "self-mesmered fool" (p. 113), entranced by a man "brave," "with valor and strength," possessing "the stature and shape of a hero" (p. 13), yet for all that a "demon" (p. 8), a "fiend" (p. 10), no gentleman, "without pity or honor" (p. 13). Rosa cannot solve the contradictions of her station in life; she only manages to convey a heart in conflict with itself. She disputes those who say she submits to her brother-in-law's offer of marriage out of desire for "possible wealth, position, or even the fear of dying manless" (p. 128). Yet Rosa's conscience doubtless is plagued by all of these self-accusations, just as she realizes she's making herself nothing but a vessel for Sutpen's design: "O furious mad old man, I hold no substance that will fit your dream but I can give you airy space and scope for your delirium" (p. 136). Faulkner here lets a whole sisterhood of abused plantation women – wives, fiancées, daughters, sisters, aunts – denounce the mad misogyny of masters who commandeered women's physical labor, administrative and financial skills, personal fortunes, and sexual lives so as to create domains they ruled, then venerated female chastity to safeguard the patrilineal descent of property and wealth. Faulkner also allows Rosa to express the ambivalence of such women, who led lives that provided advantages and luxuries they loved, and sought, and thought justified the brutalization of many around them.

Almost all the women in *Absalom* become casualties of male designs that they mistake as serving their interests. Rosa's predecessor in Sutpen's marital alliances has been her sister Ellen, both of them attractive to the ambitious newcomer because their father, Goodhue Coldfield, has a reputation for character in the frontier town of Jefferson. Sutpen has figured out how to make money; what he needs is respectability, and the Coldfield name will give it to him. Coldfield has established himself as a supplier of general goods to the planters of the newly opened Mississippi territory surrounding the town. His daughter Ellen aspires to the landowning gentry class already forming around first families like the Compsons and Sartorises. When Quentin's father tells the story of Ellen's class ascent, we can detect the mockery of someone who thinks *his* family belonged to the true elite and that crude frontier-types like Sutpen were just vulgar imitators. Mr. Compson reports (through his grandparents' eyewitness) that Ellen Coldfield "seemed not only to acquiesce, to be reconciled to her life and marriage, but to be actually proud of it" (p. 54). She grows "a little regal" in her new status as "chatelaine to the largest, wife to the wealthiest, mother of the most fortunate" (*idem*). The Civil War crushes this "bright trivial shell" when it destroys the Sutpen fortune – Ellen becomes a "moth caught in a gale and blown against a wall" (p. 67). According to Mr. Compson, "a Southern lady" is defined by ancestral pride and pretense to entitlement: it is

> as though she were living on the actual blood itself like a vampire, . . . with that serene and idle splendor of flowers arrogating to herself, because it fills her veins also, nourishment from the old blood that crossed uncharted seas and continents and battled wilderness hardships and lurking circumstances and fatalities. (p. 68)

That there's another "old blood" drawn upon – of African slaves – in addition to that of ruthlessly ambitious European ancestors does not occur to Mr. Compson, but such a truth compounds the historical obliviousness to vampirism required by the plantation ideal.

Ellen's daughter by Sutpen, Judith, gets recruited to her place in the scheme of things too. As she has been raised to marry within the plantocracy, Judith's virginity becomes her leading asset; her parents plot the alliance that will advance their standing. Sutpen needs neither wealth nor respectability at this point; but Ellen realizes what they do need is refinement, some attainment of taste and elegance that will make Sutpen's earlier crude (and intermittently criminal) phase of accumulation fade from memory. Charles Bon, a classmate of Henry Sutpen's at the fledgling University of Mississippi, seems just the right acquisition: a stylish young cosmopolitan from New Orleans. Shreve imagines how Charles courts Judith:

> And he spent ten days there, not only the esoteric, the sybarite, the steel blade in the tessellated sheath which Henry had begun to ape at the University, but the object of art, the mold and mirror of form and fashion which Mrs Sutpen . . . accepted him as and insisted . . . that he be (and would have purchased him as and paid for him with Judith even). (p. 256)

Judith's commodification under marital custom spreads from a plague of commodification that compromises the plantation South. Humans of every sort get turned into instruments of advancement and enrichment.

Sutpen's rise to chief planter of Yoknapatawpha earns him a hanger-on, a fan named Wash Jones who reveres the Colonel. When Sutpen fails to inveigle Rosa into a trial copulation, he turns to the only unmarried female at hand: Wash's teenage granddaughter Milly. Sutpen simply exercises droit de seigneur over her, impregnates her, then roughly tosses her and their useless infant daughter aside – to Wash's incredulity. Sutpen treats Milly like a mare – worse, he says with deliberate insult, because if she'd been a horse he'd at least been able to offer her a stall. This unbelievably explicit dramatization of the plantation ethos of female (re)productivity brings to conclusion a long line of incidents in which we witness the brutalization of women. We could include Thomas Sutpen's first wife, the daughter of a sugar plantation master in Haiti, whom Sutpen puts aside when he begins to suspect she has black ancestry. Or Charles Bon's first wife, a woman of mixed race, a courtesan in New Orleans, who also gets put aside when Charles decides he wants to marry Judith. Or Clytemnestra, Sutpen's child by a slave woman, who gets assigned lifelong domestic duty because black daughters present their fathers two reasons not to recognize them.

Such mistreatment of women provokes an array of responses. Ellen implodes in a puff of self-delusion, while Rosa explodes into a burst of vituperation after four decades of complicit silence. Judith acts out a truly scary drama of self-denial; we see her as a child enviously devouring the power of men to get things by violent force, then we watch her turn herself to salt as her brother murders her fiancé, that brother flees forever, her mother floats off, her great-aunt elopes, her father quashes the independent sisterhood that has formed in his absence, and her beloved's child by another woman presents himself for mothering. Stoicism hardly begins to describe how terribly Judith sub-zeroes her emotions. Clytie ends up just burning the whole Sutpen mansion down, something that probably should have been done the first time any of this accursed clan of women ever set eyes on the "ogre or djinn" (p. 16).

Faulkner surveys the lives crumpled by the power of wealthy white planters in the antebellum South, some damaged even in the process of elevation. Through his multiplex narrative, Faulkner can show how the devastation affects numerous groups, clustered in various combinations of sexual, racial, and economic disadvantage. The stone of insult ripples outward along subterranean channels into countless pools of human suffering, some generations in the future. Even those enjoying the system's greatest benefits pay a price by having to repress the costs of self-mastery. We shall see how Sutpen desensitizes himself to the sort of sympathies that would spoil the inhuman perfection of his ideal. In surveying so much injury, character by character in *Absalom, Absalom!*, Faulkner also suggests a principle of the mentality that held together Southern elites – and perhaps those of any society: collective fictions affirm the legitimacy of a system that affords you advantage, while justifying the disadvantages borne by everybody else.

So, for example, it takes Rosa forty-three years to confront the fact that, like all would-be plantation mistresses, she possesses value only as a uterus under title. Yet being treated brutally by Sutpen – like a dog – never prompts her to see how her own fantasy of social standing leads her to treat others the same way. Rosa ridicules the poor white Wash Jones, mocking his way of speaking ("hit won't none of mine nor hisn neither") and deeming him nothing but "an animal" (p. 108): "that brute progenitor of brutes whose granddaughter was to supplant me" (p. 107). Rosa hurls the word "brute" so compulsively at Jones that we must read for anxiety. In fact, it was landless white men like Jones who filled an indispensable buffer zone of plantation oversight and wage labor between master and slave, and whose standing had at the same time to be denigrated because it reflected back at their "betters" the tenuousness of social status. That Sutpen later stoops to supplant a Coldfield with a Jones exposes how fluid class positions had become after the war, but also how fluid they must have been at the outset of frontier plantation society as well. Rosa even turns her confused sense of class superiority on Sutpen himself, complaining that he was "underbred" (p. 34), and must have fled to Jefferson from "some opposite of respectability too dark to talk about" (p. 11). The historical problem for Rosa's pride in ancestry is that many of the first families of the Deep South drew their stock from obscure origins, as had many of the Virginia Tidewater gentry themselves. Sutpen is just an earlier, more ruthless Jones, as we realize when we discover that Sutpen begins in Appalachian poverty. Likewise, though Rosa considers herself the essence of respectability, she knows that her father was no more than an adventurer from Tennessee who wandered into Jefferson with a wagon full of junk. Rosa's insistence that Joneses are brutes corresponds with her disdain, too, for the Africans her world depends upon. She exaggerates the subhuman status of the slaves Sutpen brings to town – from "whatever dark swamp he had found them in" (p. 17) – as she recoils from Clytie's touch of restraint when she charges into the Sutpen mansion the day Henry murders Charles: "Take your hand off me, nigger!" (p. 112). Rosa can't stabilize her position because, as becomes apparent, social standing actually is *constituted* by successive acts of insult: aggression, competition, domination, then subsequent denial.

Faulkner's presentation of Rosa introduces an insight he has arrived at about the plantation South and its heirs: that they always *knew* their edifice to be founded on the sands of "oppression and exploitation," yet they *acted* as if they did not. At the moment Rosa flings her insult at Clytie – "nigger!" – she has already confessed how human touch "abrogates, cuts sharp and straight across the devious intricate channels of decorous ordering" that constitutes the nonsense of race: "But let flesh touch with flesh, and watch the fall of all the eggshell shibboleth of caste and color too" (p. 112). Each of the novel's principal narrators circles around a refused recognition, the denial of a truth already known too well. Such disavowal protects the South's umbilical connection to New World colonial plantation slavery, even as each version of the South's story betrays such knowledge in every sentence.

As someone who no longer seems to have anything to gain from the defunct plantation regime, Mr. Compson sorts out some of its enabling myths more disinterestedly than Rosa. Mr. Compson has lost faith in all human aspiration because the world his grandfathers made, once revered as the ideal of grace, leisure, and refinement, has been thoroughly discredited by the acknowledgment of its inescapable foundation "on the shifting sands of opportunism and moral brigandage." Rosa Coldfield has herself been an enfranchised beneficiary of the plantation South, willing to marry up into it, composing poems in honor of the Confederate dead, and trying to stop her life at the moment of the Old South's demise in 1865. Mr. Compson, on the other hand, represents the next generation, born after the war, and grown weary of the veneration of Lost Causes. He's dissolute, sardonic, despairing, also deeply erudite – as we recall from *The Sound and the Fury*. He wants to save the life of his son, who he knows is shadowed by the temptation of suicide, yet he can't figure out why even his own life is worth continuing.

The bleakness that comes through Mr. Compson's narrative reflects a moment of grave regional and national uncertainty as well. In 1898 Southern soldiers had been welcomed back into the federal armed forces, and the reunited nation, as if to confirm its rediscovery of white solidarity, marched off to subdue colonies of darker peoples. During the Spanish-American War the US seized its first non-contiguous territories: Cuba, the Philippines, and Puerto Rico. Surely the bad vibes of imperial arrogance irritate Mr. Compson into imagining the contradictions of racial discrimination in colonial settings (exemplified in his portraits of French antebellum New Orleans). Mr. Compson is especially struck by the figure of Charles Bon, with whom he no doubt identifies, who is something like "a youthful Roman consul making the Grand Tour of his day among the barbarian hordes which his grandfather conquered" (p. 74), viewing the Sutpens as "not quite yet emerged from barbarism," in contrast to his own "Latin culture and intelligence" (p. 75). Mr. Compson demystifies the imperial pride that afflicted the South but hardly originated there. The Greeks scorned the "barbarians," the Romans the Saxons (as Conrad reminds us in *Heart of Darkness*, published nine years before Mr. Compson pictures his own Roman consul amid the conquered), the Louisiana French the frontier Americans, Southern masters enslaved Africans, eventually the US North the Confederate South: all figments of superiority required by colonial domination.

Mr. Compson sees through the forms of oppression and exploitation buried in the plantation South's foundation: he understands the connection between the abuse of women and slaves, imagining that Sutpen comes "to town to find a wife exactly as he would have gone to the Memphis market to buy livestock or slaves" (p. 31). He sets out the sexual-racial hierarchy bluntly: "the other sex is separated into three sharp divisions . . . the virgins whom gentlemen someday married, the courtesans to whom they went while on sabbaticals to the cities, the slave girls and women upon whom that first caste rested and to whom in certain cases it doubtless owed the very fact of its virginity" (p. 87). Mr. Compson perceives the double exploitation of African women as "commodities" (p. 93) of labor and sex, the mixed race courtesans of New Orleans "the supreme apotheosis of chattelry, of human flesh bred of the two races for that sale" (p. 89). He mocks Ellen Sutpen for having "escaped at last into a world of pure illusion in which, safe from any harm, she moved, lived" (p. 54), taking her as the emblem of the whole town's ambivalent efforts to disavow complicity with the criminal Sutpen while swallowing the fruit of his success. Mr. Compson even seems to see through the contradictions of Southern racial formulas. He gives a sympathetic account of Charles Bon's determination to rescue his octoroon lover by marrying her in a morganatic ceremony (these were known as plaçage marriages, and they accorded protective rights such women otherwise would never have had). He repeatedly hints at the idea that there is no fundamental difference between races – noting, for example, that Henry's life as a young man does not differ from the lives of "the negro slaves who supported" him, all of them "with the same sweat, the only difference being that on the one hand it went for labor in fields where on the other it went as the price of the Spartan and meager pleasures which were available to them because they did not have to sweat in the fields" (p. 78).

Compson even identifies the social pathology that at once enables and deranges the planter classes. He supposes that when Charles Bon shows up he fulfills some already extant fantasy of self-love at the heart of the Sutpen design: "a myth, a phantom: something which they engendered and created whole themselves; some effluvium of Sutpen blood and character, as though as a man he did not exist at all" (p. 82). It's only a short step for Mr. Compson to hypothesize that what was going on was some kind of "pure and perfect incest" (p. 77), Charles having "seduced [Henry] as surely as he seduced Judith" (p. 76), all of them in love with each other, the "sister's virginity" a "false quantity which must incorporate in itself an inability to endure in order to be precious, to exist," and so the brother "taking that virginity in the person of the brother-in-law, the man whom he would be if he could become, metamorphose into, the lover, the husband" (p. 77). This tangle derives from the determination of an elite group to reproduce itself from within. Poe's "The Fall of the House of Usher" provides an analogue; Roderick refuses to admit any alien blood to the line of Usher, and, in love with himself as his sister, he consummates the impulse to incest in an act that fatally destroys those it means to reproduce. Incest doubles as the perfection of purity and the blast of corruption. The flaw in the House of Usher might be traced in Compson's version of the House of Sutpen, not to mention the House of Compson – since the story Mr. Compson aims at his son clearly means to illuminate Quentin's own diseased overvaluation of his sister's virginity and his desire to commit incest with her. It's a Southern thing, Mr. Compson seems to be assuring him; don't think it's just you.

For all his insight, though, Mr. Compson still comes up short in his effort to explain the novel's central mystery: why, upon their return from the war, on the eve of the wedding, at the gates of the Sutpen homestead, does Henry Sutpen murder Charles Bon? Rosa won't even try to solve that puzzle, insisting the act took place without rhyme or reason. Mr. Compson proposes that Henry and his father must have taken exception to Bon's earlier marriage to his octoroon mistress, and that the problem was "bigamy." But toward the end of his account, Mr. Compson confesses that his hypothesis does not satisfy him: "It's just incredible. It just does not explain" (p. 80). As in Rosa's version, though, I think we may find the answer in an earlier insult that Mr. Compson infers but won't admit. At a few points in his story Mr. Compson seems to betray his suspicion that Charles Bon is actually Thomas Sutpen's own son. He refers to Sutpen's having named "Clytie as he named them all, the one before Clytie and Henry and Judith even" (p. 48). And when Mr. Compson explains the mistake Sutpen makes in his first marriage in Haiti, he points out that "if he had acquiesced to it [it] would not even have been an error and which, since he refused to accept it or be stopped by it, became his doom" (p. 41). Given Mr. Compson's description of Charles as an "effluvium" of Sutpen "blood," doesn't it seem possible that Mr. Compson has deduced that Charles Bon must be "the one before Clytie"? Sutpen's "doom" comes down to the startling reappearance in Mississippi after thirty years of that first child from Haiti. Seemingly with the murder in mind, Shreve refers to Sutpen's dilemma as witnessing "his children . . . destroying each other" (p. 147), a comment that makes Quentin think he "sounds just like Father." The obstacle to the marriage may not be bigamy but the menace of literal incest. Admitting *that* would make a shambles of Mr. Compson's argument to Quentin about symbolic incest, but it would also explain why incest so haunts the Southern imagination: the South is full of unrecognized cast-off sons and daughters who jeopardize the integrity of blood and family.

We're not quite done, though, because what Mr. Compson flees from – into the conclusion that "that's it: [the facts] dont explain and we are not supposed to know" (p. 80) – is an even more shattering truth, one he already knows but acts as if he does not. If we look closely at Mr. Compson's words above, we may notice they betray the inescapable conclusion that Charles must be something other than just Sutpen's firstborn child. Once you figure out that Sutpen fathered a son whom he immediately repudiated, you have to come up with a reason for a parent to act so heartlessly. Compson notes that Sutpen might have "acquiesced" to the "mistake" he made, so whatever is objectionable must be all but undetectable. To a man set on redeeming his scorned white ancestors, avenging a racial slight, and establishing a dynasty of heirs "riven free of brutehood," what is the only condition that could disqualify a son from being instrumental to that design – other than a compromising of the very basis of superiority Sutpen means to claim? Sutpen might have accepted his son's ostensible whiteness (even as an adult Bon passes for white), but the *suspicion* of "black blood" itself proves to be decisive, however much of a chimera race proves to be. The pattern repeats once Sutpen sets up in Jefferson: he fathers a daughter by a slave woman but would never think of acknowledging Clytie as a blood relative, and seems surrounded by other tokens of unbridled paternity, including his driver, Sutpen's "face exactly like the negro's save for the teeth" – a connection under-scored by the description of his two legitimate white children bearing "two replicas of his face in miniature" (p. 16). So, as it's not the bigamy, it's also not the incest. It's the miscegenation. (Ironically, Sutpen cannot oppose this threat as the incest it actually would be, since for him to recognize Bon as his son would be to recognize a black man as his son, a concession that would ruin the racial revenge and class aspiration behind his design.) Mr. Compson knows a wrong has been done: a brother human being has been reduced to the subhuman "negro." He knows, but he's not telling. That's the way the plantation South worked.

Quentin and Shreve base their explanation of the Sutpen catastrophe on their explicit speculation that Bon must have been Sutpen's first child, repudiated for bearing the unrevealed African ancestry of his Haitian mother, the son later returning to seek recognition from, if not revenge upon, the monster capable of treating him with such insult. The climax of their narration comes when they imagine a scene during the war in which Colonel Sutpen calls his son Henry to his tent, finally to reveal that Charles possesses African ancestry. *"So it's the miscegenation, not the incest which you can't bear"* (p. 285), Charles sneers at Henry when his friend reports what he's found out and announces that he must now oppose the marriage he'd earlier accepted. Quentin hints that this knowledge eventually comes to him from the dying Henry Sutpen, whom he questions when he accompanies Miss Rosa to the mansion. But Bon's ancestry – both as Sutpen's son and as a negro – seems to be a kind of unacknowledged realization haunting all the accounts. Even Rosa may know more than she lets on. When she refers to Henry as "a murderer and almost a fratricide" (p. 10), she's pointing to the obvious closeness of the two college friends, but the word "fratricide" strikes unnervingly close to the aura of incest among the Sutpen children and the new suitor, and incest strikes unnervingly close to Mr. Compson's question of why a brother born is a brother no more. And what more might lurk in the ambiguity of Rosa's characterization of Sutpen as having "created two children not only to destroy one another and his own line, but my line as well" (p. 12). Judith and Henry are the two children Rosa knows about, but they don't exactly destroy each other. Henry and Charles are certainly two who destroy each other, but they haven't both been acknowledged as children of the same father.

Arriving at Harvard already depressed by the doom overshadowing his family, Quentin no doubt offers up some pretty lugubrious tales when he's goaded by his new Northern friends to tell them what the South is like. As he gets ready for college, he spends a long day listening to Rosa's histrionic denunciation of the world Quentin's people have made, then suffers through his father's morbidly sardonic chaser, in which the great families of the South rise and fall through the same cycles of hubris, fatal flaws, and ruination as their mythical predecessors in Greek tragedy and Biblical saga: Agamemnon and Orestes, David and Absalom, Sutpen and Henry. It is no wonder that Mr. Compson cautions his son that he will have to listen to Southern ladies like Rosa being ghosts because Southern gentlemen made them into ladies, and then the war made the ladies into ghosts. It's a sober narrator who describes Quentin as a schizophrenic son of the South:

"two separate Quentins now talking to one another in the long silence of notpeople in notlanguage" – the one Quentin "preparing for Harvard in the South, the deep South dead since 1865," and "the Quentin Compson who was still too young to deserve yet to be a ghost but nevertheless having to be one for all that, since he was born and bred in the deep South the same as [Miss Coldfield] was" (p. 4). Quentin: one of the living in a ghostly South, or a ghostly Southerner in a living North – the difference hardly matters; Quentin's a dead man talking. A freshman who's been sent off with his father's observation that "the field only reveals to man his own folly and despair, and victory is an illusion of philosophers and fools" (*The Sound and the Fury*, p. 48), might be forgiven for acting catatonic most of the time.

In the dead of winter a letter from Mr. Compson arrives informing Quentin of Miss Rosa Coldfield's death. Leaping into a story he's evidently heard numerous times from his peculiar roommate, Shreve immediately begins retelling what has happened the last time Quentin saw Miss Rosa, the evening in September they rode to Sutpen's Hundred together. Quentin plainly does not want to play, "his face quiet, reposed, curiously almost sullen" as Shreve caricatures his "Aunt" Rosa, "this old dame that grew up in a household like an overpopulated mausoleum" (*Absalom, Absalom!*, p. 144). The South as Gothic House of Horrors has already gotten old for Quentin, but Shreve zeroes in on Sutpen's insulting proposition to Rosa and develops a head of steam that will carry him through a long night of breathless storytelling. Quentin reluctantly capitulates to Shreve's requests for confirmation, information, and correction. Shreve has learned that insult is the nerve of the plantation South: he begins with Sutpen's "outrage and affront" to Rosa (p. 145), follows the ripple to Sutpen's callous insult of Milly Jones, and on to the still-incredulous Wash's reciprocal counter-insult to Sutpen's divine aura: "I'm going to tech you, Kernel," he says, as he slices his fallen idol's neck with a scythe (p. 151). Where does all this affront and retaliation come from? Quentin and Shreve take up a segment of the story we haven't heard much about: Sutpen's origins.

Shreve owes all his knowledge to his roommate, of course, while Quentin seems to have gotten most of what he knows about the early Sutpen from his grandfather, General Compson, who befriends the newcomer when he shows up in Jefferson around 1833, and who periodically provides legal advice to him. Sutpen is reported to have related significant portions of his life story to General Compson on at least two occasions: once when the two of them are out for days on the trail of Sutpen's architect, who is fleeing his madman employer, and the other when Sutpen is trying to solve the unspecified problem around Judith's marriage that threatens to destroy the planter's design.

Quentin and Shreve trace Sutpen's magnificent obsession to a traumatic moment in his youth. After spending his childhood in a roughly egalitarian Appalachian hamlet, Sutpen "falls" with his family back into the rich plantation society of Tidewater Virginia around the time his mother dies. The Sutpens find employment as field hands. The inexperienced child Thomas misreads his status on the plantation, figuring that the white workers' slight advantage over African slaves equates to general racial superiority. Sent to deliver a message to the plantation master Pettibone, however, Sutpen makes the mistake of knocking on the mansion's front door, at which a black butler imperiously sends him around to the back. Thomas recoils in total confusion, blasted with humiliation, and retreats to a wombish tangle of uptorn roots where he can sort through what's happened. He re-emerges realizing that "the monkey nigger" (p. 189) at the door is not the problem; rather, it is the plantation master whose view of poor whites he has misunderstood. To Pettibone, Sutpen realizes with burning shame, he and his kind are nothing but "cattle, creatures heavy and without grace, brutely evacuated into a world without hope or purpose for them, who would in turn spawn with brutish and vicious prolixity" (p. 190). At first Sutpen gets no further than the reflex desire to *become* the one powerful enough to insult. But soon he realizes that what he really wishes to be able to do is "take that boy in where he would never again need to stand on the outside of a white door and knock at it" (p. 210). He wants to redeem even the "descendants who might not even ever hear his [the boy's] name" so that they would be "riven forever free from brutehood just as his own [Sutpen's] children" would be (*idem*). Recall that "brute" is the key word for Rosa as she seeks to differentiate herself from those who are exactly like her, and we see that Sutpen's "design" stems from the contradictory impulse to convert insult into redemption by reproducing further scenes of inclusion and exclusion. It's not surprising that the passage about ripple-effect follows this one about getting riven of brutehood, since the "nub of the insult" in the South has to do with who gets to reduce whom to brutehood.

The narrator speculates that the Sutpen family may actually be returning to its Tidewater beginnings, after attempting to move westward. In that case, "the first Sutpen had come . . . when the ship from the Old Bailey reached Jamestown probably" (p. 180) – that is, the first Sutpen arrived as a criminal, to join waves of other debtors and indentured servants. Such temporary debt slaves in fact did form the first contingent of coerced labor in US colonies; only when indentured servants began gaining their freedom and swelling the ranks of freed whites did planters decide to replace them with the sort of laborers who could be kept in permanent subjection: African chattel slaves. The insult Sutpen suffers at the hands of Pettibone's black domestic slave, then, rebounds from the stone of debt enslavement structuring Deep South colonial plantation agriculture. In probing the rotten foundations of New World design, Faulkner discovers layer after layer of insult, of "oppression and exploitation."

As Faulkner excavates the US South's planter society, he allows Quentin and Shreve to turn Sutpen into a recapitulation of its entire history. Having learned that he'll never be much more than a clod of white dirt in the established squirearchy of Tidewater Virginia, the young Thomas Sutpen leaves the old colony to start over in the West Indies. A schoolteacher has told him that's where "poor men went in ships and became rich" (p. 195). Sutpen gets a job as the overseer of a sugar plantation run by what he assumes, given his light education in Caribbean history, are "French" planters. Sutpen makes his mark during an insurrection by black field workers, and the young man is rewarded with the planter's daughter and the expectation of a future in sugar. Except, of course, that when his wife presents him with their first child, Sutpen recoils from something that seems to matter only to him. Sutpen believes his father-in-law has kept secret the one piece of information that would matter most – presumably that the family has African mixed into their French ancestry – and he promptly makes arrangements to divorce the woman and leave the island.

There's a problem with the historical chronology of this episode, however, since Sutpen, born in 1807, leaves Virginia around 1820, marries in Haiti in 1827, and fathers Charles in 1831. By 1833 he has arrived in Jefferson, Mississippi, to start over in cotton. Puzzlingly,

Sutpen seems to experience events that could not have happened as he thinks they have if he is indeed in Haiti during the 1820s. By 1804, the western half of the whole island of Hispaniola had undergone a revolution led by mixed-race insurgents, most of them merchants and smaller plantation owners seeking citizens' rights under the new spirit of the French Revolution emanating from the empire's metropolis in Paris. After a decade of bloody revolt, military suppression (in one phase by Napoleon's forces), and secondary rebellions by fuller-blooded African slaves (the *noirs,* as opposed to the hybrid *jaunes* [French for "yellow"]), Haiti became the first free black republic in the New World. This outcome terrified planters of the US South, who feared the spread of slave revolt throughout the plantation world. But the anachronism of Sutpen's story remains to be dealt with. Perhaps Sutpen, telling the story to his fellow planter Compson, exhibits the sense of panic that made this first revolution seem perpetually immi- nent, a kind of live volcano that might erupt anywhere again. Or perhaps Sutpen's "mistake" represents the inability of the planter class ever to recognize the emancipation of slaves, a symptom of masterly denial. Associating Haiti with racial turmoil might also reflect unrest on the island contemporary with the novel's appearance, which involved US military occupation during the 1920s to safeguard Ameri- can financial interests and the native elite who profited from them. Haiti gets projected as an emblem of "the negro problem" in the US at a time when African Americans were agitating for long-deferred politi- cal and economic rights, and when the Caribbean was becoming a source of inspiration for New Negro political and cultural solidarities. Surely all of these senses resonate in Sutpen's putting down what he takes to be a slave rebellion in a republic that had already enacted emancipation.

On the other hand, it is just as likely that the events as described are the products of Sutpen's ignorance. He may never have heard of the revolution on Haiti; it wouldn't be in his schoolbooks, and wouldn't immediately reach field workers and sailors. Instead, what Sutpen may have encountered on Haiti was one of the many local revolts by members of the *noir* laborers, who, in fact, after the establishment of the republic, had been returned to a kind of servitude by their mixed- race governors in an attempt to restore the country's ruined economy. After the last French planters had fled (many others having been slaughtered), the *jaunes* filled vacancies in the planter stratum. Sutpen may have stumbled into a family that would never think to mention their black ancestry, since anyone of French descent left in Haiti after 1804 would also have to be of color; what Sutpen's father-in-law does mention is that his wife has some Spanish blood. As a result of his lack of interest in history, Sutpen construes the sugar planter's omission as a deliberate insult: "I was faced with condoning a fact which had been foisted upon me without my knowledge during the process of building toward my design, which meant the absolute and irrevocable negation of the design" (p. 219). Needless to say, Sutpen feels no compunction about passing along that insult to the wife and child he spurns.

My point in exploring the famous central anachronism of *Absalom* involves seeing how completely it illustrates a refusal to act upon knowledge that is already possessed. However we interpret Sutpen's missteps, they were as avoidable as the whole colonial enterprise they represent. He might have known better. The abuse of others – the rampant reduction of human beings to instruments or commodities – constitutes the willful insult required by New World settlement. Faulkner traces the ripples without identifying any single original stone. It's as if what is responsible for the effect of insult is less a given act than a condition, a mentality. Faulkner ties the abusive treatment of individuals to an epistemology, the very way we process reality and arrive at conceptions. For him, as for many other moderns, the project of European colonialism, the surge of capitalism, the spread of slavery and racism, the rise of violent nationalisms, the eventual birth of modern fascistic states, all stemmed from an excessive devotion to abstract reason. Whatever the progressive legacy of the Enlightenment – such as the concepts of radical equality, individualism, and personal freedom so honored in the West, and by Faulkner as well – slavish obedience to abstraction also desensitizes people to the claims of particular experience, logical contradiction, categorical mixture, the uniqueness of living bodies. Faulkner makes Sutpen an example of this mentality as he links him to a cold, unfeeling "logic and morality" (p. 224, *passim*): as the planter patiently explains to Grandfather Compson's legally trained mind, there must be a tactical error in the design that now threatens to cancel itself, if only he can find it in "that picayune splitting of abstract hairs" (p. 218). It's the madness of reason that sustains the unnatural fantasy of property, whether of land or other humans; the mountain boy is shocked when he first glimpses "a country all divided and fixed and neat with a people living on it all divided and fixed and neat because of what color their skins happened to be and what they happened to own" (p. 179). Against the delusional mathematics that categorize an "eighth part negro mistress and the sixteenth part negro son" (p. 80), for example, recall how Rosa once admits what she has been trained to deny: "let flesh touch with flesh, and watch the fall of all the eggshell shibboleth of caste and color too" (p. 112).

The austerity of abstraction leads Sutpen to talk about his life as if it belonged to someone else. (In fact, when he does tell his own story to Grandfather Compson, his auditor notices how he doesn't seem to be talking about himself, just someone named Thomas Sutpen.) He explains bloodlessly that "to accomplish [his design] I should require money, a house, a plantation, slaves, a family – incidentally of course, a wife" (p. 212). If you refer to your wife as an incidental part of a plan, you're already in big trouble. When he needs to get rid of her, Sutpen explains to Compson, he "found that she was not and could never be, through no fault of her own, adjunctive or incremental to the design which I had in mind" (p. 194). Shreve finds Sutpen hilarious here, and no doubt exaggerates the "bombastic phrases" he guesses would have characterized Sutpen's stilted manner of speech.

Yet it is true that Sutpen leads his life as if he were following a script someone handed him just before show time. Shreve picks up on that, too, noticing how awkwardly Sutpen does everything demanded of him by his ambition, still with his "innocence" "intact," the clumsiest plantation grandee you ever saw. In fact, Sutpen's naïvete matters a great deal to what Faulkner is attempting in *Absalom*. Sutpen functions as something of a fool, a buffoonish, if also lethal, maladroit who ends up tripping into the draperies and exposing the South's suspect machinery. It's difficult to think of a single step in his climb to becoming the county's biggest plantation master that he doesn't do badly. He blows into town like a gunslinger from nowhere; humiliates himself by hanging out at the tavern without having enough cash to buy drinks; gets half a house built then disappears, having drawn the town citizen of greatest probity into a deal so smarmy the tightfisted merchant withdraws at a loss; returns with what looks like a whole steamboat full of loot with "stolen property" practically stamped on it (did I mention a band of feral slaves?); extracts a marriage agreement from his shamed ex-partner, who then has to bail him out of jail when the town spits the bit of his outrageous larceny; insists on a church wedding ceremony that degenerates into a public scene of garbage-throwing; mistreats his wife, withdraws from family obligations, behaves with maximum rudeness, wrestles in a filthy barn pit with slaves to remind them who's boss; turns tail on his own Civil War company after they vote him out of his colonelship; returns from the war to mortify his sister-in-law, barrel over his daughter and her half-sister servant, seduce an ignorant teenager, insult his loyal retainer, and, in a curtain call, tumble out of his own casket on the way to the cemetery. My God, this is not *Southern Living*.

Cleanth Brooks, a prominent literary critic who wrote early influential studies of Faulkner, and was himself a genteel Southerner, found Faulkner's caricature of the Old South so objectionable that he wanted to give Sutpen back – to the obvious place such an offensive person had to have come from: Sutpen is really a Northern Yankee, Brooks decided.[2] Take away Brooks's Southern partisanship, though, and we might use his observation to isolate a key feature of Sutpen's significance. Sutpen is an outsider who wants in. What everyone finds unforgivable about Sutpen's rollerballing through Jefferson is that he's indiscreet; he does and says openly the things everyone else has had to do or say behind the scenes, long ago, elsewhere. He's a little like Jay Gatsby, who follows the guidelines of the American Dream so exaggeratedly that he reveals all that's corrupt at its core. Sutpen's offense is speaking aloud the unspeakable. In order for a collective fantasy to work, you can't have someone walking around rehearsing in front of the audience, muffing lines, and declaiming the stage directions. The effect of Sutpen's unpracticed performance is to lay bare the complicity in "oppression and exploitation" of those who hide behind discretion, as if excused from responsibility for the South's more egregious sins. Sutpen's loud, awkward execution of Southern formulas calls attention to their crudeness and violence. Sutpen disrupts the tactful silence that passes for innocence. And in so doing he not only puts on trial the rest of his community, he also invites the rest of the continent to wonder what its relation is and has been to a Deep South plantation world from which it drew mutual nourishment. It is no wonder that the Canadian Shreve and the Mississippian Quentin are described as joined by the great North American "umbilical" river that runs down the Continental Trough (p. 208).

The narratives that make their way to us also count as ripples from a stone dropped long ago. Faulkner understands the past always to be sounding in the present. At its most oppressive, the burden of history threatens to overwhelm Southerners: Quentin, for example, whose "very body was an empty hall echoing with sonorous defeated names; he was not a being, an entity, he was a commonwealth. He was a barracks filled with stubborn back-looking ghosts" (p. 7). But the voices that finally erupt in *Absalom* share a determination to talk back to those defeated ghosts, to protest their own fates as ghosts, to confront the reasons for the Old South's failure. Both the structure and style of the novel reinforce how difficult it is to create counter-narratives to a society's dominant myths. Rosa indulges an hysterical tirade against her oppressors, even as she betrays a deep investment in their purposes. Her rhetoric bristles with self-defense, often employing the language of the courtroom to try to prove her innocence. The breathless sentences ride on rage, even as they are extended by ambivalence and indecisiveness. Mr. Compson's wryly cool version of Sutpen's follies subjects the whole project of the Old South to corrosive irony. Compson wants to discredit the South's fetishization of virginity, purity of blood, honor, and shame not only because he knows such values are going to be worthless in a post-Southern modern world, but also because he's worried they're going to cost his son his life. It is to the suicidal Quentin that Mr. Compson directs his stories of how Southern families sidestep incestuous narcissism, for example, by taking in strangers like Bon, or how Judith rejects the idea of killing herself over lost love. Quentin and Shreve, though they once attain a "happy marriage of speaking and hearing," ultimately fail to create anything new in their rendition of the fall of the house of Sutpen. All the stories vivify the participants and make us feel how these are individual human beings who have suffered incalculably from the senseless ways some people force others to be and behave simply because they have the power to do so. But when Shreve and Quentin solve the puzzle of Southern history, they end up in the same old cul de sac of racial obsession: as the child of Jim Crow, Quentin informs Shreve with the dread of racial degeneration through "miscegenation." Sutpen's last descendant, his mixed-race, mentally defective great-grandson through Bon, turns out to be the fulfillment-as-destruction of the great planter's design: "One nigger Sutpen left." And that, according to Shreve's cavalier mockery, is the destiny that awaits "us" all: "I who regard you will also have sprung from the loins of African kings" (p. 302). Here's the old insult come home to roost, the appearance of the long suspected "nigger in the woodpile somewhere" (p. 56). "Why do you hate the South?" Shreve taunts. "I don't hate it he thought, panting in the cold air, the iron New England dark: I don't. I don't! I don't hate it! I don't hate it!" (p. 302). Faulkner leaves Quentin dead-ended in Southern denial.

The main protagonist of *Go Down, Moses* (1942), Faulkner's cycle of short stories about another plantation family, occupies a position similar to Quentin Compson's in *Absalom, Absalom!* Isaac McCaslin also confronts a nightmarish tangle of "moral brigandage" and insult at the bedrock of the Old South, only his personal anguish may be even more intense than Quentin's since what he uncovers is the morally repugnant behavior of his own grandfather. Faulkner clearly conceived of these stories involving a young man's "straddling" the shrinking wilderness, on the one side, and advancing commercial development, on the other, as another dimension of Quentin Compson's struggle with his Southern heritage under the pressure of modern change. Perhaps Faulkner's best known story, "The Bear," recounts Isaac (Ike) McCaslin's efforts to honor the ethos of Native American regard for the land, in opposition to the mounting encroachments of timber, railroad, and agricultural enterprises. When Faulkner published a preliminary version of the story in 1931, as "Lion," the protagonist was Quentin Compson and the interlocutor of his hunting experiences his father. Faulkner rewrote the story for *Go Down, Moses*, converting the two principals to Ike and his older cousin Cass, but the question of a conflict between the legacies of wilderness and plantation remains central.

Like his predecessor, Ike, too, shoulders unwanted knowledge of ancient dishonor and the shame it continues to create. And, also like Quentin, Ike seems to come into possession of such truth through a devastating initiation – a moment that apparently shocks him with the unsuspected enormity of his own past, and forces a long-deferred confrontation with the horrors of plantation history. Yet as we see throughout *Absalom*, the secret to be revealed is actually already known, however much held at bay by disavowal. Faulkner intensifies his probing of Southern foundations exactly at the nub of insult he has identified in his earlier plantation novel. When Charles Bon insists that Henry admit it's the miscegenation and not the incest he objects to, Faulkner not only exposes the racism at the heart of Southern family and community, he also confirms the aptness of incest as a metaphor for the racial and class narcissism of the plantation elite. Under this logic, incest and miscegenation limit desire as polar opposites: love of the same versus love of the other. In *Go Down, Moses*, Faulkner pursues the knotty relation between these forms of sexual and racial transgression to arrive at an even more powerful insight: that both incest and miscegenation are secondary manifestations of a more fundamental social deformity. In poring through the ledgers that have been kept by his family of planters, Ike "discovers" that his grandfather not only fathered a child by one of his slave women, but that he also in turn fathered a child upon that very daughter. That Carothers McCaslin commits both incest and miscegenation in this single act of "boundless conceiving" (*Go Down, Moses*, p. 251) seals the doom of the plantation ethos for Ike.

But the issue that ripples through the seven stories of Faulkner's cracked-up plantation novel in *Go Down, Moses* involves less the vile acts of sexual violation performed by the planter, than the rights of property such acts presume. That is, the notion that any portion of nature – a human body or a piece of wilderness – might be brought under title, and become subject to rights of use, purchase, and sale, and even destruction, ultimately beggars Ike's moral imagination. From this standpoint, incest and miscegenation become less the opposing poles of blood purity that they are for the Sutpens, and more equivalent kinds of transgressive possession.

Ike begins his descent into the planter past as a student of his family's historical record. As a sixteen-year-old, newly initiated by his mentor Sam Fathers into the spiritual brotherhood of those who hunt the big woods with "reverence for the blood they spill," Ike finds himself examining the shelf of bound volumes in the plantation commissary that

> probably contained a chronological and much more comprehensive though doubtless tedious record than he would ever get from any other source, not alone of his own flesh and blood but of all his people, not only the whites but the black ones too, who were as much a part of his ancestry as his white progenitors, and of the land which they had all

held and used in common and fed from and on and would continue
to use in common without regard to color or titular ownership.
(p. 256)

Ike is thinking this in the early 1880s; much of his ideal about black
and white common ancestry and use of the land will prove to be a
cruel delusion historically, after the onset of Jim Crow and the systematic expropriation of black landowners, and the commercial takeover of large white family plantations. As the teenaged Ike picks
through the cryptic entries made by his father and uncle, Buck and
Buddy McCaslin, he lingers over something that seems to have
puzzled him before. One entry of fifty years earlier reads: "June
21th 1833 Drownd herself" (*idem*). The report of suicide pertains to a
slave woman owned by Lucius Quintus Carothers McCaslin, the infamous "old Carothers," who founds the plantation dynasty that ends
with his grandson Ike. Eunice evidently kills herself the same month
her unwed daughter gives birth to a son named Turl. The ledgers
record a bequest of $1,000 to this boy from old Carothers at his death,
without explanation: just "Father's will" (p. 257). Ike takes these fragments and pieces together the only explanation that makes sense:
Eunice must take her life because she discovers old Carothers has
forced himself on their own daughter, Tomasina. Child of incest and
miscegenation, Turl embodies the unspoken barbarity of racial chattel
slavery.[3]

Ike notices how his planter ancestors habitually evade the recognition of such outrages. His father and uncle refuse to "discuss" the
curiosity of a slave suicide, and fail to register the blatant admission of
paternity represented by their father's bequest to Turl. In the pages of
the ledger, the twins communicate with each other, but also with the
future. Their cryptic style serves as an emblem of the way they
simultaneously record what they know but disfigure it so it may be
ignored. Both suppression, as practiced by Buck and Buddy, and open
denial, as performed by old Carothers, attempt to manage unwanted
knowledge. Buck and Buddy react to the unacknowledged sins of the
father by becoming opponents of slavery (albeit of the slave-owning
sort). But their solution to a contradictory predicament depends
mainly on evasiveness. They decide to exchange domiciles with
their slaves, for example, putting the chattel in the big house and
living in a slave cabin themselves; they allow their slaves to roam free

every night, so long as they return to their places behind the locked front door each morning. Such a charade maintains the ambivalence of their compromised lot, and illustrates the desperate measures resorted to by those who know wrong yet act in disavowal of that knowledge.

Over the course of the scene in the commissary related in "The Bear," Ike seems to come into possession of the definitive truth about why Eunice kills herself and why old Carothers includes Turl in his will. But in fact Ike's inference seems more like a creeping confirmation of a long-held suspicion than a new "ah-ha" moment of enlightenment. It's not clear when Ike has begun reading the ledgers. At sixteen "[i]t was neither the first time he had been alone in the commissary nor the first time he had taken down the old ledgers familiar on their shelf above the desk ever since he could remember" (p. 256). When he stops at the entry about Eunice, Ike is already "finding, beginning to find on the next succeeding page what he knew he would find, only this was still not it because he already knew this" (p. 257). At some point he draws the conclusion that Tomasina is old Carothers's "own daughter," and that Eunice has figured out that the infant is "her daughter's and her lover's (*Her first lover's* he thought. *Her first.*)" (p. 259). Yet the insistence on Ike's familiarity with the puzzle suggests that Ike "already knew" what he is about to find out. That is, though we see Ike patiently working through the evidence of garbled inscriptions in the ledgers and what he's heard from other sources (and even observed, as in the case of Turl's unusually light complexion), Ike solves a mystery that is already known by the community to be part of its unmentionable past; the yellowed pages of the ledgers with their now avowed truth are said to be "as much a part of his consciousness and would remain so forever, as the fact of his nativity" (*idem*). Ike is born *into* a knowledge that possesses him before he possesses it; initiations involve acknowledging what you already know. And even when he finally does admit the truth to himself, moreover, he cannot entirely free it of the customary denial that neutralizes such recognitions: "His own daughter His own daughter. No No Not even him" (*idem*).

Faulkner initiates the reader into the tragicomedy of Southern evasion in the first story of *Go Down, Moses*, "Was," which tells how Ike's parents come to marry. Faulkner frames the tale by introducing its teller as Ike's older cousin, Cass McCaslin, who as a child participates in the outlandish escapade that leads to Ike's eventual father, Buck, getting snared by his future wife, Sophonsiba Beauchamp, who lives on a neighboring plantation and has long had her eye on the shy bachelor. Since Ike is born into his father's old age, he needs Cass's help in reconstructing the circumstances of his remote family history. The story's frame delineates the characters of Cass and Ike by contrasting their relation to what will become the master theme of the novel: property. Cass, descended from old Carothers through his mother, the planter's daughter, ends up the "inheritor, and in his time the bequestor" of the patrimonial land and fortune. Ike, though a lineal male descendant of the founder, has renounced his birthright; he "owned no property and never desired to since the earth was no man's but all men's" (p. 4).

Ike's outright refusal to accept the fruit of an unjust economic and social system culminates his predecessors' reluctance to perpetuate the bogus world into which they have been born. Old Carothers McCaslin's sons want nothing so much as to escape their ordained roles as plantation masters and slave owners. "Was" recounts a semi-annual ritual in which one of their male slaves sneaks off to romance a young woman on the Beauchamp plantation. Buck methodically hunts down Turl, typically visiting with his friend Hubert for a few hours while fending off the romantic wiles of Hubert's sister, Sophonsiba, then returning home with the escapee before much damage is done. On the occasion of this story, however, things grow stickier, and what has formerly been practiced as an idle exercise in preserving the status quo produces ostensibly unwelcome resolutions of several sorts. Buck and Buddy (named Theophilus and Amodeus by their father) appear to be determined to bring the ancestral line to a close; they bachelor up in that slave cabin, and attempt to curtail the love life of Tomey's Turl – who, we realize, is not just a McCaslin slave, but a McCaslin: that very child of Tomasina, hence both the son and grandson of old Carothers, and hence the half-brother of Buck and Buddy. Moreover, as the abolitionist twins find themselves already enslaved by slavery (they "had so many niggers already that they could hardly walk around on their own land for them," Cass jokes crudely [p. 6]), they resolve to acquire no more. They don't want to buy Turl's beloved Tennie from Beauchamp; in fact, they try to rid themselves of the slaves they already own, offering to let them pay for their freedom in labor amounting to their market value.

Faulkner's story proves a riotous exposé of planter equivocation. On the one hand, no one involved in mastering, maintaining, or passing down a plantation seems to have his heart in it. The episode takes place in 1859, on the eve of the Civil War, and there's a sense of futility in the tracking down of fugitive slaves and the arranging of antebellum planter weddings. If the *three* brothers were to remain childless, the ripples of original incest and miscegenation would subside. Perhaps even more importantly, old Carothers's primal sin against the land might be expunged as well. In "The Bear" Ike thinks that his grandfather's folly has been the flaw of the entire South: Ike rues

> the tamed land which was to have been his heritage, the land which old Carothers McCaslin his grandfather had bought with white man's money from the wild men whose grandfathers without guns hunted it, and tamed and ordered or believed he had tamed and ordered it for the reason that the human beings he held in bondage and in the power of life and death had removed the forest from it and in their sweat scratched the surface of it to a depth of perhaps fourteen inches in order to grow something out of it which had not been there before and which could be translated back into the money he who believed he had bought it had had to pay to get it and hold it and a reasonable profit too . . . (p. 244)

The excesses of property coincide here: landholding, slave-owning, profit economies. In "Was" the McCaslin heirs begin the process of divestiture that their son Ike will complete.

But if everyone seems to know better, that doesn't stop them from acting as if they don't. Although Buck lets it be known he wants nothing to do with women in general and Sophonsiba in particular, he prepares for his visits to the Beauchamps like a man going courting, donning a necktie he wears for no other occasion. He flirts with more risks than he should, too. Everyone knows Buddy is the one who should go since Sophonsiba has no interest in him, and Buck makes so many willful errors in tracking down Turl and then misreading the bedroom arrangements in the Beauchamp house, once his dallying forces him and his nephew to stay the night, that we might wonder how much romantic ambivalence hides in the term "footdragging" used to describe his awkward bows to his guileful hostess. My point is that although Buck *claims* he wants to avoid marriage, he does everything he can to put himself in harm's way. Similarly, although the twins want to dispose of Turl as a troublesome possession – by fobbing him off on Hubert – they treat him ambivalently as the human relative he actually is, looking the other way each time he escapes and only pretending to hunt him as a fugitive slave.

The whole system lurches into its next phase of reproduction, in fact, by the end of the story. Faulkner changed the title of the manuscript version from "Almost" to "Was" for good reason. When Sophonsiba "tricks" Buck into mistakenly bedding down with her, thereby compromising her honor, the disputing parties turn to a game of poker to settle the score. The game is notoriously difficult to follow (Faulkner himself couldn't recall the details some years later when he was asked about it). But the gist is entirely clear: Buck tries to wager his way out of marrying Sophonsiba; Hubert gains the upper hand and adds the question of Turl's ownership to the pot; Buck gets deeper in trouble, then calls in the expert Buddy to help out. The game ends when the players leave the last hand "uncalled," Hubert to take Tennie, Buck to make good on his obligation to Sophonsiba's virtue. The narratives end in two portended marriages: the one between Buck McCaslin and Sophonsiba Beauchamp will produce Ike; Tennie and Turl's will produce several children, including a son named Lucas, who will figure in the modern saga of the McCaslin family. Both marriages will perpetuate a defunct system that survives in part because its participants remain half-willing to play on.

In the poker match, as the bidding grows more complex, the stakes higher, Buddy and Hubert experience an odd moment of stoppage: "For a minute it was like he and Uncle Buddy had both gone to sleep" (p. 27). The incident captures the element of forgetfulness or unmindfulness at the core of all social systems. Ideologies work by enveloping you in a fantasy of justified relations to what is real. Such fantasies require a disavowal of knowledge that would contradict them. But at certain odd times – particularly at moments of crisis or failure, as, here, a Southern slave-owning plantation elite sensed in 1859 – the habit of disavowal grows awkwardly noticeable.

The whole story spotlights the ambivalence of playing along with ruses you know not to be true anymore, if they ever were. The characters all get caught up in relations to reality like the sort fostered by

Sophonsiba, whose devotion to the cavalier ideal leads her to refer to the broken-down Beauchamp place as "Warwick," as if it were an English country manor. Her fantasy creates the impression that "she and Mr Hubert owned two separate plantations covering the same area of ground, one on top of the other" (p. 9). Ignoring such discrepancies, the South marched on, knowing full well that it couldn't continue to treat men like caged animals, to hunt them down like quarry and trade them like chips, to use women like "spittoon[s]" (p. 258), or to desecrate the land you love. Caught in the vortex of their game's increasingly "serious foolishness" (p. 23), many Southerners longed for the outcome to be taken out of their hands, even as they wouldn't take responsibility for ending play: "I pass" (p. 28).

If the later white McCaslins wish to dispossess themselves of ill-gotten gain, "black" McCaslins like Tennie and Tomey Turl's children demand entitlement in the very system that refused them for so long. Lucas Beauchamp, Tennie and Turl's youngest surviving child, emerges as a brilliant improviser of problems for a plantation regime that has already outlived itself. Lucas stands as the most deeply imagined black person in Faulkner's fiction; he will reappear as the protagonist of the novel *Intruder in the Dust* in 1948. As a person of color in the Jim Crow South, Lucas suffers from being dispossessed of family and community privileges. As a character, he suffers from his author's uneven success in overcoming dominant habits of representation that discount black subjectivity, and in penetrating sensibilities that have learned to protect themselves from masterly intrusion. Beginning in the second story of *Go Down, Moses*, "The Fire and the Hearth," Faulkner attempts to render black experience and mentality, exemplifying the risks, failures, and intermittent breakthroughs that come with all efforts to reverse legacies of insult and denial. Although we witness Dilsey's pain and perseverance, we are left only to infer her feelings and state of mind. In Lucas we learn how a man might reason and react as a world that has resolutely excluded him now threatens to vanish without having recognized his past or provided for his future.

Lucas straddles irresolvable contradictions in his efforts to carve out a life of dignity and self-determination in a place that has forever denied both to him and his kind. Lucas wrestles with a schizoid legacy his whole life. His past talks to him out of both sides of its mouth, the result of his in-between status as a man of mixed race and divided descent negotiating the fissures of colonial plantation society. Now in his late sixties, he continues his lifelong determination to create problems for his would-be masters. At every opportunity, Lucas plays out the illogic of a system that has dispossessed him of name, family, land, patrimony, manhood, racial pride, fortune. Diminished as he has been, he nevertheless looks for every opening to take back some of what has been taken from him. He bids for mastery, autonomy, and the occasional triumph by exposing and exploiting the ambivalence of those who know they rule illegitimately. By 1941, Lucas is dealing with a fifth generation descendant of old Carothers, "Roth" Edmonds, while Lucas himself boasts of being the founder's grandson, if only via the unrecognized "black" line.

Lucas resides on a parcel of land set aside for him at the center of the large plantation, and he values it as "his own field, though he neither owned it nor wanted to nor even needed to" (p. 35). The paradox of possessing your "own" land without owning it thrusts to the tangle at the heart of *Go Down, Moses*: is the land for private property or common provision? Lucas stages the problem by farming the land fitfully, enough to support himself, while also hunting every foot of it. The land is and is not his, just as it was and was not old Carothers's to plant and profit from. As the last of a long line of family planters, Roth tries to make Lucas responsible to the demands of commercial cotton agriculture. Lucas deliberately frustrates such purposes because he rejects their premises, even as he tries to keep them in play long enough to gain from them. The split over how to use the land structures every one of Lucas's enterprises, even the ones that look the most harebrained.

At the outset of "The Fire and the Hearth," Lucas is about to abandon his small-scale (and illegal) moonshine business because he has found a coin in a mound of earth near his still; he's convinced he's discovered a cache of McCaslin valuables, rumored to have been buried for safekeeping during the Civil War. Lucas's gold fever leads to his stealing one of Roth's mules, purchasing a metal detector with the pilfered equity, and finally jeopardizing his marriage of forty-five years as he all but kills himself digging for buried treasure night after night. Lucas's folly might be understood as a kind of "serious foolishness," since at least symbolically what he's after is some token of the original

McCaslin fortune that he can call his own. He wants the land to enrich him as it did the first Carothers – and he acts out both his ancestor-worthy dream as well as his pitiful limitations in the gold-hunting scheme.

The minor skirmishes in which Lucas tries to outwit Roth or score symbolic wins over other rivals descend from more serious confrontations that Lucas recalls setting the temper of his oppositional existence. One long sub-narrative relates Lucas's challenge to Roth's father, Zachary Edmonds, who one day casually instructs Lucas's new wife Molly to move to the big house to care for the recently widowed planter's infant son. Molly has just given birth to her own child, so at a stroke Lucas is deprived of his whole family. Marriage means everything to Lucas and Molly since it represents the one institution of social and even economic stability permitted black people after Reconstruction; the events of the story are set in 1898, the nadir of black dispossession and peril in the Deep South. Eventually, Lucas realizes, he will have to demand that Zack return Molly, so one night he invades Edmonds's bedroom and confronts him physically. When Lucas gains the nerve to fire a pistol at his antagonist as they wrestle across the bed, he realizes that he is reprising the original trauma of the McCaslin house: racial division and violation at the site of sexual reproduction. Lucas experiences his courage as a revivification of old Carothers' manly will ("Old Carothers, he thought. I needed him and he come and spoke for me" (p. 57). To *be* old Carothers is a way to say "I'm a man now. I can do what I want" (p. 105). Yet Lucas also understands that he must reprove old Carothers as well, that the planter's monstrous legacy must be repudiated even as it is remembered. Lucas has thought to kill himself after avenging himself on Zack; now he taunts his cousin with the prospect of another black suicide: "say I just use the last [bullet] and beat you and old Carothers both, leave you something to think about now and then" (p. 56). To *beat* old Carothers and his white sons must also be part of Lucas's contradictory project. Even Roth appreciates what Lucas pulled off in this long ago triumph, and how it must sustain his proud defiance of every successive McCaslin/Edmonds:

> And by God Lucas beat him, he thought. Edmonds, he thought, harshly and viciously. Edmonds. Even a nigger McCaslin is a better man, better than all of us. Old Carothers got his nigger bastards right in his back

yard and I would like to have seen the husband or anybody else that said him nay. – Yes, Lucas beat him, else Lucas wouldn't be here. (p. 112)

Faulkner's regard for Lucas's resilient, stubborn, courageous determination to expose the moral bankruptcy of a society that dispossessed him in the very act of creating him inspires the balance of the deeply troubling stories about black life in *Go Down, Moses*. If you let the novel center on "The Bear," as so many readers do, given that story's monumental grandeur, this fragmentary novel becomes an elegy to the primeval "unaxed" wilderness as it falls to modern use. But if you read the stories sequentially, you realize that the first three establish the priority of racial slavery and plantation culture as the work's dominant concern. I've argued that the connection involves Faulkner's probing behind racial insult to a fundamental economic edifice built on the illegitimacy of property. But soon we'll be in a position to question whether the apparent "destination" of the narrative – the hunting episodes taking place in a wilderness seemingly beyond ownership – might not itself be a last lingering symptom of the Southern denial of plantation slavery. Faulkner's broken saga of a ruined family hinges on the fiction of human property, its elegy not of ruined land but of exterminated people. Lucas mounts a project of counter-possession; the protagonist of "Pantaloon in Black" suffers a catastrophe of dispossession after temporary gain; while the woeful soul of the final story, "Go Down, Moses," proves that it's not just the South but a whole nation that refuses to count black people as enfranchised citizens.

"Pantaloon in Black" has always seemed the anomaly of *Go Down, Moses* since it is the only story whose characters are not related by blood to the vast McCaslin clan, of white and black, male and female descent. In making the issue of relation problematic, however, Faulkner may be questioning the legitimacy of the very concept of *belonging* to Southern family and community – to the extent those institutions are predicated on the violence of exclusion and subordination. Rider is not related to the McCaslins because no black person is really related to them, even one like Lucas who is. The ideology of "blood" stumbles over an exposed contradiction: blood is held to determine race (where it is in fact a fiction) while it is permitted to deny kinship (where it is in fact a fact). By contrast, Rider does belong to the only nexus of relations that ultimately matters in plantation society: he's related economically, leasing a cabin from Roth Edmonds while he works as a wage laborer for a sawmill company. Evidently the orphan of a local family (he retreats to his aunt and uncle when disaster strikes), Rider admires the assertiveness of his neighbor Lucas Beauchamp, and emulates him by building his own "fire on the hearth" in affirmation of the sanctity of his marriage. Rider has had his good time before settling down, but when he meets the ambitious Mannie, he renounces his wastrel past and resolves with her to practice self-discipline, frugality, circumspection. Rider and Mannie represent the sort of "good" negroes like Will Maye in "Dry September" who think they can prosper by conforming to white bourgeois standards. The couple makes a ritual out of payday, reveling in the

> bright cascade of silver dollars onto the scrubbed table in the kitchen where his dinner simmered on the stove and the galvanized tub of hot water and the baking powder can of soft soap and the towel made of scalded flour sacks sewn together and his clean overalls and shirt waited. (p. 134)

The pride in order, cleanliness, thrift, and consumption mark Rider and Mannie as New Negroes in the making. Predictably, such pride also marks them as doomed.

The couple's "problem" has something to do with their going too fast for local racial customs. Rider makes "good money," has been promoted to head of a timber gang, and, thanks to Mannie's careful budgeting and banking, they look to be in sharp ascent. The effects of excessive velocity trouble the narrative: Rider marvels that Mannie is "de onliest least thing whut ever kep up wid me one day, leff alone fo weeks" (p. 135), and even Mannie's ghost moves too quickly: "But she was going. She was going fast now" (p. 136). After Mannie's startling and apparently causeless death, Rider acts out a frenzy of the impatience that has proven lethal to the couple's dreams: "wolfing" down food, gagging on whole jugs of liquor, careering wildly from pillar to post. In a world where black people were told for a century to go slow on their march to freedom and equality, this is one negro who does everything fast. Rider demonstrates his inconsolable grief over all he has lost in Mannie – her person, to be sure, but the whole way of life she embodied as well – by rushing to the sawmill the day after her funeral, seizing the heaviest log anyone's ever lifted, and hurling it ahead of him as he rides the chute for the last time. The gesture inscribes Rider's acceptance of precipitous descent, of abandonment to his mysterious loss, of the infuriating disappearance of a better life so tantalizingly within his grasp.

Rider's refusal to accept his loss quietly draws out the social symbolism of Mannie's death. There's no reason offered for her death; it comes as an unanticipated blow, in much the way the racial violence of Jim Crow surprised its victims. Rider hasn't done anything, or Mannie, or Will Maye, or the other thousands of African Americans who lost their lives to lynching. What Rider does manage to do, in his grief, is to point to the corrupt system responsible for black misfortune and fatality. Rider gets drunk enough to challenge the crooked dice game his white foreman has been running for years, cheating black workers out of their painfully earned and desperately needed pay. Rider seizes the white man's hand to expose a second set of dice, altered so they have what Rider calls "miss-outs," duds that rig a game blacks just can't win. On behalf of all those who miss out, Rider takes a white life to even his losses, then submits to the fate of lynching, his body displayed for public edification in the "negro schoolhouse" by the avenging relatives of the murdered foreman.

The power of continued denial prevents stories like Rider's from unduly bothering modern white Southerners. The deputy sheriff tries to entertain his wife with this amusing, if puzzling, story about a mammoth negro who doesn't even take a holiday after his wife's burial, waits fifteen years to call out the boss man for cheating, then goes crazy in his jail cell as he tosses the vigilantes one by one into a pile before succumbing to his mob murder. The deputy won't admit that he's curious about what must be torturing Rider; he begins from the premise that "[t]hem damn niggers . . . aint human" (p. 149). And his story falls on deaf ears, his wife interested only in finishing dinner and getting to the movies. But if his wife evinces total indifference, the deputy betrays a waver of uncertainty that maybe the fallen giant isn't just the insensate beast he's taken as. Rider's perplexing last words draw an unexpected eloquence, and perhaps some thoughtfulness, from this ostensible defender of Southern justice: Rider weeping with tears big as glass marbles running across his face and down past his ears and making a kind of popping sound on the floor like somebody dropping bird eggs, laughing and laughing and saying, "Hit look lack Ah just cant quit thinking. Look lack Ah just cant quit." And what do you think of that? (p. 154)

The story of a black man's anguished dispossession lies unexplained – but not inexplicable – at the center of Faulkner's anti-plantation masterpiece.

Rider can't win no matter how scrupulously he plays the white man's game. His execution prefigures the death sentence enacted upon the protagonist of the title story of the novel, Samuel "Butch" Beauchamp, Lucas and Molly Beauchamp's grandson. Like Rider, Butch runs afoul of the law, but Faulkner suggests how the law always is gamed by race in the South, if not the nation at large. When the adolescent gets caught breaking into the plantation commissary, Roth Edmonds immediately bans him from his home and exiles him to Jefferson. Before long Butch has fled Mississippi for Chicago, where he expunges the marks of his origins and outlandishly attempts to possess himself of the American Dream. He learns to talk in "a voice which was anything under the sun but a southern voice or even a negro voice" (p. 351), dresses in "fine Hollywood clothes" (p. 352), and reports that his occupation is "[g]etting rich too fast" (*idem*). Like other naïve black youths who came North to claim their stake in the American Dream, Butch ends up as criminalized as Bigger Thomas in Richard Wright's *Native Son*, and as disillusioned as the protagonist of Ralph Ellison's *Invisible Man*. Butch runs numbers in the Chicago underworld, eventually murders a policeman, and comes "home" as "the slain wolf" (p. 364) to be buried among his people.

Who are? Gavin Stevens, Jefferson's chief lawyer, helps Molly bring her lost grandchild home, in an act of sympathetic if paternalistic courtesy. In the course of making the arrangements, he's startled to realize Molly is the sister of a black man living in town, Hamp Worsham, the servant of a woman whose family had owned Hamp's grandparents. An unsuspected relation among blacks underscores habitual white obliviousness to the actualities of African American ancestry and connection. No white person cares who Molly is related to. And nobody but his grandmother cares who Butch is related to either, including Butch. There's a census taker who tries to get the inmate to provide information about his past, but Butch won't co-operate – or maybe he's just giving the answers that feel the most true to him: "Parents?" "Sure. Two. I don't remember them" (p. 352). Blacks like Butch just don't count as belonging to America; here Faulkner widens the aperture of his portrait of segregation to touch on the national scale of "the negro question" in 1942. Numerous black townspeople show up to meet Butch's coffin at the train station, but only a few white idlers. Molly intones "Go Down, Moses," the spiritual that laments how African Americans age after age have been sold into oblivion by white pharaohs, and insists that the notice of her grandson's death appear in the local newspaper. Molly understands her Samuel's fate historically, as a tragedy of American bondage. As with the stories of Lucas and Rider, this one threatens to give even unrelated white people like lawyer Stevens something to think about.

When Isaac McCaslin attempts to explain to his cousin why he has repudiated his patrimony, he concentrates, as we have seen, on the illegitimacy of property. Ike believes that he cannot even "relinquish" the family land because it can never be his enough even to relinquish, just as it was never old Carothers's enough to bequeath. Nor can "the human beings he held in bondage and in the power of life and death" (p. 243) who extracted a plantation from the wilderness ever receive more than just a little of the "amelioration and restitution" due them for the "injustice" they suffered (p. 250). Ike turns all of human history into a drama of one false possession displaced by the next:

> Dispossessed of Eden. Dispossessed of Canaan, and those who dispossessed him dispossessed him dispossessed, and the five hundred years of absentee landlords in the Roman bagnios, and the thousand years of wild men from the northern woods who dispossessed them and devoured their ravished substance ravished in turn again and then snarled in what you call the old world's worthless twilight over the old world's gnawed bones, blasphemous in His name until He used a simple egg to discover to them a new world where a nation of people could be founded in humility and pity and sufferance and pride of one to another (pp. 247–248)

– yet that land "already accursed" by "what Grandfather and his kind, his fathers, had brought in to the new land," the "white man's curse" of slavery (*idem*).

From the plantation old Carothers scratches into the land, as from the entire history of Old and New World possessiveness it epitomizes, Ike flees to the forest. The woods represent a counter-historical narrative: not for anyone

> to hold suzerainty over the earth and the animals on it in His name, not to hold for himself and his descendants inviolable title forever, generation after generation, to the oblongs and squares of the earth, but to hold the earth mutual and intact in the communal anonymity of brotherhood. (p. 246).

So from the defiled bed of his grandfather Ike recoils as well, in horror at the "unregenerate old man who could summon, because she was his property, a human being" to serve his lust (p. 281). Ike welcomes his initiation into the alternative ethos of the wilderness, one that regards the land and all its creatures as belonging to all, and so belonging to none. As Lucas Beauchamp resists the exclusively commercial use of his land by hunting it as well, Ike and his fraternal band stage a retreat each year to

> the big woods, bigger and older than any recorded document: of white man fatuous enough to believe he had bought any fragment of it, of Indian ruthless enough to pretend that any fragment of it had been his to convey. (p. 183)

The wilderness myths recounted by Ike's mentor, Sam Fathers, usher the boy into a spiritual relation to the created world. The rituals of the hunt mean to embody the "communal anonymity of brotherhood" that ought to share the land, as the sacrament of marking the hunter's face with the blood of the life he sheds means to detoxify the shameful sham of race blood. Ike clearly takes the wilderness ethic as the inspiration for repudiating his patrimony. In the long conversation with his cousin Cass that occupies almost all of section 4 of "The Bear," Ike explains his view of history and the purpose of his renunciation, the only imaginable antidote to this primal sin:

> the land, the fields and what they represented in terms of cotton ginned and sold . . . that whole edifice intricate and complex and founded upon injustice and erected by ruthless rapacity and carried on even yet with at times downright savagery. (pp. 284–285)

Always, against the plantation fields, Ike withdraws, the woods seeming to erase any relation to the world of property, commerce, history: "the wilderness closed behind his entrance as it had opened momentarily to accept him" (p. 187). Ike even dreams of a counter-family to replace his own: with Sam as his true father, "[i]t seemed to him that at the age of ten he was witnessing his own birth" (*idem*).

It is Sam's Native American ancestry that bestows on him the authority to re-imagine the land apart from a surrounding history of colonial possession, plantation economy, and slavery. Though Sam, as we recall, has an African mother, the lineage that counts in the wilderness derives from "the Chickasaw chief who had been his father" (p. 158), the "savage king" Ikkemotubbe himself. That's the "blood" that allows Sam to mark Ike "forever one with the wilderness" (p. 171), as he initiates this white renegade into the ways of the "old people," teaching him a purer tongue as he salutes the forest's great stag: " 'Oleh, Chief,' Sam said. 'Grandfather.' " Here's a grandfather to make you forget your own unforgivable one. There's no question Faulkner wishes to include the story of Native American dispossession in his chronicles of Yoknapatawpha. Recall that even Rosa Coldfield, though with her usual insulting tone, refers to the way Sutpen "took" the land "from a tribe of ignorant Indians, nobody knew how" (*Absalom, Absalom!*, p. 10). At least symbolically, Faulkner's Indians represent a "green" use of the land before that colonial edifice founded on injustice and erected on rapacity takes over.

Yet the glimpses we get of Native American life in Yoknapatawpha mainly reveal its mimicry of white plantation society. The Indians' earlier communal use of the land survives only in myths about the "old people," fantasies of a past that inspire Ike's utopian dream of a society beyond property. More worrisomely, once we see how thoroughly the wilderness has already been domesticated by its interrelations with the plantation world, as well as with oncoming commercial development, we might wonder if retreats to the forest aren't more escapist than revolutionary. I use the term "mimicry" as it has been used in post-colonial cultural studies to describe the phenomenon of imitation by colonial subjects of their conquerors.[4] Only select individuals among subjugated people may be permitted to ape the manners and values of their "betters," but the class of "mimic-men" that emerges serves to exemplify the "elevating" potential of Western civilization, as well as to buffer relations between the mass of the colonized and their foreign rulers. The catch in such mimicry involves a contradiction: colonized persons, if they are truly "inferior" enough to justify domination and "civilizing," ought not to be able to reproduce the colonizers' culture flawlessly. The partial or garbled version of it that results opens up discrepancies and creates ambivalence at the sites of imitation.

When in "A Justice" we find the newly "cosmopolitan" Ikkemotubbe having developed a taste for European finery and usurping the Chickasaw chieftainship by resorting to the poisonous methods he's acquired in New Orleans, we are meant to see through Native American mimicry to its vicious colonial model. Faulkner's point in locating slaveholding among the Indians has to do not only with the historical contagion of brutality (and Native Americans like the Cherokees *did* practice the enslavement of Africans), but also with the critique of a corrupt system made possible by its imperfect replication. In "A Justice," as we've seen, the Chickasaws create a spectacle of the pointlessness of slave empire in the laughable project of hauling an entire steamboat overland. The injustice of bondage twists into the charade of adjudicated rights arranged by Ikkemotubbe, in which the master's raw power gets imposed on humiliated subjects forced to pretend they have been accorded justice and not just "a" justice.

In "Red Leaves" (1930) the same Chickasaw clan has prospered enough to produce "solid, burgher-like" (*Collected Stories*, p. 313) citizens. Idle and indulged, a couple of rank-and-file Indians recognize that "slavery . . . is not the good way" (p. 314). But it's not until we see the effects of mimicry on Ikkemottube's successor, Moketubbe, that we recognize the decadence inherent in colonial ways and can appreciate one elder's observation that the world "is being ruined by white men" who "foisted Negroes upon us": "In the old days the old men sat in the shade and ate stewed deer's flesh and corn and smoked tobacco and talked of honor and grave affairs" (p. 323). Now, the tribe is led by a grotesque embodiment of consumption – an immense bloated youth who must be carried about on a litter, his useless feet ornamented with high-heeled red slippers, his face bearing "an expression profound, tragic, and inert" (p. 325). The Indians can express their ambivalence because of their lower investment in the system, while their inexperience with its excesses allows this figure of dependence to get out of hand. Likewise, the novelty of slavery makes the Indians notice things about African chattel that white habitués to black suffering do not. The tribe's custom is to bury necessary possessions with the departed. At Ikkemotubbe's death, one of his slaves, facing live interment, flees. As he's patiently hunted down, the Indians register his all-too-human desperation – the "faint ah-ah-ah sound" of his panting and the terror-stricken gagging as he's given a last gourd of water. The slave's predicament relocates, and so both refracts and highlights, the real human suffering entailed in the social death that was slavery, just as the junior chief's spoilage points to the degenerative effects on the master class of massive greed and dependency on others' labor.

In the comic story "Lo!" Faulkner takes the Mississippi Indians' mimicry even further, concocting a tale in which a chief of mixed French and Chickasaw ancestry leads a delegation to Washington, DC, to demand ratification of their rights to the land they occupy. The story involves a complication of title, however, since the chief has first sold a microscopic bit of his land to a clever white settler, who thereby acquires exclusive access to the only ford on a boundary river for three hundred miles. When the settler erects a toll booth, the Indians revise the deal by murdering the speculator. Chief Weddel (or perhaps Vidal – the ambiguity indicates the linguistic hybridity of the frontier) takes a throng of his people fifteen hundred miles to confront an Andrew Jackson-like President of the United States. They want the murderer officially exonerated. Among themselves the Indians speak condescendingly of "white man's honor," which makes their adversaries act "like children" (p. 383). But they do conform to their rulers' customs, even dressing like white men for their visit – with the exception of the pantaloons they prefer to carry under their arms rather than don over their woolen drawers. The Indians' determination to scandalize colonial rule politely but, you can't help but conclude, mockingly, thrusts at the conceit of Jacksonian paternalism governing US Indian policy in the nineteenth century. The President in effect sanctions the murder and restores title, doubtless aggravated not only by this public exercise of Indian opposition, but also by the reminder of how white westward expansion relied on the forcible, murderous dispossession of native inhabitants. The Chickasaws' invasion of the capital constitutes a kind of resurgent Indian raid, a reverse conquest – the "entire Atlantic seaboard north of the Potomac River overrun by creatures in beaver hats and frock coats and woolen drawers, frightening women and children, setting fire to barns and running off slaves, killing deer," reports a cabinet member (p. 387). Lo and behold! – the partially clad native threatens to show you more than you want to know, and about yourself as much as himself.

Despite Isaac McCaslin's fidelity to Native American ideals that deny the right of any individual to take land as private property, Ike's views of slavery and race fall considerably short of universal egalitarian brotherhood. The most disquieting feature of the wilderness ethos as celebrated in *Go Down, Moses* proves its *compatibility* with Southern racism. In "Delta Autumn," when he is an old man, Ike speaks less guardedly, and so more offensively, about the mongrelization of America. In his ugly remarks about "Chinese and African and Aryan and Jew, all breed[ing] and spawn[ing] together until no man has time to say which one is which nor cares" (*Go Down, Moses*, p. 347), Ike seems to be laying the corruption of the "ruined woods" to racial promiscuity. Even in his youthful mood of reverence for Sam Fathers's Indian "blood," Sam's native ancestry is repeatedly distinguished at the expense of his African descent. It is fair to ask whether Ike's consistent racism might not actually be finding solace in his withdrawal from society, and in his idealization of the mythical wilderness as the only place free of the taint of ownership.

As a matter of fact, the hunting parties organized by Colonel Sartoris and General Compson through the big bottom land owned by Major de Spain retain all of the social discriminations and entitlements seemingly suspended during the retreat. Negroes remain servants; lower-class half-breeds like Boon or the negro cook Ash remain butts of humor; and the language of blood purity and royalty saturate the language of the hunt – in the breeding of dogs, in the behavior of the great animals, in the dignity and courage of the great hunters. It's as if the social discourse of Southern plantation society and the succeeding Jim Crow regime are being sanctified by wilderness ritualization. One unnerving manifestation of this is the way the wilderness itself sometimes seems like a racial entity. When Ike sees Old Ben for the first time, he has the sensation that he is encountering something already familiar – "not as big as he had dreamed it but as big as he had expected" (p. 200), something that does not arrive from somewhere else but somehow just materializes, "just there, immobile" (*idem*), almost like the incarnation of an idea. Retrieving an overly eager fyce nearly from Ben's grasp, Ike "could smell [the bear], strong and hot and rank" (p. 203). Odor is always the sign of negroes to Faulkner's whites, and the connection is underscored when we see the eventual death scene of the mammoth creature, which almost exactly reprises the wrestling down of Rider at the end of "Pantaloon in Black." That Old Ben acts like a rule-breaking predator – all but the black beast of racist fantasy – deepens the hallucinatory racial subtext of Ike's wilderness experiences.

It's not that Faulkner is fashioning a simple fable of race, so much as that the portentousness of the woods captures something of the indistinct yet ominous racial confusion of Ike's South. "The Old People" eventually delivers Sam Fathers and his young charge to a moment in which nature presents itself with pristine purity to those who revere it – in the form of the great buck that appears after Ike slays his first deer. But what precedes that moment freights the rituals of killing and blood-marking with troubling social significance. The more the story labors to free the hunters from the trappings of society, the more it reinforces a preoccupation with the need for racial differentiation. Thus, Ike is "the white boy" (p. 159); Sam is the old man "who had been a negro for two generations now but whose face and bearing were still those of the Chickasaw chief who had been his father" (p. 158), who knows "that for a while that part of his blood had been the blood of slaves" (p. 161); old Carothers is "the white neighbor" (p. 160); Boon's grandmother had been a Chickasaw, "although the blood had run white since and Boon was a white man" (p. 163); Jo Baker, Sam's friend, is a "full-blood Chickasaw" (p. 165); Cass is regarded by Sam as the child's "kinsman and chief and head of his blood" (p. 167); and so on. We even learn that Sam's mother has been a "quadroon slave woman" (p. 160), a fact that complicates Sam's race even further since in order to "be" the negro Jefferson insists he is, not only must his Chickasaw ancestry be ignored, but his rarely mentioned *white* ancestry must be denied as well. By the time Ike gets to the wilderness, with its "impenetrable walls" (p. 170) looming "tremendous, attentive, impartial and omniscient," one can't help but feel that the woods have become an objective correlative for the thicket of racial ideology that Ike cannot surrender even as he does surrender fraudulent title to the land. After Faulkner's preambles, you can't see the word "blood" in connection with the slaying of a deer and not think of race, any more than you can think of "race" or "game" or "buck" without thinking of their double meanings from "Was" forward.

If race turns out to be encrypted throughout the wilderness, so, sadly, are the rights of property. General Compson praises the idealistic young Ike for preferring the woods to the commercial world of town, where "Sartorises and Edmondses invented farms and banks to keep [themselves] from having to find out what this boy was born knowing and fearing too" (p. 240). Yet Ike's dream of the unaxed primeval wilderness hardly protects against the commercial fate that always already awaits the woods. The year after Old Ben meets his end and Sam Fathers dies, the owner of the bottom land, Major de Spain, himself one of the celebrants of the annual hunting ritual, sells the timber rights. Ike is mystified by this apparent betrayal. He visits the camp one last time, but finds log trains coursing through the forest and a planing-mill already partially constructed. Arriving at a favorite gum tree, Ike encounters Boon frantically assembling his rifle under boughs laden with squirrels: "Get out of here! Don't touch them!," Boon warns, "They're mine!" (p. 315). This epitome of human greed and possessiveness summarizes the history of New World settlement. Once the land was touched by the curse of property, and compounded by the insult of human chattel slavery, the wilderness was never other than a commodity-in-waiting. In effect, the local capitalist class practices the hunt as a form of recreation, its rituals sustaining the myths of blood, race, natural authority, and title. Perhaps it's those like Isaac McCaslin who actually have to invent the wilderness to forget about banks and farms.

Faulkner's plantation fiction includes one other major work, *The Unvanquished* (1938), a cycle of related short stories that, like *Go Down, Moses*, the author insisted was a kind of "novel." Although Faulkner published most of the pieces in magazines as he completed them, the eventual work they composed has a more integrated structure than any of his plantation works since *Flags in the Dust*. Yet the ostensible unity of the narrative belies the jarring effects of its story: all of the principal characters get caught up in violent upheavals caused by the Civil War, and all come to see that the struggle to perpetuate an unjust way of life exposes the incoherence of its core beliefs.

At the outset of this chapter I suggested that the pressures of modernity pushed Faulkner toward a serious inquiry into the historical foundations of Southern plantation society, the system that dominated his natal region but that also provided a material basis for national prosperity. In *The Unvanquished* Faulkner imagines the social volatility of modern America as traceable to the event of the US Civil War. The stampede to freedom by emancipated slaves that so startled their Southern masters, like the demonstrations of combative independence by women on the home as well as military fronts, forced puzzled reassessments of the very values being fought for. Faulkner describes how the web of rationalized insult structuring Southern society tears apart when its fragile network of coercion and provision breaks down. The Civil War triggered the discrediting of central antebellum ideals about what it meant to be a planter, a gentleman, a lady, a poor white, a negro; subsequent social convulsions over the next century of progressive enfranchisements continued to be haunted by the specter of civil war.

Drusilla Hawk, a young woman of the Jefferson planter elite, loses her fiancé in the battle of Shiloh early in the war, but refuses what is expected next of her: "the highest destiny of a Southern woman – to be the bride-widow of a lost cause" (p. 448). Instead, Drusilla decides she'd rather join the troops herself, so, "unsex[ing]" her boyish frame and womanly grief, she heads to the front lines, where she is welcomed into her kinsman Colonel Sartoris's regiment. Drusilla violates the narrow code of Southern femininity in numerous ways: even before the war her mannish skills as a rider cause comment, and when she finally returns from the front in a flurry of stories about how she has casually bedded down with John and his men through months of soldierly intimacy, Drusilla's mother finally issues an ultimatum. Aunt Louisa can't believe Drusilla's assurance that she and John have not committed adultery – a word hardly anyone is even brave enough to say aloud. The "strange times" (p. 453) of war jumble sexual mores, but also allow someone like Drusilla to act, however fleetingly, upon her longing to be emancipated from (her single) gender.

Young Bayard, John's son, who narrates the stories, sympathizes with Dru's renegadery; he's sorry that the older women finally succeed in "defeating" her by insisting that she agree to marriage and respectability. Drusilla continues the fight, though, by spending most of her time helping John Sartoris defend planter privilege against Yankee carpetbaggers intent on getting freedmen elected to office. The two of them actually end up killing two such intruders and rigging an election to prevent a black man from gaining office. Paradoxically, Drusilla becomes politically activated in the service of regressive purposes, but she does manage to "forget" her marital promise in so doing. As we shall see throughout the stories, the ideologies of antebellum plantation society break apart in unpredictable and contradictory ways: their former subjects often act at cross-purposes during this period of fundamental reorganization.

For all her insubordination over gender, Drusilla remains powerfully attached to the dominant code of honor and shame to which Southern gentlemen swore allegiance. She's the one who presents the seductions of revenge to young Bayard after his father has been slain by a longstanding adversary. Even before the Colonel's murder Drusilla has attempted to eroticize the South's romance with violence:

> There are worse things than killing men, Bayard. There are worse things than being killed. Sometimes I think the finest thing that can happen to a man is to love something, a woman preferably, well, hard hard hard, then to die young because he believed what he could not help but believe. . . . (p. 474)

Later, when Drusilla is trying to get Bayard to avenge his father's honor by going after the murderer Redmond, she exults: "How beautiful: young, to be permitted to kill, to be permitted vengeance, to take into your bare hands the fire of heaven that cast down Lucifer" (p. 481). Of course, the more attuned you become to Drusilla's "rapport for violence" (p. 489), the more you notice the madness behind it. Bayard resists her temptations to both sex and violence several times, finally growing alarmed by the crazed fervor with which she urges John's dueling pistols on him, the two barrels, as she puts it, "slender and invincible and fatal as the physical shape of love" (p. 481). Drusilla's spiraling incoherence may result from the confusion of wanting desperately to be a man in a world in which women are such defeated creatures. Yet to be a Southern gentleman is to be something mad and futile in Reconstruction Mississippi, too. The consequence is that Drusilla expresses hysterically the otherwise inexpressible: "suddenly she began to laugh again. It seemed to come not from her mouth but to burst out all over her face like sweat does and with a dreadful and painful convulsion" (p. 485).

The whole society seems to be having a panic attack. John Sartoris, for example, at first follows a predictable course: he fights on behalf of the Confederacy, tries to keep his farm intact, returns to Jefferson to rebuild, and organizes resistance groups to frustrate federal Reconstruction. Yet he also fails to find a viable way to reinvent himself. He turns on his former partner in railroad speculation, apparently for no reason but the Colonel's "violent and ruthless dictatorialness and will to dominate" (p. 472). That's an ambitious planter's nature, to be sure, but Sartoris has been further damaged by having had "to kill too many folks" in the war. It's as if the violence of the code of masculine honor has run amok in combat, so when Sartoris tries to re-domesticate himself, he finds he can't stop provoking Redmond. An ideology has taken possession of him demonically; he just won't relent, and Redmond finally puts a stop to it after a decade of abuse. Too late, even Sartoris recognizes the pathology of Southern violence; he goes unarmed to his confrontation with Redmond, musing, "I am tired of killing men" (p. 477).

Similar kinds of breakdowns plague other members of the Jefferson first families. Rosa "Granny" Millard has been galvanized into becoming a mule thief during the war, figuring out a way to scam overly courteous Yankee brass out of packs of mules, reselling them at steep profits, and distributing both monetary and muletary largesse to the suffering non-combatants on the homefront. Granny meets her match, though, when she crosses a vicious mercenary named Grumby, who murders her in an act of panicked self-defense. Granny's punctilious observance of the niceties of Southern decorum – she's always punishing Bayard and his negro sidekick Ringo for using swear words or lying – proves an absurd façade once events reveal that the Confederacy's struggle is going to be a fight to the death.

One of the most remarkable features of *The Unvanquished* is its mood of feral desperation, a kind of wild determination to survive no matter what, which just pulverizes any pretense to genteel mannerliness. Granny proves capable of stony ruthlessness; Grumby shoots a cowering old woman; two teenagers murder in cold blood. There's a way in which the entire code of Southern gentility collapses under the weight of altered economic circumstances, suggesting further that even in its heyday it might have been nothing but billowy crinoline concealing the furtive violence of self-interest.

Likewise, the white delusion of slave loyalty largely gets swept aside by acts of ferocious courage performed by blacks at the news of emancipation. Yes, Bayard continues to see negro freedom in the terms of his class interest and conditioning. He notes smugly that negroes are hardly welcomed by racist Yankees who don't want to have to provide for massive defection; individual servants like Louvinia are too scared to try the unknown; clever players of angles like Ringo try to calculate where their best interest lies, and are capable of the self-deprecating comedy of minstrelsy: "I ain't a nigger any more," he announces to Bayard after a visit to town, "I done been abolished" (p. 454). Of course, the idea of "nigger" *was* in effect abolished under the terms of the thirteenth and fourteenth amendments. Ringo spots the potential for profit in the mule scheme before anyone else, and he clearly relishes this opportunity to use his wits, nerve, and newfound independence – even if he has to help his Confederate family in order to assist his own suffering people. Ringo's father Loosh frightens white innocence with behavior emboldened by emancipation. He does violence to childish games and announces freedom's arrival. At one point he "kind of surged up out of the darkness right beside us" (p. 334), like a presence that's been there but ignored all along. He shows up "torn and muddy" (*idem*) as the result of his defiant forays to the front lines for news of Yankee success. Such unexpected materialization of black agency culminates in the apocalyptic scenes of slaves nightly marching north. Bayard listens to their "panting murmur" as they approach, "a kind of gasping, murmuring chant" (p. 375). This freedom march hardly seems real to former masters, and the panting may as much be the anxious Bayard's as the fugitives'.

Faulkner treats these vignettes of the Reconstruction South as part of an extended narrative of Yoknapatawpha plantation society. Members of the inter-related plantocracy appear in cameos, Thomas Sutpen, for example, again depicted turning down Sartoris's invitation to join the Ku Klux Klan (as in *Absalom, Absalom!*), or Mrs. Compson conspiring with her friend Rosa Millard, or Buck and Buddy shown working out the details of their anti-slavery experiment. In fact, we get a distinctly deeper portrait of the McCaslin twins' revolutionary project here, with Colonel Sartoris admitting that "they were ahead of their time" by "maybe fifty years" (p. 351) in espousing a method of using the land in a communitarian manner. Buck and Buddy endow the slaves with eventual survival disciplines by letting them earn their freedom via labor on the plantation; more radically, the two idealists convince poor black and white landowners to combine their small holdings with the McCaslins' and to share the proceeds equally. This is the kind of new political and economic reality that at least momentarily staggers the racial and class codes of the Old South. All the odder, then, that Buck McCaslin should also be the strongest instigator of Bayard to revenge (after Drusilla). Buck turns out to be absolutely sick with desire to avenge his old friend Granny Millard, and when he sends the boys off in pursuit of Grumby, he begins "to holler, with his face flushed and his eyes bright, taking the pistol from around his neck, and giving it to me, 'Catch them! Catch them!'" (p. 438). Again it appears that progressive and regressive ideas about social relationship may co-exist in a single moment of extreme historical transformation. An emergent radical idea like racially desegregated farm collectivism somehow lives in the same mind as a primitive code of bloodthirsty revenge.

In this novel about the deformation of belief systems associated with a condemned way of life, Faulkner comes up with a description of how ideology works. When Drusilla urges Bayard to avenge his father's honor, she suddenly seizes his trigger hand: "she had bent and kissed it before I comprehended why she took it" (p. 481). Bayard feels her "hot lips and her hot hand still touching my flesh, light on my flesh as dead leaves yet communicating to it that battery charge" – "a touch" that "goes straight to the heart without bothering the laggard brain at all" (*idem*). The short-circuiting of the mind is what ideology is all about; it's conditioned reflex, not thought. Bayard gets the same sensation when he's touched by a member of his father's former troop. The men think he's on the way to confront Redmond and act on behalf of the Sartoris name; one ex-soldier fumbles a pistol into Bayard's pocket, "then the same thing seemed to happen to him that happened to Drusilla last night when she kissed my hand – something communicated by touch straight to the simple code by which he lived, without going through the brain at all" (p. 487). This is not the touch of flesh on flesh that Rosa experiences as *disrupting* the authority of accepted beliefs by making one self-conscious. Instead, it's a *confirmatory* touch framed *by* a "code" that has been so deeply inculcated into the individual that you find it in the very muscles. Yet Bayard's very consciousness of these acts of ideological activation already point to its weakened condition. There are questions put, and moments of delay. And finally, after making his way to the waiting Redmond's office, Bayard has the sensation of moving in a "dreamlike state" (p. 488), where both antagonists are free to resort to "a queer ducking motion" (p. 489) as they elude the perpetuation of pointless violence. As at many other points in *The Unvanquished* there's not exactly a name for this new practice, the product of renouncing old ways, but there is the undeniable effect of releasing yourself from the grip of the past.

CHAPTER 5

Seeing a South Beyond Yoknapatawpha

Over the last fifteen years of Faulkner's life, from the late 1940s until his death in 1962, dire changes in global politics shifted the author's literary attention and challenged his imagination in new ways. First came the long-expected collapse of the arrangements made in the Treaty of Versailles in 1919 to settle the Great War. Burdened with heavy payments of reparation, Germany's economy struggled, and its working class soon grew susceptible to promises of a militaristic return to national glory. Militant fascism arose in Italy as well, and as Hitler and Mussolini identified common purposes in Europe, Japan decided to confront Russia's perceived expansionist tendencies in the East. These three Axis powers launched a World War II, triggered in 1939 when Germany invaded Poland. By the time the war ended in 1946, Europe faced ruin; Russia, as one of the victorious Allies, looked to emerge as a new global power; the US had inaugurated the age of atomic weaponry in two attacks on Japan; and the fully revealed extent of the Nazis' extermination of Jews raised devastating doubts about the course of western post-Enlightenment civilization. America's own pledge to defend liberty, once the nation was drawn into combat by Japan's attack on Pearl Harbor in 1941, again had to confront contradictions on the home front – most conspicuously the continued disfranchisement of African Americans – that compromised the social ideals being fought for. Efforts to reconstruct ex-combatant states and a world economy by the two most viable allied powers emerging from the war, the United States and the Union of Soviet Socialist Republics (or USSR, the communist regime anchored in Russia that descended from the Bolshevik takeover in 1917), soon led to a confrontational global politics. The so-called Cold War struggle between democratic capitalism and communist totalitarianism (at its simplest) turned much of the world into a checkerboard of opposing interests. US nuclear capability provoked an arms race that endangered the entire planet and locked the superpowers into paranoid schemes of mutual deterrence through incessant intimidation. The extent to which the terror of global destruction preoccupied the civilized world might be measured by Faulkner's speech upon receiving the Nobel Prize for Literature in 1950. The entirety of his remarks address the prospect of atomic holocaust, and speak bravely of humankind's determination not just to "endure but to prevail" over this unprecedented menace.

Faulkner's late fiction takes up a number of these issues. His novel *Intruder in the Dust* (1948) addresses the interminable embarrassment of Southern racism; it brings back an elderly Lucas Beauchamp, now as the victim of a frame-up and potential lynching, in order to propel white shame and guilt about racial oppression toward constructive purposes: acknowledging past evil, doing something about present injustice, and working toward a genuine post-racial mentality. A film made from the novel the next year augmented Faulkner's stature as a Southern artist willing to imagine the reform of racist habits of thought, laws, and social mores.[1] In world politics, the burgeoning pieties of Cold War antagonism led Faulkner to re-examine the claims of both capitalist freedom and proletarian justice in the final two novels of the Snopes trilogy, *The Town* (1957) and *The Mansion* (1959). In the early 1950s Faulkner responded to the emergence of US imperial democracy – a paradoxical creature, for sure – by diagnosing in *Requiem for a Nun* (1950) the unhealed trauma of the plantation South's violent origins in New World colonialism, then by turning in *A Fable* (1954) to consider an emerging new form of global domination: a transnational complex of financial and military powers.

World War II intensified pressures within the United States to deal with the persistence of legal racial disfranchisement as well as informal everyday racism. When the question of American involvement in the war comes up in "Delta Autumn," a story in *Go Down, Moses* that takes place around 1940, Ike and his hunting companions agree that there will be no shortage of defenders of the republic when the call finally goes out to "cope with one Austrian paper-hanger" (*Go Down, Moses,*

p. 323). They put off their suspicion that the US might have its own fascism to worry about in the form of "Roosevelt or Wilkie or whatever he will call himself in this country" (p. 322), but not before the point is made that even Southerners who admit the evil of racism, like Ike and his friends, detest the idea of federally dictated social policies, particularly ones enforcing racial equality. Ike will end up in the story rejecting an overture by his cousin Roth Edmonds's mistress to gain his blessing on their union (and the infant it has already produced). Roth has, unawares, taken into his bed a descendant of the long-lost "Tennie's Jim," which means his consort is not only a negro but an actual kinswoman. For Ike to sanction their love would be for him to set aside Southern fetishes of miscegenation and incest. He can't do it, at least not yet, and urges the woman to head north, where she can "marry a black man" and sidestep the still-lethal quicksand of Southern racism. The very notion that white and black might intermarry openly, that a racially divided people might declare itself a unified human family, panics Ike: hence his screed about "Chinese and African and Aryan and Jew, all breed[ing] and spawn[ing] together" (p. 347).

That some white Southerners could identify FDR with the same threat Hitler posed reflects the region's continued defense of the racial status quo during the 1930s and 1940s. Gunnar Myrdal's magisterial study of US racism, *An American Dilemma* (1944), zeroed in on the contradiction between a national creed of equality and the practice of systematic legal discrimination against negroes. The motives for going to war against Nazism only upped the ante, since it was even more incomprehensible that Americans – especially African Americans – should be asked to give their lives in defense of an ideal of freedom, and in opposition to ethnic persecution, when such regard was denied as a matter of policy to so many of the country's own citizens. German propaganda found this sore point (and the Soviets would make even more of it during the Cold War). As they had in World War I, African American leaders used this moment of ideological vulnerability to press for expanded rights, gaining concessions that led to the partial desegregation of the military and greater protections in economic life. By the late 1940s a broad civil rights movement had developed momentum, and blows soon began to be struck against the system of legal apartheid that had ruled much of the South since the 1890s. In 1954, for example, the Supreme Court overturned policies that had restricted

African American access to public institutions of higher learning. Over the next long decades of adamant demand for racial equality and often violent opposition, the South would be transformed, the long-deferred promise of real emancipation finally coming into view. Faulkner reluctantly edged into the public debate, obliged in part by a sense of civic duty expected with the world attention of the Nobel award, and compelled by the horror of Southern bloodletting. Although Faulkner's remarks on racial politics run a gamut from resolute affirmation of the principle of equality to, on one unfortunate occasion, an ugly racist condemnation of Northern interference in what he considered a Southern problem, his public letters and statements do add up to a clear commitment to the justice and inevitability of full black enfranchisement, desegregation, and the eventual discarding of the very concept of race.[2]

Faulkner's fiction through *Go Down, Moses* tends primarily to be diagnostic about race – figuring out its roots in plantation slavery, tracing its reinvention after emancipation, dissecting the way it preoccupies modern social life. In *The Unvanquished* we glimpse the rush of blacks toward freedom, the force of moving bodies capturing an historical reality in 1863, as well as registering reawakened motion among blacks in the late 1930s. In the period after World War II, Faulkner joins numerous other intellectuals and artists in imagining how a nation might finally liberate itself once and for all from the burden of racism. In *Intruder in the Dust* Faulkner wonders what must be done to free negroes from the false charges that imprison them, and what price whites must pay to lift the guilt and shame that haunt the future of race relations. Thomas Jefferson famously remarked that getting rid of slavery would be like figuring out what to do with a wolf you were holding by the ears. The next step doesn't look simple. What makes Faulkner's casting of the problem so original and astute in *Intruder* involves his refusal to represent the question of black enfranchisement as it was usually posed: what to do with the negro? Faulkner's ultimate answer seems to be: abolish "negro." Also abolish "white," along with the entire figment of race.

Lucas, a widower now and deep in his sixties, finds himself accused of a murder. He has stumbled across a backwoods scheme in which a white man is swindling his twin brother and another business partner out of a share of timber the three have contracted to have cut and sold. The offender, Crawford Gowrie, gets wind of Lucas's suspicions, and tricks his brother Vinson into confronting the meddlesome old man. In a sleight-of-hand, Lucas ends up holding a smoking gun after Crawford shoots his brother in the back. Crawford murders a second person, a timber agent, when he concludes he's liable to blackmail. Arrested, Lucas offers no immediate defense, instead waiting patiently to present the facts that will exonerate him to an elderly white friend of his wife's and a young white boy, Chick Mallison, the nephew of the county attorney. The plot revolves around the efforts of Chick, his negro "boy" Aleck Sander, and Miss Habersham to exhume the buried bodies, insist on their forensic examination, and stare down the various crowds that gather around the Jefferson town jail as reminders of the customary fate awaiting negro murderers of white men. Faulkner presents the injustice of Lucas's plight with decided sympathy and indignation. Yet the spectacle of an accused negro having to rely on assorted white champions to accomplish his emancipation has raised questions about Faulkner's capacity to imagine black agency. Lawyer Gavin Stevens, Chick's uncle, once explains that the white South no longer has any quarrel with the idea of negro enfranchisement: "Sambo is a human being living in a free country and hence must be free. That's what we are really defending: the privilege of setting him free ourselves" (*Intruder in the Dust*, pp. 400–401). From this standpoint, the duty of white liberators in *Intruder* nightmarishly repeats the farcical task Tom Sawyer and Huck Finn set for themselves in *Adventures of Huckleberry Finn*: "how to set a free nigger free." In his novel of 1885, Twain was actually putting that question to the Jim Crow South, since he could see that the institution of legal racial segregation would re-imprison negroes. Free negroes *would* have to be set free. But unlike Twain's Jim, and Stevens's Sambo, Faulkner's Lucas opts out of this game altogether. Lucas's lack of agency is less a symptom of his inability to work on his own behalf than a refusal to recognize the legitimacy of those who hold power over him.

As Stevens's habitual use of the word "Sambo" might suggest, the Lucas Beauchamp who is arrested for murdering a white man and who spends the novel waiting to be freed by white exertions, has little to do with the person Lucas Beauchamp takes himself to be. "Sambo" was a term of derision used by Southern whites for African Americans. It has a murky origin, became a popular epithet in minstrelsy, and here reflects Stevens's jokey nonchalance toward Lucas's troubles. The very first sentence of the novel makes clear that what has been committed according to the community is a racial crime: "Lucas had killed a white man" (p. 285). Everything in Lucas's environment reveals how thoroughly racial difference has been inscribed on its surfaces, relations, bodies. Knowledge of others is a function of race (Chick is said to know Lucas as well "as any white person knew him" [*idem*]; social events like hunting excursions include casual references to white people's indispensable equipment: their dogs and their "boys" ["Does his boy run rabbits too?" (*idem*) his uncle jokes about their equivalence]; and we may notice how minutely partitioned social life is in the Jim Crow South – with mentions of white and black schools, and separate jail compartments for "regular" prisoners and negroes. The threat of lynching aimed at Lucas depends solely on the racial definition of the alleged crime: "the death by shameful violence of a man who would die not because he was a murderer but because his skin was black" (p. 338).

Lucas, however, behaves not as a negro falsely accused of murdering a white person, but as a person falsely accused of being a negro. Nor is it that Lucas actually wants to pass for white, or even claim the white portion of his ancestry from old Carothers; he just doesn't want to be reduced to "nigger" or "Sambo" or any other designation of inferiority. He responds to all situations with a militant indifference to their standard racial significance. The novel begins with Chick's recollection of just such a defining act of stubbornness, when Lucas spurns the youngster's offer to pay for hospitality after he accidentally falls from a bridge into an icy stream, then is warmed and fed by Lucas and his wife Molly. Chick burns for years with the shame of Lucas's deliberate incomprehension of the coins the child offers – "What's that for?" The elder makes the point that he acts as heir and host on the McCaslin plantation, not as a darkie expecting a tip. As we may recall from "The Fire and the Hearth," Lucas models himself on old Carothers McCaslin, speaking like him, wearing the beaver hat he has bought (he takes pains to point out) from him, coming to town when he pleases, and dressing as well as any planter. The plunge that upends Chick, and that constitutes his symbolic initiation into an order of human relations that sees past race, produces this insight: that what looks back from inside Lucas at the disoriented white boy is not a negro, but something that just happens to be "inside a negro's skin," something that "had no pigment at all, not even the white man's lack of it, not arrogant, not even scornful: just intractable and composed" (pp. 287–

288). Chick has been shocked into recognizing that epidermal chance and essential character have nothing to do with each other. Lucas conducts himself throughout his arrest in just that "intractable and composed" manner because he will not recognize the authority of his community to "make" him the nigger murderer of a white man. Race *is* the frame-up. Lucas's refusal aggravates his white townsmen, who have always insisted that "We got to make him be a nigger first. He's got to admit he's a nigger. Then maybe we will accept him as he seems to intend to be accepted" (p. 296). But Lucas will have no part of such qualifying submission to racial categories he considers illegitimate.

Lucas expresses his will to self-determination through the right to spend money, which, he has discovered in *Go Down, Moses*, is color-blind. In "The Fire and the Hearth" he learns he can keep funds in the bank like anyone else, and by the time he's orchestrating the dismissal of his charges in *Intruder* he's determined to use cash to isolate himself from the morass of guilt, shame, obligation, compensation, charity, paternalism, and so on that bedevil any effort to attain equal footing and get on with things. Lucas wisely offers to pay for everything he asks for, including his legal defense, and carries the principle through to the novel's tab-clearing last line: "My receipt." Lucas serves as a harbinger of the only kind of equality under the law the country has ever achieved: to get it, a black person (like O. J. Simpson, say) has to be wealthy enough to prove he isn't a negro who has killed the white woman he sleeps with, but a rich man whose wife has been murdered.

Newly disturbed in Faulkner's post-World War II South is the traditional privilege of whites to imagine blacks as they chose. In part that shift comes as a result of changes in historical circumstances: the belated modernization of Southern agriculture and the accumulated losses of blacks to the North in the inter-war years transformed the racial landscape. Blackness was felt as an unfamiliar absence, and some African Americans who remained in the South began to experience new small courtesies and forms of regard from some whites. Chick experiences the sensation of black *self*-representation when he inspects the portrait of himself Lucas displays: "there looked back at him again the calm intolerant face" (p. 293). Later, Chick notices a black field hand as he and his uncle speed by: "he and the Negro behind the plow looked eye to eye into each other's face" (pp. 395–396). Those kinds of exchanges imply the emergence of black people from behind the stereotypes that once made them conspicuously invisible to racists, and suggest the mutual humanity that awaits a final repudiation of racial thinking.

Lucas can choose to ignore a history of whites trying to "make" him into a "nigger" because the crimes against him they've framed are their business, not his. But for Chick, as for other white Southerners who come to their senses belatedly, it's not so easy to declare the past dead, or even past. Faulkner's novel wonders whether any good might come from guilt and shame. Chick's preoccupation with his faux pas functions as a synecdoche for white mortification over a long history of insulting blacks. Chick keeps trying to make amends to Lucas, wanting to feel let off, forgiven, his debt paid. But he knows the freedom of moral exoneration is something he'll never be able to realize until he actually does something Lucas asks of him – that is, until there's a new Southern ethics that recognizes all its members as reciprocal agents. Part of what shame might accomplish is to force whites to dig more deeply into why racism has mattered so much in societies like the South's. What Chick's adventure in exhumation comes up with is a kind of fable of racism's historical utility. In that one white man frames a negro for the murder of another over a business deal gone bad, we might say that Lucas functions structurally as a sacrifice or scapegoat to white solidarity. Vinson Gowrie's sharp business practices pay no mind to clan loyalty, and Crawford responds in kind by cheating his own too-successful brother. Their strife lays bare the ruthlessness of market relations and the furious resentment of its victims. Making a black man the fall guy draws on the tried-and-true Southern method of deflecting economic resentment by uniting rich and poor whites around racial hostility, but Faulkner suggests that such ruses no longer can be counted on to keep market casualties buried.

Moreover, Lucas disturbs racial norms by behaving arrogantly; the Gowries have long identified Lucas as a prideful negro, one who needs taking down a peg. From this standpoint Lucas highlights the function of black people in the South as reassuring a "buffer" class of poor whites. Such a stratum was necessary to white elites since it performed indispensable kinds of labor and services, but such second-class whites rarely rose into the ranks of landowners, let alone full-scale gentry. People like Wash Jones in *Absalom, Absalom!*, for example, might take pride in only one thing: they were white, and that made them better than black slaves, or so they thought (recall Sutpen's shock of recognition when he realizes how contemptible laboring whites like him really are to a planter). Poor whites could be kept down by giving them the consolation of apparent racial solidarity with their betters. When facts come to light in the novel, however, it turns out that what was staged as an inter-racial conflict has actually been an intra-familial one. Faulkner cleverly turns the novel's exercise in excavation into a metaphorical confrontation with the economic grounds of Southern racism. The novel presents that insight as Chick's several times over the course of his adventures: he thinks of "the whole dark people on which the very economy of the land itself was founded" (p. 356); "it seemed to him now that he was responsible for having brought in to the light and glare of day something shocking and shameful out of the whole white foundation of the county which he himself must partake of too since he too was bred of it" (p. 388).

To recognize as Chick does that there's something shocking and shameful in the foundation of the life he enjoys puts him in the position of many of Faulkner's young protagonists. But unlike Quentin Compson, who is paralyzed by such knowledge, or Ike McCaslin, who simply parts ways from its effects, Chick understands that he must "partake" of a responsibility that comes with being "bred" of a past. In his efforts to atone for insulting Lucas years earlier by working on his behalf now, Chick develops a new sensitivity to the losses people outside his privileged set have endured. Unlike his uncle, who confirms his superiority by affably ridiculing others' misfortunes, Chick is startled to learn that black people and poor people share common human sentiments behind their protective masks. Encountering Lucas in town one day, but seeing no flicker of recognition, Chick concludes that the old man has finally forgotten him – until Chick later realizes that this was about the time Molly died: "thinking with a kind of amazement: He was grieving. You don't have to not be a nigger in order to grieve" (p. 302). You may hardly believe a lesson like this would have to be *learned*, yet just a lifetime ago in our own country African Americans were still arguing for their basic humanity. In 1948, Harry S. Truman's presidential platform included a plank opposing lynching. For decades Southern congressmen had blocked the passage of federal measures outlawing it. Chick also is taken aback by

Nub Gowrie's reaction to the discovery of his murdered son's body: *"Why, he's grieving*: thinking how he had seen grief twice now in two years where he had not expected it or anyway anticipated it" (p. 406). As the glare of day hits the foundation, Faulkner wants to register this genuine – if scandalously belated – sensitization of the South's white majority to unsuspected suffering. It is Chick's working through his own shame and guilt that enables him to locate corresponding, if far more damaging, experiences of "minority" grief.

Chick is in the position to help short-circuit Southern reflexes because he's got no stake in them yet. Like his partners, Miss Habersham, an eccentric survivor of one of Jefferson's now-irrelevant founding families, and Aleck Sander, who sees a chance to help a revered racial elder, Chick is freer to flout social norms than many. The novel calls this quality "fluidity," which women and children especially, as semi-outsiders, seem to share: "not just a capacity for mobility but a willingness to abandon with the substanceless promptitude of wind or air itself not only position but principle too" (p. 363). That's to be prized since so many of the positions and principles in this novel need to be abandoned. Chick exposes the unfairness of a lot of favorite Southern beliefs. When Lucas takes him home after his icy dunking, Chick recalls being enveloped in the cabin's "unmistakable odor of Negroes" (p. 291). That's such an automatic part of a white Southerner's "heritage," Chick muses later, that he would never have questioned it had he not inadvertently shamed himself before his host. But insulting Lucas forces Chick to think, and what he realizes is that if negroes smell different, it's because "of a condition: an idea: a belief" that they are "not supposed to have facilities to wash properly or often or even to wash bathe often even without the facilities to do it with; that in fact it was a little to be preferred that they did not" (*idem*). That is, the odor of negroes is a sign of the power of ideology: to frighten negroes into being "passive" about their unequal material conditions, to stamp them with the very aroma of subhuman inferiority ("a little to be preferred" by their betters). Likewise, Chick suffers a belated epiphany about the food he's served: heavy fried "nigger food" which, at twelve, he believes is what black people preferred, but as a grown man realizes that "this was all they had had a chance to learn to like" through generations of slavery (p. 293).

It's the way reality is represented that governs how societies work. Or so hypothesizes a theorist of ideology like Slavoj Žižek, who delineates how those in power construct fantasies that *produce* a reality justifying the status quo. *Intruder in the Dust* not only tells a story about the way conditions and sensibilities must change in the modern South, it also dramatizes the struggle to find new ways of representing human relations. A stylist like Faulkner is especially attuned to the social rhetoric of Yoknapatawpha. Numbed by his uncle's windy repetitiousness, Chick marvels at "the really almost standardized meagerness not of individual vocabularies but of Vocabulary itself" (p. 343). Faulkner emphasizes the ideological investments of the prevailing vocabulary when he has Miss Habersham explain to Chick that Lucas refuses to divulge to his Uncle Gavin the extenuating facts of the murder because "He's a Negro and your uncle's a man" (p. 350). This strikes Chick as exactly the truth, though not at face value; to be "a man" is every bit as much to occupy an artificial category of power ("Men like your uncle and Mr Hampton have had to be men too long," Miss Habersham observes [p. 351]), as to be made into a "nigger." The rhetoric of race is toxic:

> the deliberate violent blotting out obliteration of a human life was itself so simple and so final that the verbiage which surrounded it enclosed it insulated it intact into the chronicle of man had of necessity to be simple and uncomplex too, repetitive, almost monotonous even. (p. 350)

Repetitiveness dulls the critical edge of self-consciousness; monotony makes the merely asserted seem truer, more inevitable. Faulkner reproduces this aspect of bad social language in his own style; notice how he dizzies us with unnecessary repetition: "blotting out obliteration"; "surrounded it enclosed it insulated it." Faulkner does this throughout the novel, heaping up the synonyms senselessly so that we are forced to confront the lethal effects of mindless repetition.

But Chick also concludes that a statement of truth like Miss Habersham's can in its simplicity deflate the authority of a society's vocabulary: all you have to do to get to the truth is "to pause, just to stop, just to wait" (p. 351). Once a gasbag like Gavin Stevens gets going, it's like everyone around him gets caught on a "treadmill not because you wanted to be where the treadmill was but simply not to be flung pellmell still running frantically backward off the whole stage out of sight" (p. 433). Stevens sometimes is mistaken for Faulkner's mouthpiece in *Intruder* and elsewhere; but we shouldn't forget that Stevens is the one responsible for the ludicrous – and clearly discredited – speech at the end of *Light in August* that tries to explain Joe Christmas's behavior as a slapstick melodrama of black and white "blood." Chick keeps his distance from this nauseating relative when he can, referring to the "significantless speciosity" (p. 344) of his uncle's voice, and finally nerving himself up to contradict the blowhard: "That's not true," he says as he tries to shut off yet another of his uncle's turgid digressions. The compulsive repetitiveness of the novel's rhetoric, then, also suggests the sheer volume and momentum of ideological reproduction that has to be overcome to change things.

Chick gets caught up in the book's over-the-top style for another reason. Since he's seeing the world upside-down for the first time, Chick has lost the self-possession of an established class and develops real anxieties on behalf of others. While his uncle makes fun of Lucas's tall tales and uppity ways, Chick notices a truly unsettling consequence of the negro's false arrest: every African American in town seems to have disappeared. Jefferson's blacks go into hiding for the very good reason that a lynching is in the air, but Chick seems to take the transformed scene as an emotional event. He knows that black people in Jefferson "were still there, they had not fled, you just didn't see them – a sense of feeling of their constant presence and nearness" (p. 356). But when Chick gets on the road to the graveyard, he panics that they're "not here, no sense feeling here of a massed adjacence, a dark human presence biding and unseen" (*idem*). This has something to do with his being in Beat Four, Yoknapatawpha's notorious bastion of clannish white supremacy. But it also reflects a repeated dread about a world "empty, vacant of any movement and any life" (p. 394). Chick senses that the outflow of millions of negroes from the South over the first half of the century might permanently alter, and diminish, the region. The novel's prose sometimes reflects the turbulence of a world undergoing rapid transformations, its social rhetoric struggling to keep up with new realities, as if you were neck-deep in a flooded stream, feeling for the bottom with your toes.

That Chick is thinking in terms of crowds of blacks and not just Lucas's individual dilemma also signals a new stage in Faulkner's consideration of social issues. You'll recall that in *Pylon* the formation of various kinds of masses interested Faulkner, no doubt in connection with the rise of fascism abroad and demagoguery like Hughie Long's in the US. But in some of his later works Faulkner revisits the question of crowds, masses, collectivities – to wonder about political agency, and to question elements of the ideal of American individualism. In addition to the absent black mass in *Intruder* – one that will rematerialize as the mass activism of the civil rights movement – Faulkner also registers the historical force of lynching mobs. Chick compulsively describes the march and flow of Beat Four's vigilantes into town, as well as the clotting and dissolving of various town groups – some seeming to threaten lynching, others seemingly gathered to enforce restraint. Chick may be admitting that the future of the South will depend on collective determinations, on political force wielded by groups of people to counteract a whole system's failures. The confederacy of Chick, Miss Habersham, and Aleck Sander is a hopeful beginning. The crowd Lucas joins on his way to ask for his receipt represents a further possibility: "the sidewalks dense and massed and slow with people black and white" (p. 462).

Faulkner pursues the question of guilt and shame in his next fictional work, *Requiem for a Nun* (1950), a hybrid of narrative prose and dramatic dialogue. A long chapter prefaces each of the three Acts, and together they recount the phased history of Yoknapatawpha in the most chronological version Faulkner ever attempted. It's still a highly selective and idiosyncratic account, but it confronts with bitter candor the pageant of ignoble behavior that established Southern plantation society and shaped the modern South. It also places that history in a global context, suggesting the complex web of hemispheric colonialism that crisscrossed national, as well as sectional development. Alternating dramatic scenes stage later events in the life of Temple Drake, now a married woman in her mid-twenties, mother of two, whose infant has just been murdered by the African American she employs as a nursemaid. That woman is Nancy Mannigoe, the protagonist of "That Evening Sun," here condemned to death after having been given a chance at rehabilitation by Temple and her husband Gowan Stevens (Gavin Stevens's nephew, and Temple's feckless escort in *Sanctuary*). Gowan has married Temple mostly to make up for the shame of abandoning her at the Frenchman's Place; Temple seems to have hired Nancy mostly to exorcise a secret shame of her own. These suffering sinners want to confess their wrongs, turn the instinct for revenge into acts of atonement, and believe there's redemption to be had through mortification. But I find *Requiem for a Nun* Faulkner's bleakest work, offering no salvation, no grounds for faith, little reason for hope. A requiem mass is a Roman Catholic ceremony bestowing repose upon the dead. A nun, like a monk (her male counterpart), devotes herself to solitary service to the faith. In Faulkner's book, devotion seems meaningless and repose unattainable, turning the title coldly ironic.

By 1950 something has thrown a cloud over Faulkner's more upbeat vision of domestic racial progress in *Intruder in the Dust*. That novel culminated a project that had occupied Faulkner through the 1940s: black civil rights, an issue of growing urgency during the inter-war years and of renewed activism in the post-war era that eventually led to legislative, social, and cultural breakthroughs in the 1950s. But as the modern South became increasingly integrated into national mentalities, unprecedented global conditions created new sources of anxiety for the country as a whole. The US had initiated the atomic age by dropping A-bombs on Hiroshima and Nagasaki in the closing days of World War II. That the emerging struggle for global domination between the USSR and the US would resort to mutual nuclear threat generated a kind of deep-to-the-bone terror: your own vaporization was only the touch of a button away, an atomic holocaust could end planetary life. Faulkner put this bluntly in his Nobel Prize acceptance speech, delivered in Stockholm in 1950, when he complained that fear on such massive scale would destroy the human spirit. No writer could concentrate on "the problems of the human heart in conflict with itself," he said, when the only question had become: "When will I be blown up?" Faulkner went on to insist that mankind could conquer such fear if writers would lead us to think again about the universally human issues of "courage and honor and hope and pride and compassion and pity and sacrifice which have been the glory of his past." Humans will prevail, not just endure, Faulkner concluded, because they will never allow that "last ding-dong of doom" to toll (*Essays, Speeches, and Public Letters*, pp. 119, 120.)

Although *Requiem* nowhere refers directly to the atomic age or to the geopolitical squaring off that would become the Cold War of the 1950s, I believe the book is Faulkner's most telling – if admittedly most cryptic – description of that era's mood of anxiety, futility, and despair.

FIGURE 4 Faulkner boarding his flight to Stockholm for the Nobel Prize awards ceremony in 1950. His wife Estelle sees him off; his daughter Jill (on right) will accompany him. Cofield Collection, Southern Media Archive, University of Mississippi Special Collections. Reproduced by permission of *The Memphis Commercial Appeal.*

An apocalyptic desperation circulates through both of the work's tangentially related stories: the development of Jefferson and the US South, on the one hand, and the humiliation of Temple Drake on the other. Both narratives involve monstrous acts of seizure and violation, brutal self-gratification at the expense of others, unimaginable acts of complicity with evil, devastating shame, and fruitless contrition.

In attempting to understand how the modern nation finds itself on the brink of (self-) destruction, Faulkner traces lines of historical continuity to the sweeping movements of exploration, colonization, settlement, indigenous removal, slavery, civil disunion, and the absorption of region into the modern national state. Temple Drake's horrific story shadows that national narrative like an antic commentary, neither tale suggesting that there's much to be gained from confessing past evil, even though the afflicted seem incapable of leaving the past alone. The logic of *Requiem* suggests that history will just end in black-out. At the conclusion of the first narrative section, Faulkner repeats lines from his Nobel speech, minus the hopefulness: the birds nesting in Jefferson's courthouse explode from their perches at each ringing of the hour; their scattering should be understood as doing nothing more than "adding one puny infinitesimal more to the long weary increment since Genesis" (*Requiem for a Nun*, p. 505) – nothing new, nothing significant. But it seems each time "as though" they "had shattered the virgin pristine air with the first loud dingdong of time and doom." It may be a mistake to over-react to signs of apocalypse, in other words, since the earth continues as ever on its weary round; still, that virgin air *has* been shattered, and somewhere up ahead time *may* end in doom.

What *Requiem* has lost is a sense of history's purpose. While Faulkner retells the chronicle of Yoknapatawpha with surprising comprehensiveness, he nonetheless can't seem to figure out where it's all going: "One nation: no longer anywhere" – "one universe, one cosmos: contained in one America: one towering frantic edifice poised like a cardhouse over the abyss of the mortgaged generations; one boom, one peace: one swirling rocket-roar filling the glittering zenith as with golden feathers," humankind bowed by "the vast and terrible burden beneath which he tries to stand erect and lift his battered and indomitable head" which is "murmurous with his fears and terrors and disclaimers and repudiations and his aspirations and dreams and his baseless hopes, bounding back at him in radar waves from the constellations" (pp. 638–639). Notice Faulkner's trademark style morphing yet again in this work, the heaping of connectives and the frenzied excesses now indicating a kind of authorial anxiety. His evocation of explosions and fears may hint at atomic age dread, as does a later reference to "the iron and fire of civilization" rendering a farm into a "desert" during the Civil War ("assuming that it was still there at all to be returned to") (p. 646). It's as if the specter of utter annihilation has triggered a confession that regional and national history has never been anything other than a meaningless scramble toward apocalyptic doom.

From the opening page of *Requiem*, the unifying theme of American history appears to be plunder. Beginning with the origins of Yoknapatawpha's county seat, the town of Jefferson, each of the subsequent inter-chapters widens its scope, the preface to Act Two recounting the founding of Mississippi's capital city of Jackson, that to Act Three carrying the story forward to the merging of the modern South with late 1940s America. It's soon apparent that the jaded narrator believes nothing has ever happened on the continent that wasn't motivated by greed and accomplished through chicanery. The town gets pushed to build its courthouse only because it was "going to cost somebody money" not to, and the records of the settlement eventually archived there constitute "the normal litter of man's ramshackle confederation against environment": documents recording the "dispossession of the Indians," "bills of sale for slaves and other livestock," "counting-house lists of spurious currency and exchange rates" (p. 475). It's no wonder this paper trail first gets stored in "a sort of iron pirate's chest" (*idem*). The initial trio of white settlers arrives at what is already a Chickasaw Agency trading post, an enterprise that will eventually lead the entire tribe into debt and the forfeiture of its land. As Holston, Habersham, and Grenier flourish, the Chickasaws fall for the worst in colonial culture. The tribe's matriarch, Mohataha, takes to dressing in European finery and being waited on by negro slave girls; eventually she signs off as a "kingdom passed to the white people" (p. 487), with the Chickasaws beginning their own terrible enactment of removal westward (pp. 621–622). Meanwhile, Holston establishes the settlement's hotel, Habersham becomes its physician, and Grenier sets up as its first cotton planter and slave owner. The pageant of acquisition and competition continues with the arrival of a second generation of would-be patriarchs: a Compson, who swaps a race horse for the most prized square mile of town real estate; a Sutpen, who scandalizes his coevals with his naked rapacity; a Sartoris, who promises to outdo the Sutpen. The town even gets its name in an act of bribery; a US postal employee, Thomas Jefferson Pettigrew, forgives the loss of a lock that is federal property in exchange for having a new town named after him.

By the time the narrator has tracked the engine of greed through the construction of the golden-domed state capitol in Jackson, he's reached a more furious degree of contempt:

a new time, a new age, millennium's beginning; one vast single net of commerce webbed and veined the mid-continent's fluvial embracement; New Orleans, Pittsburgh, and Fort Bridger, Wyoming, were suburbs one to the other, inextricable in destiny; men's mouths were full of law and order, all men's mouths were round with the sound of money; one unanimous golden affirmation ululated the nation's boundless immeasurable forenoon: profit plus regimen equals security: a nation of commonwealths; that crumb, that dome, that gilded pustule, that Idea risen now, suspended like a balloon or a portent or a thundercloud above what used to be wilderness, drawing, holding the eyes of all . . . (pp. 543–544)

It's a short step to later fulminations about a rapidly homogenizing national culture of consumption,

the county's hollow inverted air one resonant boom ululance of radio: and thus no more Yoknapatawpha's air nor even Mason and Dixon's air, but America's: the patter of comedians, the baritone screams of female vocalists, the babbling pressure to buy and buy and still buy arriving more instantaneous than light, two thousand miles from New York and Los Angeles. (p. 637)

The narrator uses two master terms to describe the course of history: progress and obsolescence. The first certainly is meant ironically, since there's nothing that could be considered an advance in the narrator's increasingly outraged chronicle of American materialism. The second is an anachronism of sorts, a term associated with advertising lingo: the artificial speed with which modern consumables fall out of fashion and are supposed to be replaced. Projecting that idea backward – even the Chickasaws are said to become obsolete and thus must be discarded – amounts to flattening all of national history into a fable of accumulation and dispossession.

Something bad happens to the very idea of history as a result too, since there's no forward motion to it. By the end of the preamble to Act Three, the narrator has begun speculating that the South no longer has any special meaning – except perhaps that it represents the past to a generally amnesiac society. But the idea that history is nothing but a kind of personal enrichment, something to intrigue you with long-ago days of Cavaliers, or move you with a romantic tale such as Cecilia Farmer's courtship – for that kind of history you may as well go to Disney World. The feebleness of Cecilia's scratch on the pane of the jail – "this was I" – points to the meaninglessness of human life: its end – its termination, but also its purpose – is death. *Requiem for a Nun* intuits a connection between the death-haunted future represented by nuclear holocaust, and the death-haunted past of American materialism. This is an association Don DeLillo will make consummately in *White Noise*, where the longing to fill spiritual vacancies with consumer goods opens traffic with a zombie realm of commodity fetishism. That novel's airborne toxic event is an objective correlative for a contamination that engulfs the soul. For Faulkner, the consequence is to reduce the American experience to a story of imprisonment. Crude inscriptions cover the walls of Jefferson's jail with a dense palimpsest of human striving; the scrawls all mean to say "no to death," but ultimately the generations of prisoners may be imagined posing "the old same unanswerable question three centuries after that which reflected them had learned that the answer didn't matter" (p. 617). It's the palpability of imminent annihilation that puts the nation's history under a death sentence in *Requiem*.

The narrative portions of *Requiem* suffocate with anxious repetition. You get multiple versions of many key events, such as the departure of the Chickasaws from town, as if the narrator has not been able to assimilate the record of brutalization and rapacity that traumatizes its witnesses. The story of the US from trading outpost to modern superpower does not unfold smoothly. The narrator exercises little mastery over what he tells; instead, partially processed scenes of Southern shame keep disturbing him. The narrative itself is less a story than a set of obsessive tableaux. The narrator confesses as much when he describes the Chickasaw matriarch leading her people out of Jefferson, looking "like a float or a piece of stage property dragged rapidly into the wings across the very backdrop and amid the very bustle of the property-men setting up for the next scene and act before the curtain had even had time to fall" (p. 622). As a presentable narrative of the South breaks down into a simple ledger of rapine, "the South" gets exposed as an ideological projection, a fantasy to fulfill needs; the movie *Gone With the Wind* is mentioned several times as moving Southerners with its "truthful" depiction of their suffering. When a band of prisoners escapes from the preliminary jail early in the life of the settlement, they go to the trouble of mocking the residents by dismantling an entire wall of the structure, "leaving the jail open to the world like a stage" (p. 484). It's precisely the theatricalized nature of this account – with its entertaining, larger-than-life figures and arresting tableaux – that also separates it from the kind of discourse that would constitute self-analysis, confession, atonement, relief.

The same quality of nightmarish repetition afflicts the other half of *Requiem*, Temple Drake's belated effort to save the life of Nancy Mannigoe, convicted of the murder of Temple's infant daughter. Temple remains tortured by the event of her rape eight years earlier – not just by what happens to her but also by her inability to figure out what to make of it. Temple cannot get over the fact that a mere lark like jumping off a college excursion train and meeting a date could lead to such catastrophe. What starts as a brazen defiance of paternal law, as we saw in our discussion of *Sanctuary*, turns into a horrible re-provocation of violent male power. Temple is drawn to Nancy not, as crude speculation puts it, because they have something "professional" in common as women of ill-repute, but because both have acted out against men's abuse. Nancy, you'll recall, was made pregnant by one of her white patrons, who knocks her to the ground and tries to kick in her teeth when she confronts him over his refusal to pay his sex tab. Nancy falls even lower after her imprisonment – becoming what Stevens repeatedly calls "a dope-fiend nigger whore" (p. 515). When Gowan and Temple give her a second chance, she reforms, then ends up crazily killing a child on behalf of the ideal of family. Nancy smothers the Stevens baby because Temple has decided to leave Gowan and her family for another man, the brother of the lover she takes at Popeye's insistence in *Sanctuary*. Temple seems determined to act yet again in defiance of paternal law – here embodied in her husband and uncle, who condemn her incessantly, mistrust her implicitly, and even accuse her of enjoying her time in the Memphis brothel.

What Temple also shares with Nancy is an inability to work through the shame and regret manacling them to the traumas they've suffered. Temple remains helplessly locked into cycles of reproducing the conditions of her own abuse. Besides her literal violation by a series of surrogates representing the father's right to govern his daughter's body, she "falls in love" with the gangster Red, then with his brother Pete, also a thug, but one who looks "like the general conception of a college man" (that is, also like her husband Gowan, the perpetual undergraduate gentleman). Equally bewilderingly, Nancy decides to kill a child on behalf of defending the sanctity of children within the family. Neither woman has figured out how to remove the wall from her cell, neither has found a way to express herself in an authentic vocabulary, neither has found a source of significance beyond her suffering at the hands of men. Confronted with the incomprehensibility of her crime, Nancy can only manage to assert that there must be some purpose in suffering, even if she does not know what it is:

NANCY: I dont know. I believes.
TEMPLE: Believe what?
NANCY: I dont know. But I believes.
(p. 661)

Nancy's inability to break out of empty repetitiveness here corresponds to Temple's stifled powers of expression. When she's forced into bondage by Popeye, Temple responds by forging a passion for his stand-in. She writes lascivious letters to Red, once again seeking independence through deeper subjugation. The letters later show up as part of a scheme by Pete to blackmail her, but Temple refuses to destroy them when they come into her possession. It's as if she still values their potential for accomplishing their real purpose, which is the scandalizing of the seemingly numberless phalanx of males who claim custody of her. Although Temple recognizes that she's being asked to tell her complete story to the governor, she also realizes that this is not the sort of self-inquiry that might allow her to work through her past as *she* might wish to. Quite the contrary: Stevens constantly hijacks Temple's account and stuffs in his own version instead. Her confession is hardly her own; it is contrived to save Nancy, directed at paternalistic state authorities, and further violated by Gavin and the governor when they arrange, out of solidarity with an offended husband, for Gowan to overhear Temple's confession. Gowan springs out of hiding to denounce Temple when he learns of her adultery – and the likely bastardy of his son. It's no wonder that *Requiem* ends with Temple as submissively in a man's tow as at the end of *Sanctuary*:

GOWAN'S VOICE (OFF-STAGE):   Temple.
TEMPLE: Coming.
(p. 664)

Nancy has been criminalized for her acts of non-compliance, Temple hystericized. The trauma attendant on their defiance of male authority breaks down both victims. Temple admits that she cannot cry – "If I could just cry" (p. 606) – presumably about either her dead child or her horrific assault. When she tells her story to Horace Benbow in *Sanctuary*, she's clearly in a state of dissociative denial – performing for him a "bright chatty monologue." In *Requiem* Temple repeats herself psychotically – much like the narrator of the inter-chapters, actually – as if she's terrified of telling all and having to remake herself. Under such repression, Temple's very body manifests her anguish; notice, for example, how many times we're told about her fidgeting with cigarettes: "Temple (takes cigarette from box on the table: mimics the prisoner; her voice, harsh, reveals for the first time repressed, controlled, hysteria)" (p. 508). Having failed to find a language for her defiance and suffering, Temple takes to murmuring in the same despairing vein as the narrator of the inter-chapters. In fact, they both quote from the same soliloquy of *Macbeth*, Temple distractedly repeating "tomorrow and tomorrow" (p. 662) like a shade of Quentin Compson, that "sound and fury" fellow, who would concur with her that life signifies nothing. The narrator chooses other lines from Macbeth's despairing last words to capture the tragedy of national rapacity: the wanton Anglo Saxon pioneer destroys the bountiful wilderness, and so himself: "disappeared, strutted his roaring eupeptic hour, and was no more" (p. 542).

The story of Temple Drake and the history of the plantation South coincide at junctures like this. Temple's assault reprises the whole nightmarish orgy of ravishment that constitutes the region's traumatic foundation. Temple is despoiled by Popeye at the so-called Frenchman's Place, the ruined mansion of the first plantation in Yoknapatawpha, which belonged to Louis Grenier, a Huguenot settler of Frenchman's Bend. Stevens notices Temple's compulsion to replay the accident there – "he will wreck the car again against the wrong tree, in the wrong place, and you will have to forgive him again" (p. 611); perhaps the ultimate source of the trauma is historical and involves the sedimentation – Benjy-style – of an entire archive of past brutalizations not yet laid to rest. Temple is a vessel of unprocessed, still raw pain caused by the endless re-enactment of trauma at this psychic site. The narrator refers to the amoral early settlers as a "simple fraternity of rapine," and to the surrounding nearby wilderness as "three hundred miles of rapine-haunted Trace" (p. 481). Such "rapine-haunted" memories elicit descriptions of the violent deflowering of the wilderness: "the hands, the prehensile fingers clawing dragging lightward out of the disappearing wilderness . . . the broad rich fecund burgeoning fields, pushing thrusting each year further and further back" (p. 499). There's something eerily Popeye-like about those fumbling fingers and that thrusting insistence. Sexual rapacity empowers the Anglo-Saxon "pioneer," "spawning" children out of "his over-revved glands" "behind the barricade of a rifle-crotched log," and "at the same time scattering his ebullient seed in a hundred dusky bellies through a thousand miles of wilderness" (p. 542). The original "underworld[s]" Jefferson denies having traffic with were the long ago bandit realms of River and Trace (p. 477). The settlers insist instead on the illusion of legitimacy. When Jefferson's founders lock up their first offenders, they slip a wooden beam in place across "the door like on a corncrib." The haunting memory of intercourse with the underworld returns in the person of the gangland Popeye, as the memory of ruthlessly violating the virgin land resurfaces in the trope of the corn/cob/crib. The language and imagery of Temple's rape repeats and betrays Jefferson's rapine-haunted past.

Temple gets accused of loving her ravishment, and she later admits that she could have escaped Miss Reba's whenever she wanted. Negro slaves are imputed with pride at the construction of so magnificent an edifice as the courthouse. Part of the continuing psychosis of the South, according to Faulkner's brilliantly troubled work, is that privileged Southerners refuse to confront their own complicity in unspeakable practices. Instead, the guilt shows up symptomatically, even, worst, in the attribution of willing complicity to its victims. At one point the national and personal narratives touch – on the question of how both stink: Temple refers to foreign travel as a way to "fumigate an American past" (p. 577), but then admits that "I didn't want to efface the stink really" (*idem*). There seems no exit from the sense that the imminence of global extinction has demystified the record of human striving, revealing it as a tale signifying nothing. Faulkner's black mood in *Requiem* descends from the dread of total human annihilation – a prospect that reduces the entirety of human accomplishment to a wan inscription: "we were here." Without even the assurance anyone will be around to read it.

At its publication in 1940, *The Hamlet* reflected a time of both national and global inconclusiveness on the eve of World War II. You'll recall that at the end of this first novel of the Snopes trilogy, the share-cropper Mink Snopes is left incarcerated, while the speculator Flem seems destined for dominance; the metropolis beckons while the provinces languish; the ambitious adopt national models of success – "Wallstreet," "Montgomery Ward" – while local fiefdoms fade. The novel's lurch toward modernity corresponds with world developments as well: working-class retreat before corporate advance; the rise of state nationalisms; and the stirrings of anti-colonialism, anti-racism, and women's equality that jostled uncertainly during the war years. In the decade and a half between *The Hamlet* in 1940 and *The Town* in 1957, however, many of these conflicts within modernity came to be subsumed under Cold War priorities. As Odd Arne Westad puts it in his study of the period, the global Cold War emerged after World War II as perhaps the central discourse of the later century's international history.[3]

In the mid-1950s, Faulkner globalizes Snopesism as a Cold War drama. The later trilogy places the regional story of Flem's rise and Mink's resentment into the context of the conflict between the two principal narratives of Western progress: the spread of freedom and the advance of equality. As the Cold War hardened ideological differentiation, freedom became the watchword for US capitalist democracy, while a vision of egalitarianism inspired Soviet-style communism. Faulkner himself understood the "battleground" between the era's "two mighty forces" in these terms. In a pamphlet addressed to Japanese students in 1955, he emphasizes that the only hope for humankind rests in the ideal of "freedom," although, he hastens to add, such liberty "must be complete freedom for all."[4] Elsewhere, speaking against US racism, he insists that the defense of freedom cannot be separated from a commitment to equality: "we cannot choose freedom established on a hierarchy of degrees of freedom"[5]; "belief in individual liberty and equality and freedom . . . is the one idea powerful enough to stalemate the idea of communism" ("On Fear," p. 102).

In resuming the Snopes trilogy at this point, Faulkner reflects a shift in national mood. The dread of nuclear holocaust that overshadowed the early 1950s had eased somewhat by mid-decade. The USSR's ruthless and unpredictable dictator, Joseph Stalin, had died in 1953, and was succeeded by Nikita Krushchev, who in general pursued a more rational foreign policy, and seemed to regard nuclear warfare as a last resort to be avoided. In 1955 the Geneva Conference produced some accord between the US, USSR, and other former Allies about what to do with the defeated European states. Faulkner joined into the Cold War's cultural competition with the Soviet Union by agreeing to foreign tours sponsored by the US State Department. He hated to travel, hated to take time from his writing, but evidently undertook this duty as a representative of international good will and cross-cultural understanding. By the middle of the decade, some of the despair over total destruction that paralyzes *Requiem* had eased; perhaps the Cold War would be a contest of beliefs that could actually produce, if not an outright victory, than at least a survivable "stalemate." Even so, Faulkner refused to side uncritically with USA-ism during the 1950s standoff of superpowers. As Cold War opposition to communism became a national preoccupation, Faulkner put difficult questions to capitalist democracy's certitudes.

In *The Town* Faulkner picks up the story of Flem's ascent where it left off in *The Hamlet*, relating the newcomer's early Jefferson phase by incorporating wholesale the already published short stories "Centaur in Brass" and "Mule in the Yard." The novel's format complicates the presentation of these episodes, however, since instead of a bemused anonymous town narrator, we have several identified members of Jefferson's offended establishment chronicling the Snopes invasion. You may recall that *The Hamlet* employs third-person narration throughout, although it also uses a lot of free indirect discourse to convey the speech and point of view of Flem's principal antagonist in Frenchman's Bend, V. K. Ratliff. The sewing-machine salesman reappears in *The Town*, but now only as one of a set of rotating narrators who speak in their own voices through a sequence of named sections. In *The Town* Faulkner opens his account of Snopesism to multiple perspectives, the effect of which is to make the reader think harder about the conflict of interests – economic, social, personal – that dictate how events are told. Although all of the narrators Faulkner chooses have reason to oppose the spread of Snopesism, they begin to respond with a wider range of comprehension and discrimination than we've seen before. As Chick Mallison observes when he listens to Flem and his Uncle Gavin discuss a legal dispute: "And that's when Uncle Gavin found out that he and Mr. Snopes were looking at exactly the same thing: they were just standing in different places" (*The Town*, p. 148).

From Gavin Stevens's point of view, "Snopes" amounts to nothing but "a whole family's long tradition of slow and invincible rapacity" (p. 29). To him it hardly matters which Snopes he's dealing with, "they none of them seemed to bear any specific kinship to one another; they were just Snopeses, like colonies of rats or termites are just rats and termites" (p. 36). Gavin's grievance with this new species of predator involves more than the fact of their subhuman greed; deep down he also resents that they have overturned his own kind's economic advantage. He seethes with mocking self-contempt as he imagines how one day the Sartorises, Ratliffs, and Stevenses will themselves require the protection of the Snopeses; having gained the whole town, they will have to "defend and shield us, their vassals and chattels, too" (p. 39).

When he urges Eula Varner Snopes's teenaged daughter Linda to flee town when she chooses a college, Gavin insists that Snopesism has entirely overrun his cherished place: "Jefferson was Snopes" (p. 191). Gavin begins his tutelage of Linda as a kind of war against Snopesism – its vulgar materialism, its small-town imitation of everything modern, its bourgeois provincialism. Flem has installed his trophy wife Eula in a starter house decorated, Stevens sneers, as if from a photograph in *"Town and Country* labeled *American Interior"* with "the added legend: *This is neither a Copy nor a Reproduction. It is our own Model scaled to your individual Requirements"* (p. 194). JD and PhD that he is, Stevens acknowledges that Flem doesn't even have a business education, let alone a general one (p. 231), so you could hardly expect more of him than magazine style. When Flem builds his own place, he decides on something straight out of *Gone with the Wind*: in Ratliff's words, a mansion with "extry big" "colyums" across the front, "like in the photographs where the Confedrit sweetheart in a hoop skirt and a magnolia is saying good-bye to her Confedrit beau" (p. 309). Gavin takes as his mission the rescue of Linda from this cesspool of modern middle America. It means everything to him that Linda should get to a place like Greenwich Village, a kind of "college" all its own (p. 307), "with a few unimportant boundaries but no limitations where young people of any age go to seek dreams."

Stevens attempts to oppose the "Snopes industry" (p. 111) with his cosmopolitan refinement, mulling lines from T. S. Eliot as he contemplates his disgust with modern life. When he begins meeting Linda after school at the ice cream shop, the middle-aged Stevens wonders what he is doing trying to enlighten a high school teenager, and a Snopes one at that: "the interminable time until a few minutes after half past three filled with a thousand indecisions which each fierce succeeding harassment would revise" (p. 181). Stevens resembles the J. Alfred Prufrock whose "Lovesong" he alludes to here, since both spin a cocoon of super-refinement to rationalize their fear of change and refusal to engage modernity. Yes, the Snopeses endanger the cultivated way of life that better off Jeffersonians have come to expect as their due. But it's the terror of losing his economic advantage that creates Stevens's extreme condemnation of everything Snopes, in much the way Quentin can't find anything to his taste in the new world he's been kicked into. Stevens' family does not belong to the plantation gentry, and the professional classes who used to live off that system now must confront an unappetizing new clientele: muddy men on the make like the Snopeses.

Gavin amasses a lavish education (Harvard, Heidelberg) only to end up in the Jefferson City Attorney's office of his grandfather. The lawyer retreats to a fantasy, reviving the local cult of Eula Varner-worship. To Gavin, Eula inspirationally defies the soul-sapping conformity and respectability of small town middle-class America. She takes up with Manfred de Spain, son of Major de Spain and president of the Merchants' and Farmers' Bank, the two of them scandalously zipping around town in the banker's red convertible. All of those bemoaning the damage inflicted by the Snopeses' obsession with money admire the couple's zest, especially Gavin, who dubs it "the divinity of simple unadulterated uninhibited immortal lust" (p. 13). Stevens is using Eula as the menfolk in Frenchman's Bend did, as a fetish object that transcends the commodification of everything. She's exalted as too much to incorporate into familiar economies of domestic desire – "even a whole Jefferson full of little weak puny frightened men couldn't have stood more than one Mrs Snopes inside of just one one-hundred years" (p. 65).

Faulkner condenses the whole modern trend toward commodifying pleasure in the activities of a Snopes named, appropriately, Montgomery Ward, who opens Jefferson's first pornography shop upon returning from YMCA service in Paris during the war. Faulkner will have more to say about this escapade in *The Mansion*, but for now we might note how Monty seizes on the genius of the modern entertainment industry, without ever needing to visit Hollywood. The war canteen he runs in France proves the army's most popular because of an innovation he comes up with: "a new fresh entertainment room with a door in the back and a young French lady" (p. 100). The experiment teaches him the advantages of manufacturing cultural goods over making real ones: as the sewing machine salesman Ratliff concludes admiringly,

> no matter how much money you swap for ice cream and chocolate candy and sody pop, even though the money still exists, that candy and ice cream and sody pop dont any more because it has been consumed and will cost some of that money to produce and replenish, where in jest strict entertainment there aint no destructive consumption at all that's got to be replenished at a definite production labor cost ... (pp. 101–102)

Here's the formula for the eventual US global empire in information and entertainment industries. Monty's "magic lantern" is a metaphor for the way images of desirable things may be made profitable all by themselves, the gratifications of commodified pleasure epitomized as pornography.

The Town shows some awareness of the global stage on which this kind of capitalism will have its day. Chick recalls that his Uncle Gavin's nephew, Gowan Stevens, has been the source of some of the stories about Flem's initial doings in Jefferson. Gowan returns to Jefferson as a thirteen-year-old, a few years before Chick is born, when his father, employed by the State Department, is sent for a term of service to "China or India or some far place" (p. 3). Since later we learn that Gowan's parents may be stuck in their foreign posting because of "the war in Europe" (p. 92), it would seem that Flem's career gets off the ground in counterpoint to the rise of American empire during the Great War. (In fact, Gowan's father could be an appointee of Woodrow Wilson, the first Southern president since the Civil War, elected in 1912; later, Gavin Stevens will be invited to serve on a postwar European reconstruction committee (one wonders whether it is only for his having lived in Germany, or also for his Southerner's view of such programs [p. 99].) The horizon of world empire gets glimpsed only fleetingly in *The Town*, but it's enough to suggest how this second installment of the Snopes trilogy is developing a broader framework for understanding the phenomena of modernity: the aspirations and mobility of a peasant class, the emergence of finance capitalism and consumer culture, the ambitions for democratic empire through economic and cultural domination.

Stevens wrinkles his nose at these revolting developments, but Faulkner doesn't entirely side with his dismissal. The author can allow for a form of capitalism, for example, that might have more humane ends than raw profit-taking. Wallstreet Panic Snopes, for instance, gets an idea about starting a wholesale grocery in Jefferson modeled on national chains. The venture brings a greater variety of produce, more cheaply, to town dwellers, and incidentally helps him save his father-in-law's farm. Even Gavin approves Wallstreet's "simple honesty and industry" (p. 129), and Ratliff points out that at least this one Snopes has demonstrated exceptional integrity by turning down Flem's demand to invest in the business, mostly at the insistence of his wife, who loathes Snopesism. Marrying one, she gets the opportunity "to beat Snopes from the inside" (p. 132). Faulkner harbors a hope that the sort of market capitalism driven by profit-madness might be countered by a more ethical form, the tempered, personalized sort Ratliff practices in *The Hamlet*, and the kind characterized as "socially embedded" by David Harvey, who uses this term to characterize market economies that accommodate obligations to common social welfare.[6] Faulkner keeps the question open in *The Town* and pursues it in *The Mansion*.

In so doing, the author also gently mocks Stevens's impassioned denunciation of the concentric circles of "rapacity" that constitute "the record and annal" of his "native land" (p. 277). Stevens winds up a typically overblown and melodramatic survey of life's meaningless pageant of greed, above which he tries to hold himself: he views that

> fat black rich plantation earth still synonymous of the proud fading white plantation names whether we – I mean of course they – ever actually owned a plantation or not: Sutpen and Sartoris and Compson and Edmonds and McCaslin and Beauchamp and Grenier and Habersham and Holston and Stevens and De Spain. (p. 278)

As it turns out, there's no way to exempt himself from the "we" – since his "we" were part of the world created by the plantation owners' "they." Conceding that the Varners and Snopeses are only the latest and outermost of the rings of local greed, Stevens remains puzzled that life continues to beckon to him, that he can't give up. Despite the monotony of the human story, there's something about its "inconclusiveness" that makes it both tragic and vital. Faulkner mocks himself as Stevens here, a polysyllabically inclined "white-headed" "old man," who reluctantly gets drawn into the problems of Flem's designs, Eula's debasement, and Linda's rescue. In Faulknerian cadences, the passage suggests that it's deadly to oppose change, which is motion, which is life itself; instead, to be alive is to enter, yet again, into "whatever your new crisis is" (p. 279). And there, in fact, we find Faulkner at the end of his career: still fiercely taking on the most urgent new crises of his day.

Published in 1959, two years after *The Town*, *The Mansion* engages at every level with the defining geopolitical conditions of its era. *The Mansion* directly addresses numerous Cold War issues: US Communist Party activities, red-baiting, Greenwich Village bohemianism, artistic avant-gardism, and European fascism. The result is the most topical of all Faulkner's novels. Faulkner does more than offer reflections on contemporary world events, however; he undertakes a systematic exploration of conflicting Cold War principles. He shows how Cold War ideals on both sides represent legitimate aspirations for progressive change, yet how vestigial mentalities protect vested interests. Extending his earlier encounter with the history of colonialism, Faulkner now detects that history's after-life in the presumption of American superiority. In the later Snopes trilogy Faulkner criticizes the pieties of US free worldism for disregarding the casualties of injustice that strew the path of American triumphalism.

Faulkner organizes his last Snopes novel as a standoff between two powerful motives: the demand for revenge and the desire for freedom. Mink Snopes, the protagonist of the novel, waits 38 years before finally gaining his release from Parchman Penitentiary. Whereupon he makes his way to Flem's parlor to even a very old score. Faulkner tightens the bow of this narrative over the course of the entire trilogy; *The Hamlet* ends with Mink beginning his prison sentence, having been betrayed by Flem, stunned that his kinsman deems respectability thicker than blood. Mink neither forgives nor forgets. Flem knows what's coming when Mink gets out of jail, so he tricks Mink into attempting a premature prison break, and gains a second term of protection for himself.

Unlike the earlier volumes of the trilogy, *The Mansion* actually tries to understand a Snopes. In *The Hamlet,* Faulkner shows pity for damaged Snopeses like Ike and Ab, as he ridicules soulless ones like Flem and I.O. But there's no getting inside those wolverine brains. In *The Mansion,* however, Faulkner devotes the first long chapter of the novel to Mink, using free indirect discourse to render his point of view and expressive habits. We begin to grasp the world as Mink does, and learn that his singular preoccupation is the question of fairness. He pays his court-imposed fine to Houston painstakingly, for example, all the while trying to convince himself that eventually he'll get a fair shake.

> He meant, simply, that *them – they – it,* whichever and whatever you wanted to call it, who represented a simple fundamental justice and equity in human affairs, or else a man might just as well quit; the *they, them, it,* call them what you like, which simply would not, could not harass and harry a man forever without some day, at some moment, letting him get his own just and equal licks back in return. (*The Mansion,* pp. 335–336).

Mink remains partial to homicide as the equalizer of choice, and his demands for "fundamental justice" never surpass his uncle Ab's bitter vengefulness. Mink epitomizes Southern farm laborers' underdeveloped capacity to reorganize agricultural capitalism through class pressure. He does get into trouble initially because he has the audacity to launch a resistance movement of his own, however misbegotten. Mink sets his scrawny cow free one fall, letting his prosperous neighbor Houston winter it, before claiming it again in the spring as a newly identified "stray." To cover the implausibility of his ruse, Mink invents a story about selling the cow to a distant farmer, whom Mink claims to have reimbursed when he discovers the cow has wandered back. But Mink's scheme is motivated more by pure resentment than any bid to better his financial condition. He is goaded into action only because he cannot stand the sight of Houston's prosperity and, worse, the superior airs of Houston's black overseer. Mink hardly cares about the chance to turn a profit; he cannot get over the eight dollars he knows he will have to pay Houston to get his cow back, even though he knows he's far ahead on the wintering costs (and will be farther ahead if his cow is returned pregnant, as is likely). He rages at what might be called the temporality of capitalism, frustrated that he cannot gain "simple justice and inalienable rights" "at one stroke," but "must depend on the slow incrementation of feed converted to weight" (p. 341). Mink's time is never more than mere waiting, without issue – "prolongation" it is called (*idem*). The individual tenant cannot hope to turn a worthwhile profit; farming like this, as Flem puts it at the outset of his mercantile career, has no "benefit." Flem, on the other hand, understands that speculative time is fungible, figuring out, for example, how to collect nickels and dimes in perpetual receipt of interest from the incomprehending victims of his usury.

Mink's incarceration in The Prison Farm at Parchman just makes literal his economic confinement. Working the state's cotton fields under armed guard hardly differs from being indentured to Varner. He has heard of the "commonist" cause (p. 416), as he once puts it, but he never develops a political consciousness. He fumes at Houston for "being a rich man too and all you rich folks has got to stick together or else maybe some day the ones that aint rich might take a notion to raise up and take hit away from you" (p. 366). But he adds that that's not the reason he's murdered his nemesis; the killing comes from a sense of personal dishonor, the result of Houston's gratuitous assessment of an "extry" dollar pound fee. Just as he swears to get even with Flem not for duping him into trying to break prison but for the unnecessary insult of providing a woman's dress and sun bonnet to do it in, Mink repeatedly acts on trivial motives, and gains nothing from them but self-ruination. Notice how Montgomery Ward, who, unlike Mink, follows in Flem's commercial footsteps, describes what it means to be a Snopes: "I realised that I had come from what you might call a family, a clan, a race, maybe even a species, of pure sons of bitches" (p. 409). All doubtless apt, but of course what's missing from the list is "class." As we have seen in *The Town*, the businessman Montgomery Ward embraces the myth of individualism as it sanctions entrepreneurial capitalism – every son of a bitch looking out for himself. But the tenant farmer Mink will only be driven into the ground by standing alone.

Faulkner molds Mink's story around the ideal of working-class justice that inspires communism.[7] "Commonist" solutions to the excesses of property appealed to Faulkner; he imagines them most sympathetically in Uncle Ike's dream of a return to the "communal anonymity of brotherhood" under which Native Americans held the land, before any white man had arrived to say, "Get away! This is mine." Later in *The Mansion*, Mink receives help according to his need from a communitarian Protestant congregation. Faulkner also sharpens the issue of class conflict in *The Mansion* by adjusting his depiction of Houston. In *The Hamlet* Houston is barely getting by himself, having mortgaged most of his land to Will Varner, while in *The Mansion*, perhaps to underscore the tenant's resentment, he appears as a lordly man of wealth. As for Mink, Faulkner suggests that the sort of economic system that has evolved in the modern South has put the landless laborer into a state of arrested development. Mink is repeatedly described as a "small frail creature not much larger than a fifteen-year-old boy" (p. 376). The commonist fails to attain majority status.

Historically, of course, Southern workers did organize unions and other collective organizations to defend their rights. A number of the more radical activists managed to affiliate with the Communist Party, though farmers were less likely to join than urban industrial wage laborers.[8] Faulkner knows that efforts to forge common cause along class lines were often sabotaged by ideologies upholding the American way of capitalism. To begin with, there was the impregnable fiction of individual success. When Faulkner has two comic communist Finns show up looking futilely for Jefferson's "proletariat" (p. 522), they never do learn that there *is* no proletariat in Jefferson. There's not even a middle class, the poor "being convinced instead that it was merely in a temporary interim state toward owning in its turn Mr Snopes's bank or Wallstreet Snopes's wholesale grocery chain or (who knows?) on the way to the Governor's mansion in Jackson or perhaps the White House in Washington" (p. 523). I suppose the Finns would have to wait for Mega Millions or "American Idol" to get the point.

A second condition stalling class solidarity in the South, of course, was racism, a remnant of colonial ideology, invented to rationalize slavery, and reanimated to promote post-Emancipation peonage. Faulkner suggests this obstacle in having Mink misdirect his class resentment at a racial target, Houston's black employee: "I don't listen to niggers: I tell them" (p. 344). Mink's brain is as much his prison as

Parchman. He embodies the stubborn entrenchment of ruling-class fictions even in those for whom they do nothing. Mink's story validates the ideal of justice while suggesting how it has been thwarted by those who profit from injustice. Faulkner tells the story of failed working-class "commonism" from the historical perspective of the 1950s, when the fetishes of capitalist individualism and racism take on fresh life in the Cold War nation, as well as when the reflexes of proletarian resentment and class conflict seem as anachronistic as the time-encapsulated Mink.

Over the course of *The Mansion*, Faulkner enlarges the narrative of justice to touch on numerous other struggles for social equality. The novel takes seriously the determination of communists like Barton Kohl and Linda Snopes to fight against oppression.[9] Faulkner treats the couple's involvement in the Spanish Civil War respectfully; he cared about this cause himself, donating his manuscript of *Absalom, Absalom!* to a fundraising campaign on behalf of the Spanish Loyalists, and even subscribing to the anti-Franco, anti-fascist statement that accompanied it.[10] As well, the novel makes much of Linda Snopes Kohl's personal feminism: her military heroism, her wartime factory work, her physical strength, and her sexual freedom. Paradoxically, it is Linda who grows impatient with Jim Crow education in Jefferson, while a gradualist African American principal quoting Booker T. Washington asks her to stop interfering. It is left to a younger black man later to defend Linda's work on behalf of racial progress.

In these episodes it seems clear that Faulkner understands how Cold War communism was rightly pressuring traditional forms of American inequality. Although the Cold War did provide rationalizations for shooing women back toward household duties, and strengthening the defense of American economic and sexual "norms," social practices that violated the ideal of liberty and justice for all became points of ideological vulnerability during the Cold War. Truman and later John F. Kennedy were particularly sensitive to Soviet propaganda in the Third World about the shortcomings of US civil rights. For many Cold Warriors, Southern desegregation mattered as much to global politics as to domestic ones. Civil rights activists seized the moment, while, likewise, numerous women's organizations "joined together to use the Cold War as an opportunity for collective action on behalf of women" (Meyerowitz, 2001, p. 111).

In *The Mansion* Faulkner suggests that the South, as the forgotten subtext of national failure, exploitation, and hypocrisy, contradicts American pride in itself as the land of freedom, equal opportunity, and justice. The prevailing contemporary view of the South as the nation's number one economic *problem* functions critically for Faulkner by exposing the South as the country's Achilles heel. As one of its central concerns, then, *The Mansion* is determined to recognize the longings for economic justice that fail to be answered by American democratic capitalism. Faulkner's portrait of Mink Snopes represents him as a global South's agricultural proletariat, a Third World composite who awaits recognition and recompense.[11]

If Faulkner bravely defends the claims of justice associated with the left at the height of the Cold War, he likewise criticizes the so-called Free World's perversion of freedom. Faulkner begins *The Mansion* with an eye-popping fusillade directed at the commodification of everything. For page after page the novel initiates us into the subhuman mentality that reduces everything to monetary valuation. Beginning with Mink's desperate cry for help – "I'll pay you – Flem'll pay you!" (p. 333) – through the torturously obsessive calculations of Mink's cow scheme, down to an obscene allegory of market intercourse that has country preachers providing sexual favors to frustrated farmwives in exchange for home-style cooking ("the job of filling his hole in payment for getting theirs plugged . . . the wives coming because here was the best market they knowed of to swap a mess of fried chicken or a sweet-potato pie; the husbands coming not to interrupt the trading" [p. 335]) – Faulkner imagines the endless grotesqueries of the lust for money.

Faulkner responds to Cold War preoccupations by broadening the significance of Flem's career in *The Mansion*. If Flem was little more than a local redneck in *The Hamlet*, by the 1950s he bids to become an American icon. The key to Flem's ultimate ascent to the presidency of the Merchants' and Farmers' Bank of Jefferson involves his adoption of national models of managerial capitalism. When Flem succeeds to office, he makes a point of trading in his cloth cap for "a black felt planter's hat suitable to his new position and avocation" (p. 453). That hat points to the financial lineage of Jefferson's wealth, to the founders Major de Spain and Will Varner, who represent, respectively, the planter class and the commercial class of landholders. But it evokes an even more august forebear as well, the nation's Founding Planter, who inspires the banker to do an extreme make-over of his digs so they resemble Mt. Vernon. Snopes sits idly in this "monument" the rest of his days, occupying what Faulkner calls "a colonial monstrosity" (p. 513), the "Snopes-colonial-mausoleum" (p. 645). At one point, Flem has a piece of wood affixed to the mantel where he props his feet, to remind him, Ratliff speculates, of his origins, but practically to protect the finish from wear. It's as if Flem imagines his place in the pantheon of American capitalists, his house already "the solid ancestral symbol of Alexander Hamilton and Aaron Burr and Astor and Morgan and Harriman and Hill and every other golden advocate of hard quick-thinking vested interest" (p. 470). Flem wants to be careful; he figures someday there might be tours.

The utter vacuity of Flem's life calls into question what the US thinks it is doing in the Cold War. As Faulkner suspects, the empire of freedom looks mainly like an imperial free market, its only rule the "trompling" of the poor on the road to the palace of leisure. If Flem's mansion stands as the culmination of New World plantation colonialism, then Faulkner has indeed unearthed the bloodline of Cold War capitalism. One character summarizes US foreign policy after World War II as all a matter of dollars: "If they had let us lick the Russians too, we might a been all right. But they just licked the Krauts and Japs and then decided to choke everybody else to death with money" (pp. 427–428). Or as Montgomery Ward Snopes puts it drily, having been framed by his cousin Flem, he welcomes Parchman because at least he'll be "safe from the free world, safe and secure for a little while yet from the free Snopes world" (p. 406).

Patterns of colonial domination organize modern American consumption as well. Even an expanding market does not enfranchise equally. Montgomery Ward's infamous Atelier Monty brilliantly symbolizes Faulkner's conviction that profiting off of the wants of the needy amounts to a sort of pornography, that behind the traffic in consumer desire is "what you might call a dry whorehouse" (p. 379). French erotic postcards may enflame male lust in Jefferson, but they function like all capitalist spectacle to represent the barrier to gratification as itself the source of pleasure. Miss Reba, the mistress of a bordello in Memphis who has heard about Monty's enterprise, underscores the distance between classes of consumers:

> just looking at pictures might do all right for a while down there in the country where there wasn't no other available handy outlet but . . . sooner

or later somebody was going to run up enough temperature to where he would have to run to the nearest well for a bucket of real water. (p. 402).[12]

It is the poor and distant who are excluded from metropolitan gratifications – at least until they break out and make a run for the real thing. Once Montgomery Ward grasps Miss Reba's point about the relation of his business to hers, he realizes that his franchise is just the "desert-outpost branch" (*idem*). Faulkner anticipates views of global modernization that emphasize the power of US marketing to Third World consumers. Figured by Montgomery Ward's repackaging of French postcards, extended in Mink Snopes's orgasmic consumption of cold Coca-Colas the minute he's out of prison, it is US-driven market domination, Faulkner suggests, that the ideology of the Free World means to defend during the Cold War.

In probing modern American capitalism and its sustaining culture of consumption, Faulkner grasps another feature of its pathology, its fundamental reliance on the abuse of women. As deeply as any book Faulkner wrote, *The Mansion* sees how masculine "self-making" involves the forcible command of female bodies and labor. The novel includes a number of episodes in which men batter women into submission: Mink, for example, having to compensate for his lost hours of work, "with vicious and obscene cursing drove the three of them, his wife and the two girls, with the three hoes out to the patch to chop out his early cotton" (p. 364). Mink knows this drill intimately, since he once recalls from "deep in memory" (p. 426) a scene in which his step-mother has been beaten so badly by Mink's father that she cannot eat. Mink remembers her as "always either with a black eye or holding a dirty rag to her bleeding" (*idem*).

Such brutal violence is the bedrock of the more genteel forms of financial exploitation practiced on women in the trilogy. Faulkner understands that misogyny is not incidental, but instrumental to an American-style capitalism based on the rights of private property (to wives, land, slaves), the legal power to coerce labor, the lawful entitlement of men to women's financial assets. Flem's scheme to have Linda make him the beneficiary of her will simply literalizes the association between dead women and living patrimonies. Even Chick can see that "the record of success and victory behind [Flem] already had two deaths in it," Eula's suicide the freshest. Faulkner provides a nearly anthropological grasp of the foundational commodification of women, tracking Eula's fungibility for her father and husband through numerous permutations, to its last word as real estate: Eula Acres.

When Faulkner gets to the cultural symbolism of misogyny, then, he makes us see sexual depravity as more than just a convenient image for capitalist corruption. Miss Reba's remark that her patrons "come in here to do business" (p. 400) conveys a literal truth, Faulkner's extensive thematics of prostitution and promiscuity throughout his fiction suggesting the conflation of sexual and financial commerce. Consider the sub-plot involving Virgil Snopes's "really exceptional talent" to "take care of two girls in succession to their satisfaction or at least until they hollered quit" (p. 398). Clarence Snopes capitalizes on his nephew's prowess by marketing him, and dreaming of his big future, "if the supply of two-dollar whores just holds out" (*idem*). The practices of sexuality are so laced with economic language, and the practices of economics with the language of sexuality, that Faulkner seems to be suggesting more than just a figurative relation between them. It's not analogy, or even homology, that aligns capitalism and sexual exploitation, but their mutual history as social institutions.

Faulkner evokes perhaps the most iconic representation of these matters in the portrait of the young Linda Snopes, who stands in a long line in American literature of fetishized nymphets representing a national psychosis: the transgressive consumption of unspoiled goods. Besides Faulkner's own Eula Varner, Temple Drake, and Little Belle Mitchell, we might think of Fitzgerald's Nicole Warren Diver and Rosemary Hoyt in *Tender is the Night* or Nabokov's Dolores Haze in *Lolita*, published in 1955, just two years before *The Town*. Such figures share defining features: they combine excessive desirability with prohibition against it, often in the form of incest taboos; despite their innocence, they are made responsible for their own violation by their purported seductiveness; they function as emblems for broader dynamics of consumption; and they are frequently associated with the vulgarity of mass culture.

Gavin Stevens wonders if he can't emancipate his Lolita instead of devouring her. Rather than succumb to temptation, Gavin perfects habits of renunciation. With her mother's encouragement, Linda meets the lawyer who is twice her age at the drugstore a couple of times a week, where "she et a ice-cream sody or a banana split and the ice melted into the unteched coca cola in front of him" (p. 451). Stevens undertakes Linda's informal education during these sessions, tutoring her in the poets, telling her about northern colleges, and mostly urging her to get out of Jefferson and leave everything Snopes behind. Stevens directs her toward New York City, not as the classic destination for materializing the American dream, but as the place where she can discover oppositional culture. Linda's escape to Greenwich Village yields her a Jewish lover, a communist sculptor committed to radical politics and experimental aesthetics. Already signaled by Gavin's refusal to touch his Coca-Cola, Linda's liberation constitutes a different kind of freedom; it repudiates "the free Snopes world" of money-making and consumption. She bids to emancipate herself from false norms of behavior attached to national origin, region, class, family, race, gender, marital relation – norms fetishized by Cold War America, but questioned here as functioning primarily to rationalize power-holding.

Faulkner's political fable in *The Mansion* exposes the shortcomings of US Cold War conflict-thinking on several counts. Not only does America's preoccupation with the defense of personal liberty deafen it to the claims of justice, but the assumption that freedom is synonymous with free marketry ignores the numerous fatalities behind capitalism's success story. Beyond this diagnostic insight, moreover, Faulkner manages to suggest longings for more authentic freedom, in which liberty and justice need not conflict, where the discrepancy between the idle rich and the imprisoned worker need not end in murderous confrontation. Faulkner hints at possibilities for a progressive modernity not adequately represented by the ideologies of either democratic capitalism or Stalinist communism. Its general principle has to do with a fairer distribution of the goods capitalism creates. The Allanovna designer ties Ratliff finds in New York appeal to his love of sensory pleasure, as does Barton Kohl's modernist sculpture.[13] Faulkner presents such experiences inarguably as elevations of imagination, expansions of spirit. Something similar occasionally lifts Mink out of his subhuman battle for survival. Mink has a thing for trains, cars, and movies. Whenever he can, he spends a night at the depot, savoring the spectacle of motion and speed, the display of means and mobility, the embodiment of freedom and distance. Mink wants to be caught up in these intersecting narratives of modernity: narratives of movement toward the metropolis, of technological transformation, of revolutions in representation. If only he could afford them.

The trilogy concludes with Mink in the midst of a reverie about the end of his life. In it, he tries to reconcile the powerful thirst for freedom with the undeniable demand for justice. He's already killed Flem, and he exults "I'm free now" (p. 720). He imagines finally being able to insert himself into the narrative of Western progress; he could head west now "since that was the direction people always went" (*idem*). Still, Mink recognizes that he'll never really catch up, never really have a mansion of his own. Only the dead are truly free, he concludes:

> the justice and the injustice and the griefs, leaving the folks themselves easy now, all mixed and jumbled up comfortable and easy so wouldn't nobody even know or even care who was which any more, himself among them, equal to any, good as any, brave as any, being inextricable from, anonymous with all of them. (p. 721)

Like so many poor people, Mink surrenders the dream of freedom and fairness for *himself*, in *this* life. Spurred on by Linda Kohl, who reviles Flem for exploiting the very conditions of inequality she fights to redress, Mink manages nothing more than the destruction of one wealthy person's obliviousness. Cocking his pistol at the bank president, all he can do is insist, "Look at me." It's not much, but it's a start.

Faulkner's fiction repeatedly stages moments in which those who are disregarded demand acknowledgment. Mink's face-to-face with Flem echoes another, Charles Bon's appearance at the Sutpen mansion to request that the planter recognize his son's mixed blood as his own. In perhaps the most unsettling of all such episodes, Faulkner concludes *The Town* with an anecdote in which Byron Snopes's mixed Mexican/ "Apache" offspring are sent home to Flem by the fugitive embezzler. The four inscrutably dark, silent, violent children terrorize Jefferson. A kinsman, paid by Flem to house the unwanted immigrants, has his face slashed one night when he sneaks into the children's room to see if they are asleep. He doesn't even realize he's been cut until he feels two "streaks of fire," the "two slashes running from each ear, jest missing his eye on one side, right down to the corners of his mouth like a great big grin that would bust scab and all if he ever let his face go" (p. 322). Flem sends the children back to El Paso, care of Byron.

This episode comes at the very end of *The Town*. It ruptures the narrative like a shard of the political uncanny. The children embody to the point of caricature every trait associated with the stereotype of "greaser." The McCarran-Walter Act of 1952 had severely tightened immigration policies, imposing measures that reflected Joseph McCarthy-era paranoia and racism. In 1954, Congress authorized a program to round up and repatriate illegal Mexican workers, and to tighten border patrol. The project was known as Operation Wetback. El Paso was a center for return. But what makes the four "Snopes Indians," as they are once called, especially threatening, is that they're not workers at all. Besides being adept at self-defense, they sneak into the Coca-Cola plant and drink the syrup; they also kill and devour a $500 show dog owned by a Yankee paving contractor's wife – "a Pekinese with a gold name-plate on its collar that probably didn't even know it was a dog, that rode in the Cadillac and sneered through the window not just at other dogs but at people too" (p. 318). The children become suspects in the dog's disappearance when one is noticed wearing the collar as a necklace. I'd say this is Third World consumption with a vengeance.

Faulkner's fantasy here suggests the connections between Cold War defense of the American way of life and the threats sure to materialize from continued imperialist exploitation and inequality. At the end of *The Town*, it is as if Faulkner fully realizes the global framework of Snopesism, one that, as we have seen, will require a more systematic consideration of Cold War ideologies in *The Mansion*. The American host's slashed face symbolizes the awful fiction of national innocence, a dopey grin that will dissolve into the wound it really is if ever he lets his face discompose. You'd like to think the aliens are safely pacified, but you're really working in the dark. Faulkner invites us to imagine a day when a stunted Third Worlder, long out-of-sight-out-of-mind, will cross a border to say, "Look at me." The Jicarilla Apache Mexican Snopeses represent the fluidity of First/Third, North/South, native/alien, "pure" blood/mixed-breed distinctions, and expose such categories as the effects of continuous migration, conflict, conquest, and exploitation. In the more overtly political novels of his later career, Faulkner displays an expanding awareness that the South he's been writing about in Yoknapatawpha shares historical roots and contemporary problems with places across the world that had been dominated as peripheral regions of production under Old World colonialism. As early as *Absalom, Absalom!*, Faulkner had traced the network of Caribbean plantation society and global slave trade that encompassed the

US South, noticing how French New Orleans and frontier Mississippi functioned as outposts of trans-Atlantic northern industrial capitalism.

As Faulkner rose to the challenge of addressing the apocalyptic mood of international geopolitics in the 1950s, he maintained a Southern perspective on world problems. This afforded him an unusual binocular view, as a citizen of the First World's foremost nation, writing from its Third World region. Given their conquest by the North, occupation by Yankee troops during Reconstruction, and continued dependence on the capital of outsiders, Southerners of Faulkner's background thought they knew what it meant for a remote power to dominate and exploit their region. I don't think there's any evidence that Faulkner had a grand scheme to organize his saga of Yoknapatawpha around the theme of colonial history. But in writing so observantly about his characters' historical preoccupations, their acute sense of place, and the singular conditioning of their lives by Mississippi's plantation society, Faulkner couldn't help but make this approach the unifying principle of much of his fiction. The result of Faulkner's project in the last decade of his life was to show how the effects of the global history of colonialism could still be seen in the modern US South: in the perpetuation of apartheid in the face of racial hybridity as portrayed by *Intruder in the Dust*, for example, or in the antagonism between an agricultural proletariat and modern finance capitalism as played out in the later Snopes novels.

A distinct, if complementary, ambition of Faulkner's writing during this period was to prophesy how a new world order altogether was evolving out of colonial imperialism. Looking back from the onset of the so-called "Cold" War, in which opposing national superpowers bid to revive the dream of world dominion, at least in the realm of ideology, Faulkner began to worry that a greater menace to human freedom and justice was arising: a transnational confederation of military, industrial, and financial interests.[14] When Dwight D. Eisenhower left the US presidency in 1961, he warned Americans that democracy faced a new threat in the nation's growing "military industrial complex." Fears for the country's survival in the age of atomic standoff, he cautioned, could lead to a dangerous surrender of authority to military professionals and captains of the defense industry. Eisenhower also might have included finance capitalists among those eager to influence foreign policy and profit from war. Americans of Faulkner's age had plenty of evidence that financiers conspired with munitions makers, other collateral industrialists, and a state-embedded military to set national agendas that were increasingly indifferent to the will of the governed.

Faulkner takes up this phenomenon as the central problem of his time, and writes a book about it that he called his greatest – his "magnum opus." He worked on this novel for nearly a decade, under the most trying of circumstances, beating back doubts of waning creativity, severe health problems, marital turmoil, romantic frustration, and chronic money difficulties, finally to complete *A Fable* in 1953. Published the next year, however, the novel has been one of Faulkner's most weakly appreciated works. Reviews tended to be respectful but lukewarm, while a few, despite the author's newfound stature as a Nobel Laureate, judged the book an outright failure. The novel is very long, and many readers find it impossibly prolix. It also meticulously – to some minds, tediously – replicates the events of the Passion Week of Christ's crucifixion in a day-by-day chronicle of a soldier's sacrificial execution during the Great War. On the other hand, a few critics saluted the novel as an ambitious new departure by America's greatest living author, and it did win both the Pulitzer Prize for Fiction and the National Book Award in 1955. *A Fable* is an extreme book; Faulkner demands as much from his readers as he did from himself in the effort to comprehend something so vast and disturbing as a new kind of world empire.

Faulkner got the germ of his novel from an independent film project pitched to him in Hollywood in 1943, just as he was preparing to return to Oxford during an intermission in his long-term contract with Warner Brothers. The idea involved working up the story of the so-called Unknown Soldier of the Great War, whose unidentified battlefield remains had been interred in 1921 beneath the Arc de Triomphe in Paris to memorialize all the war's anonymous casualties. A film honoring those willing to sacrifice their lives for fatherland and freedom might have been popular in the midst of World War II. Faulkner was supposed to produce a filmscript quickly for his partners (but was also free to develop his own separate novel from the material). However, Faulkner struggled so long to complete the project that world circumstances shifted under him; he ended up working on it through a dispiriting era of escalating techno-militarism. The awful ending of World War II in the atomic destruction of two Japanese cities set a terrifying backdrop for the sharpening of US-Soviet hostility in the early 1950s; then a civil war in Korea between the US-backed South and the communist North blew up almost immediately, while the shadow of nuclear confrontation began to stretch across the planet.

In this increasingly dire climate, the original idea for a work about the glory of military death must have soured for Faulkner. Instead, *A Fable* turns things upside-down, attributing the messianic significance of the Unknown Soldier to his *refusal* to fight. Faulkner takes the notion of heroic sacrifice and superimposes on it another kind of legend coming out of the Great War: a series of actions in which soldiers on both sides staged mutinies against further bloodshed. The result is a book that could be read, Faulkner admitted, as "an indictment of war perhaps" (Blotner, 1984, p. 453). Faulkner exploits Jesus's reputation as an opponent of evil in high places to imagine a messiah intent on sabotaging the modern war machine by spreading a message of non-violence. *A Fable* decries the birth of a heartless new master class, an anti-Christ-like beast that feeds on the poor in spirit. Faulkner surveys this emergent regime's historical roots in Western imperialism; its recourse to force to dominate the masses; its abuse of ideals like patriotism and nationalism to manipulate the faithful; the possibilities for resistance; and the role of art as dissent.

The most conspicuous power wielded in Faulkner's war novel belongs to the professional military class. In defiance of its autocracy, a young corporal in the French army has organized a mutinous cease-fire among battle-weary soldiers on both sides of the line. The agitator begins by selecting twelve like-minded disciples, who spend four years circulating surreptitiously with him through trenches and camps under the cover of official leaves. Their plot to halt combat eventually spreads to the German infantry as well, and finally a day is appointed when a French regiment will refuse an order to charge the enemy position. As the troops stand down, artillery in both camps falls silent. The stunned division commander realizes that the mutiny has been the work of rank-and-file troops; his oblivious officers rose to lead an assault that never materialized behind them. General Gragnon immediately requests that the entire regiment of 3,000 be executed. The humiliated officer argues to his group commander that such punishment is the only way military discipline can be maintained under the desperate conditions of prolonged trench warfare. Gragnon's superior, however, decides that the ringleader alone, Corporal Stefan, deserves death, to be executed by firing squad.

The commander spares the renegade regiment not because he is humane but because he has shrewdly calculated the violence necessary to maintain power. Like the corporal himself, the troops who refuse to fight are peasants from mountain villages. Only reluctantly drawn into national affairs (four of the mutiny's agents, including Stefan, aren't even French), but desperate for paying jobs, such soldiers come from families who are already skeptical about the cause for which their sons are dying. Once they realize that their relatives may actually be killed by the very army that employs them, these civilians begin to lash out against authority. The peasants flood angrily into the town where the offending regiment and its thirteen instigators are to be brought. The mass of military prisoners has also grown enraged at the lead mutineers, whom they now view as "foreigners" responsible for betraying them into disobedience. The command ranks hardly want to let this wrath find its proper target: the war machine grinding up lowly conscripts and exploited laborers all over Europe. So General Bidet excuses the ignorant rank-and-file strikers, while his superiors concentrate on putting down the more potent threat posed by would-be messiahs and their revolutionary ideas. The last thing you want if you're running a war is for the cannon fodder to be asking, "Is it a problem and harmful for men in front-line trenches to think of peace, that after all, we can stop fighting if enough of us want to?" (*A Fable*, p. 856).

The behavior of the military's upper echelon suggests that those who hold power act primarily to demonstrate that they possess it and you don't. The orders over which the regiment revolts involve an assault that Gragnon himself knows to be hopelessly doomed. The division commander understands that there can be no strategic justification for sending his men to certain destruction, yet he executes what then must be merely a show of absolute military authority. The audience for this object lesson isn't the enemy, it's the command's own troops and lower officers. Faulkner worries that a professional military may be used to subdue domestic constituencies as much as foreign adversaries, and that it seeks to legitimate raw force as a means of doing so. Elsewhere in the novel military commanders act with abrupt violence: a German general shoots his pilot at point blank range as part of a charade to disguise a meeting between German and Allied officers intent on resuming hostilities after the surprise armistice. And, ironically, Gragnon, who initially figures he will simply retire quietly from the army after his moment of infamy, discovers that he's to be sacrificed himself for the failure of the intended failure. Faulkner portrays the contempt of the military mind for the weak masses it would discipline. A corps commander explains to Gragnon that

> It is man who is our enemy: the vast seething moiling spiritless mass of him. Once to each period of his inglorious history, one of us appears with the stature of a giant, suddenly and without warning in the middle of a nation as a dairymaid enters a buttery, and with his sword for paddle he heaps and pounds and stiffens the malleable mass and even holds it cohered and purposeful for a time. (p. 693)

The language here suggests the compatibility of an independent military class and fascist dictatorships, a menace twentieth-century history had already confirmed for those of Faulkner's era.

Faulkner surely is concerned about democracies whose professional militaries understand their purpose as keeping order rather than defending liberty. Faulkner's generation had witnessed a military uprising in Spain in the 1930s that, after years of bloody civil war, installed a military dictator, Francisco Franco, to rule the republic. Franco was backed by rising dictators in two neighboring democracies: Mussolini and Hitler. Yet Faulkner's determination to comprehend fully the new amalgam of power in his age leads to an even deeper insight that modern empire is not primarily a military phenomenon, but an economic one. World-wide owners of wealth secondarily annex cultural, political, technological, and military spheres to support their ventures. The menace to contemporary democracy, Faulkner figures out, won't come from crude military takeovers, or simple domination by technology, or even the rise of a single superpower state. Rather, the core of the new global hegemony is unrestrained market capitalism.

If you look at the imagery of the lines quoted above, about the appearance of a strong leader to discipline the masses, you'll notice that the setting evokes the problem of labor and production. The "malleable mass" needs heaping and pounding and stiffening to make it cohere around *purpose* – the purpose of market production, of getting the buttery to turn out butter. Thus Faulkner's fable of military crisis metaphorically reflects capitalist anxieties. The soldiers are armies of laborers, the officers their managers, the high commanders the trustees of capital. Faulkner reinforces this trope by observing repeatedly that the allied command headquarters was once a manufacturing plant, even describing one squadron of soldiers hurrying home from their duties as resembling a "recessed shift out of a factory" (p. 794). The "machinery of war" (p. 731), then, is fundamentally the machinery of profit-making. As one commander puts it, "From the loins of man's furious ineradicable greed sprang the captains and the colonels to his necessity" (p. 715). It's the "men who, in order to become millionaires, supply the guns and shells" that constitute the motor of Western history. And that motor is "rapacity" (p. 906). Rapacity is the one constant in the human chronicle: "civilization itself is its password and Christianity its masterpiece" (*idem*). Even Jesus himself is invited to join the pageant of plutocrats:

> the generals and admirals, the corporals and ratings of glory, the batmen and orderlies of renown, and the chairmen of boards and the presidents of federations, the doctors and lawyers and educators and churchmen who after nineteen centuries have rescued the son of heaven from oblivion and translated him from mere meek heir to earth to chairman of its board of trade . . . (p. 906)

What Faulkner grasps so perceptively at his historical moment is how intersecting spheres of power – economic, military-industrial, political, cultural – were consolidating to form a global class of owners of means. It's a magnificent insight, one that is more timely today than ever. It makes *A Fable* the Faulkner novel for our times, whatever its difficulties, and no matter that Faulkner himself recoiled from his glimpse at the monster. (He wrote a never-to-be used preface for the novel in which he denied, for instance, that the book was "pacifist.") The novel anticipates arguments like Michael Hardt and Antonio Negri's in *Empire* that the "American" century has really been an era of global free market capitalism and that the relevance of political states and national societies is fading before the might of multi-national corporations. It foreshadows the development described in David Harvey's *Neo-Liberalism: A Brief History* of a revolution that began in the early 1980s dedicated to restoring extreme advantages to the world's wealthiest tier, advantages weakened by a preceding century of progressive social welfare policies.

Faulkner conveys the conflation of several kinds of privilege in his description of the Generalissimo's headquarters. The Old General has taken up residence in a commandeered chateau, so he's constantly pictured ensconced in luxury: his office

> had been merely a boudoir back in the time of its dead duchess or mar-quise, and it still bore the imprint of that princely insensate (and, perhaps one of the duchesses or marquises had thought, impregnable) opulence in its valanced alcoves and pilastered medallioned ceiling and crystal chandeliers and sconces and mirrors and girandoles and buhl étageres and glazed cabinets of faience bibelots, and a white rug into which war-bleached boots sank ankle-deep as into the mud of trenches. (p. 876)

The chamber drips with rarefied excess, while the image of the mud-deep white rug ironically accents the gulf between the accommodations of generals and foot soldiers. (It's difficult not to think of De Spain's pale carpet here, too, which so offends Ab as a sign of his worthlessness.) Of course, French duchesses and marquises learned pretty decisively that their wealth was not "impregnable," and Faulkner's novel revives that revolutionary mood.

The chateau also signals a multi-national style of imperial furnishing: the library might have been "lifted bodily from an English country home" while another room boasts "a heavyish, Victorian-looking, almost American-looking table" (pp. 945–946). Such eclecticism has historical import; Faulkner never lets us forget the succession of national territorial empires that flowed into the twentieth century's transnational capitalist sort. The same sense of entitlement and ease with the forcible extraction of wealth propels the updated version. Faulkner knows that World War I constituted a watershed in the course of Western empire. It resulted in the break-up of the Turkish Ottoman Empire, encouraged independence movements in British colonies world-wide, and blocked a budding German expansionism, at least temporarily. The war also convinced the US that the future lay not in further territorial conquest (as it had headed toward in its war over the remnants of Spanish empire at the end of the nineteenth century), but in economic domination and cultural influence.

In *A Fable* Faulkner presents the war as a curtain call of Western imperial history. One French soldier notices that the town of Chaulnesmont, where the Allied headquarters is located, has a peculiar set of guards assigned to it:

> It's like another front, manned by all the troops in the three forces who cant speak the language belonging to the coat they came up from under the equator and half around the world to die in, in the cold and the wet – Senegalese and Moroccans and Kurds and Chinese and Malays and Indians – Polynesian Melanesian Mongol and Negro . . . (pp. 959–960)

This brigade of "alien[s]" (p. 960), who "dont even think Caucasian thoughts," reminds us of that other "front" earlier advanced by militant European colonialism. French colonial outposts are mentioned throughout the novel – Saigon (p. 892), New Orleans (p. 850), Beirut (p. 937). The standard performance of colonial race merges the Senegalese of Africa with the American Negro: the African guards are described as having a "theatrical insouciance to the raffish shabbiness of their uniforms like that of an American blackface minstrel troupe dressed hurriedly out of pawnshops" (p. 787). The commander of American forces has "the face of that predecessor or forefather who at twenty-five had retired rich from the quarter deck of a Middle Passage slaver, and at thirty had his name illuminated in colored glass above his Beacon Hill pew" (p. 694). The mutinous peasant regiment looks "like harassed and harried and homeless refugees from another planet" (p. 1021), while lower officers bear the "air of oafish peasants smelling of field and stable summoned to the castle, the Great House, for an accounting or punishment" (p. 888). These bottom orders mean nothing to the generalissimo, lofty among a "triumvirate" of supreme commanders who resemble "archbishops" and "Brahmins." The jumble of nomenclature and traditions of lordship suggests that under the conditions of postmodern capitalism the downtrodden are being pulped into a single mass of exploited servers – variously pictured as foot soldiers, people of color, slaves, refugees, aliens, peasants.

A Fable seems preoccupied with matters of empire, repeatedly coming back to the term itself: the "scrap or fragment of an empire" (p. 899), "empire's carapace" (p. 905), "the vast glorious burden of empire" (p. 915). When a trio of American soldiers steps forward as a team of executioners for Gragnon, they constitute another microcosm of subalterns, this one from the world's newest empire: an Iowan, a Jew, and a "Sambo." Their place in the history of oppression is not lost on them. Following tunnels to the cell where Gragnon is held, the three sense

> the whole concentrated weight of history, stratum upon stratum of dead tradition impounded by the *Hotel* above them – monarchy revolution empire and republic, duke farmer-general and sans culotte, levee tribunal and guillotine, liberty fraternity equality and death and the people the People always to endure and prevail. (p. 1017)

It's not at all clear, though, that the People can stave off the deaths their betters have designed for them, and perhaps a more accurate characterization of the lot assigned to the rank-and-file under the new regime would be the image of the army as understood by its chief theorist in the novel, the so-called General "Mama Bidet." This Frenchman has concluded that "no army was better than its anus," and so he travels with a bidet to ensure battlefield hygiene, at least for himself. But if generals are assholes, infantrymen must be their shit. The shuffling troops amount to nothing but "a functioning machine in the same sense that the earthworm is, alive purely and simply for the purpose of transporting, without itself actually moving, for the distance of its corporeal length, the medium in which it lives" (p. 713). Eating dirt then evacuating it pretty much captures the reality of trench combat, not to mention conveying the common soldier's worthlessness in the scheme of things. Ab Snopes knows exactly what he looks like to the De Spains when he decides to smear manure onto their carpet.

Faulkner denotes the novelty of the elite that is forming by having some of its aspiring members speak in awkward new terms about it. The authorities' response to the unexpected ceasefire has been for representatives of all the combatant armies, including the Germans, to meet secretly and figure out a way to resume the killing. An allied officer later congratulates the old general for their achievement: artillery on both sides has destroyed unarmed British and German battalions meeting in No Man's Land. "'We did it', the Quartermaster General said. 'We. Not British and American and French we against German them nor German they against American and British and French us, but We against all because we no longer belong to us'" (p. 969). Ideologies of nationalism and ideals of patriotism may delude the rank-and-file into sacrificing themselves on behalf of ruling interests, but the rulers know these are ruses of power:

> that thin and tensioned girder of steel and human blood which carries its national edifice soaring glorious and threatful among the stars, in dedication to which young men are transported free of charge and even with pay, to die violently in places that even the map-makers and -dividers never saw . . . (p. 739)

There could hardly be a better gloss on Benedict Anderson's idea that nationhood functions as a fantasy, and that the proof of the fantasy's power is how patriotism actually gets ordinary people to give up their lives for their countries. Those who profit from such sacrifices, of course, appreciate that a mere fiction assures their reality: should the single word "fatherland" be effaced from man's memory, observes one commander, "that will destroy us" (p. 715). In the passage above, the quartermaster grapples with the realization that those holding power constitute a "We" that transcends national identity, the We a coterie whose only qualifying attribute is the means to get almost everyone else to do what it wants.

Faulkner's allegorical use of details from Christ's ministry and crucifixion has led many readers to believe that *A Fable* must be advancing a Christian message. Faulkner kept a chart, inscribed carefully on the walls of his office at Rowan Oak, which outlined the events of the corporal's last week; parallels abound to the Biblical story of Jesus's final days. Stefan appears to leave behind three women, Marthe (also called Magda), Marya, and a prostitute lover; the corporal is tempted to abandon his pacifistic teachings in an interview with the old general; he is executed between two other offenders; he gets a "crown of thorns" when his riddled body spills into a clump of barbed wire; his corpse disappears from its hastily dug grave, and his empty coffin inspires puzzlement among a second group of attendants. Jill Faulkner, the author's daughter, remarked that the book's "theme is religious," and thought her father probably came to accept the judgment that the work was a failure, because he was "out of his element" in taking on such a subject (Blotner, 1984, p. 589). But *A Fable* is not religious, it's messianic. Walter Benjamin has discussed what he calls the messianism of writing history in a certain way. If you represent the past so that it can be used to resist becoming "a tool of the ruling classes,"

Benjamin writes, then you have activated the messianic power of history: "In every era the attempt must be made anew to wrest tradition away from a conformism that is about to overpower it. The Messiah comes not only as the redeemer, he comes as the subduer of Antichrist." In *A Fable* Faulkner re-imagines the story of war as an anti-war story. At the moment a new global ruling class came of age during World War I, who resisted their bid to gain control over national economies and planetary resources, to command the very power of life and death?

A spark of hope arises in the past from a messianic defiance of tyranny. Adopting the meekness of Jesus, the rebellious corporal has faith that "even ruthless and all-powerful and unchallengeable Authority would be impotent before that massed unresisting undemanding passivity" (*A Fable*, p. 728). From the opening scenes of the novel, in which the mountain peasant families congregate in Chaulnesmont's public square to support the offending regiment, Faulkner is very interested in what crowds can do, what masses might accomplish. It's the genius of the corporal's mutiny that it challenges authority through a simple mass refusal to act. An aide marvels that it's the common soldiers who "are stopping it" (p. 701), and "the runner" takes pride in his small "part in bringing war to a pause, a halt, a stop" (p. 733). Not *the* war, notice, but "war" altogether. The idea, as the runner later elaborates, involves a mass insurrection through which the very concept of war is finally discredited as a tool of ruling-class domination: "just walking forward like free men – just one of us, one man; suppose just one man, then multiply him by a battalion; suppose a whole battalion of us, who want nothing except just to go home and get themselves into clean clothes and work and drink a little beer in the evening and talk and then lie down and sleep and not be afraid" (p. 955). That's a working-class vision worthy of a democratic revolution. When the Allied and Axis commanders conspire to restart the killing, Faulkner must be thinking of a common interpretation of World War I as a contrivance of financial and industrial classes alarmed by the prospect of imminent world-wide workers' revolution. The Bolsheviks had already seized power in Russia in 1917, and labor parties in numerous Western nations were stirring. One of the consequences of the outbreak of hostilities between European states was the sidelining of international working-class solidarity by drummed-up nationalistic fervor.

Images of passive mass resistance let Faulkner touch on other contemporary liberation movements as well. Besides an army of subjected workers, there are the poor more generally. The peasants turn out to be suffering from war's devastation – productive land decimated, critical labor stripped away. A woman faints from hunger in front of a sergeant policing the streets; he doesn't even comprehend her distress until it's explained to him, and he has to rely on the peasants themselves to produce a crust of bread to revive her. The hand that reaches out with the staff of life turns out to be Stefan's, and the messianism here invites us to see these peasants as universal representatives of the dispossessed. They're described in the first paragraph of the novel as rising "from the straw mattresses and thin pallet beds of their hive-dense tenements" (p. 669). Later in the novel, the corporal's step-father surveys what combat has done to his farm: "But the fields, the land. Ruined. Ruined" (p. 1033). Other victims of abuse await emancipation too. In perhaps the eeriest scene in the novel, Faulkner describes a holding pen that has been constructed for the mutinous regiment in the Allied compound. The fences have been reinforced with electrified barbed wire; surveillance searchlights and machine-gun platforms have been installed. Holding a vigil for their fathers and brothers and sons, the crowd of peasants camps outside this barricade, "lying along the barrier in an inextricable mass like victims being resurrected after a holocaust" (p. 787). The tableau evokes images of Jews in the death camps, of Japanese in US internment camps, even, bizarrely – given that it's the Senegalese guards who are "lounging haughtily overhead" (*idem*) – of African Americans corralled in penitentiaries like Mississippi's Parchman prison. All these instances of modern detention suggest the various modes of discipline being imposed by the ruling classes on their subjects.

Yet the grouped masses also exert pressure, also constitute a problem for those in command. Some people (or People?) are, after all, on the *outside* of the pen. And Faulkner's depiction of that inextricable mass of victims notices startlingly that it is as if they are "being resurrected after a holocaust." A resurrection of the masses might be just the messianic act required to challenge the "Authority" responsible for holocausts. The runner's vision of one person marching forward, joined one-by-one by others, until whole battalions form, points to mass efforts Faulkner might have been learning to appreciate in contemporary American civic life. In 1941 A. Philip Randolph called for 10,000 people to march in Washington, DC, to protest continued racial discrimination in the US defense industry. Other acts of non-violent mass protest in the 1940s, while Faulkner was working on *A Fable*, would lead to the more celebrated instances of civil disobedience that propelled the civil rights movement in the mid-1950s. So much of Faulkner's value as a modernist writer has been associated with his searching exploration and innovative expression of individual consciousness and conscience, that we may undervalue his turn in a book like *A Fable* toward large-scale social phenomena that affected whole populations.

One of the stranger sub-plots in this sprawling novel involves an episode set in the US South. The corporal's mutiny takes place in May of 1918, just months before the final armistice in November. Two years earlier, the runner encounters a peculiar outgrowth of combat subculture in a barracks near Amiens. An English private oversees a cottage industry on the front lines: he advances soldiers cash on monthly terms, he to make a profit if they survive and have to pay up with interest, they to come out "ahead" if they're killed first. The scheme is fiendishly brilliant – the sort only an actuary could love, but the story mostly matters because its roots lie in an even more legendary entrepreneurial escapade. It turns out that the private is only the local agent of a casualty gambling association run by his former partner in horseracing, a Reverend Tobe Sutterfield, who now heads an enterprise in Paris called "Tout le monde" [literally, "All the World" or "Everyone"]. Sutterfield is making money from his battlefield loan franchise, but the runner eventually hears the tale of Sutterfield's earlier, even more colorful collaboration with a twelve-year-old jockey, a three-legged race horse, and its English groom (who becomes the private). In 1912 an Argentinian millionaire sells a champion racehorse to an American oil baron. The thoroughbred is entrusted to the American's negro hostler, Sutterfield, for transit from New Orleans to Kentucky. The train carrying them has an accident, plunging through a bridge, and the horse ends up lame. Rather than allow the animal to be put to stud, its only source of value now, Sutterfield, the jockey, and the Argentinian's English groom go on the lam to let the horse do what it's been born to do. The trio make money when they show up in small towns and take bets from skeptical country folk more accustomed to four-legged racehorses. But the thoroughbred blows away the competition, and for a while the company stays a beat ahead of the law as they roam the South.

Faulkner published this set piece separately as "Notes on a Horse Thief," and its relation to the main story of *A Fable* has always seemed tangential. Seen in the context I've tried to establish, the anecdote may suggest the potential for small-scale economies to resist the consolidating imperatives of global capitalism. Within the circuitry of millionaires dealing luxury goods across the hemisphere, Sutterfield and friends intercept a transaction and divert it to their own profit. There's something about the way these scoundrels thumb their noses at officialdom that wins over little folk everywhere. In one town a crowd disarms the jail's turnkey so the thieves can escape; the fugitives also get help from the fraternal order of Masons, a secret society that admires their frontier spirit. Sutterfield's renegade horseracing prefigures his later ability to make money unofficially in the niches of the vast war machine. The novel anticipates the present burgeoning of "localist" movements – economic, ecological, agricultural, educational, religious, and cultural – seeking to provide alternatives to transnational corporate "globalization."[15]

Let's digress momentarily to discuss Faulkner's last novel, *The Reivers* (1961), since it elaborates on such informal local economies against the backdrop of modern life that, in Faulkner's judgment, had become overly administered, homogeneous, and mass-produced. I'll return to *A Fable* to consider a final problem – how art might resist the authority of the profiting classes – but in *The Reivers* Faulkner settles for a less taxing project, indulging in nostalgia for ways of life that seemed more immediate, personal, and colorful. The narrator is the sixty-six-year-old Lucius Priest, who tells his grandson about an uproarious escapade he took part in when he was eleven, in 1905. Published the year of Faulkner's death in 1962, *The Reivers* echoes *A Fable* in offering another comic tale of horse-thievery, racing, and gambling. The episode begins when Boon Hogganbeck, familiar to us from *Go Down, Moses*, and now an employee of Lucius's grandfather, decides to use "the Boss"'s automobile without authorization one weekend. Grandfather Priest has left with other family members to attend a funeral in New Orleans, and Boon sees a perfect opportunity – as "the dean of Jefferson motorcar drivers" (*The Reivers*, p. 748) – to organize an expedition to Memphis. Boon wants to visit his regular girl at Miss Reba's whorehouse, but he also welcomes the prospect of a long motor trip since he loves driving the Priest automobile, one of only two in Jefferson. He talks the youngster Lucius into going with him. Once on the road they discover that a third tourist has smuggled himself on board, Ned William McCaslin, a black descendant of old Carothers McCaslin and another of Grandfather Priest's hired men. Ned wants a weekend in Memphis, too. The adults agree to meet up again early Sunday morning after enjoying Saturday night at their respective gentlemen's establishments. Lucius is apparently due to get his own small first taste of living large; he is to pal around with another underage visitor, Otis, the nephew of one of Reba's girls.

Things go smoothly until Ned shows up in the middle of the night with a change of plans. To Boon's horror, Ned has filched the car and traded it for a race horse with a questionable track record but a gleam of promise, at least to Ned's eye. Ned's idea is to set up a match, figure out how to get the newly rechristened "Lightning" (neigh "Coppermine") to run as he never has before, then make enough of a killing on the action both to get the car back and keep the horse. More of this works than you'd think. What I want to emphasize is the way Faulkner takes such pleasure in spinning out Ned's ingenious plots and counter-plots. Ned proves himself to be the novel's comic wizard: he deftly manipulates every man, woman, child, and animal in sight, black or white, and ends up thoroughly impressed with his own cleverness, and several hundred dollars the richer for it. Ned takes zero assets and converts them into a wad by capitalizing on his official powerlessness. Ned is a black man trying to make his way in a harshly racist place and time. He manages by masking his abilities and by not worrying too much about ethics rigged to favor white folks. The novel mostly makes light of such painful realities, or ignores them altogether in the spirit of the happy outcome, yet at certain points we can see that what's at the core of Lucius Priest's memory is not just the thrill of riding his first race horse, or the fun of a first road trip with the guys, but an unwanted and extremely troubling initiation into the desperate measures forced on the disadvantaged.

Lucius is a child of privilege; the rest of the merry pranksters have no means at all. Boon, for example, isn't exactly an employee, he's property: "Boon didn't actually belong to us. I mean, not solely to us, the Priests" (p. 737). He actually has "three proprietors," so, Lucius jokes, he's really "a corporation, a holding company," in which the McCaslins, De Spain, and General Compson have – not shares of labor

– but "shares of responsibility." Ned, too, is a possession: "we inherited him in turn" (p. 749). By contrast, Lucius knows that his family belongs to "our Jefferson leisure class" (p. 754). The first thing we see in the novel is Lucius's father inculcating him with managerial responsibilities. Grandfather Priest is the president of the older of Jefferson's two banks; his son Maury runs a livery service, and requires his son to help with the books each Saturday morning so that he learns the importance of "assuming responsibility for, the space he occupied, the room he took up, in the world's (Jefferson, Mississippi's anyway) economy" (p. 725). Although the institutions of family privilege may change over the next fifty years – Lucius says that "by 1925 we could already see the doom" of the unspoiled wilderness – the command of strong multi-generational clans looks pretty secure.

At the end of the novel some of Ned's better-laid plans get disturbed when the absent white landowners unexpectedly return (Colonel Linscomb of Parsham, Tennessee, on whose pasture the races are being held, and Grandfather Priest himself). Ned grouses at first that the white folks will spoil everything, but then he figures out how to take advantage even of their paternalistic intervention (they swoop in to suspend the result of one race, putting the collected money into "escrow" – an example of the way they automatically attempt to regulate a cheerfully irregular enterprise). The agreement that resolves the numerous breaches of etiquette and custom in the races gets drawn up in the luxurious quarters of Linscomb's "plantation" office, a space that reasserts the authority of a high-blooded white ruling elite.

Ned calls the shots throughout the horse races, right down to betting against his own entry and slyly raking in even his patrons' money when he throws the final race, the consequence of his refusing to use a secret goad – the sardine that usually drives Lightning mad in the home stretch. This is all funny, but you sometimes have the sense that you're watching a cagey minstrel figure trying to outwit his Boss man. In fact, Ned is so self-effacing at first that he provokes one of the true villains in the novel, a racist brute of a country sheriff named Butch, to sneer at him as an "Uncle Remus" (p. 868). But when Ned takes Lucius aside and starts instructing him about how to ride Lightning, the child realizes he's speaking "quiet and succinct": "he was not Uncle Remus now" (pp. 871–872). It's not only that Ned seizes command of his circumstances in ways never permitted the deferential Uncle Remus in Joel Chandler Harris's tales, but also that this black uncle, unlike the Remus who is so protective of his young master's peace of mind, is apparently determined to rob one privileged white mama's boy of his innocence. At first it seems the only danger to this child is that Lucius will have to suffer the shock of learning more about sex than he's ready for. The precocious Otis (or not: he's passing as ten when he's actually fifteen) eventually gets Lucius up to speed on the practice of "pugknuckling," something Otis discovers his aunt does back in Arkansas (and which he soon figures out how to merchandise by drilling a hole into her bedroom wall and charging viewers). Sex is a little hard to avoid at a brothel, so Lucius gets an earful of dirty talk and an eyeful of indecent behavior. But there's even more he has to take in when he begins to watch penniless people making their way in a world he knows nothing about.

The grimmest realization that occurs to Lucius is that Miss Reba's whores do what they do only for money, not pleasure. Boon's prostitute (and Otis's aunt), Everbe Corinthia, takes a liking to the well-mannered little Lucius, and he gets the chance to see her at her most human. Chastened by Priest's unthinking goodness, Corrie resolves to reform; eventually she and Boon marry, after she quits her career. When Lucius sees Butch immediately try to take advantage of Miss Reba and Corrie when they get to Parsham, he can't believe the sheriff's crudeness. Later, Corrie suspends her reformation by trading her body one last time, to Butch in order to spring Lightning from confiscation, and gets thanked for it by being beaten by Boon. What staggers Lucius is how degrading the struggle for money is among the poor. Otis proves to be a caricature of their desperation; he's so lacking prospects that he's practically insane with the lust for cash, dreaming about it, plotting for it, willing to capitalize on anything in any way to get it. All wage labor amounts to prostitution (a standard association in proletarian fiction, by the way). Boon makes the connection explicit: "She's in the paid business of belonging to me exclusive the minute she sets her foot where I'm at like I'm in the paid business of belonging to Boss and Mr Maury exclusive the minute I set my foot where they're at" (p. 884). Corrie's misery over her debased life can't be laughed off as easily as the jovial versions of the shifts of the poor we get elsewhere: the infamous "mud farm" set up by a couple of idle croppers because "Mud's one of our best crops up thisaway" (p. 796), or the man in Jefferson who builds his own automobile from scratch because he can't afford to buy one, or the ever-ebullient Minnie, who saves enough money in the sex trade that she can buy a gold tooth as mouth bling.

What comes through all the novel's shenanigans for making money – and they *are* high-spirited and entertaining – is the central realization that life for poor people is just plain hard. Faulkner admires their pluck, no doubt, and has the well-off Lucius repeatedly salute their embodiment of the purest form of the American ideal: "our inalienable constitutional right of free will and private enterprise which has made our country what it is" (p. 898). But if such local enterprise is the essence of democratic freedom, we can't overlook the fact that Faulkner entitled the book in honor of his preoccupation with American rapacity ("reivers" is an old Scottish variant of "reavers," which means those who plunder or rob). In effect Ned and his sort are forced to steal what others have lucked into. Lucius observes that "Boon wasn't a banker nor even a very good trader either. But he was proving to be a pretty damned good guerrilla fighter" (p. 752). Such guerrilla economies bid to level the playing field, but they haven't made much difference yet, as the conclusion's return of all to the status quo suggests. Still, Lucius has been put through an unwanted initiation into such matters, one he constantly protests he has been inadequately prepared for: "I knew too much, had seen too much. I was a child no longer now; innocence and childhood were forever lost, forever gone from me" (p. 866). This does sound like exaggeration, all the more so in light of his incessant whining about being reunited with his mother (p. 778). Yet what he's seen is bad, and he knows it, even if he's still capable only of blaming the victims:

> I was ashamed that such a reason for fearing for Uncle Parsham, who had to live here, existed [Parsham is a black elder who gives shelter to the white Lucius]; hating (not Uncle Parsham doing the hating, but me doing it) it all, hating all of us for being the poor frail victims of being alive, having to be alive – hating Everbe for being the vulnerable helpless lodestar victim; and Boon for being the vulnerable and helpless victimised; and Uncle Parsham and Lycurgus [his son] for being where they had to, couldn't help but, watch white people behaving exactly as white people bragged that only Negroes behaved – just as I had hated Otis for telling me about Everbe in Arkansas and hated Everbe for being that helpless lodestar for human debasement . . . (pp. 865–866)

By the end of the novel Lucius's grandfather has given him a way to deal with what might be the master problem of all Faulkner's fiction: what to do with unwanted knowledge. If "Nothing is ever forgotten. Nothing is ever lost" (p. 968), then what do we do with shame and guilt? Grandfather counsels, "Live with it . . . A gentleman accepts the responsibility of his actions and bears the burden of their consequences, even when he did not himself instigate them but only acquiesced to them, didn't say No though he knew he should" (p. 969). This advice may appear weakly sententious, resting on an outdated ethos of gentility. But in light of the social traumas Southerners of Lucius's class had to reckon with – the hideous acts of bondage and rapacity upon which the edifice of their world was founded – if you actually did accept responsibility and bear the burden of consequences it would require a commitment to generations of reform and restitution. It may not be a hugely consequential insight; but it would be a hugely consequential act.

The Reivers may be the most simply written of all Faulkner's novels; at the end of a life consumed by language, the author largely sets his own aside, and, with minimal interference from his screen narrator Priest, listens to folks like Boon and Ned plot their lives and explain their ways. But before staging this act of genial surrender, Faulkner engages his style as passionately as ever in the effort to render his world. *A Fable* may be the most complexly written of all Faulkner's novels; in fact, I believe it is deliberately *over*written. In this endlessly talky book, maybe the biggest windbag of anyone is the Generalissimo, who builds up quite a head of steam as he justifies the execution of the mutinous corporal. The commander has a knack for florid imagery, and as he argues himself into the necessity of taking the life of an idealistic young man from his home region (who, to boot, may be his illegitimate son), the old soldier's language becomes more and more inflated. He pictures an apocalyptic crisis in the future in which the present path to techno-militarism has produced machines that take over the world and conduct their own battles, "two mechanical voices bellowing at each other polysyllabic and verbless patriotic nonsense" (*A Fable*, p. 994). That bleak scenario, he goes on, may lead to humankind's embarkation for a new planet altogether, amid a nuclear-like holocaust, the last sound on earth a survivor's "puny and inexhaustible voice still talking, still planning" (*idem*). Faulkner puts these words from his Nobel speech into the old general's mouth, also having him refer to "the ding dong of doom" and the belief that mankind will not just "endure" but "prevail." It is as if Faulkner has reassessed the ability of official culture to command the representation of reality. Even his own critical voice has begun to sound fatuous to his ears, its capacity for resistance co-opted by developments like Nobel recognition and deployment on presidential missions.

Thus Faulkner develops a new way to confront a tradition of representing war that masks its reality behind a thick appliqué of inspirational verbiage and "deodorizing" imagery. This "polysyllabic and verbless patriotic nonsense" obscures the awful reality of combat; "every man [who has ever been] touched by even one second's flick of its mud and filth and physical fear" knows that "Death" is the only truth of "War." And anyone who worked for the Hollywood film industry, as Faulkner did, also understood that the reality of combat was often distorted unforgivably in the patriotic pictures the government asked the studios to produce to support the war effort. The novel once refers to "a plot whose meretricity and shabbiness only American moving pictures were to match" (p. 723). Faulkner goes on to describe a young expert on military affairs as having "the face and body of a durable matinee idol" (p. 883), and the narrator later ties such deception to institutions of knowledge-production, too, like the war colleges that turn out graduates who "condone the deodorization of war's effluvium even from the uniforms they wore, leaving them simply costumes" (*idem*). (It's no wonder one of Faulkner's initial Hollywood collaborators said he didn't recognize anything of his original idea in *A Fable*.)

That conventions of representation were being hijacked to mystify violence seemed especially noticeable and objectionable to artists during World War I. At least one way to understand the determination of a generation of modernists to use language (and other media) in aggressively innovative ways is that they wanted to perform a kind of cleansing of the word from its corruption by official culture. *The Enormous Room* by e. e. cummings ridicules the bad language of journalists and war-mongers while inventing its own subversive polyglot lingo; even before the war itself, Gertrude Stein had tried in *Tender Buttons* to separate words from their bourgeois associations; Hemingway's war veteran-narrators strive to distill English to its purest essence; William Carlos Williams summarized the whole project as "no ideas but in things."

By 1954, though, the struggle to work through the excessive mediation of reality by overused and falsifying conventions of representation had to find another method. *A Fable* invents what we might identify as a prototype of postmodern aesthetics dedicated to protesting the economic, political, and military institutions of capitalist empire. Faulkner *reproduces to excess* the excesses of mediation. In *A Fable* there's nothing that doesn't betray itself as an effect of ruling discourse. The mutiny, the novel's most radical act of resistance, gets registered by the powers-that-be as a disruption of the interminable conversation of war: it's a stoppage, a silence that temporarily jams things. The only way to fight all the way through the effects of distorted representations of reality is at the level of style, Faulkner seems to be suggesting by magnifying the distortion. The more conspicuous the language, the better. Faulkner was already on the route to this strategy in *Intruder in the Dust*, in which, you'll recall, he taxes certain habits of racist rhetoric to the breaking point. In *A Fable* Faulkner exaggerates the tyranny that an interconnected mafia of economic and cultural ministers has begun to exert over world affairs. I'm going to quote a long excerpt from *A Fable* to illustrate some of these final points, as well as to close my book with the most convincing example I know of Faulkner's utter indispensability as an interpreter of our history and a prophet for our present.

> ... half Europe went to war with the other half and finally succeeded in dragging half the western hemisphere along: a plan, a design vast in scope, exalted in conception, in implication (and hope) terrifying, not even conceived here at Grand Headquarters by the three old generals and their trained experts and advisers in orderly conference, but conceived out of the mutual rage and fear of the three ocean-dividing nations themselves, simultaneously at Washington and London and Paris by some immaculate pollenization like earth's simultaneous leafage, and come to birth at a council not even held at Grand Headquarters but behind locked and guarded doors in the Quai d'Orsay – a council where trained military experts, dedicated as irrevocably to war as nuns are married to God, were outnumbered by those who were not only not trained for war, they were not even braided and panoplied for it – the Prime Ministers and Premiers and Secretaries, the cabinet members and senators and chancellors; and those who outnumbered even them: the board chairmen of the vast establishments which produced the munitions and shoes and tinned foods, and the modest unsung omnipotent

ones who were the priests of simple money; and the others still who outnumbered even these: the politicians, the lobbyists, the owners and publishers of newspapers and the ordained ministers of churches, and all the other accredited traveling representatives of the vast solvent organizations and fraternities and movements which control by coercion or cajolery man's morals and actions and all his mass-value for affirmation or negation – all that vast powerful terror-inspiring representation which, running all democracy's affairs in peace, come indeed into their own in war, finding their true apotheosis then . . . (pp. 880–881)[16]

Notes

Preface

1   Joseph Blotner's *Faulkner: A Biography* (one volume edition, New York: Random House, 1984) still provides the standard account of Faulkner's life. Frederick Karl's *William Faulkner, American Writer: A Biography* (New York: Weidenfeld & Nicolson, 1989) adds some information. *The Life of William Faulkner: A Critical Biography* by Richard Gray (Oxford, UK, and Cambridge, MA: Blackwell Publishers, 1994) concentrates on Faulkner's writing in the context of events in his life. In *William Faulkner and Southern History* (New York: Oxford University Press, 1993), Joel Williamson focuses on Faulkner's Southern past and makes several important discoveries about his family. *Faulkner, The Transfiguration of Biography* (Lincoln: University of Nebraska Press, 1979) by Judith Bryant Wittenberg demonstrates how Faulkner drew on experiences in his life for the subject matter of his novels. David L. Minter describes how Faulkner's early life formed the basis of his fiction through *The Sound and the Fury in William Faulkner: His Life and Work* (Baltimore, MD: Johns Hopkins University Press, 1980). In *Faulkner's Career: An Internal Literary History* (Ithaca, NY: Cornell University Press, 1979), Gary Lee Stonum shows how Faulkner developed as a writer by consciously setting new challenges for himself in each successive novel.

Introduction

1   An earlier moment of intense interest in fiction about the South occurred in the decades just before the Civil War, when the westward expanding

South (the areas that eventually became Mississippi, Arkansas, and Missouri) stimulated a genre of frontier humor. One magazine in particular, *The Spirit of St. Louis*, cultivated a number of contributors who profited from the craze, as did the periodical itself.

2 In *The Nation's Region: Southern Modernism, Segregation, and US Nationalism* (Athens, GA: University of Georgia Press, 2006) Leigh Anne Duck describes how the South was pictured by the rest of the country as the backward opposite of modern national progress.

3 How Faulkner made use of local history is explained by Don Doyle, *Faulkner's County: The Historical Roots of Yoknapatawpha* (Chapel Hill, NC: University of North Carolina Press, 2001).

4 See Robert J. C. Young's *Colonial Desire: Hybridity in Theory, Culture, and Race* (London and New York: Routledge, 1995) for how the concept of race was invented by European colonialism.

Chapter 1

1 Interview with Jean Stein Vanden Heuvel, reprinted in *Lion in the Garden*, p. 253.

2 An example is *Vision in Spring* (Austin, TX: University of Texas Press, 1984), edited, with an introduction by Judith L. Sensibar.

3 *The Marionettes*, edited, with an introduction and textual apparatus, by Noel Polk (Charlottesville, VA: University Press of Virginia, 1977).

4 *William Faulkner: Early Prose and Poetry*, compilation and introduction by Carvel Collins (Boston, MA: Little, Brown, 1962).

5 See D. Matthew Ramsey, " 'Turnabout' Is Fair(y) Play: Faulkner's Queer War Story," *The Faulkner Journal* 15.1–2 (1999–2000 Fall–Spring 1999): pp. 61–81, for Faulkner's exploration of homosexuality in his early career.

6 For more on Faulkner's depiction of women see Minrose C. Gwin. *The Feminine and Faulkner: Reading (Beyond) Sexual Difference* (Knoxville, TN: University of Tennessee Press, 1990), Diane Roberts, *Faulkner and Southern Womanhood* (Athens, GA: University of Georgia Press, 1994), and Deborah Clarke, *Robbing the Mother: Women in Faulkner* (Jackson, MS: University Press of Mississippi, 1994).

7 Peter Lurie describes how film stimulated Faulkner's artistry in *Vision's Immanence: Faulkner, Film, and the Popular Imagination* (Baltimore, MD: Johns Hopkins University Press, 2004). An earlier study of the importance of vision in Faulkner is *Fascination: Faulkner's Fiction, 1919–1936* by Michel Gresset, adapted from the French by Thomas West (Durham, NC: Duke University Press, 1989).

8 *Visual and Other Pleasures* (Bloomington, IN: Indiana University Press, 1989).

9 See John Duvall's *Faulkner's Marginal Couple: Invisible, Outlaw, and Unspeakable Communities* (Austin, TX: University of Texas Press, 1990) for a study of unorthodox sexual arrangements in Faulkner's novels, including *Pylon*.

10 Michael Grimwood studies *The Wild Palms* extensively in this context in *Heart in Conflict: Faulkner's Struggles with Vocation* (Athens, GA: University of Georgia Press, 1987).

11 The novel was published with the title *The Wild Palms* over Faulkner's objections; he wanted it called *If I Forget Thee, Jerusalem*. The Library of America edition of the novel restores Faulkner's original title (along with making other corrections based on Faulkner's typescript). However, the Vintage International paperback edition, otherwise using the corrected text of the novel, has returned to the title *The Wild Palms*, after first trying the restored title. In citing the LOA edition I will refer to the title it prefers, but elsewhere sometimes use the more familiar title.

12 See *Fictions of Labor: William Faulkner and the South's Long Revolution* (Cambridge, UK, and New York: Cambridge University Press, 1997) by Richard Godden for an interpretation of the convict's pleasure in unalienated labor. Godden's book is a Marxian interpretation of Faulkner's fiction through *Absalom, Absalom!* A more recent book continues his analysis through the later fiction: *William Faulkner: An Economy of Complex Words* (Princeton, NJ: Princeton University Press, 2007).

13 Meta Carpenter Wilde, *A Loving Gentleman: The Love Story of William Faulkner and Meta Carpenter* (New York: Simon & Schuster, 1976).

Chapter 2

1 See Michael Kreyling, *Inventing Southern Literature* (Jackson, MS: University Press of Mississippi, 1998) and Patricia Yaeger, *Dirt and Desire: Reconstructing Southern Women's Writing, 1930–1990* (Chicago, IL: University of Chicago Press, 2000). Kreyling argues that the baneful influence of Faulkner has to do with the way he was interpreted by Southern Agrarians as denying modern change, and by later Southern intellectuals who identified with the regional self-loathing they found in figures like Quentin Compson. For Yaeger, a preoccupation with Faulkner as the pre-eminent Southern modernist prevents fair attention to a host of other writers, particularly Southern women, who cannot be approached through the lens of Faulkner's ruling concerns with honor and shame, patrilineal decline, Oedipal guilt and rage, and so forth.

2 John T. Irwin's *Doubling and Incest/Repetition and Revenge: A Speculative Reading of Faulkner* (Baltimore, MD: Johns Hopkins University Press, 1975) concentrates on Freudian Oedipalism, especially in the Compson fiction. Doreen Fowler offers a detailed application of Lacanian psychoanalytic terminology in *Faulkner: The Return of the Repressed* (Charlottesville, VA: University Press of Virginia, 1997). In *Children of the Dark House: Text and Context in Faulkner* (Jackson, MS: University Press of Mississippi, 1996), Noel Polk makes the case for Faulkner's awareness of Freud's work.

3 "The Work of Art in the Age of Mechanical Reproduction," in *Illuminations*, edited and with an introduction by Hannah Arendt, translated by Harry Zohn (New York: Schocken, 1969).

4 *The Most Splendid Failure: Faulkner's* The Sound and the Fury" by André Bleikasten (Bloomington, IN: Indiana University Press, 1976) is a formalist study of the novel. The broader work from which it was drawn was published subsequently as *The Ink of Melancholy: Faulkner's Novels, from* The Sound and the Fury to Light in August (Bloomington, IN: Indiana University Press, 1990). A study of Faulkner's modernist technique is Donald M. Kartiganer's *The Fragile Thread: The Meaning of Form in Faulkner's Novels* (Amherst, MA: University of Massachusetts Press, 1979). Richard C. Moreland provides a historical context for Southern modernism in *Faulkner and Modernism: Rereading and Rewriting* (Madison, WI: University of Wisconsin Press, 1990).

5 See *Fiction's Inexhaustible Voice: Speech and Writing in Faulkner* (Athens, GA: University of Georgia Press, 1989) by Stephen M. Ross for a study of the variety of Southern oratory that informs Faulkner's writing.

6 For more on this topic see Lewis M. Dabney, *The Indians of Yoknapatawpha* (Baton Rouge, LA: Louisiana State University Press, 1974), "Faulkner's Indians," a special issue of *The Faulkner Journal*, guest editor Gene M. Moore, XVIII, Numbers 1 and 2 (Fall 2002/Spring 2003), and Annette Trefzer, *Disturbing Indians: The Archaeology of Southern Fiction* (Tuscaloosa, AL: University of Alabama, 2007).

7 *Faulkner, Mississippi*; translated from the French by Barbara Lewis and Thomas C. Spear (New York: Farrar, Straus, and Giroux, 1999).

Chapter 3

1 *False Dawn: The Delusions of Global Capitalism* (Cambridge, UK: Granta Books, 1998).

2 Jack Temple Kirby, *Rural Worlds Lost: the American South, 1920–1960* (Baton Rouge, LA: Louisiana State University Press, 1987).

3   Annette Kolodny, *The Lay of the Land: Metaphor as Experience and History in American Life and Letters* (Chapel Hill, NC: University of North Carolina Press, 1975).

4   See Charmaine Eddy, "Labor, Economy, and Desire: Rethinking American Nationhood through Yoknapatawpha," *Mississippi Quarterly* 57 (Fall 2004): 569–591, on the Snopeses' imitation of national patterns of commercial success.

5   *Modernity at Large: Cultural Dimensions of Globalization* (Minneapolis, MN: University of Minnesota Press, 1996).

6   See Barbara Ladd, *Resisting History: Gender, Modernity and Authorship in William Faulkner, Zora Neale Hurston, and Eudora Welty* (Baton Rouge, LA: Louisiana State University Press, 2007) for an account of the latter.

7   Gilles Deleuze and Félix Guattari, *Anti-Oedipus: Capitalism and Schizophrenia*; translated from the French by Robert Hurley, Mark Seem, and Helen R. Lane (New York: Viking Press, 1977).

8   Gayatri Chakravorty Spivak, "Can the Subaltern Speak?," originally published in *Marxism and the Interpretation of Culture* edited by Cary Nelson and Lawrence Grossberg (Urbana, IL: University of Illinois Press, 1988). Spivak's main point goes beyond the question of representing the lives of subjected people for them. Even the respectful request that such populations represent themselves (to an interested, but typically ex-colonizer, audience) replicates the dynamics of colonial power and dictate.

9   Any hint of sexual interest by a black male in a white woman amounted to the crime of rape under most conditions in the South.

10 See Joel Williamson, *The Crucible of Race: Black/White Relations in the American South Since Emancipation* (New York: Oxford University Press, 1984). Studies of race in Faulkner include Thadious M. Davis, *Faulkner's "Negro": Art and the Southern Context* (Baton Rouge, LA: Louisiana State University Press, 1983), Eric J. Sundquist *Faulkner: The House Divided* (Baltimore, MD: Johns Hopkins University Press, 1983), and James A. Snead, *Figures of Division: William Faulkner's Major Novels* (New York: Methuen, 1986).

11 My approach is indebted to Barbara Ladd, *Nationalism and the Color Line in George W. Cable, Mark Twain, and William Faulkner* (Baton Rouge, LA: Louisiana State University Press, 1996).

12 In *The Narrative Forms of Southern Community* (Baton Rouge, LA: Louisiana State University Press, 1999) Scott Romine shows how the expectations of the Southern community predetermine Joe's fate. Philip Weinstein explores inter-related Western ideologies in *Faulkner's Subject: A Cosmos No One Owns* (New York: Cambridge University Press, 1992), while Kevin Railey studies Southern ruling-class beliefs in *Natural Aristocracy: History, Ideology, and the Production of William Faulkner* (Tuscaloosa, AL: University of Alabama Press, 1999).

13 As I write, the state of Mississippi has begun to take the lead in bringing long-delayed justice to civil rights' era victims of white racist violence. See "Justice Plays Catch-Up," by Margaret Burnham (*The Boston Globe*, April 27, 2007): "Recently, Mississippi has shown a particularly robust appetite for revisiting its violent racist past. With more black elected officials than any other state, the political infrastructure is now there to support community reconciliation, of which prosecution is a necessary feature."

Chapter 4

1 See George B. Handley, *Postslavery Literatures in the Americas: Family Portraits in Black and White* (Charlottesville, VA: University Press of Virginia, 2000) for a discussion of Faulkner in the context of hemispheric colonialism.
2 *William Faulkner: The Yoknapatawpha Country* (New Haven, CT: Yale University Press, 1963).
3 See Erik Dussere, *Balancing the Books: Faulkner, Morrison, and the Economies of Slavery* (New York: Routledge, 2003) for the central significance of the idea of accounting and the image of the ledger in fiction about slavery, including *Go Down, Moses*.
4 Homi K. Bhabha, "Of Mimicry and Man: The Ambivalence of Colonial Discourse," in *The Location of Culture* (New York: Routledge, 1994).

Chapter 5

1 Lawrence Schwartz studies the political interests that led to seeing Faulkner as an exemplar of the artistic freedom available in a liberal democracy like the United States during the Cold War: *Creating Faulkner's Reputation: The Politics of Modern Literary Criticism* (Knoxville, TN: University of Tennessee Press, 1988).
2 In a commencement address delivered in 1953 at Pine Manor Junior College in Massachusetts, where his daughter Jill was among the graduates, Faulkner stated, "In fact, we must break ourselves of thinking in the terms foisted on us by the split-offs of that old dark spirit's ambition and ruthlessness: the empty clanging terms of "nation" and "fatherland" or "race" or "color" or "creed." The speech was published in the *Atlantic Monthly* (August 1953), and is reprinted in *Essays, Speeches, and Public*

Letters, edited by James B. Meriwether (New York, 1965); quoted sentence on pp. 142–143. In September of 1955 Faulkner issued a press dispatch from Rome on the recent murder of a fourteen-year-old African American from Chicago, who, on a visit to relatives in Money, Mississippi, was accused by a young white woman of whistling in a sexually suggestive way at her. Emmett Till was brutally mutilated and killed by vigilantes that night. The case became a *cause célèbre* of the civil rights movement when Till's mother insisted that journalists be allowed to photograph her son's body in an open-casket funeral. Faulkner's letter emphasizes the utter moral degradation of killing children for any reason, and the short-sightedness of whites – a minority of the world's population – thinking racial violence is justifiable. In his pronouncements on Southern race matters, Faulkner sometimes took up eccentric aspects of the problem (as in this statement on Till), that may have been meant to ambiguate his position for antagonistic audiences. On at least two occasions his irritation at being ridiculed by many of his family and friends for his comparatively liberal views on race led to extreme – and despicable – efforts to compensate: one instance involved an early letter that seemed to defend lynching as a desperate last measure under some circumstances; another (though here with the caveat that the British journalist eliciting the comment confirmed that Faulkner had been drinking before the interview) was a combative remark that if he had to choose between letting his state be overrun by outside agitators and "shooting niggers in the street," Faulkner would do the latter to defend the state of Mississippi. One can only observe that these are uncharacteristic remarks, and that Faulkner's fiction unquestionably imagines attitudes and narratives that transcend the often racist confines of his personal loyalties, family ties, and regional history. Charles D. Peavy provides the documentary record of Faulkner's public remarks on race in *Go Slow Now: Faulkner and the Race Question* (Eugene, OR: University of Oregon, 1971). Theresa M. Towner examines how race is represented in the later fiction in *Faulkner on the Color Line: The Later Novels* (Jackson, MS: University Press of Mississippi, 2000).

3 *The Global Cold War: Third World Interventions and the Making of Our Times* (New York: Cambridge University Press, 2005).

4 "To the Youth of Japan" (Tokyo, 1955 [pamphlet published by the US Information Service]), reprinted in *Essays, Speeches, and Public Letters*, edited by James B. Meriwether (New York: Random House, 1965), p. 84.

5 "On Fear: Deep South in Labor: Mississippi" (*Harper's*, June 1956), reprinted in *Speeches*, p. 106.

6 *A Brief History of Neoliberalism* (New York: Oxford University Press, 2005).

7   See Joseph R. Urgo's *Faulkner's Apocrypha: A Fable, Snopes, and the Spirit of Human Rebellion* (Jackson, MS: University Press of Mississippi, 1989) for a study of the later fiction in the context of the Cold War.

8   See Robin D. G. Kelley's *Hammer and Hoe: Alabama Communists during the Great Depression* (Chapel Hill, NC: University of North Carolina Press, 1990).

9   James Watson includes Linda's communist activism as part of Faulkner's favorable depiction of her "transcendent humanistic love" (*The Snopes Dilemma: Faulkner's Trilogy* [Oxford, OH: University of Miami Press, 1968]), p. 228.

10   Frederick Karl, *William Faulkner: American Writer* (New York: Weidenfeld & Nicolson, 1989), p. 630.

11   See Hosam Aboul-Ela's discussion of the Snopeses in terms of Third World class structure, in particular of Flem Snopes as a representative of a global *comprador* elite that co-operates with foreign Northern metropolitan "development" and administers the foreign exploitation of local labor and resources (*Other South: Globalization, Faulkner, and the Mariátegui Tradition* (Pittsburgh, PA: University of Pittsburgh Press, 2007).

12   Fredric Jameson proposes the pornographic dimensions of late capitalism in *Postmodernism, or, The Cultural Logic of Late Capitalism* (Durham, NC: Duke University Press, 1991).

13   Addressing Faulkner's late modernism, Catherine Gunther Kodat interprets *A Fable* as Faulkner's attempt to bridge the gap between modernist and mass cultural modes via an intermediate "sentimental modernism": "Writing *A Fable* for America," in *Faulkner in America: Faulkner and Yoknapatawpha, 1998*, edited by Joseph R. Urgo and Ann J. Abadie (Jackson, MS: University Press of Mississippi, 2001), pp. 82–97.

14   My approach here is indebted to Richard Godden's analysis of *A Fable* in his *Faulkner: An Economy of Complex Words*.

15   Paul Hawken, *Blessed Unrest: How the Largest Movement in the World Came into Being and Why No One Saw It Coming* (New York: Viking, 2007).

16   In the first edition of *A Fable* this last line reads: "all that vast powerful terror-inspiring representation which, running all democracy's affairs in peace, *comes* indeed into *its* own in war, finding *its* true apotheosis then . . ." (emphasis added). In this version "representation" serves as the general term for all the modern phenomena preceding it, and becomes the subject of the singular predicate.

Bibliography

Aboul-Ela, Hosam. *Other South: Globalization, Faulkner, and the Mariátegui Tradition*. Pittsburgh, PA: University of Pittsburgh Press, 2007.

Appadurai, Arjun. *Modernity at Large: Cultural Dimensions of Globalization*. Minneapolis, MN: University of Minnesota Press, 1996.

Benjamin, Walter. "Theses on the Philosophy of History, in *Illuminations*. New York: Schocken, 1969.

Benjamin, Walter. "The Work of Art in the Age of Mechanical Reproduction," in *Illuminations*. Edited and with an introduction by Hannah Arendt, translated by Harry Zohn. New York: Schocken, 1969.

Bhabha, Homi K. "Of Mimicry and Man: The Ambivalence of Colonial Discourse," in *The Location of Culture*. New York: Routledge, 1994.

Bleikasten, André. *The Most Splendid Failure: Faulkner's "The Sound and the Fury."* Bloomington, IN: Indiana University Press, 1976.

Bleikasten, André. *The Ink of Melancholy: Faulkner's Novels, from "The Sound and the Fury" to "Light in August."* Bloomington, IN: Indiana University Press, 1990.

Blotner, Joseph. *Faulkner: A Biography*. One volume edition. New York: Random House, 1984.

Brooks, Cleanth. *William Faulkner: The Yoknapatawpha Country*. New Haven, CT: Yale University Press, 1963.

Burnham, Margaret. "Justice Plays Catch-Up," *The Boston Globe*, April 27, 2007.

Clarke, Deborah. *Robbing the Mother: Women in Faulkner*. Jackson, MS: University Press of Mississippi, 1994.

Collins, Carvel. *William Faulkner: Early Prose and Poetry*. Compilation and introduction. Boston, MA: Little, Brown, 1962.

Dabney, Lewis M. *The Indians of Yoknapatawpha*. Baton Rouge, LA: Louisiana State University Press, 1974.

Davis, Thadious M. *Faulkner's "Negro": Art and the Southern Context*. Baton Rouge, LA: Louisiana State University Press, 1983.

Debord, Guy. *Society of the Spectacle*. Detroit: Black & Red, 1983. (Originally published as *La Société du spectacle*. Paris: Buchet/Chastel, 1967.)

Deleuze, Gilles and Félix Guattari. *Anti-Oedipus: Capitalism and Schizophrenia*. Translated from the French by Robert Hurley, Mark Seem, and Helen R. Lane. New York: Viking Press, 1977.

Doyle, Don. *Faulkner's County: The Historical Roots of Yoknapatawpha*. Chapel Hill, NC: University of North Carolina Press, 2001.

Duck, Leigh Anne. *The Nation's Region: Southern Modernism, Segregation, and US Nationalism*. Athens, GA: University of Georgia Press, 2006.

Dussere, Erik. *Balancing the Books: Faulkner, Morrison, and the Economies of Slavery*. New York: Routledge, 2003.

Duvall, John. *Faulkner's Marginal Couple: Invisible, Outlaw, and Unspeakable Communities*. Austin, TX: University of Texas Press, 1990.

Eddy, Charmaine. "Labor, Economy, and Desire: Rethinking American Nationhood Through Yoknapatawpha," *Mississippi Quarterly* 57 (Fall 2004), 569–591.

Faulkner, William. *The Marble Faun* (1924) and *A Green Bough* (1933). [Poems]. New York: Random House, 1965.

Faulkner, William. *Soldiers' Pay* (1926). Corrected text in *Faulkner: Novels 1926–1929*. New York: Library of America, 2006: 1–256.

Faulkner, William. *Mosquitoes* (1927). Corrected text in *Faulkner: Novels 1926–1929*. New York: Library of America, 2006: 257–540.

Faulkner, William. *The Sound and the Fury* (1929). Corrected text. Norton Critical edition (second edition). Norton: New York, 1994.

Faulkner, William. *As I Lay Dying* (1930). Corrected text. Vintage International Edition. Random House: New York, 1990.

Faulkner, William. *Sanctuary* (1931). Corrected text. Vintage International Edition. New York: Random House, 1993.

Faulkner, William. *These Thirteen*. New York: Cape, 1931.

Faulkner, William. *Light in August* (1932). Corrected text. Vintage International Edition. New York: Random House, 1990.

Faulkner, William. *Pylon* (1935). Corrected text in *Faulkner: Novels 1930–1935*. New York: Library of America, 1985: 775–992.

Faulkner, William. *Absalom, Absalom!* (1936). Corrected text. Vintage International Edition. New York: Random House, 1990.

Faulkner, William. *The Unvanquished* (1938). Corrected text in *Faulkner: Novels 1936–1940*. New York: Library of America, 1990: 317–492.

Faulkner, William. *If I Forget Thee, Jerusalem [The Wild Palms]* (1939). Corrected text in *Faulkner: Novels 1936–1940*. New York: Library of America, 1990: 493–726.

Faulkner, William. *The Hamlet* (1940). Corrected text. Vintage International Edition. New York: Random House, 1991.

Faulkner, William. *Go Down, Moses* (1942). Reprint. Vintage International Edition. New York: Random House, 1990.

Faulkner, William. *Intruder in the Dust* (1948). Corrected text in *Faulkner: Novels 1942–1954*. New York: Library of America, 1994: 283–470.

Faulkner, William. *Collected Stories of William Faulkner*. New York: Random House, 1950.

Faulkner, William. *Requiem for a Nun* (1950). Corrected text in *Faulkner: Novels 1942–1954*. New York: Library of America, 1994: 471–664.

Faulkner, William. *A Fable* (1954). Corrected text in *Faulkner: Novels 1942–1954*. New York: Library of America, 1994: 665–1072.

Faulkner, William. *Notes on a Horse Thief*. Greenville, MS: Levee, 1951.

Faulkner, William. *The Town* (1957). Corrected text in *Faulkner: Novels 1957–1962*. New York: Library of America, 1999: 1–326.

Faulkner, William. *The Mansion* (1959). Corrected text in *Faulkner: Novels 1957–1962*. New York: Library of America, 1999: 327–721.

Faulkner, William. *The Reivers* (1961). Corrected text in *Faulkner: Novels 1957–1962*. New York: Library of America, 1999: 723–971.

Faulkner, William. *Essays, Speeches, and Public Letters*. Edited by James B. Meriwether. New York, 1965.

Faulkner, William. *Flags in the Dust* (1973). Corrected text in *Faulkner: Novels 1926–1929*. New York: Library of America, 2006: 543–875.

Faulkner, William. "An Introduction to *The Sound and the Fury*." *Mississippi Quarterly* 26 (Summer 1973): 410–415. Reprinted in *The Sound and the Fury* (Norton Critical Edition): 228–232.

Faulkner, William. *Selected Letters*. Edited by Joseph Blotner. New York: Random House, 1977.

Faulkner, William. *The Marionettes*. Edited with an introduction and textual apparatus by Noel Polk. Charlottesville, VA: University Press of Virginia, 1977.

Faulkner, William. *Uncollected Stories of William Faulkner*. Edited by Joseph Blotner. New York: Random House, 1979.

Faulkner, William. *Father Abraham*. Edited by James B. Meriwether. New York: Random House, 1984.

Faulkner, William. *Vision in Spring*. Edited with an introduction by Judith L. Sensibar. Austin, TX: University of Texas Press, 1984.

Fowler, Doreen. *Faulkner: The Return of the Repressed*. Charlottesville, VA: University Press of Virginia, 1997.

Gilmer, Walker. *Horace Liveright, Publisher of the Twenties*. New York: D. Lewis, 1970.

Glissent, Edouard. Faulkner, Mississippi. Translated from French by Barbara Lewis and Thomas Spean. New York: Farrar, Straus, and Giroux, 1999.

Godden, Richard. *Fictions of Labor: William Faulkner and the South's Long Revolution*. Cambridge, UK, and New York: Cambridge University Press, 1997.

Godden, Richard. *William Faulkner: An Economy of Complex Words*. Princeton, NJ: Princeton University Press, 2007.

Gray, John. *False Dawn: The Delusions of Global Capitalism*. Cambridge, UK: Granta Books, 1998.

Gray, Richard. *The Life of William Faulkner: A Critical Biography*. Oxford, UK, and Cambridge, MA: Blackwell Publishers, 1994.

Gresset, Michel. *Fascination: Faulkner's Fiction, 1919–1936*. Adapted from the French by Thomas West. Durham, NC: Duke University Press, 1989.

Grimwood, Michael. *Heart in Conflict: Faulkner's Struggles with Vocation*. Athens, GA: University of Georgia Press, 1987.

Gwin, Minrose C. *The Feminine and Faulkner: Reading (Beyond) Sexual Difference*. Knoxville, TN: University of Tennessee Press, 1990.

Gwynn, Frederick L. and Joseph L. Blotner. *Faulkner in the University*. Charlottesville, VA: University of Virginia Press, 1959, 1995.

Handley, George B. *Postslavery Literatures in the Americas: Family Portraits in Black and White*. Charlottesville, VA: University Press of Virginia, 2000.

Hannon, Charles. *Faulkner and the Discourses of Culture*. Baton Rouge, LA: Louisiana State University Press, 2004.

Harvey, David. *A Brief History of Neoliberalism*. New York: Oxford University Press, 2005.

Hawken, Paul. *Blessed Unrest: How the Largest Movement in the World Came into Being and Why No One Saw It Coming*. New York: Viking, 2007.

Hemingway, Ernest. *The Sun Also Rises*. New York: Simon & Schuster, 1954. (Originally published by Scribner, 1926.)

Irwin, John T. *Doubling and Incest/Repetition and Revenge: A Speculative Reading of Faulkner*. Baltimore, MD: Johns Hopkins University Press, 1975.

Jameson, Fredric. *Postmodernism, or, The Cultural Logic of Late Capitalism*. Durham, NC: Duke University Press, 1991.

Karl, Frederick. *William Faulkner, American Writer: A Biography*. New York: Weidenfeld & Nicolson, 1989.

Kartiganer, Donald M. *The Fragile Thread: The Meaning of Form in Faulkner's Novels*. Amherst, MA: University of Massachusetts Press, 1979.

Kelley, Robin D. G. *Hammer and Hoe: Alabama Communists During the Great Depression*. Chapel Hill, NC: University of North Carolina Press, 1990.

Kirby, Jack Temple. *Rural Worlds Lost: The American South, 1920–1960*. Baton Rouge, LA: Louisiana State University Press, 1987.

Kodat, Catherine Gunther. "Writing *A Fable* for America," in *Faulkner in America: Faulkner and Yoknapatawpha, 1998*. Edited by Joseph R. Urgo and Ann J. Abadie. Jackson, MS: University Press of Mississippi, 2001: 82–97.

Kolodny, Annette. *The Lay of the Land: Metaphor as Experience and History in American Life and Letters.* Chapel Hill, NC: University of North Carolina Press, 1975.

Kreyling, Michael. *Inventing Southern Literature.* Jackson, MS: University Press of Mississippi, 1998.

Ladd, Barbara. *Nationalism and the Color Line in George W. Cable, Mark Twain, and William Faulkner.* Baton Rouge, LA: Louisiana State University Press, 1996.

Ladd, Barbara. *Resisting History: Gender, Modernity and Authorship in William Faulkner, Zora Neale Hurston, and Eudora Welty.* Baton Rouge, LA: Louisiana State University Press, 2007.

Lurie, Peter. *Vision's Immanence: Faulkner, Film, and the Popular Imagination.* Baltimore, MD: Johns Hopkins University Press, 2004.

Meriwether, James B. and Michael Millgate (eds.). *Lion in the Garden: Interviews with William Faulkner 1926–1962.* New York: Random House, 1968.

Meyerowitz, Joanne. "Sex, Gender, and the Cold War Language of Reform." In *Rethinking Cold War Culture.* Edited by Peter J. Kuznick and James Gilbert. Washington: Smithsonian Institution Press, 2001: 106–123.

Minter, David L. *William Faulkner: His Life and Work.* Baltimore, MD: Johns Hopkins University Press, 1980.

Moreland, Richard C. *Faulkner and Modernism: Rereading and Rewriting.* Madison, WI: University of Wisconsin Press, 1990.

Moore, Gene M., guest editor. "Faulkner's Indians," a special issue of *The Faulkner Journal,* XVIII, Numbers 1 and 2 (Fall 2002/Spring 2003).

Mulvey, Laura. *Visual and Other Pleasures.* Bloomington, IN: Indiana University Press, 1989.

Peavy, Charles D. *Go Slow Now; Faulkner and the Race Question.* Eugene, OR: University of Oregon, 1971.

Polk, Noel. *Children of the Dark House: Text and Context in Faulkner.* Jackson, MS: University Press of Mississippi, 1996.

Railey, Kevin. *Natural Aristocracy: History, Ideology, and the Production of William Faulkner.* Tuscaloosa, AL: University of Alabama Press, 1999.

Ramsey, D. Matthew. "'Turnabout' Is Fair(y) Play: Faulkner's Queer War Story," *The Faulkner Journal* 15.1–2 (1999–2000 Fall–Spring 1999), 61–81.

Roberts, Diane. *Faulkner and Southern Womanhood.* Athens, GA: University of Georgia Press, 1994.

Romine, Scott. *The Narrative Forms of Southern Community.* Baton Rouge, LA: Louisiana State University Press, 1999.

Ross, Stephen M. *Fiction's Inexhaustible Voice: Speech and Writing in Faulkner.* Athens, GA: University of Georgia Press, 1989.

Schwartz, Lawrence. *Creating Faulkner's Reputation: The Politics of Modern Literary Criticism.* Knoxville, TN: University of Tennessee Press, 1988.

Snead, James A. *Figures of Division: William Faulkner's Major Novels.* New York: Methuen, 1986.

Spivak, Gayatri Chakravorty. "Can the Subaltern Speak?," originally published in *Marxism and the Interpretation of Culture.* Edited by Cary Nelson and Lawrence Grossberg. Urbana, IL: University of Illinois Press, 1988.

Stonum, Gary Lee. *Faulkner's Career: An Internal Literary History.* Ithaca, NY: Cornell University Press, 1979.

Sundquist, Eric J. *Faulkner: The House Divided.* Baltimore, MD: Johns Hopkins University Press, 1983.

Towner, Theresa M. *Faulkner on the Color Line: The Later Novels.* Jackson, MS: University Press of Mississippi, 2000.

Trefzer, Annette. *Disturbing Indians: The Archaeology of Southern Fiction.* Tuscaloosa, AL: University of Alabama, 2007.

Urgo, Joseph R., *Faulkner's Apocrypha: A Fable, Snopes, and the Spirit of Human Rebellion.* Jackson, MS: University Press of Mississippi, 1989.

Watson, James, *The Snopes Dilemma: Faulkner's Trilogy.* Oxford OH: Miami University Press, 1968.

Weinstein, Philip. *Faulkner's Subject: A Cosmos No One Owns.* New York: Cambridge University Press, 1992.

Westad, Odd Arne. *The Global Cold War: Third World Interventions and the Making of Our Times.* New York: Cambridge University Press, 2005.

Wilde, Meta Carpenter. *A Loving Gentleman: The Love Story of William Faulkner and Meta Carpenter.* New York: Simon & Schuster, 1976.

Williamson, Joel. *The Crucible of Race: Black/White Relations in the American South Since Emancipation.* New York: Oxford University Press, 1984.

Williamson, Joel. *A Rage for Order: Black/White Relations in the American South Since Emancipation.* New York : Oxford University Press, 1986.

Williamson, Joel. *William Faulkner and Southern History.* New York: Oxford University Press, 1993.

Wittenberg, Judith Bryant. *Faulkner, The Transfiguration of Biography.* Lincoln: University of Nebraska Press, 1979.

Yaeger, Patricia. *Dirt and Desire: Reconstructing Southern Women's Writing, 1930–1990.* Chicago, IL: University of Chicago Press, 2000.

Young, Robert J. C. *Colonial Desire: Hybridity in Theory, Culture, and Race.* London and New York: Routledge, 1995.

Index

Note: page numbers in **bold** indicate major discussions of works.

war films 58–59
"Was" **200–204**
Wasson, Ben 88, 109–110
The Waste Land (Eliot) 24, 65
West, Nathaniel 52
Westad, Odd Arne 248
Wharton, Edith 52
white dominance 119, 155–158, 168
White Noise (DeLillo) 243

The Wild Palms 60, **68–74**
Williams, Eric 102
Williams, William Carlos 285
Winesburg, Ohio (Anderson) 10
Woolf, Virginia 23, 24, 65

Yeats, William Butler 23

Žižek, Slavoj 235